MOSCOW FAREWELL

MOSCOW FAREWELL

GEORGE FEIFER

THE VIKING PRESS \\ NEW YORK

For Tanya

First published in 1976 by The Viking Press, Inc.
625 Madison Avenue, New York, N.Y. 10022

Published simultaneously in Canada
by The Macmillan Company of Canada Limited

LIBRARY OF CONGRESS CATALOGING IN PUBLICATION DATA

Feifer, George.
Moscow farewell.
I. Title.
PZ4.F2973Mo   [PS3556.E418]   813'.5'4   75-28266
ISBN 0-670-48985-9

Printed in U.S.A.

Author's Note

Largely to protect Muscovites I lived with sporadically from 1959 to 1971—including a year as a graduate student—I have altered names, concealed identities and rearranged time sequences in this account. Without these changes, I would have had to depart much further from the literal truth by eliminating politically sensitive material. But in the sense that almost nothing has been invented, what follows is reportage of my Russian friends' lives and of my observations. To modify Christopher Isherwood on his rendering of Berlin forty years ago, it is a record more of what happened than of what might have happened to me abroad.

At the same time, my reminiscences make no attempt to describe "typical" Moscow life—the burden of many easily available books—but only what I saw, heard and felt.

Behind the Byzantine apparatus of state, life went on.
—Vassily O. Klyuchevsky, nineteenth-century Russian historian

He lies like an eyewitness.
—old Russian proverb

Contents

MOSCOW FAREWELL

1 Notes from My Window

From my window, through two panes of wobbly glass, a corner of this University, this city, this brooding country. Kremlin cupolas in the distance, jewels of possessed autocrats, shrouded by an icy fog. The seat of temporal and spiritual authority in its medieval splendor, regilded yearly and equipped with loudspeakers for big-brother Muzak.

Outside its sepia walls, the capital's sprawling center, sullen to match the setting and mood. A city landscape wanting neon and city life, as if square miles of squat buildings had been abandoned at the first November snows. No aircraft or traffic sounds but a northern folk song wailing in the back of my mind. Overwhelming sadness and strength in the subduing hush of Russia's expanse.

A broad artery, one spoke of the city center's wheel, leads in this direction toward the single bridge over the Moscow river; and along its snowy length, four lone construction trucks and five buses are gliding, past the empty intersections and sagging Glory-to-Lenin signs. The river itself is immobile and resigned, like the boarded-up summer cafés on its bank in Gorky Park; like the old women guarding the park gates, suspended in time and space. Frozen steam rises from ice packs in the water, drifts, darkens, and settles in the snowfield of the deserted Lenin stadium. One of the world's largest, it is lost in this white continent. "There is something in the Russian soul," said Berdyayev, "that corresponds to the immensity, the vagueness, the infinitude of the Russian land." I soar and sink with this understanding.

On this side of the river, everything has changed and remains the same. Flat fields, flimsy red flags, mile after mile of prefabricated apartment houses; and a scattering of furtive figures hunched into fraying collars of ankle-length overcoats. This section of the city is a showplace of postwar Soviet construction, but winter ravages new buildings of brick and cement block as relentlessly as any Volga cabin. Peeling from their dour façades, bricks plop into nets hastily hung to protect pedestrians. Joints sever, sidewalks crumble into the snow. A fortune is spent on repairing the ubiquitous cracking, flaking and cleaving, and much patchwork is abandoned midway when teams are summoned to more urgent emergencies. Even the new Palace of Pioneers, star of a thousand magazine features, has lost the battle to winter, chipping apart before it is fully fitted out. But runny-nosed children, bundled in fur until they're nearly round, are swooping down snow-covered mounds of sand and gravel left by the builders, whooping like Indians on their homemade skis.

Below me, a splendid boulevard perpendicular to the central artery separates the University from its sporting grounds beyond. Straight, broad, Olympian, it belongs to this country's Great Shining Future, for which elaborate plans are regularly remade. But it is empty now and already eroded: mournful for the present and mocking the future. A crew of women wrapped in black shawls is sweeping it clean of the new snow, swinging their witches' besoms in the age-old scything motion. Even the flanking firs and birches are stunted by the climate.

I am high in the Stalinesque tower of Moscow University,

looking north at this panorama in the light of the mid-morning dawn. It is gray: a solid plane of heavy cloud presses on earth and shoulders with a relentlessness that groans "Russian winter." And cold: icicles dangle from the skyscraper's ornate cornices, although this is the first day of December, only the beginning of the annual trial. And still: the thump of student shoes striking a lumpish soccer ball reaches me from the courtyard eighteen stories below. (Those shoes! And many must last another winter.) A raw wind sneaks through my dormitory window although it is double, like all in Russia, and workers appeared in October to stuff cotton wadding between the warped frames.

Inside, the lights are on despite the hour, the bulbs emitting a hum. This huge complex of buildings, the pride of Soviet education, is a Socialist Achievement worn in a decade to a provincial sitting room's homey dilapidation. I am Pinocchio unanimated: the weight of everything devitalizes my limbs. The Russian I hear from the corridor is like a language I knew in an earlier life rather than sounds I first heard as a Harvard senior in my typical scramble for the beautiful and true, this time in Russian courses after three prosaic pre-law years. The corridor itself seems closer to the spirit of my inner life—a hall so ordinary that it gives you a headache, but with the expectation of something ennobling at the end—than my own progression from Manhattan to Orange County with my family, then to Cambridge as their white hope. Its threadbare oriental runners discharge a smell of must and dust; in the common room, fat rubber plants compete for space with massive sofas of disintegrating leather. For show, the floors are scrubbed every month—with an acrid liquid that corrodes the once-precious wood.

A mechanic is repairing the elevator again. Arriving grimy and cheerful in early morning, he spent the first three hours flirting with a busty cleaning woman and trying to borrow tools. The elevator will break down again tomorrow, but no one will waste time lodging a complaint. Even on good days, it's shut off before midnight to save electricity for the current Five-Year Plan.

Anastasia is slipping away from me and I can't stop it unless I somehow become a better man. I'm not going to call her today; and Alyosha is still away, so there is nothing much to do with myself. It took this moment of musing to tell me how much my life here has come down to just these two people. Maybe I'll go to the library later—or on a book-buying outing into town, my standard excursion to pass time while pretending to be busy at something useful. Meanwhile, I'm going to stay here at my twelfth-floor window, watching the pickup game of soccer and the hearty, sweatsuited girl students taking their morning jogs through the snow. Just sit here, dreaming and resting. I want to merge with the mood of this place: the oilcloth on my tiny table that links me to my grandmother's ghetto kitchen; my pal, the wooden lamp on the desk. With this heaviness, sadness, acceptance of fate.

The room smells of slightly rancid lard. Roommate Viktor is frying potatoes on the old hot plate in his corner. Twice daily, after breakfast and supper, he drains the lard back into a pickle jar, to jell gray on the window ledge and be re-used until fully consumed. His skillet lacks a handle, and Viktor stoically endures every burn to his stubby fingers. My suggestion to purchase a replacement produces only bewilderment: "Ekh, but I can't waste the cooking part, the *metal!*" The potatoes come from his family vegetable patch, a major treasure of the beloved family plot. Before being sliced into the pan, each dwarfish bulblet is clasped for a tender, proprietary instant.

Viktor has enough money to breakfast in the cafeteria, for he's rich by Soviet student standards. But he's also relentlessly frugal: reads other people's newspapers to save the daily two kopeks; presses the pants himself of his single, funereal suit (it has never been to the cleaner's); dices a hundred grams of the cheapest grade of garlic sausage into the potatoes for his supper. He always goes to the movies (twenty kopeks, in one of the ground-floor auditoriums) alone, lest in a group he find himself nearest the cashier and be expected to pay for everyone, according to the loose Russian custom. He's saving money now to invest in the family plot, that precious half-acre allocated for dachas and gardens. But he would save mightily even without a specific goal; the compulsion is in his bones.

When prompted with trigger questions, he can dredge up quotations from his three decades of intensive socialist upbringing and training, reciting cram-course extrapolations from Engels on private property's psychological, sociological and familial evils. But never for an instant has he related his unfaltering ideological commitment to himself or his own treasure, the marshy little plot. Just as political evils are *over there* in the bourgeois West, his political enlightenment stops at the border—the Soviet border, on the Elbe—and in a schooldesk compartment of his brain. His real attitudes, the working ones, came with his mother's milk—in her photographs, mother is only slightly too squat and stern-looking to be the picture of the Russian peasant—and he loves what is his as powerfully as any Breton shopkeeper.

Viktor is a pudgy, Mongolian-looking man with an overdeveloped torso (he stores his weight-lifting equipment under his bed) and a mole shaped like Corsica on one starchy cheek. His smile is his most endearing feature, a sheepish, friendly grin that seems to say all this is too much for him. Being at this top University is too much; the thought of becoming a People's Judge—which he'll be "elected" soon after graduation—is too much; above all, rooming with a foreigner—an *American*—is more than he ever bargained for. Born in a village, he expected a peaceful life. The opportunities and adventures that have befallen him entirely by chance disturb more than stimulate him. Who could have guessed that his very ordinariness would reward him with such advancement? But he, the unimaginative plodder, is precisely whom the cadres-bosses recruit for the country's "leading ranks."

He is the only Communist—meaning member of the Party—in our wing of this floor of the dormitory. Other students will join in time, a handful out of conviction, most as a prerequisite for privileges or promotions; but they are still too young. Viktor is thirty-one; he was a tractor driver, a collective-farm assistant brigade leader, then an infantryman before becoming a student. (Party membership, a solid record as a soldier and a worker, and a sterling peasant-proletarian background squeezed him into the University despite his entrance exam scores.) It was in the Army that the unquestioning Young Communist of twenty-seven joined the Party itself. The regimental political officers tapped him for his "positive" attitude, stolid loyalty and, again, the desirable social origin.

During his first eight months in uniform, he did not have a single overnight pass; not expecting one, he wasn't surprised. After basic training, he was stationed for nearly three years with a border garrison some sixty miles northwest of Vladivostock and did not manage so much as a day trip to the city, much less a week of home leave. The sum of his Army wages for three years was one hundred and thirty-five rubles, the price of his black serge suit. But he's proud of the hardships of national service. "Our Army is tough," he explains gravely. "We don't pamper the men; that's why we win." Moreover, he expects the opponents to live up to *their* reputations. Raised on comic-book-level spy stories and indescribable television potboilers featuring the intrepid secret police, he wants the evil, tricky imperialist agents to put up a proper fight before surrendering. His greatest disappointment in the American warmongers was the cowardice of Gary Powers, who so abjectly confessed. He offered me condolences for the ten-year-old humiliation, just as he dutifully congratulates me when an American team defeats a Soviet one in some track meet.

I have had fierce, friendly, meaningless and painfully enlightening political arguments with many other Russian students in the dormitory; often they start at supper and continue into the night. But Viktor and I never talk about anything political. His thoughts about the nature of man and society are limited to the opening paragraphs of the morning's *Pravda* editorial.

Having scanned today's issue—saving his two kopeks—he's returned it to my table. "The struggle between the two conflicting ideologies—socialist and bourgeois—represents the greatest battle of ideas in all history. It has acquired a genuinely *all-pervading nature, and this is the principal characteristic of the contemporary stage of the ideological struggle.*" This is the kind of statement he used to repeat, indeed to *read* doggedly to me, during our first trying weeks, before we'd worked out the terms of our coexistence: political truce based on political silence. His assertions of fact during the initial jousting were on the same level: Finland attacked Russia in 1939 and (since Soviet Russia has never struck a first blow) Japan also invaded in 1945. Franklin Roosevelt was a Jew. (Viktor's clinching proof was Roosevelt's aid to fellow-Jew Trotsky in pursuing anti-Soviet subversion from Mexico.) The Communist parties of Britain and the United States are, although illegal and repressed, the people's genuine voice—because all Communist parties are by definition repositories of truth and virtue, and everyone who, like himself, knows the way the world really works is automatically a Communist. In short, his "brass tacks" arranged themselves around a powerful magnetic field. Mother Russia is right, her opponents wrong.

Despairing over the usual dead end of our debate, I asked him one day whether the Soviet government had ever committed an injustice in its foreign policy. He gave some genuine thought to this unexpected question and answered with shining eyes and quivering sincerity.

"There were a few *before* the Revolution."

Yet although the living embodiment of Emerson's "We are born believing. A man bears beliefs, as a tree bears apples," Viktor knows less about Marxism or Leninism, not to speak of any other social idea, than some Greenwich Village barbers. He's never read Marx, only the primers for schools and the Army. There's no kinder way to say it: my roommate belongs to the camp of the Communist Party whose chief characteristic is not cruelty, drive for power or even ideological rigidity, but straightforward thickwittedness, stiffened by plebeian envy of his betters. "Not *all* the dullest and dumbest are in the ranks," said a wit across the corridor. "But the less you know the better. Ol' Vik's mental equipment makes him a natural."

But this is irrelevant in a sense, since Viktor is not really interested in Marx. Nor, in fact, in anything even faintly political; and unless provoked by me, the incarnation of the ideological enemy, he'd rather not pretend. He does care about three things: the fortunes of Moscow Dynamo, his favorite soccer team, the fishing conditions compared to this time last year and, again, the family half-acre. The plot is located in a little village of unpainted, ramshackle peasant cottages about forty miles east of Moscow. Directly after his last Saturday morning class, Viktor wraps his overalls in newspaper—the ones he favors in the room to save wear on his "lectures-only" trousers—and hurries to the station. A suburban *electrichka* and a brisk walk on eroded lanes delivers him home in two hours for a weekend of family council and work. With his father, brother and brothers-in-law, he is adding a second room to the dacha for the sake of the wives (the clan's cooks, cleaners and driving force for upward mobility) and the children, the revered little heirs. For the men, there is a large pond on the other side of the village with muddy water but delicate-fleshed pike.

Obsessed by the twelve-by-fourteen-foot construction project, Viktor resents the intrusion of academic and Party obligations on his thoughts and time. (Although he attends every class and meeting of his Party section, I've never seen him open a textbook except when an exam was approaching. But sometimes he'll read a spy novel or his favorite sports magazine before dropping off to sleep at ten o'clock.) He enthuses about the joys of a country place, remonstrates against the outrageous price of lumber, describes how best to bribe an electrician to take a day off from his legal job. (The last Party session inveighed furiously against such corruption.) He can discourse too on the intricacies of plumbing and cesspools—for the new "wing" includes an internal water closet!

He's also fascinated by my toilet kit—stainless steel razor blades provoked his first suspicion about the inherent superiority of a socialist economy—and empties my aerosol cans of shaving cream in surreptitious play. After a long struggle with his self-control, he mumbled a request for one for his father's birthday. Scotch tape, ballpoint pens and my immersion heater to boil water for instant coffee also enchant him, but he turns up his nose at the toilet paper I obtain at the American Embassy commissary. "Too dainty," he complained, returning to the standard University product: ripped-up eights of yesterday's *Pravda*. On the other hand, the highly impressionistic drawing I bought from my friend Zhenya, an "underground" painter, leaves him speechless.

Viktor makes sure I'm out when, every ten days or so, he brings a girl to the room for fornication. He doesn't want me to acquire an unseemly view of Communist morality, which he's supposed to represent. Or maybe it's the girls themselves he'd rather I didn't meet. I've caught sight of several when, after the event, he'd be prodding one of them down the corridor toward the emergency stairs, tugging her anxiously away from the elevator in case a car containing an acquaintance should arrive. The girls are among the University's homeliest, and never from our department (called the Juridical Faculty). He rarely sees one a second time and never provides supper. Having safely seen the sweetheart out, he returns to the room, runs through a set of Red Army light calisthenics and lingers in the shower, repeating to himself a list of things to do.

My friends warn me that Viktor weekly informs the appropriate authorities about my visitors, activities and ideological inclination, just as he reported on his fellow soldiers in the role of company stool pigeon. Somehow this fails to disturb me. I'm told too that he probably describes me as dull-witted and harmless because this is quickest and easiest for him. He wants to avoid writing supplementary reports about any transgressions he might name and, above all, more intensive surveillance assignments that would bite into the family weekend. On the other hand, I think I sometimes see in him a certain disappointment that I'm not the slick ideological subversive he has been educated to expect.

This morning, he was up as usual before seven o'clock to polish his city shoes and darn a pair of khaki socks. Having noticed I'm not feeling my best, he presented me with a saucer of his mother's delicious apple jam, made from the fruit of a tree bordering the family garden. Then a second saucer with a glass of tea. "Gosh," he said in response to my praise of the jam. Yes, it's his smile I like best. And he likes me because he knows I don't care, so he needn't feign an interest in his legal studies.

I turn on the radio and listen for a moment, lying on my daybed and looking at the black-bordered pinup of Gagarin above Viktor's desk. (Strange how this cheapest, ugliest lump of furniture, like all my beds everywhere, has become my closest friend, although its grease-stained mattress cover made me gag when I first arrived and I could hardly touch it before, let alone after, its dusting with bedbug powder during the presemester general cleanup.) The radio transforms every voice into a thick buzz, making it tricky to follow even the news, whose phrases I know by heart.

Actually, it's not a proper radio but a speaker that transmits

Radio Moscow from a plug in the wall; like most hotels, restaurants, offices and apartment houses, the University has been wired with rediffusion points throughout, enabling the Whole Truth to ring in every room. Violins soar and the announcer's voice grows throaty: the program is about a retired machinist's love for his old lathe; and through the lathe, his factory; and through the factory, his Soviet Motherland and Lenin, "our eternal Vladimir Ilich, who is truly more alive than the living." Radio Moscow's correspondent affects profound emotion at the veteran worker's patriotism, and excerpts of his interview are transmitted, crudely spliced and laden with rallying cries, a precise copy of a hundred increase-production interviews broadcast all day, every day, and supplemented by commentary for anyone who misses the point. "Our factory carries the sacred name of Lenin; we couldn't fail our socialist duty. . . . The most satisfying day of my life was when we were judged worthy of the title, Brigade of Communist Labor. . . . An honest man loves his factory like his family, his Homeland . . ."

The music matches the ceremonial clichés. Pretending his ardor is out of control, the announcer breaks in. "Comrades! We are devoting our utmost efforts to greet the New Year of our beloved Socialist Motherland as Lenin teaches us, with new dedication and success on all fronts of labor productivity! In this way we show our heartfelt thanks to our Leninist Homeland, the world's first socialist state—and to our dear, native Communist Party, inspiration of all progressive people. Lenin inspires each of us to do his very best . . ." It's less the message itself than its morning-to-midnight incantation that has anesthetized part of my reason. This is no country, but a crypt. Everyone in it is a dervish being whipped up for self-sacrifice.

The next vignette is about a North Sea fishing captain who has voluntarily increased his socialist norm in honor of the second "decisive" year of the "historic" new Five-Year Plan—and bagged a bigger catch than ever, "as if Vladimir Ilich himself was guiding the crew." Then a little sketch about stitchers in a clothing factory mobilizing all their thoughts to increase labor productivity and regretting they weren't there to sew shirts for dear Vladimir Ilich while he was alive. It's so bad that Viktor, a devotee of propaganda soap operas, asks me to turn it off. He has finished breakfast and stripped to his bloomer-like black under-shorts—the standard, flyless Soviet model of vinegary acetate—in preparation for a wash. Last night, he interrupted our aimless conversation to declare he's keeping an eye out for a wife, damn hard to find among modern city girls who know zilch about running a thrifty house. "The University ones can't open a can by themselves and feel too important to learn. Yet I'm for women working, so what's the answer? You've got to have equality, everybody building Communism. But women are *happier* in a kitchen than in an office. It could cause trouble, this diverting them from their natural purpose."

The clique at the end of the corridor demonstrably ignores Viktor, the "hopeless square." Although somewhat disconcerted by this—his age and Party membership should make him our floor's ethical leader—he's come to terms with his unpopularity, counting its compensations: he would bitterly resent keeping up with the clique in expenditures for tobacco and drink. He shakes his head in saddened puzzlement at their camp affectations: quoting obscure hack writers of the worst Stalinist periods and smoking the cheapest *papirosi* in imitation of Volga riverboat bums. He can't even understand their idiom, a supercharged student-underground hodgepodge of jazz, criminal and labor-camp jargon. It's the latest *smart* way of talking and requires introducing everything with an exaggeratedly drawled pronunciation of the phrase "personally speaking." "Personally speaking, I could go a glass of tea"—or, "have a pee." "Personally speaking, Charles de Gaulle was the President of France." Although my Russian is now adequate for most conversations, I often fail to catch even the gist of their apparently riotous exchanges, and they are delighted when they can keep up such banter for several minutes without my understanding a word of it. But I've managed to learn a few of the more fathomable terms: a "hammer" means great guy; "old slipper," a swinging chick; "boiling derby," a smart kid.

Because its members seem Westernized in some ways of student iconoclasm, the clique illustrates the irrelevance of many imported categories and calculations—those I used to think in too—to this country. Even these jivey cats obey Russian laws of logic, confounding Western assumptions about how they *should* reason. Six or seven of them—who do not really look alike but appear to because their striving to be hip encourages conformity —comprise their tight ingroup. They are country lads with gangling arms extending inches beyond their faded flannel cuffs. All twenty-one or twenty-two years old, all sons of semiliterate peasants who nevertheless won gold medals in their village schools, they are, beneath their boisterous nonchalance, palpably nervous about the startling success and status so quickly severing their roots. In England, their type—Yorkshire working-class lads who find themselves making good in London—has been the making of much contemporary literature: the brash soon-to-be elite, with less and less to say to their village parents, yet also little to the genuine intelligentsia of Moscow and Leningrad.

But they themselves don't know they're on edge. Quick and clever, they've exploited their provincial manners to help make them the dormitory's wise guys and big wheels. Taking the University as a long, big-city spree, they devour impressions and discoveries—of theaters, girls, acquaintances working in the cultural establishment—with appetites befitting their thin frames. They are flying through the best years of their lives on their energy and wit. All my life, I've avoided the fraternity type more successfully than here; the clique somehow shames me into returning slaps on the back and repaying them with American jokes for theirs about Russia.

In their last of five years here, the members are writing theses instead of attending classes. A hundred or so pages long, these papers are the first independent scholarship required during their University careers, but thanks to agreeably low standards of research and writing, most of their day is available for loafing. (The ringleader, a caustic young man with unwashed hair and wild eyes, is writing about Vsevolod Meyerhold, the brilliant theatrical experimentalist, arguably more important than Stanislavsky, who "disappeared" in Stalin's 1937. Caught between the impossibility of an honest thesis—because Meyerhold's avant-garde theories are still taboo and his tutor wants no mention of Stalin—and the bitter pill of a phony one—because he's increasingly enthralled by his subject's genius—Number One has taken to increased buffoonery "in Vsevolod's style.") Waking late in their airless rooms, they shout the well-known slogan to each other through the walls: "Rise, workers; onward and upward!" Then they reluctantly take leave of their beds to congregate in one of the rooms, sitting against one another in underwear worn a full week, smoking strawlike cigarettes for breakfast and telling political jokes.

The gags are variations on three or four old standbys illustrating the gap between Soviet rhetoric and reality, and the nonsense of intensifying propaganda campaigns instead of tackling real work that might close the gap. Two collective farmers meet in the mud of their village street. "Hey, Petya!" shouts Ivan. "What's this I hear on the radio? Something called Communism—d'ya know what it means?" "Sure," volunteers Petya. "That's when everybody gets everything he wants." "Gee! What would you ask for under Communism?" "A good little airplane." "Why on earth do *you* need an airplane?" "I could fly to America and buy myself a bag of potatoes."

Question from "Armenian Radio": "Can a prick be a member of a Brigade of Communist Labor?" *Answer:* "No—for three reasons. It can't work seven hours a day. It frequently changes its place of employment. It is known to spit on its work partners."

Urgent archaeological exploration is being pursued on Egyptian territory soon to be flooded by waters from a new dam. An Italian team discovers a miraculously preserved tomb, but their elation turns to consternation when they fail to decipher its hieroglyphics, even to determine the buried suzerain's name. They call in an English team working nearby, but the Oxbridge experts have no better luck. A French team is summoned, then a German one; the code remains unbroken. In despair, someone thinks of sending for Professor Stukaivich, the leading Soviet Egyptologist. A telegram to Moscow produces the great academician ten days later—flanked, of course, by two KGB escorts. Shaking hands with his colleagues, whom he knows by way of scholarly journals, he enters the tomb. That evening they do not reappear. A long day and second suspenseful night pass without sign of them. Haggard and bearded, the three men finally emerge on the third evening, announcing laconically, "It's Ramses III." The astounded scientists whoop their congratulations. "Marvelous chaps, those Russians!"—but how was the mystery solved? "I don't want secrets," says an Italian over the popping of corks. "But how *did* you identify Ramses?" "The bastard," grunts a KGB man. "He confessed."

But disagreeable reaction has taught me to draw no "obvious" conclusion from these jokes. Behind the clique's sarcasm lurks an insular patriotism from which the Texas Bible Belt could take lessons. When I laugh too loudly at their failures-of-socialism stories or offer an observation of my own, they turn on me, a glint in their eyes. *They*'ll poke the fun; foreigners had better keep their mouths shut—or, as their rougher mates do with the odd cheeky Arab, be prepared for a beating one day when caught alone in some snowy field.

At bottom, they're convinced that Soviet ways are the best in the world. They accept the system's underlying axioms partly because it is easier to believe than to doubt, partly because propaganda, as E. M. Forster said, "is not a magic drug; it must appeal to something that already exists in men's minds, or its power evaporates."

The appeal to the clique of their own social system lies not so much in its being Soviet or socialist (some of their favorite jokes remind us that Marx was a bearded Kraut—no, a dirty, bearded Jew) as in its being *Russian*. And what is Russian is *ours*. The Red Army is ours, Lenin is ours, sputniks and dialectical materialism, agitprop and even meat shortages are ours. Maybe Russia isn't really best; perhaps, for the real truth, it's crude and backward. But not weak! The armed forces, biggest and best, are growing more so; let the West laugh at that! Besides, backwardness is all the more reason to defend the homeland against the richer, denigrating West. All the more reason to work for *our* people's triumph. Lampooning their political lessons, therefore, they believe in the need for them.

Work for the Soviet Union is precisely what the clique will do two or three years after graduation. Assuming success in their first jobs, as teachers and editorial assistants, where occasional reprimands for heavy drinking will not spoil their essentially favorable records, they will be recruited to operate the machinery of the state. Not the heavy machinery of the KGB or Party *apparat*—from the Party's point of view, they're too clever and sardonic to be trusted with direct political power—but the desks in the front offices which require higher education and accompanying refinements: the diplomatic service, newspaper and broadcasting editorships, control posts in cultural and educational affairs. Other students will graduate with higher distinction, but the clique's peasant-proletarian lineage will win them the administrative jobs. It's not the working-class pedigree itself that makes people trustworthy here but the attitudes bred by upbringing in laboring communities, untainted by cosmopolitanism—precisely the Russia First animus of these up-and-comers. Bright as they are, the Party knows—because it has arranged— that their education will have done nothing to undermine their fundamentalist patriotism. As they themselves recognize, they will always belong to their villages.

"We'll get ahead," Number Two assured me recently, "because we're in tune with the country. Moscow is the façade; we've always needed façades. But the truth is still the village. Everything comes from the village and is the spirit of the village. Which is why the sons of the clever Moscow intellectuals will be working for us."

This cynicism, a facet of the clique's essential dishonesty, helps put me off them. But perhaps, on the contrary, they are admirably honest to acknowledge their advantage. Maybe my unease is prompted simply by my being older—or by resentment that, like Viktor, I'm too square to make their grade.

Two nights ago, the clique had their monthly fling in one of the double rooms. The table was laden with sausage, tinned fish, sweating cheese and real butter for their fresh white loaves. The room was as stifling as a cowbarn in winter. The vodka was consumed in water glasses downed *zalpom,* eight ounces in one daring gulp. As ritual toasts were shouted and the alcohol relentlessly swilled, the boys' features grew thick along with their voices. Sweat coated their faces, somehow more lurid because of the bitter night outside. They were not twenty-one, but fifty; not even fifty, but ageless. Having joked, fought, screamed, sung, cursed Mother Russia and sworn to die for Her, they were staggeringly, insensibly drunk by ten o'clock. By midnight, having smeared the lavatory's wall tiles with layers of vomit, they were stacked across the cots like cordwood, in each other's arms and oblivion. The Chinese student who lives next door—whose presence is a mystery since all his countrymen were sent home ten years ago—was smugly disgusted. "Barbarous Russians. They will never change. *We* are supposed to learn from *them?*"

Much in Russia is opaque, atmospheric, redolent of its great literature; but there is no mystery in the clique's smells. Socks that have been worn all winter inside a single pair of shoes, now polluting the floor like fetid puddles. The shoes themselves, never dry of sweat and slush, with their own distinctive odor. Body odors distilled from cabbage and garlic sausage; tobacco tar seeped deeply into winter skin; the Clorox mustiness of men's dormitories everywhere, heightened by rarely washed laundry and never-cleaned wool. And on the morning after the spree, the vapors of adolescent puke: universal hangover stink, in no way more interesting or agreeable because it reigns here, in enigmatic Russia.

Sprees are held never less than once a month, on someone's birthday, a national or University holiday or payment day for student stipends. Whenever a few rubles come to hand, the clique casts about for a suitable event—Miners' Day or the anniversary of the Mongolian Revolution, in a pinch—to celebrate. That afternoon, money is allocated to food and drink, the purchasing logistics are planned—no less solemnly than for a feast day of the Mohawk nation—and the chosen room is arranged with tables and chairs. The agenda of the party itself varies little. The boys nibble at the bologna and salted cucumbers, clink their glasses and toss them down, emote, bare their souls, become hopelessly maudlin, then turn savage before passing out. It is a pagan celebration, a religious rite; the Russian peasants' quest for periodic escape, salvation, release from this shabby world to something higher and all-encompassing.

Delicacies such as cheese and "Doctor's" brand sausage—let alone vodka—represent a spendthrift extravagance. The party costs at least half their monthly stipend, and during the last ten days of the month they will exist solely on boiled potatoes and "white nights" tea—glasses of hot water with nothing added. ("The tea's *zhidok*," they say, ritually repeating their stale wordplay, "but the host is Russian." In this case, *zhidok* means both "watery" and "a Yid.") But this only intensifies their anticipation of the next party and broadens their grins while they plan how many cans of marinated cod and how many bottles to buy. When a Dutch student suggested they might be healthier and happier on a more realistic budget, they were contemptuous. "What are we, clerks in some goddam office? You save your own money, buy yourself a bookcase. Russians know how to *live*."

The clique is often joined by a slightly younger student whose appearance and background are as unlike theirs as was Isaac Babel's from his beloved Cossacks. Narrow-shouldered Leonid wears a clean suit and flesh-colored glasses, and is balding before his voice has fully changed. A cosmopolitan Muscovite, he is the son of well-to-do Jewish intellectuals. His father is a corresponding member of the Academy of Medicine, his mother a distinguished classicist, his older sister a cellist training in the Conservatory. Leonid himself, almost against his will, stands near the academic head of his faculty. He reads a dozen books a week in three languages, and his room in the comfortable family apartment is a substantial library.

When the drinking at the sprees has begun in earnest, a fierce Great Russian chauvinism expands within the boys as if the vodka were an acid producing a gas on contact with the soft metal of their prejudice. And integral to the chauvinism is a deep hatred of *Zhidi*, the dirty Jews. The first jokes are relatively mild. "I heard the weather was lousy on the Black Sea last summer." "Yeah, those dirty Jews." . . . An old Jew shuffling up Arbat Street is clonked on the head by dislodged fragments of a building's façade. "Goddamit, there's no place for a good brick to fall down in this country." But such witticisms are soon discarded for more direct expression of the clique's drunken wisdom.

"The Jews are scum, they stink up Russia with their sniveling fear and greed." . . . "To straighten out our country overnight, take the plum jobs from the bloodsucking Jews and send them to the front. No, they'd kiss the enemy's ass and sell us for some jewelry." Leonid lowers his eyes and plays with the oilcloth. When he offers a comment about a subject under discussion, he is told to shut his mouth. Everyone knows a Jew's opinion is worthless because a Jew understands nothing but money and hoarding—certainly nothing about Russia or Russians. "We'll ask you when we want to know about Moses."

One morning, when Leonid was catching some sleep in my

room after an especially hard party, I asked him why he put up with the awfulness. Sparked by the victory of the Six-Day War, fired by hope of a huge immigrant column trudging to Israel, the Zionism of some Jewish students is fierce. Children whose parents kept resolutely "assimilated" households for decades, denying their Jewishness for the higher cause—socialism was going to make Judaism and all "petty nationalism" obsolete—are among the most implacable Israeli patriots, perceiving antisemitism even where it's absent (a considerable feat in contemporary Russia) and sneering disgust at every aspect of Soviet rule. Among many Moscow Jews, not an hour passes without specula-tion, calculation and agonized deliberation whether to take the do-or-die steps toward leaving—and questions, questions, ques-tions to me, who, as a Westerner, *must* know what a Tel-Aviv dentist earns in terms of a kilo of stewing beef.

Leonid belongs to this category precisely. Some of his friends have left, and even his well-established parents are locked in the frightening debate of whether to throw everything up and face the persecution accompanying an application to emigrate. But the meek young man himself has pledged never to "quit." The last thing he'll become, he says, is another unemployed Israeli intellectual. "They have a surplus already, while Russia goes hungry."

"But why subject yourself to abuse from boys half your worth?" I repeated. "*You* have no illusions about inherent proletarian wisdom. Is it masochism?"

He hesitated again and I was sorry I'd pressed him. Day by day, he was being grinded between the clique's "anticosmopoli-tan" arrogance and soaring Jewish tribalism. "Because I want to be a writer," he said at last. "I want to write about the Russian people, and these are real ones, not the sophisticated types my family has always known. The truth frightens my parents largely because they've always hidden from it—masked it with political dreams. . . . Besides, I like the boys. Underneath, they like me. They're my best friends."

And they are: for Leonid *personally,* the clique has only respect and affection. They are unhappy when Lenya, as they call him, spends the night at home instead of squeezing in to share one of their cots. Once they actually postponed a party because flu had him bedridden.

As for drinking, Leonid himself is a slouch only in comparison to the clique's hard core. The boy-intellectual started in order to be accepted and to demonstrate his affinity for the muzhik, but by now enjoys inebriation in and for itself.

"If you lived here, you'd drink too. It's less the thing to do than the thing you must do. Vodka is essential to everything."

To pursue his interest in "real Russians," Leonid would like to live with the clique rather than in the grandish family apartment, but manages only occasional nights sharing one of their narrow cots. Students whose families reside within fifty kilometers of the University must live at home even if they'd prefer the dormitory (just as Muscovites may not take a room in a Moscow hotel). This restriction reflects practical as well as political needs: even without the Moscow contingent of students, the dormitories are badly overcrowded. The University's enrollment, like that of almost all Soviet institutes, strains its physical plant.

Next door live three girls in a room meant for two: Raya, Ira and Masha. Coarser than Chekhov's Three Sisters, they provoke the occasional association nevertheless, specially in their delight at inhabiting *Moscow* after wholly provincial childhoods. Raya and Ira, who share the same plainness and freckle patterns, spend their spare time sewing curtains, doilies and what they think are pretty little things for their bathroom. (Why no pretty dresses for themselves?) Stendhal novels opened, they listen to Tchaikovsky on the portable record player for which they saved all last year.

Sometimes they attend one of the Saturday dances in honor of Soviet–Burmese Friendship Day, the Fifty-fifth Anniversary of the Young Communist League and similar holidays featuring a revolutionary or peace-and-friendship theme. The evening begins in the main auditorium with political lectures, expressions by Asian and African students of gratitude for the magnanimity of Soviet foreign policy, academics citing the latest production targets—cement production will be increased threefold by 1977!—and a professor of literature holding forth on the current slogans. Then the main event itself, which, in the central building's main hall of columns and a splintering floor, reminds me of my parents describing their 1930s dancing days: a big, sloppy student band playing that kind of fox-trot, boys and girls displaying their Sunday best—purple dresses and ties with metallic threads—and hundreds of couples swaying almost in time to the beat while crowds of singles eye each other across the floor.

"She's not bad, the one with that belt."

"Are you serious? Scary as war."

"And gives. She loves to put out."

After their afternoon of ironing blouses and washing their hair, Raya and Ira arrive looking less attractive than almost anyone else and move quickly to a corner. Their spirited talk there is about the same subjects, and in the same tone, as all day and all week. After dancing with each other half a dozen times, they leave together, arm in arm. Do such girls still exist in America? The homely but kindly ones, waiting for husbands without a word of distress, a hint of complaint or, of course, of aggressiveness? I'm always too embarrassed to thank them, as I'd like to, for being their unadorned selves.

That Masha gets on beautifully with them is a case of total opposites attracting. Raya and Ira leave early for class, holding hands and stopping en route for a cafeteria bun and a glass of muddy coffee; Masha, on the other hand, sleeps until eleven if possible (despite the strict requirement, accompanied by elaborate machinery for strict enforcement, that attendance is obligatory at all lectures). Masha then knocks at my door, her yawning face puffed by too much sleep, and, when Viktor's at class, comes in to breakfast on Nescafé and an American cigarette. A strong, sourish smell surrounds her, proclaiming who she is—a miner's daughter—and the spicy foods she likes to eat: an intriguing scent to someone raised with Colgate and Arrid. Tipped by wide purple nipples, her breasts swing heavily under the gauze of her nightdress. Masha is a geology student and my oldest female Russian friend. When she was young, she says, she adored making love. Now she can take it or leave it—nothing personal intended. Next month she'll be twenty.

On the day Masha and I broke the ice as neighbors, she told me about her first love. Amply developed physically, she was otherwise a schoolgirl in uniform and braids whose knowledge came from chaste novels and classmates' reveries. She did dream about romance—but more about Ulanova and Plisetskaya, for she was attending a special high school for ballet. (Masha a ballerina? With that low-slung bottom and the matching Russian thighs? Photographs of her at sixteen, when this happened, indicate that she had already acquired her womanly sponginess, together with a lower body designed more for cross-country skiing than for the stage. Nevertheless, her teachers assured her she had promise.)

This was in her native Perm, the industrial center of the middle Urals, which is off limits to foreigners because of defense plants and military installations. In such "closed" cities, the role of the secret police is significantly greater than elsewhere in Russia, another way of saying it is very great indeed. The KGB closely watches all aspects of municipal life: roads into the city, airports, streets and squares, and every institution on these same streets and squares. The central headquarters for the huge staff required for this myriad activity was a large building some fifty yards from young Masha's school.

It had a staff cafeteria, of course. Every Soviet institution has its basement cafeteria—one of many reasons why cities are so bare of places where a private citizen can eat. When this one was closed for repairs and repainting, several junior agents walked next door for dinner, to the opera theater's canteen. One day, Masha's class, which had been rehearsing for a recital on the theater's stage, was also eating there. As the lusty girl with the face flushed by her pirouettes stood in line at the counter, a young man approached—who, however, did not seem young at all to the sixteen-year-old. It was the handsomest of the agents.

"That's a terrific pair of tits, lassie—and a luscious ass. Shall we road-test it this afternoon?"

This was not the first time Masha had heard such words. Like most city girls, she had accustomed herself early to propositions and sneered obscenities by toughs loitering in courtyards and back streets. But no man had ever explored her eyes while mentioning her private parts. And such a fine-looking man, with clean blond hair and an open face! Why did he talk that way? Did he suppose she was no longer a virgin?

Blushing fiercely, she wondered where to hide. Then something wholly unexpected and even more pleasant happened: *he* blushed to the same hue. It was clear (he explained later) that he'd misjudged her; he regretted his insult. He hadn't even checked out her face at first—only the body, which certainly *looked* of age and experience to pop straight into bed.

Still intrigued, he recommenced on an entirely different tack. He carried her tray to her seat, withdrawing immediately so as not to embarrass her before her girl friends. Leaving *his* friends, he waited outside the canteen and persuaded her to meet him after class. Walking her home, he made her laugh. It was a week before they actually slept together: seven unhurried days and evenings of courting, coaxing, reassuring and good times, filled with as many movies and meals together as they could sneak time for. By then he had grown fond of her, and she, needless to say, loved him breathlessly. He was a hail-fellow-well-met, liked by the town's successful young men, not least because of his repertoire of political anecdotes. (A KGB man joking about the Soviet system? Yes; and less improbable than Masha's dancing ambition.) Charming and unusually energetic, he drank moderately, spent freely and treated Masha with tenderness and respect.

And made love to her wildly. Never, he exulted, had he known such passion; certainly not with his wife, a good-looking, well-dressed blonde whom, however, he didn't like even before, as now, she became a source of guilt and resentment. For hard as he tried to remain a husband to her and good father to their boys, he was increasingly entranced by Masha and soon loathed time spent at home. Although unfaithful to Masha as well as to his spouse—he couldn't help it, he told her—his other conquests were mere one-shot pickups. On top of everything, family finances virtually collapsed under the drain of entertainment and gifts for Masha. To the wife who formerly budgeted his monthly pay, he brought home nothing.

His superior officers posed the greater problem. To maintain the KGB officer's public image of a hardworking, clean-living

Builder of Communism marching in the vanguard of political
and ideological campaigns, all drinking, joke-telling and forni-
cating are kept scrupulously private. The behavior of Masha's
man caused increasing displeasure at headquarters. The couple
had been seen in the city's handful of restaurants. Their affair
was far too open; talk swelled about the failure to uphold
family-man standards—and about Masha's age. He'd even
ignored friendly front-office advice to drop her. Divorce was out
of the question: an agent who leaves his wife, especially for a
younger woman, is a discredit to the service. Something had to be
done.

A less popular and competent officer might have been
discharged. Masha's man was offered alternatives: accept transfer to a distant city or resign. Masha begged him to think of his
family and career—and he agreed. Their last evening together
foundered. In the morning, he left for his new post two thousand
kilometers away, and she never heard from him again. A year
later, there was an epilogue. Masha was in trouble for associating
with a young chemist who read and passed around Andrei
Sinyavsky's *On Socialist Realism*. Out of affection for his departed
protégé, the KGB captain conducting the investigation dismissed
her with a warning. Nothing incriminating entered her dossier.

I hadn't intended to dwell so on the KGB. This is the style of
the diplomatic crowd, belaboring its *idée fixe*. (My main grudge
against the Embassy is grounded in its security lecture the day
after my arrival, whose dwelling on "sexual fraternization"
dangers gave me weeks of frustration and a mortifying hour of
impotence at my first serious attempt with a puzzled Russian
girl.) Even now, much of the American colony remains constantly ALERT, refusing to set foot in a Russian apartment.
Provocations are indeed staged; but what really terrible thing
can happen to someone with diplomatic immunity? But, paradoxically, this preoccupation does reflect a partial truth about
the secret police. The same isolation that shields Embassy officers
from the institution's "human" side—KGB agents are people,
after all; viz. Masha's paramour—also prevents them from
personally seeing how thoroughly police penetrate daily life.

Last week, a school friend of Raya's passed through Moscow

from their native town and told the story of a neighboring family's distress. It began when their cottage burned to the ground, the blaze consuming their last book and wooden spoon. In despair, the widowed mother of three approached the local Red Cross for assistance, and her persistence was rewarded with fifteen rubles—food for a week. "But the Red Cross is supposed to *help;* it's supposed to be for emergencies just like mine," she wrote in gentle protest—adding, in a petition to her local Soviet, that during her own dozen years as a volunteer member at her factory, her dues alone exceeded the sorry offering. The result was a KGB visit and warning that continuation of such attempts to "create a disturbance" would be dealt with as an antisocial act. "How," asked the officer in charge, "will imprisonment help your children?"

My mistake was to have pictured the KGB crushing only political dissent, whereas any little display of any kind of independence may incite them. At the same time, there's a wider area of uncertainty and more room for play than I'd expected. It's less sinister when you know it, and more depressing.

It's cosy to have women students in the dormitory. Quarters are assigned helter-skelter in the Russian way, with men and women often in adjoining rooms. For four years in the 1960s, women were segregated in a specially guarded wing of the main building. Now that the sexes are together again as they should be, there is speculation about what caused their seclusion and why it was abandoned. Three theories are popular. It is said that foreign students, who began arriving in numbers in the late 1950s, could not take the mixed arrangements in stride; their antics and tittering warned the authorities of damage to the University's reputation. Alternately, it is argued that a shocking number of (free and legal) abortions proved the need for remedial action. But later, segregation was found not to have appreciably reduced the demand on the University clinic, perhaps because hundreds of male students managed to sleep in the women's section every night. (Of course another elaborate system of check-in and check-out operated to prevent this, including watchwomen at the entrances and midnight patrols checking rooms. But where else is it so easy to fool or bribe the checkers by distracting attention, switching documents, sliding a chocolate bar into a granny's pocket? Or, if you're caught, to plead your way—"I throw myself at your mercy, please-oh-please don't be cruel to me"—out of being reported? Petty Soviet authority is often a peasant *babushka*, unquestioning in political faith, impervious to logic, but with a *heart* waiting to be moved so she can forgive her errant charges. In any case, hordes of men sneaking into the women's section was acknowledged to be a disturbance greater than those of the old system.)

But now a new theory is gaining sway concerning the first secretary of the University's Party organization. A Georgian obsessed, like most men of his nation, about female virtue in his family, he became anxious when his own darling daughter was about to enter the University: clearly, the traditional dormitory arrangements would not do for *her*. With a lofty preamble about Communist morals, he issued the segregation ukase. In vain, the University's Young Communist League protested on humanitarian grounds, as did several deans on bureaucratic ones: scattering students of the same faculties increased paperwork. Unhappy years passed, ended at last by a happy discovery that the Georgian had been stealing and reselling textbooks and office supplies (or, in another version, that he persisted in speaking well of Khrushchev). Dismissed after a confidential Party investigation, he was ordered to an obscure Siberian post while the old system was quietly restored. *Sic in Muscovy res geruntur. Sic*, in any case, is the nature of the rumors.

Last night, I again heard one of the University's most popular stories. Unwashed and unshaven, a young law student is bodily in attendance at one of his droning lectures in a large amphitheater. His attention wanders (as does that of his fellow students, who are doodling, chattering and reading novels: it is the rare lecturer anyone actually listens to, if only because most parrot the plodding textbooks). Three rows below and a dozen seats to the right, he spies a pretty girl he'd never noticed before. Scribbling her a note, he has it passed on, hand to hand. "I like your looks. Come to my room tonight at seven o'clock, we'll fuck." The well-groomed girl pens her answer in the margin and returns it by the same route. "Will be there at seven. Understood your hint."

The old chestnut always gets a big laugh—because, the students say, it's so true. They're surprised to hear that even after all recent permissive developments, sex at Harvard is less plenteous and informal. And I still wonder at what can be had here almost for the asking.

Some professors apparently have as much trouble as I concentrating on work. Students say the "boss" of Scandinavian languages, for one, is better at philandering than philology. Inviting undergraduates home, he mentions their doubtful grades and "screws us like mad," as a self-confessed victim put it. Other teachers too are known as notorious womanizers, and their conquests, very easy anyhow, are augmented by a tricklet of girl students to *them*. . . . All this is true, I swear it; but not the implication about my personal riches. Even here—especially here, with robust sex all around me—I manage to jinx things at the last moment, and get less than I should. When I'm blue, I long to bury myself in the oblivion of passion. Like artichokes, Russian femininity seems to grow directly from the earth. Strong, supple arms and the slight bulge of vulvas through skirts beckon with the lure of all the high-school seniors I used to fantasize about. The flesh seems so *pliant*.

Miner's daughter Masha is the strongest female personality on our floor, but the prettiest girl—the most enchanting I saw anywhere in Moscow until I met my own Anastasia—is sylphlike Natasha. Perhaps, however, her braids distort my judgment. She's the only girl who still wears them—the traditional flaxen plaits that fall to the small of her back, ends gladdened by snippets of ribbon. Sometimes she winds them around her head, exposing her creamy neck. She has a roundish face, limpid eyes and classic Slavic features. Her mouth is almost too perfect for kisses. When she sits in the common room, head tilted, humming to herself, I think I'm looking at the model for a Russian Renoir.

Natasha teeters on the border of serious academic trouble. Her mind wanders, she says—superfluously, for her most characteristic expression heralds this. She wafts along the corridor, daydreaming about her future. Every few days she comes into my room and, if I'm alone, sits on my cot, squeezing her hands and sighing. She is so beautiful and unaware of it that I wish we could fall in love and live happily ever after. Occasionally she talks about her married sister in Moscow—who, as I found when I tried to track her down one day, doesn't exist: there is no building at that address. The thought of schoolteaching, her given destination, appalls her. She hasn't the slightest interest in Soviet history, her major, or, indeed, in history in general.

"What *do* you want to be, Natasha?" runs the game played daily on our floor.

"An actress."

"In films or the theater."

"The theater." (Sigh.) "I think my place is on the stage."

She goes quickly to the cot of anyone who says she has the makings of a natural actress, but bursts into sobs after perceiving she's been duped. (Aside from a high-school play three years ago, she has never acted.) Her weeping used to be heard more often from several rooms, but some older boys have recently assumed the role of her protector, and have stopped sleeping with her themselves—because, they say, taking advantage of a child spoils the fun.

The boy who loves Natasha more than anyone is Kemal, but she won't even have supper with him: like many girls here, she has a visceral repugnance for "black" skin. Kemal's color is in fact a delicate umber—which, on his ankles, looks like suntan against the white of his adored sheepskin slippers from Harrods. He pads back and forth along the corridor, studying while in motion like a guru and inviting every English-speaking soul into his room at each encounter.

"I'll make us a cup of tea?" the singsong Indian voice asks in English, with a trace of a Russian accent.

"Sorry, Kemal. I'm late for the movies, just can't stop."

"You are too pale. You will need some good tea."

Kemal lives next to the kitchen in a room he's had for four years. (He swears he found a microphone under the bed his first winter—if true, the only tangible discovery of the bugging of foreigners' rooms that Russians take for granted.) The son of a wealthy Delhi manufacturer, he came to Moscow to study instead of to his beloved Oxford for what he calls "unfortunate political reasons." Declining to elaborate, he will, however, reveal how he copes with another inherited problem. Like his moneyed father, Kemal is short and slender, with full black hair and an unusually meager penis. The shortcoming troubled him severely until a wise man near the family's summer residence taught him the elements of hypnotism. He used this power primarily to convince conquests that the member they were enjoying was "very full and fat," and now insists Russian girls are his best subjects. "They are susceptible to it, you understand. Because they are always flooded with statistics to convince them they have three times what they actually do. Production figures, production reports—it comes to the same thing, you know. It is a nice setup for my little deception."

Kemal questions me for hours about the chances of fulfilling his dream: graduate study at M.I.T. on the basis of his Moscow degree. (When the application forms arrived—imagine the problems *they* inflicted on puzzled postal censors!—I spent days interpreting questions and helping phrase his replies. He saw hidden meanings and rewrote answers like a prisoner composing a stay-of-execution plea.) He also tries to establish something like an English-Speaking Union with the new crop of American and English exchange students every September. But his closest friends are a Russian couple who befriended him during his first week in Moscow, two hundred and thirty-three weeks ago, "not counting the days." The couple live together unofficially two floors below, and have established a kind of University record for a love affair's durability. I know the girl, brown-eyed Anna, moderately well: a Belorussian with the intensity of a Radcliffe student who suspects she's unattractive. But human-dynamo Sergei avoids me: he's planning a government career, hopefully in the diplomatic service, which fraternization with an American might prejudice. According to Anna and Kemal, Sergei, the product of a poor family, will stop at nothing to make his way.

Now Kemal is bitter on Anna's behalf. The four-year affair has come to an end. In fact, Anna and Sergei have just married other partners, although they still share an occasional night.

"In my four years with him," says Anna, "I didn't know other men existed. I've never slept with anyone else, before or after. I can't sleep with this person called my husband. I belong to Sergei."

The end was sour. Despite his unfaithfulness and her brittle resentment, their *de facto* marriage was surprisingly solid—until October, when Sergei became apprehensive. Since neither he nor Anna were Muscovites, both would be sent, upon graduation in June, to a village or town for fulfillment of their obligations at jobs assigned by a state commission. The prospect of a three-year "sentence" to the provinces was very bad; worse was their slim chance of ever securing the residence stamp that would permit them to live again in the capital. Sergei proposed the standard subterfuge: he would marry the first suitable *Moskvichka* who came his way; Anna the first bachelor *Moskvich*. Thus they would remain in Moscow, free to continue almost as before. After a seemly interval—not less than two years, because the police have begun revoking residence permits obtained through obvious marriages of convenience—they would pay their partners whatever was necessary, divorce them and come together officially.

Anna reluctantly agreed when she realized that, under the circumstances, this was as close as possible to a marriage proposal. But when Sergei actually made his choice—a shy girl he met in the library and proposed to immediately—her self-control shattered. Weeping, cursing, begging, she fell upon the mortified fiancée with fists and nails. His resolve stiffened by just these hysterics, Sergei carried through his plan.

To spite him, she too married the first interested man—a minor official of fifty—for *her* Moscow permit. But Sergei was happy with his docile bride and Anna succeeded only in increasing her misery by pointing up his lack of jealousy. Now she's trying to cultivate friends in high places, for she is determined to be more successful than "that shallow careerist I thought I once loved."

There are worse troubles than Anna's. Last month a girl hanged herself in a room on the adjoining corridor. She looped a belt through the handle of a cupboard over the doorway, and the wood held just long enough to achieve the strangulation. It is said there are a dozen suicides a semester in the dormitories.

Most victims jump from the upper-story windows after prolonged fits of winter melancholy. The incidents are never reported; on the contrary, the University administration painstakingly hushes them up. A constant buzz of rumor therefore surrounds the circumstances of each episode. Was the boy who died in October the son of a certain minister?

Last month's victim had been discovered stealing from a roommate—single rubles from pockets from time to time and bits of clothing which she sold. The roommate reported her suspicions and, on the morning the investigating commission was expected, left to meet them in the main foyer. Returning to the room twenty minutes later to question the suspect, they found her body on the floor. She had left a note: "I cannot face my guilt nor the shame of a Comrades' Court. Please forgive me. Something went wrong."

Chingiz came in to tell me. The dead girl had been his lover. He sat on the floor, fingering the books she'd left him the evening before and speaking in staccato. "Galya stole because of hunger for affection. It's the most basic psychological reaction. She needed more than we gave her; and tomorrow, when our guilt wears off, we'll be as selfish as ever. Why the 'brotherhood' pretense when we're all *alone?* Damn the lies we live."

It was not the first suicide Chingiz knew. He's a type—unhappy himself, yet solid—reached for by people who feel they can't cope. Foolish as the premonition is, I'm convinced bad news of our own will pull us together.

Chingiz and I hadn't been close before that morning but sensed the time would come. Passing in the corridor, we always smiled comfortably, pleased at biding our time. When the suicide was discovered, it was natural he came to me; natural, too, to go to a movie instead of demonstrating proper mourning.

Dreamer, libertine and former laborer, Chingiz looks exactly like what he has been and is. He's tall and lean, with a cowboy's slouch and mane of dark hair obscuring an Apache-Asian face. Except for his eyes, which are often impenetrable, he reminds me of a less-dented Jack Palance. In the freeness of his spirit, he resembles a younger Alyosha except that he, my friend of friends Alyosha, is never moody.

Black-eyed Chingiz was born in the vast semi-arid steppe
north of the Caucasus. His people are hybrid Russians and
Kalmyks: seminomadic Buddhists who speak Mongolian and
raise sheep. The feeling of something very close and very
good—his mother, who rode with him strapped to her back—was
the first emotion he remembers; wanderlust was the second.
Mother and father adored and spoiled him, the settlement's
young darling, but by the time he could master a strong horse, he
knew he had to explore. After half a dozen adolescent attempts to
run away and a score of odd jobs on trucks and construction sites,
he found his way to Odessa and became a sailor; then a leading
seaman, next an officer; then an officer on ships *going abroad.*

No matter that the crew was watched incessantly to prevent
defections and the ship's political officer made him sick; he had
found his calling. Movement and open air soothed him, while his
quiet hard work earned him regular promotions. He entered the
University two years ago because his ambition is to captain his
own vessel—to be his own boss—and a Soviet master's license
requires a University degree. In any field whatever; for lack of
another academic interest, Chingiz chose Russian literature. And
now the sea has a strong competitor; he has discovered that
poetry puts him in communion with the Large World much as
dawn perceived from the bridge of a solitary ship.

Mayakovsky is his hero. (*"I will make myself black trousers of the
velvet of my voice."*) Chingiz knows his long poems by heart and
loves to recite "The Cloud in Trousers."

> Your thought
> musing on a sodden brain
> like a bloated lackey on a greasy couch,
> I'll taunt with a bloody morsel of heart;
> and satiate my insolent, caustic contempt.

I'm not sure precisely what I admire in Chingiz. We still
haven't fully opened up about ourselves, although I know he's
troubled by "sensitive" political issues and detestation of repression lies in his bones. (Did I know why Mayakovsky really
committed suicide? he once asked me. Why almost all the real
revolutionary poets killed themselves by 1935?) In fact, we rarely
discuss anything at length. On a "walk" last Sunday in Moscow's

outskirts, a six-hour hike through tumbledown villages and disconsolate woods, we hardly exchanged a sentence. It was enough to absorb the countryside's tranquilizing current, transmitted through the immense, inspiring silence and icicles of sunlight. Chingiz never speaks of his girls, who are legion, or how he wins swimming meets without training. He broods, drinks, enjoys his hard-won privilege of being left alone by the clique and by Komsomol activists trying to recruit "volunteers" for their latest project to raise political consciousness.

His schedule conforms to the general pattern. He attends lectures and seminars throughout the day: forty long hours of classes a week, for Soviet pedagogues prefer group study and textbook-spooning to independent reading and research. Like military service schools, this educational system assigns certificates on the basis of course hours attended rather than individual achievement. Evenings, Chingiz plays dominoes in the common room, goes walking in town, or entertains a girl in his room. Not what but *how* he does things is different; even reading in bed, he's more alone and intense than the others, yet the whole range of University activities seems a mere distraction for him, as if he's marking time for something more important.

It was from Leonid I learned that Chingiz's father was one of the first Kalmyk Communists, a Robin Hood admired by the local shepherds as much as they despised the ruthless commissars dispatched from Moscow. A victim of one of the earliest purges, he was taken away before dawn one morning after holding Chingiz's forehead through a fit of vomiting that very night. Chingiz never saw him again, nor heard what happened to him—not a word in thirty years, until a letter for his mother arrived in 1958, posthumously rehabilitating her husband, sharing her sorrow over the unfortunate mistake, promising the Party would never again tolerate the "isolated violations of socialist legality" permitted during the "personality cult." His mother threw away the paper. Someone looking back to the promise of the Khrushchev days once lauded the Party for rehabilitating purged Communists; Chingiz stood up and left the room, his silent fury ending the argument.

Another student told me that Chingiz recently spoke at a Komsomol meeting for the first time. The discussion concerned an unruly troublemaker whom the Presidium had recommended for expulsion. The activists were startled, then angered, at Chingiz's extemporaneous speech in his defense: such challenge to the leadership at an open meeting was insolent. (Not quite unprecedented, however: similar democratic gropings had been ventured during the heady days of Khrushchev's liberalization.) When the vote was taken and the recommendation defeated, several kingpins succumbed to rage. Chingiz quietly left, reappearing with a large Lenin emblem pinned to his black turtleneck.

His father's reverence for Lenin is clearly sire to his own assumption that a return to genuinely revolutionary principles would set the country straight. In other words, his "opposition" is uncorruptedly Leninist. Students of Leonid's sophistication, by contrast, have come to feel that just this Leninism—its dogmatism, intolerance and repression of dissent, born of the narrow-minded ruthlessness of the man himself, who discarded centuries of wisdom for his Marxist "answers" to everything—was Russia's greatest tragedy. Is it a law of nature that Leonid knows more yet does less to ameliorate present wrongs? That his greater understanding only inhibits him in comparison to the strong-willed Chingiz?

Is it in keeping with some other law that the one student I know who has actually participated in a form of organized political dissent is among the least likable personally? Long-legged Pyotr has never said precisely what he does and I don't ask, of course; but to an American, he's willing to hint that he once helped collect samizdat materials documenting political persecution. In other words, he was an authentic member of the now almost-extinct "democratic movement": one of the handful of "underground" fighters for civic rights whose persecution, as reported in the Western press, has brought them awesome international admiration.

And Pyotr obviously *is* brave; his political principles—for which labor camp and a mangled life are the most probable rewards—*are* exemplary. But the question of why he and his fellows attract so little sympathy from the Russian people for whom they volunteer to sacrifice themselves is complicated by matters of personality. For all his social high-mindedness, Pyotr is a self-righteous petty tyrant, not unlike some American salon revolutionaries. Russians' perverse resistance to enlightened efforts to improve their condition is hardly new; but in this case at least, there is good reason why few are moved to clasp hands with Pyotr the Prig. I must not reveal more about him. But if there is more to say about Soviet villains than fits into newspaper accounts, there is also more to examine about those I once accepted, *ipso facto*, as saintly heroes.

When Chingiz is in a talkative mood, he sometimes alludes to goings-on in the University and city which I hear about nowhere else, although I'm supposedly deep in native life, sharing the authentic Russian experience. Students expelled from the University and exiled from Moscow for challenging some of the more fatuous The Party Saved Russia myths of the (obligatory) History of the Communist Party course; several professors dismissed from their jobs—with confiscation of manuscripts on which they'd been working many years—for having signed petitions about the twelve-year sentence awarded Vladimir Bukovsky; assorted intellectuals demoted or blacklisted for having befriended Westerners who later published articles "slandering Soviet reality." (In some cases, prior authorization to invite the Westerners to their apartments had been quietly obtained, but the police officers resented their misuse of the privilege: the hosts obviously failed to exercise proper control of their guests.) Chingiz says the KGB network in the University is almost as active, and its control almost as strong, as in the armed forces and the Party itself. One of his closest friends, a rebellious history student, was expelled for challenging a lecturer to admit Trotsky was the father of the Red Army.

"Why don't I hear about these things from anyone else?" I ask.

"Who'll tell you? Dissenters are cut down soundlessly, to avoid publicity. People who do learn about specific cases know that they can expect the same if they talk. It's a protection racket: victims' lips sealed by fear. Outsiders like you are hard put to learn how things really work."

Chingiz is almost as disgusted with foreigners who misinterpret Soviet life as with the KGB apparatchiks who, as he sometimes says, are the country's real government. He considers the naïveté of Western leftists as boundless as the dictatorship's hypocrisy:

"the two feed on each other." When he was at sea, roughly a third of the crew was permitted ashore in capitalist ports; the others were not trustworthy enough—that is, not ideologically resolute and genealogically pure. (No one with a relative anywhere in the West or connections with foreigners in Russia was even considered.) Those with the coveted permission could leave the ship for no more than four hours at a time, only in a group, solely on central streets, always shepherded by a KGB overseer. The watchdogs too were watched by a secret informer in the group, as well as by KGB personnel in Soviet trade missions in the ports themselves.

"Much of our free time went to receptions by friendship societies. Gentlemen in tweeds would shake our hands, pleased with themselves. Happy to pretend that everything was normal—simply some Soviet lads abroad, you see, just like ordinary sailors, only better, of course. They'd talk about Soviet culture and achievements. If you tried to tell them two-thirds of the crew couldn't set foot in their city, they wouldn't believe you. But the point is, nobody did try. Goons with sharp ears were busy mixing in that merry hall—a word from them and you'd join the stay-aboards."

But Chingiz too must be seen in the Russian, rather than the Western-liberal, context. To start with, he's suspicious of liberalism and the societies that nourish it. "Russia is subjected to enormous Western influences," he says. "Unfortunately, most are harmful. Ninety per cent of what our people want is the cheapest, most vulgar of capitalist glitter. This applies to our high-school generation in particular, whose ideals are down to chrome and bubble gum. And artists too: the blind imitation of phony Western trends can make you sick. So many 'smart' people fawning, posing, plagiarizing; passing off their worthless copies as art because they'd sell in San Francisco. . . . The paradox is that our campaigns against Western commercialism encourage more empty imitation. Prohibitions only weaken us for more debasement and demoralization by the tawdriest Western junk."

In short, Chingiz is a neo-Slavophile, convinced that Russia must develop along its own lines, avoiding Western excesses. He doesn't realize that just this attitude, with its unrealistic idealism and unwillingness to take freedom's bad with its good, is itself a reflection of Russia's enduring troubles. Like Solzhenitsyn, he's far better at diagnosing ills than at concocting home remedies.

Still, all this is secondary. It is the condition of the country's peasantry that disturbs Chingiz most strongly. Twice a year he visits his mother, who moved to a collective farm north of Moscow after the war. Unable to exist for more than a week on her infinitesimal pension, she returned to work—for a monthly sack of flour and a few rubles in cash—at the age of seventy-three. This provides sufficient bread to fill her stomach, but she doesn't see potatoes for months (except for her own fowl, there is no question of meat), until Chingiz appears. "*I* take a sack of potatoes to *her* on the farm; that's what country life is like. Hardly any able-bodied men are left on her farm: they've all escaped, even without papers. Women, children, pensioners do the work. Animals should get better feed."

Although Chingiz seems resigned when talking of such matters, I'm afraid he'll explode one day and quickly join his expelled, exiled friend. Last week, surely in sublimated protest against authority, he went to the apartment of a history professor who had been entertaining Natasha and other pretty, academically troubled girls. In the fierce argument following Chingiz's demand of an end to such exploitation, each threatened to ruin the other. In the end, Natasha was liberated. Like the rescued heroine of a real-life drama, she waits outside Chingiz's door with adoring eyes.

Two dozen suicides a year; but some say many more. The surface motive is rarely Harvard's scourge, fear of academic failure. In some psyches, the succession of winter days produces a cosmic depression formerly called "Arctic hysteria." As dense as a morning's frozen mist, vapors of purposelessness descend, obliterating all traces of a path or a refuge. With nowhere to go and no objective to sight upon, the country's burdens become personal, therefore intolerable. The nostalgia of threadbare workmen for the late hangman—"In Stalin's day, you could get a mug of real beer; he cared about the people"—bespeaks its impossible demands. The cold mercifully numbs the pain; you feel only that the infinite outdoor void has captured your insides, and that death might be a sensible escape from the domination of the gray forces.

Surely it's these phantoms that crank up my own depressions to a grotesque pitch. Sometimes I'm so stricken that I can drag myself up only for the toilet. On top of my familiar feelings of worthlessness and being trapped in petty spites, a dread I've never known before keeps me prostrate in my unchanged sheets, grateful, at least, for the deep overcast that helps me feign sleep. I am surrounded by adventures, new impressions, eager friends; I have only to open my senses in order to absorb the unique excitement of living in Moscow. But when the self-doubt strikes, I'm too weak to lace my shoes.

What am I doing here, cut off from all I know and everything I am? Deprived of my bourgeois ways and New York comforts? All my life I've roved off my beaten track to demonstrate I'm more swashbuckling than a garment-district salesman's academically achieving son. Football with Irish bruisers, pig farming in Canada, Palm Beach lifeguarding instead of summer camp—my ventures into what my family considered enemy territory were intended to show that I have the brawn to cope with low life and danger. Some ended in humiliating tears, and this time I fear another debacle. I plead to be delivered from this dismal room and the pretense that has driven me across the earth to this blankness.

The real me is no intrepid explorer but a puzzled little kid who happened to grow tall and strong—and somewhere felt so small that he had to act out the adventure fantasies of all Jewish boys. The real me visualized himself listening to Mendelssohn in Carnegie Hall all the time he worked in an Oregon sawmill and, when the moods strike now, whimpers for a Sixth Avenue corned beef on rye, not a Russian salad of despair and freakish visions. Once I actually daydreamed of my parents arriving to take me home.

Mad as it seems, I lose control partly out of infatuation with socialism. Anyone would think that firsthand acquaintance with the hypocrisy sneered in its name here would beget immunity to its false promises, and on most days this is true: I so hate the gangsters who rule me that I pray for economic collapse. I visualize war with China sparking explosions of nationalism in the non-Russian republics and outbreaks of popular revolt, in which I play a daring oratorical role, like a reverse John Reed. But at other moments, I surrender to socialism's essential truths and cheer for its victory. One hundred and seventy-two million tons of steel annually at the end of the Five-Year Plan? Splendid, comrades; how can I help? Twice as many pairs of shoes per capita, three times as many eggs? Yes, the country *is* marching toward plenty for all, while we claw and pollute, and our blacks still grovel. The Soviet representative has consistently called for complete, unqualified disarmament throughout the Geneva negotiations? Well, I don't know Kissinger's answer, since it is never printed. But it seems fine, and I wonder why our militarists won't agree. As never before, I see that capitalism, driven by selfishness, is degrading by its very nature, whereas socialism at least appeals to better instincts and therefore *does* represent a higher stage of civilization.

How terribly wrong it is, how ugly, that powerful individuals own oil produced by geological processes over millennia, surely a nation's *common* property. That grasping hands determine the distribution of wealth; that good people suffer from poverty while vulgarians gorge themselves on obscene consumption. Only socialism can wash away the anomalies and bitter injustices of private enterprise—which, before this extended contact with even perverted Marxism opened my eyes, seemed to me God-given. Only socialism offers us all the means to love and respect ourselves by working for the common good rather than for the appetites within us that we least respect. Even if all this is utopian, even if Soviet State capitalism is more exploitative than our corporate variety, I know I'll never again be happy living and working under the American system's legalized greed. Hypocritical as they are, newspaper articles here about pet shops where more is spent on poodles' coiffures than some black families can afford for food fill me with shame. *Pravda* makes me shudder about much I never noticed before.

But most of my depressions are more personal. These brief breakdowns are mainly in reaction to the breakdown of my career. I can't picture my place in the America I've come to disvalue. Nothing will be found for the everlasting student who—it's absolutely certain now—will never fulfill his promise.

It's clear now I'll never teach. This encounter with Russian life, which was supposed to complete my education, has crippled me for scholarship. As Florence forces amateur painters come there for inspiration to abandon their puny efforts, the confrontation with Russia's unbalancing spirit vitiates archival labors. I can no longer see the country in terms of paradigms, Party infrastructure and intergroup pressures, the concepts of my trade. Like my Russian friends, I'm too confused and oppressed for sober monographs. They've taught me to shut out everything unrelated to the individual people who bear directly on my life; to swap detachment and rationality—those foreign conceptions —for subjective sensations. Having learned the Slavophile's truth, how can I devote myself to scholarship? "Russia is not to be understood by intellectual processes," said Tyutchev. "You cannot take her measurements with a common yardstick; she has a form and stature of her own."

No job, no future. Nothing from which to exorcise the success so long expected of me; no hope, at this age, of mastering another profession. This once-in-a-lifetime year is slipping by and I'm wasting it; I can never have another. To be a nobody at this supposed prime of manhood is intolerably shaming. I simultaneously plunge into an abyss of degradation, as when I used to masturbate to relieve the guilt of masturbation, and cling to the rock face of existence with fantasies of rescue through confession and self-enslavement. I'll tell the world how useless I am; I'll work for anyone who supplies my daily bread. If only I had a genuine skill, the training of any honest craft, instead of the hot air of my liberal education!

This angst and I were companions fifteen years ago, during my normally abnormal teens. How surprised I am at its regeneration now; how I dislike myself for it when I'm unable to laugh. Some days, the thought of facing the music of my failure in New York is worse even than the loneliness of my exile. Since what is happening to me here has rendered me unable to be the success-type I must be there, perhaps I should somehow arrange to remain in Moscow: become a translator, a secretary, anything to keep myself alive.

In this world, I'm still a somebody. After all, "Westerner" by itself is a title. At the lowest level, it gives me access to chewing gum and Camels, which buy the same kind of deference and accommodations from the same kinds of postwar Europeans who serviced GIs. At the highest, my opinions are solicited by intellectuals far more accomplished than I merely because I'm from "over there." How ironic that I, who had the usual youthful scorn for capitalism, feel a plutocrat for the first time in the Motherland of Socialism! The restaurants are inferior, but in what other capital could I afford the very best, together with front-row seats for every play at every theater?

No other city's luxury is so at my disposal; nowhere else am I made to feel so close to the Big Time—so important to myself. The same me who is one of ten million at home has ballooned into a personage here: an attraction and a celebrity, without achieving even false success. So the temptation to stay is very great, even though I know that no Westerner can hope to settle in Moscow without eventual impressment into KGB service.

In the nadir of my self-pity, my thoughts sink from this level to the basest visions of myself, and I groan into my pillow. But the panic of what will become of me is distant today, and I luxuriate in the respite of a patient between attacks. Weeks sometimes pass in blissful freedom from conscious dread. ("What are you going to be when you grow up, fella?" "I won't.") Meanwhile, the soft ache that is my closest friend throbs greetings from inside, and I exist in perpetual limbo. Knowing the disgrace that awaits me, I drift like the bum I've always wanted and feared to be, hoping this eerie year is over quickly to end my apprehension—and, at the same time, that the refuge of suspension lasts forever.

Maybe this was my year to crash and it would have happened anywhere. Perhaps it was inevitable that as I approached the last turning point to "maturity" and the professorship to prove it, I'd discover my unsuitability and flee. Or is Russia responsible for the collapse of my props of conscientiousness and orderly habits: of everything needed—especially a deaf ear to my deepest anxieties—to support me in the world of professional upper-middle class? Perversely, the only activity I perform well here—submerging myself into the joys and maiming sadnesses of daily life—is the one that has tumbled me. But maybe Mother Russia herself will somehow save me. Or I'll straighten things out with Anastasia and we'll be happy forever after.

Marusa has just opened the buffet for her afternoon trading hours. It's an ordinary single room at the end of the far corridor converted to a miniature grocery: a dusty cubicle with oilclothed shelves, what we used to call an icebox, and bins of brown loaves delivered twice daily. In addition to the bread, Marusa sells sausage, cheese, milk, yoghurt, sugar, and, occasionally, a few runty, blemished apples costing (at state prices, for her little establishment is an offshoot of the Grocery Trust) the equivalent of $2.75 a pound. The yoghurt is natural; the bread sour, delicious and full of life. The other products might have come from flood relief. In the main cafeteria too, even in the higher-priced one patronized by the staff and by richer students, the food gets steadily more lumpish. Apparently this tendency is typical of every winter as all fresh produce disappears; but recent crop troubles have reduced even the kasha and macaroni to mush.

Marusa is a firebrand: I picture her tongue-lashing top-hatted bankers and foreign monopolists during the civil war. She's petite and bleached blonde—good-looking in a tarty way despite her soiled smock and the heavy makeup that only emphasizes the signs of wear in her face. (She's been married three times, most recently to a truck driver whom she says she can drink under the table.) She alternately flirts with her male customers and screams at them in a shrill working-class patois. Like most Russians of her background, she's a zealous socialist who hates the thought of capitalism only less than the reality of work.

"Get the hell out of my hair, you vultures, and don't waste your time standing on line. There's no more sour cream. None. You can rot there all day, I'm not serving another person."

But students keep joining the line nevertheless. (It's shorter than the hour's wait at the cafeterias, where standees read novels to pass the time. Besides, not every student can afford sixty kopeks for a proper meal.) They know that if they beg, plead, coquet, cajole, Marusa will eventually serve them all, even with magically found jars of sour cream. Why can't she simply do her job without first the cursing, then reconciliation and finally the peace offering? Why can't the most routine transaction in this country be completed without steaming it into a crisis? To buy a can of herring here is to expose yourself to a sociological adventure. It's never an offer of mute money for an inanimate tin, but a human barter in which a chunk of self must be invested by both sides: fitting frustration, then satisfaction, exchanged.

Marusa the socialist. I intend nothing ironic by this, for she's utterly convinced that socialism is progressive, uplifting and morally irreproachable, whereas capitalism produces degradation and cheating as well as exploitation. Her own cheating in no way invalidates the general principles but, rather, is simply how things are done.

She makes an elaborate show of weighing everything to the gram, adding and removing a daub, adding again, then removing the final speck of bologna or cheese to balance her scales. Yet everyone knows she is busy fleecing customers and the house— i.e., the state; everyone accepts that fiddling is part of the job of every saleswoman and counterclerk in the land. Scales are tampered with, products weighed with wrapping paper to add the odd gram, a cheaper grade of cheese substituted, bread cut to leave a slice for the slicer at both ends—only a kopek's worth on each purchase, but enough to eke out a living for the perpetrators, which their tiny wages alone don't provide. It is as endemic to the system as the stupendous precautions against theft—literally nothing movable is left without a giant padlock—and occurs for some of the same reasons.

In Marusa's case, the cheating is as much professional habit as profitable enterprise. The items in her meager buffet hardly justify the effort: no wine to water, no coffee beans to spill (and later gather), not even lemons to steal. (A grade-A lemon costs more than her hourly wage. For many unskilled workers in the city, and almost all peasants outside it, taking tea with a sliver of the prized fruit is a holiday extravagance—if they can find it on sale.) And Marusa's fudging is also essential to the traditional game of tease. "Hurry up, for God's sake," shout the ravenous boys at the end of the line. "If you cut the show with the scales and speed it up, we'll give you a *bonus* for exceeding your cheating plan."

Marusa fairly spits with fury, but when someone winks and runs his eyes over her figure, she shams suppressing her smile. "This miserable life of mine," she moans, wiping a jagged knife on the hip of her smock. She can survive bombing, famine, and purges with heroic nonchalance, can fight at the front in fierce civil and national wars. But the daily routine of her job in the buffet—working by the clock and actually serving people—is too much.

Why was I surprised to find such a variety of personalities here? The range may be no wider than elsewhere but it appears more diverse because I'd expected uniformity, as if the two hundred and fifty million would arrange themselves into the four or five categories of my textbooks; and, I think, also because the personalities seem larger than life: extravagant theatrical characters against the dull gray backdrop of the Russian *mise-en-scène.* Just as the bleached blonde hussy in a Moscow restaurant is the quintessence of bleached blonde hussies, the studious lad, the enthusiastic joiner and the soccer fan are all classics of their type.

Even the sprinkling of foreigners seems more interesting in this setting, their awareness of themselves heightened by the undercurrent of potential drama. A large, amiable Bulgarian student, for example, shakes my hand with splendid gravity whenever we pass in the corridor. He seems to feel we have something profound and risky in common, and although I don't know what, I somehow share in the assumption. Month by month, his smile broadens. What are we in together?

Naturally, the range of Russians is broader. There is misanthrope Igor, who had been in the Air Force until his MIG crashed ten years ago, mangling his splendid body. Miraculously, he was revivified and fitted with artificial limbs; but his spirit never recovered and his self-pitying bitterness casts a pall when he enters the common room. He had been a blond, blue-eyed fighter pilot, the elite of Soviet warriors, with all the money he needed and a new girl every week. Now he's a scarfaced cripple, unable to intrigue himself or anyone else. He drinks up his pension alone in his room, hardly pretending to study.

And Sergei Alexandrovich (no one calls him Seriozha or just Sergei), another older man (Soviet higher education institutes accept students to the age of thirty-five), who avoids Igor out of fear and detestation. Big and blubbery, Sergei Alexandrovich is the only obvious pederast I've seen in the University; but the official attitude to homosexuality makes him exceedingly careful.

A graduate student in English literature, he lavishes his love where it is safe, on dead writers of a distant land. A distant era, too, for he's convinced the summit of English literature was reached by Dickens, and grieves over the language's subsequent debasement. Months ago, I fulfilled his request for a copy of *Dictionary of American Slang*, without which Russians can hardly decipher contemporary novels in English. But although he thanked me for the gift, he hates what it represents.

"Those dreadful words. So degrading, so *unnecessary*. And to use them in *literature*, whose function is to uplift. To compile a scholarly *dictionary* of them, ugh!"

He prefers memorizing *Bleak House* to reading anything of the last fifty years—Joyce, Waugh, Bellow, Mailer—for the first time. This will make him the perfect high-school teacher: for political reasons—his picture of rapacious English capital and a hungry working class—Dickens is the backbone of the Soviet curriculum. Odd that Sergei Alexandrovich's students will know as little of contemporary literature as the government wants, but for very different reasons.

Edward too wanted a *Dictionary of American Slang*, but not for academic reasons. Craving everything Western, he lets it be known when he's wearing Eminence underwear or a (somewhat soiled) Liberty foulard (the former was bought from a French student, the latter exchanged for an out-of-print Russian book) and tries to keep his tone casual when comparing the cut of Brooks Brothers to Savile Row. (The jewel of his wardrobe is a gray pin-striped suit only one size too large. Many tourists remove labels as a precaution, but this one was intact and his "dealer" imposed an onerous surcharge for it.) Edward's Western name and appearance—he's tall, slim and dressed like a neat prep school graduate—are sadly fitting. He's the most persistent and pathetic of the Russian hangers-on among the French, English and, especially, American students. Always in a Westerner's room, denigrating everything Russian; always offering clever comments on movie reviews—of movies that will never be shown in Russia—in back issues of newsmagazines he's managed to obtain and study; always laboring to be fluent in the latest trends and slang. (To be au courant with this season's trouser widths and Washington scandals is evidently not enough. Once he tried to engage me—"Like, what do you dig about it, man?"—in a discussion of gold stock futures.) Like a newly rich African entrepreneur after a grand European tour, he has rejected his own society's every value, even—or especially—Russian folk music and folk art, which enchant the angriest dissenter. Because he can never actually become one of us, his rich, white Western gods, his highest goal is to win hourly demonstrations of our acceptance. Like a Harvard freshman desperate to join a snobbish final club, he is at the heels of one or another foreigner every free moment of the day.

That he reports to the KGB is acknowledged even by a grunt of "no comment" from Viktor: otherwise, of course, he would not be allowed to devote his life to Western decadence. Soon after he began dropping in on me, Edward himself told me how he had been recruited. In recognition of his Young Communist organizing efforts years ago he was chosen for a student trip to Geneva. The morning before the never-in-his-wildest-dreams departure, his crisp new passport was delivered (he had never seen one before) and he was summoned to an interview. "You're a good chap," began a KGB officer briefed on Edward's weakness for "foreign" and "abroad." "We've heard you're planning a jaunt to Geneva. That's fine; travel is always beneficial. . . . You know, I think, that we can easily, er, postpone your journey. Someone else can be found to take your place. But I'm certain there will be no last-minute difficulties. Help us out with a little something, and I guarantee you'll stay on the list."

What was wanted of him, predictably, was to report on the behavior of the others in the group, including informers planted earlier. Given the afternoon to ponder, Edward became ill. It was the opposition of his unusually principled girl friend that tipped the balance, giving him the fortitude to decline. Crying in the officer's presence, he regretted the decision bitterly even as it sounded on his lips. His passport was taken from him before he completed his explanation.

Edward's self-pity dilated to greater size and weight with every memory of the injustice earned by his noble refusal. In the absence of any hope for travel, he became obsessed by Western possessions. This demoralization made him more promising to the KGB than if he had accepted their conditions for the Geneva trip—in which case he could have claimed he'd seen nothing worth reporting. When a second officer offered him a chance for redemption by "helping out" in the dormitory, fresh tears—this time, of relief, anticipation and self-reproach—accompanied his acceptance.

But now his sorrow for himself swelled yet faster: he was not just a victim, but simultaneously an informer—a pimp for pimps. It was not only Western *things* that had beguiled him all his youth, but also Western notions of privacy and individual dignity, from which his voluntary peonage had excluded him forever. To assuage his remorse, he took to cautioning foreigners about himself, cursing his weakness and pleading for understanding; mixing *mea culpas* with tortuous explanations. (It was Edward who, days after my arrival, motioned me into the corridor, away from the bugs, to give me my first whispered warning. "You're the new American? Beware. Your moves will be watched, every word recorded. Believe me, there's a microphone in your room; I've heard the recordings. I tell you this as a friend, someone who hates treachery.")

Sometimes the spectacle of his self-incrimination moves Westerners to soothe him with gifts of rock'n'roll records and James Bond paperbacks. Other times, the trinkets are an inducement for him to quit their rooms at last. Far from evil, Edward makes it as plain as anyone that only the accident of birth has given me the luxury of not having to be a hider or a liar. But his piteous attempts to win approval by confessing sins to the very people on whom he practices them are authentic Dostoyevskian self-destructiveness. Each admission sucks him deeper into the whirlpool of self-pity and self-loathing; lowered even further in the eyes of his masters and his quarry, he tries harder to please both. There is no escape, only the solace of new items of secondhand clothing, which, by compounding his debt, also fuel the dismal cycle. Ruined at twenty-four, he can only hope that the police retain him in this petty servitude and allow him to keep his loot. And, as his spirit descends, he can trade up: from a two-year-old London Fog to an almost-new Burberry.

Edward's roommate Yuri, by contrast, is so oblivious to clothes and other worldly goods that Edward's degradation is beyond his comprehension. Yuri the Righteous: so quiet, kind and selfless.

So devoutly *virtuous* that he gives me a queasy sensation of being in another age; in ours, I was certain, such rectitude no longer existed. Yuri of the steel-rimmed spectacles and churchgoing radiance, who can't tell a lie even to save himself from the most boring invitation, and who spends a morning searching for the saleswoman who undercharged him by ten kopeks. He's more the Puritan settler than anyone in contemporary Massachusetts.

It's curious how virtues as well as vices seem larger than life here, undiluted from biblical models. More than anything, this country is *old-fashioned;* the fundamental qualities of people and things are as plain as Colonial furniture. The dormitory houses many of Yuri's kind, young women as well as men. Sober-faced and morally scrubbed, their high-mindedness gleams all the brighter in contrast to their washworn shirts and dresses. They really do live by the Moral Code of the Builder of Communism—which, after all, is the Ten Commandments, slightly revised.

And if there are a score of conflicting types among the students I personally know, what of the twenty-five thousand as a whole, coming and going in ceaseless streams from the metro station and bus stops? Most seem supremely ordinary; I've been picking out the personalities because of their stories. Bland, conventional, insufferably dull! Some days, the huge building shrieks of boredom, and if one more small-town, small-minded Russian asks me the horsepower of a Ford, I'll punch his philistine nose. If one more businessman slinks into my room with a handful of greasy rubles for my ties, underwear, socks . . .

Among the twenty-five thousand, odd things stand out. One is that the proportion of military officers is even greater here than in the city as a whole. In crumpled uniforms, clutching tattered briefcases, they contemplate their physics texts, even when stuffed into the dark, impossibly overcrowded elevators. The Army is never out of sight. Rumor has it that the main building's entire eighteenth floor—at which the elevators never stop and for which there's not even a number on their floor indicators—is reserved for tapping equipment and war research.

Last war's casualties are as numerous but more depressing. Armless and legless men are everywhere among the professors and older students; pinned-up sleeves, timeworn crutches, black plastic gloves over wooden hands and clumping artificial limbs.

Their numbers too are greater here than in the city generally: disabled veterans are given preference in the severe competition for University places, and the age limit is often waived. Maimed and mutilated bodies are an integral part of the national scene, living exhibits of Russia's misfortunes.

But why so many clubfeet and bone malformations among the students of my generation? Here the forgotten word "rickets"— no less unpleasant in Russian: *rakhit*—is in common usage, and the familiar hunchback of Russian literature still casts gloom on daily University life. Standing abjectly on cafeteria lines, they are reminders of a tubercular uncle of mine, symbols of a particular sadness.

Student privation is a lesser manifestation of the same problem: the stark lack not only of pretty things to wear and interesting objects to buy, but often even of nutritious food. This country's poverty is a baffling phenomenon. Even amid the University community's relative plenty, scarcity is seemingly incurable. It's not the poverty of the East; no one is near starvation. Things *are* getting better all the time. But everyone except progeny of the Moscow bourgeoisie struggles near slum level. A single shiny suit hangs in the otherwise bare wardrobes of most male students; girls wear one grubby sweater week after week. (It is to save body heat and a few kopeks rather than in pursuit of chic that some wear them with undershirts rather than brassieres.) And a professor full of years and the authority of papers in international journals spends hours telephoning friends to help him acquire the prize of a Belgian raincoat: it's no classic trenchcoat he wants, but a plastic imitation that is all the rage.

Noises from the communal kitchen now, complementing Marusa's yelps. Dented pots and kettles clanging on the old black stoves; an anonymous tenor crooning "Strangers in the Night" while hands plop lunch potatoes into water; children of maintenance personnel supplying motor noises for their tinny toy cars. A white-tiled, dairy-smelling chamber next to the common room, the kitchen becomes a midday center of activity on the otherwise listless floor.

It's extraordinary how easily people who share it—of every generation, sex and cultural level—get along. Patrician graduate students with uncombed women floor-waxers, the shy young bride of a linguist (living illegally in his room) with the members of the clique. There is neither condescension nor self-consciousness as each tends his own pot on the stoves; no surprise that such an eclectic menagerie, complete with children and grandchildren, inhabits a university dormitory. Russians can be as selfish and snobbish as anyone, and their inequality of wealth and life-styles are often enormous. But when pushed together in the business of living, they display a natural egalitarianism whose source must surely be older than the Soviet propaganda they ignore. At some level, they are joined by a common history and fate: the intense experience of being Russian, which pulls people together like soldiers under fire. All belong to the continental family nourished by the Russian earth.

The matriarch of this tiny wing of it is Zaiida Petrovna, chief biddie of the twelfth through fourteenth floors. Everyone is required to deal with his own kitchen mess, and once a month we all serve on the morning cleaning detail which scrubs—is supposed to scrub—stoves, tables and walls. Nevertheless, Zaiida Petrovna is always left with a filthy kitchen (if you believe her complaints), and displays her neat bulk at lunchtime to remind the kitchen-users of their duty. Heard as well as seen: in her alto wail, she carps at everyone in sight, interrupting her own ceaseless monologue about intolerable slovenliness and disrespect for the elderly.

"Such people! Leave their mess every day for a weary old woman. Dear God, it's shameful. For the likes of us, never a moment's rest."

Yet rest, of course, is what she does most of the day. Otherwise she's busy hoarding things: bits of paper and string; rubber bands and sardine keys; almost everything, on the you-never-know-when-it'll-be-available-again life principle. Since my own mother threw out almost everything, I couldn't account for my familiarity with Zaiida Petrovna's attitude until I remembered my grandmother, and my wincing for her when my mother assailed these same Old Country habits. I wonder whether this is why I sometimes feel I've come home to this distant land.

It's hard to imagine altering a single detail of "Auntie Zina's" countenance. Every feature and bulge of this quintessential

Russian *babushka* is in place, starting with the round, frostbitten face and ending in legs grown loglike with the arduous years. She's a grandmother in fact as well as in shape, and three or four times a week brings her grandson Shashinka with her to work. (Her daughter is a secretary in a ministry, where children are not welcome; and in any case, infants are granny's rather than mother's responsibility during the working day.)

Shashinka has become *primus inter pares* among the children smuggled into the dormitory, and a mascot to the students. (Raya and Ira, however, try to keep him out of their room because he prefers dismantling their lacework to enjoying their cuddles.) He waddles up and down the corridors and wanders into any room, a bundle of pink fat sweating in leggings, sweaters and white knitted cap. Winter having arrived, Auntie Zina will not dream of removing another layer of his clothes, even when the steam heat is working—even when Sasha wilts in the kitchen heat. When tired, he falls asleep in the lap of any cleaning woman available: all are his *babushki*, for he already senses he belongs to the one big Russian family.

Zaiida Petrovna also takes Shashinka along to the obligatory political lectures for service personnel after work on Thursday afternoons. She likes the meetings for their churchgoing warmth, the feelings they give her of belonging and doing good, but she would not understand less if the lecture were a Mass spoken in Latin. The child sits on his grandmother's lap while she tries to knit, not listening to a word or even pretending to. (Toward the rear of the room, farthest from the red flags and busts of Lenin, workmen are cleaning their nails and noses, and one swigs surreptitiously at a bottle.) "What's Shyria?" the tyke asked one day when I saw them leaving the session. (That afternoon's sermon had been on the righteousness of supplying Israel's enemies with arms.) "I don't know, darling," she answered, buttoning his thick fur coat. "I don't know a thing." She believes in Communism just as, and in the same way as, her people believed in God, heaven and forces for greater, higher good—forces that will insure, in this life or the next, that justice is done for the long-suffering little people. Nevertheless—or perhaps consequently—the thought that she or anyone she's fond of must work hard to achieve Communism has never occurred to her.

She's always admonishing me to *take it easy,* lie down and have a rest.

"But what about building Communism?" I ask her. (It's not an entirely facetious question; she assumes that, being here, I'm of course a Party member.)

Waving her hand "No," she casts about for a place to settle her bulk. "Communism can be built one day later, lad. Young people mustn't work so hard. You should be having a good time—a person must think of his health."

In this even more than in her appearance, she symbolizes her people. The principal concern is to avoid exertion, to cut down on *work.* Not advancement but peace of mind is the *summum bonum*—and a layer of fat for protection against famine and cold.

At the window again, gazing at my world. The University's central skyscraper, a monstrous stalagmite misplaced in residential tundra, with red running lights to caution aircraft. Acres of formal gardens where Stalin's wraith lurks, keeping them rigid and unused. . . . Across the river, my Moscow in nightdress: dusk in mid-afternoon. Ten thousand streetlamp specks interspersed in the great expanse like the diesel-generated lights of some oil port. Neon chiefly in a scattering of signs sputtering: "GLORY TO THE COMMUNIST PARTY!" "GLORY TO THE SOVIET PEOPLE!" "GLORY TO COMMUNISM, SHINING FUTURE OF ALL MANKIND!" I understand the spell of the Russian countryside now, but what is it in this drab urban scene that also tugs at my heart? Why does the whole human condition, its futility and mine, seem *there,* in the despondent expanse?

Below me, the great iron fence surrounding the University grounds and the stone blockhouse guarding the gate—a working battlement, as if Moscow State University were a tsarist outpost subject to Mongol raids. A light breeze plays dry snow through the bars of the fence and the branches of young trees, which, in the burning cold, are as stiff and black as the metal.

A crowd is bunched outside the guardhouse. Evening session is about to begin, and everyone waiting to enter the grounds is rummaging in a pocket or handbag for his pass, a little cardboard folder with a photograph of the bearer and, of course, an official stamp. The rules are universal: passes required for entrance into the University, as for every office and institution of this People's State; no citizen allowed where he doesn't belong; old men or women camped inside every door in the socialist land, checking credentials and intentions. *Citizens! Produce your passes!*

I once asked an assistant rector whether all this was necessary at an institute of higher education. Didn't I see? he responded fervently. Grounds accessible to ordinary members of the public, to anyone with a whim to look in, would lead to intolerable chaos. Operating a great university without passes was unthinkable. And it's true that this institution, an impressive luxury in the context of Russian life, attracts crowds of gawkers and gapers. Despite all fences, vagabonds are found encamped in dormitory rooms after every vacation.

But the examination of passes is brief. Negotiating a narrow passage through the guardhouse, each holder shows his document to a team of fieldhand women bundled in overcoats and the inevitable woollen scarves. When the women are grumpy and examine photographs, the line-standers, late and cold, mutter under their breaths; when they are gossiping, a mere motion toward a pocket that might contain a pass suffices. And when you've forgotten your pass or have none, you can usually heartthrob your way through the emergency.

A standard performance is required: ten minutes of pleading in deeply tragic tones to demonstrate why *this* exception to the rules is justified by higher human considerations. In the manner of a Soviet criminal defendant—and in the tradition of mercy for the errant in Russian literature—you must show yourself to have been the victim of cruel fate, prove yourself profoundly repentant, throw yourself at the women's boundless mercy. "Just this once, I'll never ask again, I promise. If I don't get in to fetch a certain book now, the whole semester's wasted. My pass was stolen yesterday, together with all my money. I've had only a glass of tea today. I know it's wrong of me to ask, but I'll be grateful to you forever. Sure you have a fine son about my age; think of how you'd want *my* mother to treat *him*."

It helps to have given the women a bar of chocolate on Women's Day or the Anniversary of the Revolution—not at the moment of pleading itself, however, for a direct bribe may be insulting and even dangerous. But even without goodies or a month of smiles to build you a credit of goodwill, a passable actor melts their village hearts. A humble lad's lamentations means so much more than rules they themselves don't understand.

But if this fails, there is a last resort: an enlarged space between two bars in the fence on the opposite side of the dormitory, which all but the fat can negotiate after removing their coats. Nine out of ten people who *must* gain entrance to the University will find the means; the whole pass system, with all its paperwork, procedures and shifts of a hundred guards, is a gigantic waste of time. The regimentation breaks down when brought into contact with the human factor: iron and discipline corroded by neglect and compassion—the pattern of many phases of Moscow life.

Each fall, whole classes of students are dispatched to the countryside to dig potatoes—the usual forced labor, hailed as "volunteer." The October countryside is a sea of slime, and living conditions on the collective farms are kindly described as "primitive": pig sties converted to barracks or leaky tents without latrines, and food fit only for the starving. But the students have potato fights, songfests and alfresco love affairs; and those who truly detest the prospect of a full month of cold and wet can usually feign illness or buy a faked medical exemption. Russia has more restrictions, prohibitions and bureaucratic imperatives than all of Europe combined, but most are easier to evade than in countries of sensible, and therefore seriously taken, regulations. A law of compensation operates: where the burden of rules is most impossible, petty officials seem most persuadable to ignore them.

Someday this aspect of the national character must be explained. The Russian propensity to laziness and anarchy frightens the rulers, who promulgate tomes of unworkable controls. The old habits of "fix-it" and "make-do" encourage people to ignore and evade them, an essential element of the Russian way of life. The rules are augmented by yet another series of ukases, accompanied by propaganda campaigns for strict observance. Do the drafters themselves, I wonder, take their own decrees and campaigns at face value? No one seems to, yet someone must.

Besides Chingiz, my friends are nice, middle-class boys. Lev—Dustin Hoffman with a beard—actually studies evenings, a wondrous strange pastime when exams are not imminent. In dread of the three years' service in the provinces after graduation, he is determined to make the top five per cent of his class, thus exempting himself from such bondage so he may proceed directly to graduate school. He's on the economic faculty and wants to write a book about Robert McNamara. (If he's accepted for graduate work by the institute of his choice, he will have access to such research materials as old *Time* magazines and the Congressional Record.) For relaxation, he plays Monopoly on a set left behind by a former American exchange student. Delighted by the incongruity it represents in this citadel of Marxist-Leninist learning, he swears that the game has taught him more about capitalism than four years' reading of Soviet texts.

Pavel comes from Tbilisi, where his father is a high official in *Pravda of Georgia.* Once a month, a brother brings him a package from home containing smoked meat, jars of pickled delicacies and three bottles of home-brewed vodka, against which all Soviet newspapers, his father's included, wage a fierce, permanent campaign. Pavel's greatest problem is whether to follow in the paternal footsteps—and use his influence—toward a Party career or to struggle alone to become the artist he would like to be.

And there is Semyon, who is not, however, a friend, but for some reason an antagonist and a tutor. Semyon has no friends. Sometimes he seems to have no physical substance. He is all brain waves, nervous tension and irritation: the Doom of the Intelligentsia incarnate.

I think I see as much of him as anyone in the dormitory—which speaks of his terrible loneliness, for he is impossibly distant from me despite our hours together. Hours entirely tête-à-tête, for if a third person approaches, Russian or foreigner, anyone except Chingiz, he slinks away, without a good-bye or acknowledgment of the intruder (but directing an evil glare at me). To avoid this, he almost always contrives to see me after midnight.

The first time was frightening. He slipped into my room without knocking one night when Viktor was at his dacha. When I awoke, my traveling clock's luminous hands indicated 2 A.M.

Switching on the overhead light, Semyon walked toward the bookcase. I'd never seen him before, or anyone so loathsome. He had an embryo's body and ballooned forehead: facial skin stretched taut over visible skull, scalp depositing live flakes on pathetic shoulders. He was clearly much older than the typical student, like a veteran circus dwarf among newcomers. A nervous twitch clutched his lips, revealing stubs of chlorine teeth.

Without more than a (scornful) glance at me, he ran his eyes over my bookcase like a thief contemplating new loot. He took down three or four volumes by Trotsky and Deutscher (among the most heretical, therefore the most interesting and dangerous, of the country's hundred thousand banned books; it was only through a friendly diplomat that I dared get them in) and opened to their title pages to check the editions. Then he selected several other studies of Russian history, tucking them under the decomposing sack of wool and canvas that served as his jacket. Finally, he acknowledged me.

"I n-need a book c-called *The Agrarian Foes of B-bolshevism* by Radkey, the American, and the l-last edition of Kerensky's *Russia's Turning P-point*, p-published in 1970. I expect you can obtain them. I'll be b-back to check n-next week at this t-time, when I will return these."

"Who are you? What are you doing here? Books like that can get you into trouble."

With a leer—although he might have intended it as a smile—he was gone, ashes from his trembling cigarette leaving a trail on the floor.

It was months before I found out anything about him. He seems to have no animal needs: I've never seen him eat, sleep, or use the toilet, and I can't picture him in the cafeteria actually mixing with other students. After we've talked for several hours, he sometimes pours himself some water from the washbasin and drinks a few sips. (Disliking myself, I wash the cup with soap afterwards.) Otherwise, he feeds on a surprisingly expensive brand of tobacco, books, and a kind of nihilist self-torture best portrayed in the doomed souls of *The Possessed*.

Just twice—the second time when a sensational rumor about a Politburo conflict was circulating and I wanted the opinion of Moscow's best analytic mind—have I visited him. The smell of the clique's dens after a hard night is disagreeable enough, but Semyon's room had the stench of a condemned man's cell. The deposit of his scalp coated the sheets. Like beach party refuse, sticky jars and tins were scattered on stacks of books. In one corner was a pile of rotting laundry. These unwashed clothes, including several white shirts, were a mystery, for I've never seen Semyon in anything but his prison-like gray suit, sagging with dirt. The puzzle of why the Sanitary Commission (appointed by the student government to make weekly rounds of all the rooms) tolerates Semyon's filth is more intriguing. Perhaps they want to spare themselves the sight—or have been told to give him special treatment? How else is he left in peace—although watched—to live his asocial, even "antisocial," life?

He appears in my room once a week after I've switched off the light, always in quest of more volumes whose possession, especially as Brezhnev and company intensify their suppression of dissent, might be used as evidence in criminal proceedings. He never asks for this literature but demands it as his right.

"It is your d-duty as a citizen of the free world to supply the intellectual m-material I require."

There is something more sinister about Semyon than even the cynicism, scorn and smoldering hate that sputter out of him. But he is also the only genuinely brilliant man I know, and more erudite and lucid about political affairs than all my professors together. From tourists and exchange students, "underground" archives and Moscow's network of dealers in "rare" (read "prohibited") books, he's obtained and absorbed an immense body of literature in English, German, French and Swedish on all aspects of history, sociology, politics and philosophy. (Although his reading knowledge of these self-taught languages is excellent, he can barely utter an intelligible sentence in any of them.) Semyon thinks much of this scholarship has merit only in comparison to Soviet drivel. Human motivation, he says, is too complex for successful analysis, certainly by New England political scientists who *feel* neither Russia nor Marxism, and whose interpretations are burdened by academia's self-perpetuating pedantry. To demonstrate this, he takes an event such as the collectivization of agriculture—incomparably more brutal, traumatic and significant to the country, he claims, than the Stalinist purges which so fascinate Soviet specialists—and talks about it spellbindingly for hours, commenting on Marxist, non-Marxist, and anti-Marxist theories, and drawing Russian geography, climate, history, psychology, national character, culture—the whole of Russian civilization, with special emphasis on the shaping-*cum*-reflecting role of the Orthodox church—into his extemporaneous discourse.

Semyon is especially scornful of Western social scientists who predict an early liberalization (normalization!) of Soviet rule—in stupendous ignorance, he says, of the central shaping forces of the Russian mentality and way of life. But he is hardly less contemptuous of foreign writers who treat the widely heterogenous members of the underground "democratic movement" as selfless heroes one and all, carrying the banners of Virtue, Good and Russia's Hope. Some dissenters glorified in the Western press are vainglorious and intolerant as well as courageous, he says; and only the superficiality of Western analysts—who portray in a single dimension, omitting everything but the dissent itself—fails to recognize the tyrannical potential of those fighting the present tyranny. "Lenin t-too was a dissenter in his d-day, you know. How m-many times have Western analysts got things wrong? Swallowed n-novelistic nonsense about Russia's *new* saviors? Sacrificed their intelligence because *they* needed p-political heroes?"

That Russia's present martyrs are brutally repressed, he says, does not in itself make them virtuous, any more than the long oppression of American blacks has made *them* the country's natural leaders. The contribution of Soviet dissenters and protestors is their recognition of the society's grave illnesses—from which they themselves are not immune. The unqualified adulation of Solzhenitsyn, for example, is based on a publicity trick: a "pre-packaged 'solution' for m-minds that, to recognize b-black, must have an opposing white." The first thing Western students are taught about Leninism, he continues, is that its narrowness developed in reaction to the autocracy it opposed. "Yet Western teachers s-somehow can't apply the same analytic concept to Solzhenitsyn's n-nature, shaped by the society *he* opposes. He is in the Russian tradition: religious, mystic, p-potentially dictatorial. *P-plus ça change.* But for all their l-luxurious libraries to draw on, not one p-pampered Princeton 'scholar' writes a word of this.

"And by the way, if it's democracy they really w-want for Russia, as they claim, the Communist Party happens to serve quite well. In the t-true sense of the word, it's relatively quite d-democratic: consisting, and r-reflecting the views of, society's lower elements. The scholars haven't even got their t-terms straight, meaning their ideas. And here, the p-problems are far deeper than scholarly."

In short, Semyon's prognosis is profoundly pessimistic and, as with much debunking, has a realistic ring. But sneer as he will at Western naïveté, he can't keep himself from his addiction to forbidden books. He knows they will land him in trouble again; it's said that one of the KGB informers on our floor (a misery of dourness, while the other is a handsome ladies' man) was assigned to watch Semyon more closely even than the Western students. "Sooner or later, they'll have to p-put me in a l-labor camp. It's convenient, you know, to have a State t-that lays down hard laws about sin. That caters to one's own shilly-shallying death wish."

In all, Semyon has vouchsafed a dozen sentences about himself. Discussion of personal affairs is frivolous; it is the affairs of state that merit attention—above all, the *philosophy* of state power. By what means do some men dominate others? Hypotheses, abstractions and analytical formulas are his companions; personality—of the Lenins, Stalins, Nassers and Joe McCarthys —enters only as a factor in these equations. His is the ultimate of that well-known phenomenon, the human condition studied by someone isolated from ordinary human contact. Surely his insatiable passion for everything historical, anthropological and sociological is a partial substitute for the personal exchange from which he feels his ugliness excludes him.

What I've learned about him seems all political, too. Born in Rostov-on-Don, he moved to Leningrad with his mother while his Cheka father, whom he rarely saw, roamed the country on extremely secret—presumably murderous—assignments. In Leningrad he read, kept to himself, and entered the University, from which he was expelled seven years ago for participation in an "anti-Soviet" political cell. The "cell" was in fact a half-dozen students who met to discuss the Russian past and future in terms of heretical concepts such as humanism, agrarian socialism, and "genuine" Marxism (as opposed to Marxism-Leninism, the illegitimate and corrupt distortion of Marx's theories and ideals). The group was heavily influenced by Nikolai Berdyayev, the early twentieth-century philosopher who wrote of creativity and the free human personality as the central meaning of Christianity and the hope for Russia's salvation.

After months of discussion and extremely difficult preparation, the group "published" a "journal," using—at great risk—a mimeograph machine in a government office to which a member had access. It was a collection of essays about the drift of Russian history interrupted by Bolshevism, and was designated "Volume I, Number I." There was no second number. The KGB unearthed the authors within days, and they were imprisoned for ten months while the case was investigated. Tried in secret, the moving spirits were sentenced to five years of labor camps and exile.

Semyon spent some months in prison, too, but his monkish personality apparently saved him from serious punishment: although a charter member of the "cell," he had attended only two meetings and could not face the personal involvement of long "underground" editorial conferences and secret working shifts with the mimeograph machine necessary to produce the journal. Or did his father's influence save him? In any case, his present enrollment in Moscow University—rather than chopping logs in exile—is puzzling.

"How did it come about?" I asked him when he confirmed the Leningrad episode. "Surely you can't be expelled from one university, have that on your record, and go to another?"

"These things happen. N-not everything in this country is as efficiently t-totalitarian as your p-political scientists imagine. . . . Don't worry," he added, implying that I might suspect a *quid pro quo* had been demanded for allowing him to continue his education. "I'm hardly the informer t-type."

On his next visit, more of his background emerged. I had asked something about Leningrad and he was lecturing me, in his contemptuous yet brilliant style, about the city's Party organization as a traditional power base in Politburo intrigues.

Having tossed off plot-and-counterplot biographies of Zinoviev, Kirov and Zhdanov as examples, he suddenly froze, staring at the window's blackness. When he snapped back, it was to say something wholly extraneous to his previous associations.

"More Leningraders expired d-during the Nine Hundred Days" (the Wehrmacht seige of 1941–43) "than Americans in their w-wars combined. I m-mean all the wars in the history of your country, including the Civil W-war."

He stated this as dry fact, perhaps implying that Leningrad's tortured political history—the purges and bloody retributions, execution and exile of hundreds of thousands of her best people, including the best Communists—cannot be understood without a grasp of the tragedies that were *not* self-imposed. This is an underlying theme of much he says about Soviet—and tsarist— rule: cruel acts of nature visited upon Russia sustain an atmosphere and mentality that encourage the politics of masochism. But surely the statement about the Nine Hundred Days was also a hint about his personal history? For until the children could be evacuated, he himself endured the seige.

Semyon once described the experience to Chingiz. His family —grandmother, mother and an aunt; his father was still away on special duty—lived in a largish room of a relatively comfortable downtown apartment. A month after the German invasion, little remained of recognizable life; the blockade's sealing in September introduced them to hell. Semyon's grandmother died first: too old to work, she was not allotted bread enough to live, even lying all day in bed. Semyon hid when her corpse was carried out. His aunt was then killed in a cellar hit by a shell.

That winter, his mother's daily bread ration was two hundred and fifty grams (roughly nine ounces); his own, half that. Every day, she gave him half her own—*and he seized it,* knowing she was starving to death, like granny. She died of pneumonia in March. Semyon grew up in orphanages, drawing attention to himself by his precocity and urge to hide.

"Perhaps he'd have been troubled anyway," said Chingiz. "But war made it certain. His first perception of the world was in a city that suffered more than any other in modern history. He was intelligent enough to understand that he wanted his mother's crust more than he wanted her to live. . . . Yes, we won the war, survived the purges; but the damage to the living sometimes exceeded that to the forty million dead."

Last month, Semyon's interest was piqued in Freud and he set out to obtain something of his legally. There had been a rumor—one of the daily clusters of rumors—that despite the general intellectual constriction, censorship was being quietly relaxed in selected disciplines considered necessary for the country's development. In the Lenin Library, Semyon tested this by submitting a slip for *A General Introduction to Psychoanalysis* together with requests for eight Soviet works on Marxist-Leninist Pavlovian psychology, most containing indignant attacks on Freudianism. Producing the approved books, the librarian made no mention of the Freud.

"Where's the ninth?" asked Semyon, deadpan. With a cautionary squint, the librarian said she could not issue "such material." Semyon persisted. She pointed to a door behind her counter.

The office was sparsely furnished. Lenin's portrait hung low over the desk; beneath it sat a man in a pulpy suit. He studied Semyon's request, then his petitioner's splotchy countenance.

"Why do you want to read Freud?"

"I d-don't want to read him. It's essential—for my work."

"I do not think it is essential. Dozens of our texts will explain what you need to know about Freud. You understand his 'theories' are pornographic and unacceptable?"

"I think I do."

The official frowned. "Listen, young man. I'll give you this book if you insist. But take my advice and don't. Why have such things in your record? Be sensible: pick up your other issues and go."

Which is what Semyon did. The episode, he said, did not refute the rumor about the easing of restrictions. A harder man, or the same one with sterner instructions, would have informed him the book was missing, entering a damaging notation in his dossier.

Semyon encountered a friendlier form of censorship in connection with his honors thesis on the Yalta Conference. It was a hack job, culled from standard Soviet sources and free of any reference to scores of Western analyses which Semyon could have demolished—but had no business knowing. Approving a preliminary draft, his tutor suggested that the phrase "the Soviet representative" replace "J. V. Stalin" throughout the text. "Between us, it's safer that way. Why expose yourself? No one knows what the attitude toward Stalin will be by the time you're ready to submit."

Sure enough, the official attitude is steadily hardening—that is, softening toward Stalin's crimes. Publications have resumed praising his "historic work" building socialism and Soviet might, no longer mentioning what used to be called "unfortunate negative factors." Even the scholarly press faithfully supports the rehabilitation by going mute again on huge chunks of history. Semyon's tutor gave sound advice: liberal or conservative, the readers of the Yalta thesis need not trouble themselves with the political implications of mentioning a former Great Father by name.

The line shifts. Yesterday's saints become today's Judases, then heroes again. History is hastily rewritten to document the latest immutable truth. But a portion of the slag heap of superseded literature finds some use. In a reeking latrine the other day, a copy of the obsolete 1967 *History of the Communist Party of the Soviet Union* was braced between the tiles and drain pipe, its pages extolling N. S. Khrushchev's inspiration to progressive mankind to be ripped out for toilet paper as needed. But no irony was intended: the convenience was an unconscious acquiescence to the law of shortage requiring maximum recycling, and acceptance that the yellowing pulp now best serves for this.

But why such emphasis on this kind of observation? Most Russians I know well, on this floor and others, are less keen than I to spot the aberrations of government and state. Here politics is impenetrable, like the low cloud cover sealing us in from one horizon to the other. Something suffered and accepted, not puzzled over or pried into: given, like the weather. It's snowing again, and the radio predicts a—normal—night of twelve to fifteen degrees below freezing.

And so, when Andrei Amalrik received his terrible second sentence last week, the trial's whys and hows were hardly discussed. A few people felt a tug of hurt, the kind Russian peasants experienced when prison convoys trudged past them on their way to Siberia. (Peasant women pressed loaves badly needed by their own families into the desperate prisoners' hands.) Several passionately "literary" students, the lovers of Mandelshtam, Pasternak, Tsvetaeva, Akhmatova, turned aside for a dry cry, and perhaps more people than I know felt wounded. But most neither knew nor cared; and even the "activist" minority produced a low moan rather than shrill noises of shock or outrage. Such tragedies are expected; no one can prevent them. What hurts most is not being able to comfort the victims.

And in a way, some of the same minority are proud of, as well as appalled by, government persecution. Russian life is hard—but isn't challenge the psyche's daily bread? Doesn't the highest satisfaction lie in surviving a difficult environment, winning out over severe obstacles and dangers? It is Russia's paradoxical good fortune that the pressures of her life—weather, war, shortages, tyranny—are external, often producing a unification of self and a rising to the challenge, rather than the anxieties and neuroses germinated by affluent liberalism, where you have only your flabby self to blame. No one need feel confused or guilty about the too-soft life here; primeval forces prevail, to be faced and overcome.

A bony girl at the end of the corridor is soon to leave the country forever. After nearly a decade, and the new arrangements between East and West Germany, her exit visa has been granted, and she will join her only surviving relative, an aunt living in Frankfurt, whom the Germans took for slave labor during the war. Even by Russian standards, Olga's life has been unusually cruel. Stalin deported her entire people, the Volga Germans, to Siberia in 1941. Her father died of exposure during the journey; her mother, who built a hut with her bare hands in the wilderness of their exile, succumbed within the year. In their grim settlement, half the children with living parents expired; Olga's orphaned childhood was an animal struggle for existence, won only by her lusty constitution. After the rescinding of the exile in 1957, she continued to bear the stigma of "traitor." Smuggling herself into Moscow, she spent every free hour for years in ministry offices, pleading to join her aunt.

But now a new theme—Siberia's natural beauty—is modulating her lament of hard times. "Yes, winter was brutal. And in the six weeks of summer, the mosquitoes ate you alive. But the rivers! The lakes and the *trees!* Germany will have nothing like it. Can it be true I'll never see that glory again?"

As her time to leave approaches, Olga becomes less certain and more nostalgic for the places where she suffered extreme adversity. "How does a person live outside of Russia? My aunt's rich, she has her own apartment and car. But what happens to your insides when everything's so easy? When you can do what you want, buy what you like; everything's there for the asking? Maybe I'll be back home in two weeks."

It's time now to attend to my correspondence. I don't write home often because the outside world has become an illusion, obscured by paralyzing, eternal Russian isolation. By the sense of existing in a separate cosmos, cut off by dusky space and aeons of time: this has contrived to stay in power, despite everything shrinking the twentieth-century world.

The technical marvels exist somewhere here: BEA Tridents from London four times weekly, the BBC Russian service three hours a day. But electronic communications and speed-of-sound jets are as extraneous to our lives as horseflies in this winter landscape. They do not penetrate the ironclad, snowbound Russian remoteness; cannot affect the heavy, fated way of life. Like the dazzling achievements of Soviet science we read of, they are not bogus but exist by and for themselves in some sealed laboratory, and therefore are irrelevant to the likes of us. A brilliant young professor I know works on computer design in the mathematics faculty's research department. But when his wife asks him to bring home some meat, he slips away early to stand on an hour-long line for a ham in an outlying store where his luck has been good before; then stuffs the precious, *Pravda*-wrapped kilo in his battered briefcase while the counterwoman bends over an old abacus to do her sums. This is the technology we live and understand.

Perhaps it is to the credit of the otherwise lumbering Russian state that it has kept pace with every kind of dizzying technological advance in its methods for preserving the ancient isolation.

Telecommunications with the outside are effectively nullified because not one knob on a single control board can be touched without the Party's authorization. The BEA flights are chimerical because even the buses delivering passengers to planes are searched by armed guards, and not one Russian in a hundred thousand can approach as close as the check-in counter. Tapping apparatus clearly superior to the telephone system itself, jamming equipment more powerful than any transmitter—everywhere in modern life, restraint covers progress like paper, in the old game, over rock.

But censorship and controls are not enough to keep us apart. Insouciance and profound passiveness are powerful allies: the *internal* isolation that hundreds of years of backwardness and hardship has bred into native bones. Russians are cut off and know it. And if they think of the possibility at all, many do not want to close the gap: too much effort is required, too much disappointment awaits them. Dream as they do of transforming themselves, they fear that any attempt to reach European standards would stop at the visionary talk stage, like the plans of Chekhov's doctors. For, if successful, would the executors not have ceased being Russian? And if they weren't Russian, would there be need for agonizing self-analysis, dreams of shining new worlds and futile crusades?

Life here is different. As on a ship at sea, special rules apply; distinctive prohibitions and dangers condition mind and movements. Although some of this country's distinctions from Europe are subtle, the overwhelming whole is far greater than the sum of its parts. Sometimes I scrutinize people and places in an attempt to define them more sharply; but nothing I can specify in their appearance or moods captures the underlying *feeling*, every day in every setting, that this is another world. "There are parts of what it most concerns you to know that I cannot describe to you," wrote Plotinus. "You must come with me and see for yourselves." Or, to take a less common quotation, I can cite an underlined first sentence of a Frenchman's book lying on a cluttered, unoccupied desk in the Lenin Library yesterday: "If there is a country in the world that seems destined to remain unexplored and unknown by any other nation, either nearby or far away, that country is surely Russia, at least as far as her

Western neighbors are concerned." The article was written in 1861, the year of the emancipation of the serfs.

For centuries, European residents in Russia have been overpowered by the same sensations. The observations of the Marquis de Custine (French Ambassador to St. Petersburg in the nineteenth century) and Sigmund Von Herberstein (Ambassador of the Holy Roman Empire to Muscovy in the sixteenth century) are as relevant to contemporary attitudes as any analysis of the socialist system and Soviet regime. Both were followed, deceived by obsessively secretive bureaucrats, alternately exhilarated by the irrepressible Russian spirit and horrified by the slovenliness and dirt; both described precisely the sense of wilderness that grips me this minute.

This is why I've lost contact with the outside world and write but a few dutiful lines to America, as if to another planet, every other week. Besides, my mail is opened. Crudely: little drops of brown glue decorate the envelopes, symbolic of Russia's odious acts, and of the coarseness with which she performs them. I confine myself, therefore, to picture postcards and small talk. My correspondents read about the weather and stirring performances at the Bolshoi.

But what would I write if I were free to describe my real feelings? On bad days, I so despise this country and all it stands for that I dream of guiding B-52s to the Kremlin with a flashlight. The honored assistant rector has lied to me outright, announcing blandly that a meeting I'd asked to attend as research, and which was being held that very minute, had been cancelled. My faculty advisor, who is fond of jeering at "bourgeois" scholarly integrity, counsels me to measure Soviet public opinion by "the best documentary evidence": the 99.7 per cent election majorities and unanimous votes of the Supreme Soviet. A professor of political economy cites the New York garbage strike as living proof of the American workers' exploitation and capitalism's disintegration, never mentioning actual wages even before the dispute because he knows that skilled Russian mechanics, who can't strike anyway, earn one-sixth as much.

Not ideological commandments but cynical deceptions like these, on which the country is governed at every level, reduce me to a nonentity. My movements restricted, intelligence sneered at, individuality violated, I choke with rage. *How dare they do this to me? I was born a free man!* This country is ruled by cousins of the redneck sheriffs of the Mississippi town where I spent a crow-eating summer as a civil rights worker. It's not enough that they can crush you at a whim; they want you to grovel by applauding their lies.

But the subduers of happiness are usually less specific: the weight of everything, the inexorable presence of melancholy and misfortune, the absence of a moment's diversion by a pretty, airy thing. All my childhood presumptions—a four-lane highway of goodness and progress, leading onward and upward for the world and me—are vaporized in this gloom. I spend hours on the daybed, leafing dog-eared copies of *Time*. Despite the snowfall's chalky reflection on the walls, these are the darkest days—and the longest—I have known.

Sometimes I tell Russians about Paris, Rome, the Greek islands: all the lush places I'll revel in when I return to civilization. I do it for spite, to hit back—unfairly, but in the only way I can—at the coarse hands controlling me. My listeners know they'll never see the color of the Mediterranean, sip a drink in a real café, own a suit even like the Barney's sale one I bought specially to wear out here or to give away. Some quiver when questioning me: they're envious, as I intended.

Few suspect that I'm as envious of them: that I often wish that I'd been born to their deprivation and pressure. What they lack sometimes seems inconsequential compared to what they have: ingenuous talk in place of sports cars; homemade singing instead of discotheque noise; hair worn long not to be with it or to conform, but to postpone the sacrifice of thirty kopeks for a haircut; guitars which represent neither revival nor fad—Russians have always played. . . . They are more natural and whole than any young people I've known; their student life is the kind I've always wanted. And this is no less true because caused by Russia's old-fashioned poverty.

What do I really want to tell the people I write to? I am a second generation New Yorker. My grandfather fled from a Polish ghetto after a pogrom. My father used to talk to me about man's dignity under Marxist socialism—until Stalin destroyed his faith and made him a cynical reactionary. Both hate Russia for what it did to them and theirs; both begged me not to come. How can I explain to them that the worst of what they believe about this country is here, practiced and suffered every day, and that I love it nevertheless? That when I'm in my gloom or Leonid lowers his eyes at the clique's obscenities, I feel as cursed as the hunchbacks in the corridors, yet grateful for the glimpse of man's tragic essence that has replaced the complacency and false security of my former existence.

For I have begun to sense what Russian writers have long revealed: that this is a place where the human spirit is made to struggle, thereby becoming fuller as well as more repressed. Their nineteenth-century phrases—"the vulgarity of life . . . the meanness of man . . . the tragic nakedness of human existence" —still afford the deepest reportage of the Russian scene and soul. The truths they lay bare uplift as well as demean. My senses are sharpened here; I know that I am me. It's not despite Russia's fated tragedy that warmth and emotion flourish here, but because of it.

"Great God!" wrote Leontiev, "am I a patriot? Do I despise or love my country? It seems to me that I love her as a mother loves, and despise as one despises a drunken thing, a characterless fool."

And Rozanov: "Russian life is dirty, yet so dear."

And an ill Yuli Daniel from his labor camp: "I loved you so much, my Russia—even more, perhaps, than I loved women."

Although depression never fully leaves me, I've somehow come to cherish the spell I'm in. If this is what the great writers knew, a particle of their insight has been given to me. The sense of abandonment and cosmic loss that haunts me simultaneously draws the rest of creation to my side. For the first time, I see I am part of everything. Anastasia and Alyosha are here, who are all to me that my family wasn't. This is why I yearn to escape this room, to flee Russia and never return. And why I know I'll always long to live this year again.

II To Town

Today it is colder. Rings of rime coat streetcar cables and stunted poplars; the ground is a glacier of soiled ice.

Nightgowned Masha feels her way into my room an hour earlier than usual, a night of love accentuating her usual essence. (She sleeps with Chingiz for fun; with a pallid young physicist from town for a restaurant meal or emergency rubles. When she slept with me, I was intimidated by the warmth of her body and my thoughts of her total availability: too easy, still too sensuous for a boy like me whose mental energy for years went to fantasizing precisely this kind of sex.) She drops a cigarette from her fingers and fumbles for another, then ambles to the window and stares at the numb outdoor expanse. In their gelid states, every substance is alike, fusing into a single mass. All molecules are frozen immobile, and the suspension of icy fog in the air is like iron.

A growl of protest rises to Masha's throat. "This rotten cold, it makes me sick. What's wrong with these matches?"

I make her a cup of Nescafé with my immersion heater and gather some papers into my briefcase. She closes her eyes to savor her sips.

"Aren't you used to the weather? You've had it all your life."

She turns to me with no expression. "Sometimes, friend, you sound positively patronizing. No visiting-scholar anthropology today. I have a headache; I've got to go *out*."

Someday, I'll write an essay about Russian winter. *Russkaya zima*, the great depressant of spirit and waster of life. We live in a no-man's land, enveloped by the seamless, soundless mist. Isolated even from the sky: it's been weeks now since enough sun has forced through to be able to guess its position.

The cold of this country has a freakish quality. Each moment outdoors is a confrontation with a vast antagonistic force. Your cheeks burn and nerves are permanently tensed; not even a dash to a mailbox can be taken for granted. Freezing the tears it has drawn from your eyes, a light wind raises the discomfort to genuine distress. You cover your face with your gloves and hurry for shelter, hearing your child's voice pleading for relief.

Mere temperature is not the crippler; Vermont and Minnesota—even Iowa during severe cold snaps—can produce harder spells. The difference is the immutability: the grip of the Russian freeze—and of its mood—never lets up. Winter lays hands on you in October, takes command of you, throttles you straight through until April. Week after week, a slate-gray cloud bears down on the squat skyline and people are made numb or sullen. Your skin flakes and shoulders ache; in time, your psyche also suffers. Irrationally resentful, you begin to take the punishment personally, and by late February—after the January thaw fails to appear—you recognize traces of persecution anxiety. A snapshot of a friend enjoying the Bois de Boulogne in a mere raincoat and muffler arrives (after its sixteen-day delay by the censor), filling you with envy of everyone "outside." Some days, the resentment snaps your will and turns you passive—as the Russian people are so enduringly passive? Now and then, it blinds you—like them?—to good sense in your urge to rebel. Always, you are conscious of living in a land where *nature has gone wrong* and appeals do not lie to justice or reason.

Seven months of such seige each year; and a total far greater than the sum of its parts. For winter is not a season like other seasons, but a state of mind, saddening even summer—which is too short to soothe the sense of hurt. Russian winter is the song of Russian life: submit, you lost lambs, to your fate of inexplicable hardship. You were born and you will die in a place of aberration—a cruel accident, but also your hope of salvation through suffering.

The inhuman weather and feeble human responses to it; how little I knew about these keys. I was a certified Soviet specialist, qualified to lecture about this society and its politics; yet the thousand books and treatises I've read revealed less than Masha's response to the look of February through my wavy glass. In a sense, all I'd mastered about the structure of the Party, the exercise of power, the channels of absolute authority, took me steadily farther from a native's perspective. For stifling as it constantly is, deceitful and vengeful at the slightest provocation, the dictatorship is but a marginal addition to Russia's older, heavier burdens. Although worse than I had imagined, the brutalization of political life is also less important because it is subsidiary to climate, geography and mood, the chief oppressors of everyday life.

Occasionally there are gifts. A bright day is polished turquoise; the air scrubs your lungs, the sun on the snow's crust makes you squint. Faces flush with bonhomie and the exalted beauty, people talk of the wholesomeness of Russian winter and of the good old days when frosts were really that. But such prizes are as rare as roses in December. Moods sink with the reappearance of the overcast, and the cumulative effect is disastrous.

Winter is a struggle to wage, a cross to bear. Day after day for half the year, half their lives, Russians pay groaning tribute in energy and fuel for the concession of staying alive; their children's swaddling and their own mountain of clothes are never enough to dispel the shock to skin and stiffness of limb. Cautious intellectuals can go months without an encounter with Party or KGB, and millions never think of the Kremlin at all except with vague patriotic pride. But no one escapes from the tyranny of the freeze. Each step from shelter to street is a slap in the face by searing air. Each buckling of boots for the venture outside is a reminder to respect your betters. You are humbled by dumb, blunt forces, the parents of Politburo satraps.

Someday, I'll document my insight into the Russian personality. The elements are hostile here; this is the *fons et origo* of hulking buildings, strident newspapers and absent amenities—of everything that village-bred, disaster-fearing men (for these are the kind who control all public reactions as well as rule) make ponderous, laborious and inimical to public amusement. Where life is a struggle to fend off such giant forces, why build cafés to serve aperitifs or coffee? No matter that even more northerly countries are far less grim; in Russia, encumbered by backwardness, the environment is *perceived* as hostile. With their mothers' milk, children are given to understand that their hot, cramped homes are love, but that the world outside is essentially unfriendly to human habitation.

The Party unconsciously understands this awful truth, which is why it protests so shrilly to the contrary. A million messages a day about its glorious victories; two generations of pleas, proofs and exhortations about remaking society and forging the New Soviet Man—and all, as they somewhere know, in vain. For Marx himself teaches them that "environment determines consciousness"; and above all, it is the weather which controls the environment, making mockery of their agitated efforts. All the propagandists' exhortations and the people's sacrifices have done nothing to loosen the grip of today's bleak iciness and mood. Pathetic posters proclaiming the achievement of "HAPPINESS!" under socialism hang from every other wall, railing futilely against the pervading sadness; for Russians will not be remade nor their sense of having been mistreated by nature relieved until something drastic is done about the Russian winter. Nor will the quiet sore of guilt from having caused their own troubles be healed—an irrational oppression, as in children who blame themselves for their family's bickering. "Russia is a freak of nature," wrote Dostoyevsky, always stressing how much heavier the psychological burdens are than the merely physical.

All this I know more certainly than anything tangible I observe. The personal questions are harder: Why am I so at home with this futility and guilt? What pulls me closer to myself here than elsewhere; puts me in communion with the universe through a sense of cosmic depression; allows me to welcome my inner ache?

Masha yawns, scratches her hips and settles into my desk chair, exchanging her empty cup for my shaving mirror and examining her face with undisguised concentration that makes her self-absorption seem artless. Had Huxley not usurped the word, I would have thought of her flesh as pneumatic. Hard work and deep sleep have given it a springy plumpness that somehow magnifies the dimensions of her bottom and breasts.

Yesterday morning, she wasted an hour scouring my room for a mislaid book; although still unfound, it is quite forgotten. Shivering at a gust that has breached the window and grazed her neck, she again affirms that the cold goes right through her. "I detest winter; always have, always will." Yet she apparently hasn't considered wearing something over her redolent nightdress or on her tawny feet.

I promised myself to be in the Lenin Library by now but postpone my departure while she lingers to enjoy another Camel. Happy thoughts dominate her bemusement; a distant smile puckers her chunky lips. Her presence in the room is deeply comforting, as if contact with someone so sound in mind and body will help me pull through my troubles and find my adult feet. Sometimes I think of asking her, this miner's daughter reluctant to stretch her thoughts beyond a given day's physical satisfactions, what I should do to make something of my life. When she's with me, my anxiety about career and reputation loosens its grip; I understand that I needn't be more than what I am. People are really meant to procure and consume their daily bread, raise their children, enjoy their morning Nescafé and thoughts of chicken for Sunday dinner. To live the days as they come without sweating to make some mark of significance—and therefore, without suffering a self-made sense of failure. With a tenth of my prospects for success, riches and worldly stimulation,

Masha is ten times more contented. Unperturbed by the bad, she congratulates herself for the good, and when she's near, I believe I can learn her secret.

"What are you thinking about, Masha?" I've never asked her before, and wonder whether it might be a mistake.

"Oh, nothing. I have to get my boots repaired."

This is declared with a loud blankness that breaks the meditative spell. My regard for Masha sometimes reminds me of a friend who disdains Italian opera because, he insists, the dandified singers trilling dolorous heartbreak are in fact concentrating on their post-performance spaghetti.

"I have to go out this morning," Masha adds. "And my guests are coming," she informs me, using the incongruously dainty slang for the arrival of her period (and probably explaining the source of her sharp smell and uncharacteristic headache). "Can you get me more jiggers?"

Although she could barely believe her eyes when she first saw them mere months ago, she already regards Tampax, the "jiggers," as indispensable. She had never heard of them, had never used more, in fact, than a handful of cotton wool positioned in her panties—even when available, Soviet sanitary napkins are too coarse and too expensive for regular use—until I ran into her one fall afternoon while wandering on a busy street behind Red Square. It was shortly after I'd first arrived; months before I could make sense of the ensuing hour.

Recognized and beamed at, I was gaily invited to join her looking in on a friend in a nearby, green-painted building—a temptation in itself, for each step into a Russian apartment carried the excitement of forbidden adventure. The Embassy had frequently warned of the drugging-and-photographing dangers of risking this alone, and somehow official Russia too made it clear that while Moscow's main streets were open to the likes of me, the people's living quarters were off limits. Entering the musty structure had much in common with visiting a Harlem tenement at midnight, which I once did in tow of a burly black friend.

The apartment behind GUM was less demoralizing than the one on 119th Street, but darker and more threadbare. Following Masha up a dank staircase to an attic, I found myself in the company of five young women smoking and drinking cheap wine like sorority sisters. Galya, Maya, Ina and Ida; but there was barely time for these first-name introductions before I triggered the puzzling incident.

As I took off my coat, my fortnightly bag of purchases from the American Embassy's commissary fell from my hands, revealing, *inter alia*, a box of Tampax destined for a French girl in the dormitory. The girls' giddy exuberance in retrieving the carton suggested they envisaged a treat of foreign bonbons for their party. My offer of a box of tea bags as a substitute was ignored as hands ripped at the tantalizing Western cellophane, symbol of everything "brand-name"—imported, and therefore deluxe—as opposed to "Sov," the contemptuous epithet for domestic production.

It was Masha who tore off the lid and sniffed. Perplexed by the unchocolate-y savor, she examined the leaflet—and then experimented. In the failing afternoon light, her large dusky triangle beckoned like eggplant from beneath her raised skirt. What the hell is this, has she forgotten I'm here? Are Russian girls the way Swedish ones used to be imagined? But while *my* excitement was driven by thoughts of the coming orgy, Masha's was expressed in marvel at the ingenious device. Nonsense, she assured the others, it doesn't hurt a bit. "Doesn't even tickle—it feels *nice.*"

Shame-shaming and cajoling, she persuaded the others to drink up and follow her lead. (The staunchest holdout was concerned about sanitary considerations and possible infection.) Swiftly removed and scrunched into balls, four more pairs of panties were tucked beneath the cushion of a broken chair; the girls seemed more embarrassed by their old-fashioned underwear than by exposing themselves to a total stranger. Squatting on the square of ancient carpet, bumping backs and steadying one another's legs, they passed the box back and forth as if it indeed contained chocolates. For having tried one, tipsy delight prompted them to test their skill with another; and then a third . . . a game of inserting, cooing, giggling and withdrawing that climaxed in a romp for the last tampon. Girlish squeals echoed from the barren walls as the happy friends demonstrated "how *I* look" and tugged at the others' strings.

Neither the strangeness of the scene nor the girls' playfulness blunted my excitement as I waited for *my* fun. But in five minutes, the novelty had worn off. The new toys were withdrawn for wrapping in the inevitable *Pravda* and discarded under the communal kitchen's corroded sink. The empty carton was just an empty carton; the Russian compulsion to splurge had been indulged and satisfied. (Even the most expensive Swiss chocolates, each one a rare luxury, would have been consumed to the last piece, just as every bottle of vodka, port or brandy in the country is drained to the last drop in the same session it is opened.) The girls were now discussing a handsome actor's film debut, and my attempt to steer the conversation back toward the seemingly promised sex drew rebuking glances. It was my turn to be baffled. I like to claim that I introduced tampons to Russia, and maybe I did; but if I were to write a story about the episode, wouldn't it need a better ending?

"Can you get me more jiggers?" Masha repeats. When the party broke up, she popped off to a movie with the other girls and did not mention Tampax for weeks. But she asked for some when her next period began, and I've been a faithful source of supply ever since.

"I will if you promise to finish the story about your brother's girls."

Masha tells dozens of tales about life in Perm, often not realizing why they're amusing. Yesterday she reminisced about the first time she was old enough to vote in a Supreme Soviet election. Oversleeping, she did not report to her polling station by noon, the hour at which election workers like to have the show wrapped up. When a representative knocked at her flat to inquire what was the matter, her mother, who had already voted, volunteered to run down again and drop her daughter's pre-marked ballot into the box. The officials were delighted: with the vote unquestioned in any case, their principal interest was in winning the competition to be the first district to report the unanimous "Yes!"

But my favorite story of Masha's is about the schoolteacher who replaced the KGB agent as her lover. The young man's provincial political staunchness helped get him selected to a small student delegation to Austria, from which the political careerist—who else goes abroad?—returned "with an even bigger head and all the Western glad rags he could buy or beg." But because a Young Communist secretary, which he was, would court scandal and downfall by being seen in such foreign gear, his new wardrobe never saw the light of Russian day. Instead, he modeled his mod shirts and tight trousers in the safety of a sidekick's flat, a treat to which he sometimes invited Masha until she "wised up" and left him.

The radio bleeps ten o'clock. Masha pulls herself up and suggests we ride into the city together in fifteen minutes or so. "But don't keep me waiting, please. My boots are falling apart, I mustn't be late."

She's going to an Armenian called "Uncle Grisha," a war invalid permitted to operate a private repair service. Uncle Grisha is rich on his reputation as the only Moscow cobbler able to cope with new Western platform shoes (he fabricates soles from old vegetable cartons) together with his skill in fooling the inspectors who check on him constantly to impose crippling taxes. Since only the smart set has this footwear, he's patronized by many of the city's lovelies, some of whom allow him to lavish his earnings on restaurant meals for them, and a few of whom even grant him their favors. It's as entertaining to visit his workroom as the studio of Zhenya, my highly talented painter friend.

Meanwhile, I sit down to tackle Leonid's novel, his one effort he likes enough to have shown me. He's rewritten it four times in response to changing political desiderata, for he much hopes to have it published *and* preserve some of its truths. The story is about the entwined fates of a Moscow lad and a Luftwaffe pilot he first "encounters" when he sees his bomber overhead in 1941. The more I read, the more it reveals itself as a feeble imitation of *The Young Lions*. There is even a scene, remarkably like Irwin Shaw's, of the seemingly doomed pilot regretting all the women he could have had and didn't; and I wonder what to say to Leonid, who is hanging on my "Western" verdict.

The disappointment of the first chapters prompts me to nag Masha that her "fifteen minutes" elapsed half an hour ago. After an additional quarter-hour, she is wrapped in her mottled acetate coat, topped by a pink acrylic hat: ready! I'm going to the Lenin Library at last; she to the basement workshop of her cobbler. The cold is as severe as it appeared from the window; we set out to make the ten-minute walk to the metro station in eight. On the way, Masha tells me not about her brother but about a Marxism-Leninism teacher of the old generation, who bristles at "insults to revolutionary sacrifice" and tends to flunk students who appear before him in clothes with any trace of style. His examinees are careful to dress "proletarian," the boys in open collars and no jackets, the girls without makeup or high heels. Masha herself is planning to go in overalls from her native Perm.

Soon I'm telling her about the summer *I* spent in overalls, when I was a high-school senior trying to "return to the land." The old farmer I slaved for, whose nastiness to me and his animals I took very seriously at the time, was named Blackcock. Doubled up at my attempts to render this in Russian, we lose the path and sink into the snow.

At this moment, I catch sight of a laborer on the skeleton of a new University building. A pretty girl with a peeved expression —no doubt bricklaying was not her first choice—she peers down from her scaffold, picking us out from the pedestrian stream trickling into the station. Construction in this temperature? Yes, on it goes, despite the vast extra effort and waste. (Even if the girl were not partially paralyzed by cold and clothes, would she give a damn where she slapped her mortar?) Somehow, I know this daily walk will go into my memory with the image of this tough-but-fragile worker: trowel dripping half-frozen mortar, smatterings and gobs from the head to the toe of her weather-beaten laborer's quilts, a thick smear of carrot-colored lipstick to proclaim that she's a woman.

Twenty thousand identical colleagues are putting in their eight hours at a swarm of nearby sites. I look back and wave to this one. Her cheekbones remind me of my Anastasia, and the day takes on another dimension.

III The Lenin Library

The Lenin Library flanks the city's epicenter, a short block from the northwest hypotenuse of the Kremlin walls. You rarely give it a glance except when the guide of a passing busload of winter tourists summons attention to the landmark: a pile of gray masonry and casement windows in the style of the functional office buildings of the first Five-Year Plans. It was designed in the early 1930s before the birth of Stalinist architecture, and although built as a monument, with statues of peasant and proletarian heroes, its slap-dash construction shows in the uneven wear of the spacious steps and porticoed façade.

The main entrance fronts on Kalinin Prospekt, a hundred yards south of the Central Military Department Store. Rows of Zils and new black Volgas are parked in an inlet between the two institutions, their chauffeurs waiting hours in the cold with the help of cigarettes and cheap novels. The cars are assigned to several high commands and war colleges in adjacent side streets, and from time to time, a gold-braided general appears, a boulder of a man with an ankle-length overcoat and a face bloated by peasant choler and peasant success. Bulling his way through knots of trudging shoppers, he disappears behind the drawn curtains of his sedan, like a caricature of himself.

The other exposed beam of the building faces a stark asphalt artery for cars and trucks speeding toward the Moscow River. A short walk down this icy avenue—still called Makhovaya by old Muscovites, although it's been renamed Prospekt Marx—rises the former Pashkov House, an elegant eighteenth-century palace with a memorable rotunda. This was the site of the Rumyanstsev Museum, a private collection nationalized after 1917 to become the Lenin Library's foundation. The great state institution has grown phenomenally since: two thousand seats for readers (the guides intone); three thousand employees and two hundred and fifty kilometers of shelves. Very big, very rich, very revered.

At the entrance, a metal grating is built into the pavement, designed for hot air to be blown through and melt the snow from users' boots. But something is permanently wrong with the mechanism: what air does appear has the force and warmth of human breath, causing mounds of gritty slush to pile high every morning—and more work than ever for the cleaning women. Bent over the foyer floor, they sop up the mess with grimy rags and mops.

Above the grating stands a block of doors with the weight of a fortress's outer portals; it takes the full force of your body—oomph!—to swing one open. There are eighteen in all, positioned six to a set in outer, middle and inner rows, a yard or so apart. But only one door in each row is ever unlocked—at opposite ends, to keep out the cold as people enter and leave. Because you never know which one is in service on a given day, you must yank at several: one of the country's hundred daily tests of your patience, endurance and strength.

I used to wonder about this while struggling through the maze each morning. Why do they always humiliate you? If doors can't be used normally, why don't they at least post signs indicating which ones work? Why build grandiose entrances—twenty-four

portals, for example, at the University's "parade" entrance—
only to make you grope and squeeze your way through like a
laboratory rat? (Half the front doors to everything in Moscow are
permanently locked. Unless you're in some foreign delegation, you
must search for a grimy staircase—appropriately called "black"
in Russian—somewhere at the back.) And if protection against
the cold is really the purpose, why do they keep the system
operating throughout the summer? Even in the minor, nonpoliti-
cal matters, convenience for the public is the last consideration.
Moscow's entire center is closed to stage some old Bolshevik's
funeral and a hundred thousand unwarned shoppers freeze on
cordoned-off streets. Metro stations are cattle-car packed, but
one of the escalators is shut off on bureaucratic schedule, forcing
you to butt in even harder toward the working one and to feel
even more misused and helpless. Why the vast expenditure for
show everywhere, and the maddening disregard for how things
actually work?

Still, the Lenin Library is more comfortable than most
buildings. And the time I waste finding my way into it and
bemoaning such affronts to my dignity postpones the moment
when I must open my books. Russia supplies so many good
excuses for your own procrastination and failures.

The room just inside the entrance is equipped with the usual
petitioning window for offices that receive the public: a small
opening—at chest level to reduce the petitioners to a suitably
humble crouch—with a wooden cover for slamming shut when
the bureaucrat inside wants to terminate a too-persistent supplication. The line for passes to use the library begins here and curls
around the waiting room's walls, which are lined with library
instructions-*cum*-prohibitions and posters illustrating Lenin's love
of learning. The last person to join the line, a breathless woman
with a briefcase, is solicitously reassured by her antecedent that
the wait will be less than an hour.

The first person, a large man with an asthmatic wheeze, is
pleading his case at the window. He *must* use the library for a
week, it's *essential* for his research. He's come *all the way to Moscow*
for this, and his institute is *counting* on his report. . . . But the
secretary with the stringy hair and limp cardigan is unmoved.

She's sorry, she says—bored even with the bureaucrat's satisfaction of being haughty to aspirants—but rules are rules; he doesn't have the proper documents.

"How can I get all those signatures now? I told you, my institute's in Kharkov. I just *came* from there."

"And I suppose you can go back? The regulations weren't made yesterday, and we're not changing them today. Signed and stamped statements from . . ."

(Under his breath): "—and grab your mother by her fucking leg—"

". . . your organization explaining on what grounds their request for you is based. Full details. We can't let people in off the street, Citizen."

"Just a week. Three or four days. I'm *asking* you."

Suddenly the secretary's contempt elevates to rage. "You are wasting my time, Citizen. You are *not* going in. NEXT!"

The man moves away with no discernible expression, stops, returns to the waiting room and joins the end of the line for another try.

The lines in the main foyer are shorter but take more time. Eight or ten of them stretch from the vast open cloakrooms on both sides, where users of the library must leave their outer clothing. For it is gravely *nekulturno* to enter an office (or a theater—and, in the case of prudes, a living room) in outerwear; and whatever was bad manners under the ancien régime, the new Soviet functionaries fear and despise more than Wall Street or a free idea. Therefore the operation of divesting oneself of overcoat, overshoes, scarf, hat and gloves is performed a hundred million times a day at the entrance to every public building; performed solemnly, for it is as much a social ritual as a matter of convenience or, as is sometimes argued (with reference to germs transported in overcoats), of public health.

The holdup in the library is caused by an insufficiency of hooks to accommodate the daily legion of readers. All are taken by nine o'clock, just as every chair of every Moscow restaurant will be occupied twelve hours hence. The elderly attendants, therefore, gossip among themselves, read handed-along newspapers and sip tea to pass the time behind their counters. They can do nothing until someone leaves the building and claims his things, liberating a hook for the person at the head of one of the lines. Knowing they may have to wait until lunch time, those near the end of the lines make use of their hours. Upright and sweating in their overcoats, they read their current "queuing" books, stuffing scraps of notes into their pockets.

Sometimes I wait with the Russians too: it is another way to postpone my work while feeling virtuous. I tell myself I'm learning something about local life by living it as a native. But this morning I won't waste the time. Two good hours remain before lunch, and I feel clearheaded and determined: this is the day I'm going to shake off my inertia. I make my way to the counter on the left and ask to be served next. (This is my right as a foreigner, and I'm encouraged to exercise it to jump lines at restaurants, movies, theaters and stores. But it too is part of the syndrome of show-before-people. Why does the Soviet government excoriate the Western bourgeoisie in every newspaper, lampoon them vulgarly or viciously in every other cartoon—then bow and scrape to them shamelessly when they appear on Soviet soil?)

I hand my things to the old attendant when the next hook is freed, pocket my metal claim check, squeeze through the one-person-at-a-time railings to the checkpoint guarding the main entrance, display my pass to the scowling, scrutinizing matron behind the desk, collect my daily attendance slip, nod to the smiling, scrutinizing policewoman beside her and mount the wide, worn stairway to Reading Room Number One.

The plaque on the door proclaims:

SCHOLARLY-SCIENTIFIC READING ROOM NUMBER ONE
For Doctors, Professors, and Members of the Academy of Sciences

And, of course, American graduate students. VIP treatment— in the Soviet hierarchy, a doctor, let alone a member of the Academy of Sciences, is an exalted personage—for the likes of obscure me. What a way to cop a birthright! In reverse proportion to the lower standards here, I'm closer to this country's richest and best than I'll ever come in my own.

Scholarly-Scientific Reading Room Number One is my work-room, the place I'm meant to put in my forty hours. A stately hall whose wood paneling insures an appropriate solemnity despite large windows on both long sides. Big brown desks—individual, in contrast to those of the Library's lesser reading rooms—with inkwells and lamps of editor's-visor green. Persian runners in the spacious aisles, chandeliers as if designed to spoof everything proletarian-pompous, and Lenin's collected works— in three editions, but not the unexpurgated first—for handy reference on both sides of the room. I love this hushed sanctuary and the headache it gives me: my old friend, the pressure of undone homework.

Maya's on duty behind the counter this morning. She'll be leaving soon for her three months' maternity sabbatical, and if she stays away longer, I'll be back in New York and may never see her again. The bubble on her slender frame has swelled day by day since October, making her face correspondingly more luminous with expectation and motherly pride; sometimes her space-staring gaze makes me want to cry. But Maya herself is no longer crying; she's actually happy that her great tragedy ended as it did. She's even taken to giving me mini-lectures, apparently genuinely oblivious that they deny everything she had been saying, hoping, praying just months ago. Her theme now is the need for maturity, responsibility and compatibility of background in lasting love. Don't marry one of us, she keeps whispering. No matter what she promises or pleads, don't become involved with a Russian girl. Because it can't work: your outlooks would be too irreconcilably different. Even before you'd leave the country, the great burden would be on her. Like white hunters taking native wives, it's always an injustice.

Bending awkwardly when she sees me approach, she fetches my books from the reserved shelves behind the counter. Then she blows a "haaa" of hot breath on her rubber stamp, punches it smartly on my slip, scrawls a big "5" in the corner with a red pencil and hands me the slip together with my books. She recognizes the titles by now: the same five I've had out since last month.

"How about some work, Comrade?" she teases. "You're getting like the old ones." The old ones are elfish men in prewar suits too big for their shrinking bodies, who daily collect and return the same small pile of books. Two are waiting behind me now—surely distinguished men to have survived the purges and earned the honor of the use of this hall, but who have become the very picture of an old age of useless scholarship. Their type slumbers and slides toward death everywhere in the world, but somehow seem more archetypal because they are Russian.

I pick up my pile and look for an empty desk near the windows, where the clear light and steady draft will keep me invigorated. How hard it is to work in this room—not only because the conditions are so good and it seems so easy, but also because its air brings on daydreams like the ones induced by dentist's gas. The very pretense that it's a reading room like any other adds to the mystical qualities and sense of encapsulation in this strange country. But enough of this goddam musing. I think of my future and take a deep breath. I *will* make headway today!

Every few minutes the door opens with just enough noise to draw your head up to see who's entering. The 10:45 arrival is Ilya Alexandrovich. Striding to the counter, he picks up his books and settles his large frame at his usual desk. Within minutes, however, his arm is lying across his books and his head is resting on top, as if they were a pillow. Weariness overpowers him more and more often now, yet he feels it is his duty not to die until his clandestine work is done.

Why Ilya Alexandrovich told me his story is mystifying unless you know that Anastasia was with me, and that some people want to reveal their secrets to her. (And, despite his eighty-two years, Ilya Alexandrovich has an eye for pretty girls.) He spied her waiting for me outside the library late one afternoon, and when I appeared, invited us home for tea. Following his brisk pace to his nearby apartment, Anastasia and I wondered what to expect. It was one of those winter dusks of opaque colors and severely beautiful façades flanking empty streets, as if someone had designed a Winter Palace setting for the coming narration. Inside, Ilya Alexandrovich settled us in heavy armchairs and made the tea himself, serving it and an excellent pepper-vodka with black bread and his own marinated mushrooms. Of course we knew his famous surname, but none of the rumors about him were as strange as his facts. We listened, postponing our questions.

He was the last living member of one of Russia's most noble families; owners of thirty thousand serfs, holders of respectful attention in the courts of a dozen tsars. As a young man—a latter-day Vronsky, with dark good looks, huge energy, and impeccable lineage—he was sent to the Imperial Naval Academy in Saint Petersburg, a highly select institution that was one of backward Russia's islands of technical and professional excellence, on a par with the best in the West. It was intended as a kind of reform school for the *enfant gâté*, but he trained hard and won firsts.

After graduation and commissioning in 1912, he was assigned to the cruiser *Border Guard* under Admiral Alexander Vasilevich Kolchak, whose personality would leave a deeper impression on him during the next eight years than even the incredibly tumultuous events the two men were to grapple with together. Kolchak was simultaneously Captain of the *Border Guard* and flag officer of its squadron in the Baltic Sea; but these were the least of his duties and concerns. At the moment, he was desperately trying to prepare the entire fleet for war with Germany, which he predicted would start by 1915. Matched by towering integrity and power of leadership, Kolchak's energy and intelligence had driven him to involvement in almost every phase of naval operations and strategy, from Admiralty staff work (where his presence had been the dominating factor before returning, recently, to sea duty) to hydrology and submarines. More than anyone it was he who cast aside the tsarist bureaucracy's mountainous deadweight, inspiring and reorganizing the Navy's rebirth as a modern, technologically oriented force after its catastrophic 1905 defeat by the Japanese—during which Kolchak himself was taken prisoner, suffering from wounds that never fully healed.

With the outbreak of the First World War, Kolchak's stature grew yet greater. On land as well as sea, he was a hero to all younger officers and a teacher of most older ones: a kind of Commander of the Battle Cruiser Squadron (Vice-Admiral Sir David Beatty), Commander of the Grand Fleet (Admiral Sir John Jellicoe) and First Lord of the Admiralty (Winston Churchill) in one.

Ilya Alexandrovich followed him everywhere as a personal

aide—even, after the Revolution, to Kolchak's native Siberia where, in a much better-known period of his life, he commanded one of the Civil War's most powerful and ruthless White armies. When the Admiral was finally defeated in 1920 and dispatched by a Red firing squad in Irkutsk, Ilya Alexandrovich was awaiting his own execution the following morning. He escaped, lived like a hunted leopard for weeks and finally smuggled himself abroad, joining the great White emigration as his great family's sole male survivor of the national bloodletting.

He lived in Berlin, Amsterdam, Paris, trying to feed himself and make sense of émigré politics. But the Second World War found him in Yugoslavia, where he fought bravely with the partisans and organized liaison with the approaching Soviet Army staff. Russian generals wined and dined him, and—on orders, of course—urged him to return to the Motherland's forgiving embrace. Tears of love for Russia fell into cups of vodka. Not nearly so naïve to believe the "times-have-changed, Russia-needs-its-best-sons" orations, Ilya Alexandrovich nevertheless felt alone and weary of exile. And curious.

On the plane to Moscow in 1946, the tone of the accompanying officers changed in one breath from respectful to reviling. The next moment, handcuffs went on. "Counterrevolutionary!" "Enemy of the People!" "Traitor to the Motherland!" Perhaps Ilya Alexandrovich *had* been a trifle naïve after all: he could not quite banish images of the Leningrad apartment and curatorship of a small handicrafts museum he had been promised for a modest but comfortable—and contributing—middle age. Instead, he was treated to the zombie conditions and surrealistic interrogations of Lubyanka's basement. (Relatively few questions were put about the former Prince's prerevolutionary life or even his Civil War activities; it was émigré affairs in Paris and, especially, aspects and personalities of the Yugoslav partisan high command that concerned his inquisitors.)

Two years passed. The trip from the Moscow military airport to jail had been in a Black Maria. Aside from his jailors and interrogators, Ilya Alexandrovich did not, in that period, see another soul, Russian or otherwise.

Suddenly—and mysteriously, for 1948 was a time of big leaps in repression and terror, especially after Tito's break with

Stalin—his imprisonment ended. And means for him to contribute to the Motherland were indeed found: after a period of rest and rehabilitation, he was served up to foreign dignitaries, delegations, and the occasional visiting newsmen as evidence of Soviet goodwill to former class enemies. What more satisfying proof of the harmony of all peoples under socialism than this still-robust man, with the name second only to Romanov, thriving in Moscow? And happy in his humble but honest job—for one had been found for him, teaching Slovenian in a language institute.

Substitutes frequently took over his classes, however; Ilya Alexandrovich was always on call to be driven with a group of foreign visitors to one of the family's former estates, now an orphanage, in a lyrical valley southwest of Moscow. "How happy I am that these buildings are being used for the good of unfortunate children instead of ludicrous private privilege," he would say (in French, Italian, German or Dutch—but, most typically, to a British trade union delegation tearing with joy for the use to which the magnificent mansion, like the Botanical Gardens and the Bolshoi Ballet, was being put under Soviet *love for the people*).

"I myself have a comfortable apartment in Moscow. (You must visit me sometime.) What on earth could I have wanted with a time-wasting extravagance like this? I can only thank the elected representatives for freeing me of endless roof-repairing and wrangling with gardeners; and bless them for making it possible that my family's wealth and greed, so often the source of hurt to others, is at last contributing to my people's happiness."

KGB officials stood at both elbows, and the tour leaders—also secret policemen, of course, like the picked chauffeurs—strained for his every word. But Ilya Alexandrovich's declarations were not pure hypocrisy; he was not lying even when he suggested that in their common recognition of service as man's redemption, Communism and the Orthodox church were far from incompatible. Whatever else he felt—and it was not, despite everything, that his homecoming had been an unqualified mistake—the former heir to literally incalculable wealth did not want his estates returned. In this sense, he *was* grateful to the Revolution.

But he was no less grateful to be relieved of his role and left in relative peace. This happened gradually in the 1950s, as his novelty value declined in proportion to the greater numbers of foreigners admitted to post-Stalinist Russia. Finally, he was freed entirely of his burden (together with the obligation of having to sign his name to the occasional article about aristocratic perfidy in general and his family's debauches in particular) and treated as a private citizen—in which capacity he turned his full attention to teaching. Lacking a family, he gave his free time to compiling a Slovenian-Russian dictionary. It was a tolerable end to a full life, affording even a degree of dignity, provided he kept his mouth shut. But—and this was the point of his story—he had not seen the last of his trials.

To aid his labors on the dictionary, he was granted use of the Lenin Library—even assigned to Reading Room Number One. During breaks, he took to reading about the cataclysmic civil war in which he had played a minor part. What deprived him of a quiet old age was not the textbooks—teaching had fully acquainted him with the appalling distortions codified there—but that even in scholarly works, even archives, a great mass of evidence had apparently been destroyed. The Russian people were being deprived not only of the truth but also of the means of ever resurrecting it.

His dismay centered around Kolchak, the dazzling naval hero turned anti-Bolshevik war lord. Ilya Alexandrovich had long questioned the Admiral's Siberian adventure: having mistakenly involved himself in politics, he thought, the professional sailor had been inevitably sucked into the deception and terrible cruelty practiced on both sides. But what of his earlier brilliance in Russia's service? The supercharged dynamism and dedication to standards, the furious resolve and labors that had transformed the Navy from feudal stagnation to a modern force—and gave splendid victories to the Admiral's squadrons on the high seas? All this was gone, together with any hint of Kolchak's magnificent patriotism and courage. Portraying him only as an arch enemy of revolution, Soviet historians had ruthlessly eliminated every reference to his prerevolutionary virtues and achievements —even to his existence. Like Trotsky, he had been made into a counterrevolutionary villain in a state fable.

After all Ilya Alexandrovich had made peace with in his own life, the odious assassination of Kolchak's memory became unbearable. The Admiral's execution began to dominate his memories. ("I've looked death in the face more than once," the condemned man had answered the officer in charge. "Thank you for your offer, but I have no need for a blindfold now.") Ilya Alexandrovich became possessed by the knowledge that in another decade, no power on earth would be able to rescue Kolchak from the quicksands of ideological villainy and insensate myth. Eyewitnesses and subordinates would all be dead, and even if tsarist archives had been preserved somewhere, a fair history of the leader and his contribution—even his tragedy— could never be produced. And if understood, this very tragedy— symbolic of so many of Russia's—of a good man's destruction contained more potential enlightenment than the hate-provoking official liturgy of Red saints and White devils. How did this officer whose honesty and chivalry approached the quixotic become a Caesar, presiding over (if not personally directing) a brutal tyranny?

This was Ilya Alexandrovich's new trial: for lack of anyone else, it had fallen to him to assemble a chronicle. Accepting the challenge, he felt a resurgence of his youthful commitment to honor, duty and country, as if this was the culmination of his cadet training. Secret research became the lonely man's obsession. Stealthily excerpting from rare naval histories and classbooks, warily tracking down former naval officers among the handful who survived, the octogenarian was assembling the makings of a monograph on his former commander and was dieting carefully so as not to die before completing it.

But then what? With whom would he leave it? And knowing that one word to the authorities would be its ruin, why did he entrust his secret to Anastasia and me? "Perhaps," he said, refilling our glasses, "my subject holds enough interest for publication in the West. If you believe it is worth something, you might help me in this endeavor." (Eyes on Anastasia.) "But let's turn to lighter subjects. How did such an enchanting couple meet?"

He saw me in the library often after that but never so much as alluded to Kolchak again, let alone my smuggling out his manuscript. As he's doing today, he alternated between intervals of great bounce and equal exhaustion, in which his age seemed to vary by thirty years. Now he's deep in his books again, apparently revived by his nap. He's wearing a handsome new tie to go with his cream-colored shirt: he still takes pride in his appearance.

Drifting and daydreaming; staring at and somewhere absorbing, but unable to focus on or fully comprehend the sights of this room. Steeped in the smell, a muskiness of newsprint and pulpy scholarly journals. Lulled by the sounds: of Prospekt Marx's snow-muffled traffic outside and the swish-swish of whispered Russian, with its consonants, here and there inside the hall. Benumbed by the mood: of the huge rubber plants, a plaster bust of Lenin, marbled columns, and the long-unanswered ring of a telephone in the librarians' anteroom.

Were I able to fix the meaning of even a few of the images before my eyes, something might be clear about why Russia has a life unlike any other. The shaved head of the man at my right, a bullet-like skull sitting evilly on a bureaucratic torso, the chandeliers' reflection gleaming in the oil of its pores. Good God, is he really the sinister Stalinist he seems? Or, on the contrary, does he look like that because he himself suffered? Why *do* Russian academics still shave their heads? . . . The man in front of him, no less pear-shaped and serge-suited, but sharing a desk with a woman lipsticked and bleached like the most blatant Broadway tart. And a third man, older and more shriveled, steering a shaky course down the aisle toward the door with a cane in one hand and a square of trembling newspaper in the other: yesterday's newspaper, which this corresponding member of the Academy of Sciences—like all Russians, no matter how august—has trained himself to carry in pocket or briefcase for when the call of nature sounds. Somehow it seems not humbling but democratic when done with his dignity.

From the desk to my left, the guttural whisper of two wiry Iraqi students, no doubt discussing girls, careers in state petroleum monopolies, and the intrigues of the University's Arab factions. Dressed in chain-store sports jackets and nylon shirts, they are nevertheless a sartorial cut above Russian students; and the Russians, bitter at Mother Russia's additional levies to enrich distant ingrates—and repelled by colored skin—keep a sullen distance from their "Arab brothers." The book on their desk is a standard American chemistry manual: after three years here, their Russian is still too weak to struggle with Soviet textbooks on subjects unavailable in English. They have come all this way, supported by fat stipends, immense economic investments and international commitments, to learn their formulas from pages printed in New Jersey.

To the Iraqis' left, the reedlike Nigerian with an Italian suit cut to accent his superbly haughty bearing: a chieftain's son popular in the University's smartest black circle, not least for his denigration of everything Slavic. Flaunting his English like his wardrobe, he insists—reverting to Russian on these occasions, and making certain he's overheard—that the natives will remain ignorant muzhiks until colonized by a superior civilization. In the same spirit, he encourages his scholarship colleagues to refuse their turns in dormitory cleanup details: although students from Eastern and Western Europe all pitch in uncomplainingly, Africans, he says, should not stoop to sweeping Russian floors.

The Nigerian's warrior face is sometimes pulpy from the fists of townie-type Russian students; during the last ambush, when a cooperative blonde lured him from the path to the metro, his always-worn dark glasses were ground to bits in a mortar-mixer. His answer was to have a smarter pair air-mailed from Paris, exhibit himself in the company of his latest sexy conquest (won partly with a half-dozen bottles of Revlon nail polish and a purse atomizer of Madame Rochas) and again swear to dedicate himself, after returning home to a place in his government, to the cause of weakening Soviet–Nigerian relations.

The North Vietnamese students with their Mao uniforms and relentless industriousness—are they my enemies? They never so much as glance at me and, in fact, hardly look at anything except their books. The well-groomed West German girl who has come from an incredibly richer, slicker world to study Lermontov . . . BUT NO MORE: I *must* get to *work!*

At first, I had the crazy idea that I was going to reform Farmer

Blackcock. Then I hated him for killing my idea of finding myself through tilling the soil.

He was impatient for the days when his bull was scheduled to service a cow. The wet summer kept their rear ends dripping, but he never missed a milking time to tell his joke about why the shit didn't swim up their "cunts." I had to laugh hard enough to keep his temper down, but not too hard because he was trying to bait me for sodomy. His other conversation piece was how they loved "that kinda thing" down old Marne way, which he'd noticed in '18, under Pershing. Lifting tails, he'd inform me that Frenchy liked to sniff his food.

Blackcock himself treated food as feed, consuming just enough to stoke his scrawniness. Once he missed dinner while attending to the tractor in town, and his wife gave Jim and me more. Most days, we felt too intimidated to ask. "Cut that up with yer 'tatas," he'd instruct, nudging his knife into the slice of pork fat representing our meat. "Protein builds yer sinews."

We finished quickly because we had fifteen free minutes while Blackcock cheered Fulton Lewis, who was cheering McCarthy, on the radio. Jim didn't lie down. He played with his pile of old comics. He was fourteen, already stunted by undernourishment.

The New York State orphans' bureau paid twenty dollars a week, or something, for his maintenance. Blackcock didn't spend three on his food, and no more than twenty a year for clothes. His one pair of sneakers was rotting from sweat and lime. He wore them all day, every day, like a depression kid. And Blackcock squeezed even more out of him than me—Sundays too—because the kid knew all the machinery and procedures. Work was over when it was too dark to see. We went up to our attic without washing. At dawn, his wife woke us with the fire-gong.

It was easier on the days I worked alone, away from his exhortations. The farm was at the tip of the state, twenty miles below Canada. I rested on my pitchfork and watched in case a car would appear on the rise across the fields. Each one was my spaceship back to civilization. A '49 Buick speeding toward Burke, then on to Malone, which had a movie house . . . It was breaking loose from here! I loved its chromy glint and pictured the lucky driver. He was *free.* Zooming toward *the city,* carnival of lights, drugstores, traffic and crowds: of everything I loved with a refugee's longing for his homeland. When the car was gone, an incredible emptiness gripped the fields. No human in sight, even from the top of the pasture. When someone did appear it was Blackcock, who was coming the back way to check on my hay mounds.

I knew what kept me in his power. Having made the dramatic move of leaving school to become a farmhand, I couldn't return at least until fall. Why I went on these escapades in the first place was harder to fathom. My mother and father constantly fought, but whose parents didn't? As long as I can remember, they both worked—and I felt so alone that I concocted quixotries like returning to Mother Earth. To escape solitude, I fled to that geezer's forsaken farm where—this was the laugh—my loneliness was unbearable.

I crept out of the attic in the dead of a September night, walking to Malone without hitching in case a neighbor reported me to Blackcock. When the stores opened, I spent my last five dollars on a pair of white sneakers for Jim. . . .

I slump in my seat, remembering my pastoral summer with tender relief. When things are punk, it's a comfort to relive something much worse. Having pulled through the genuine misery of Blackcock, I'm not going to surrender to today's petty panic.

What's the great death blow if I drop my dissertation, don't get my Ph.D., never become a professor? That's no cause for these waves of self-contempt. The irony is that I never really wanted the academic life—until this year, when I realized I'll never get in. Being a professor was my last substitute after the fiasco of doing something "basic" through farming. And now I've convinced myself, for some self-destructive reason, that I'm too old and have come too far in graduate schools to switch to anything else: if teaching's out, there's no other way to earn and justify my existence. How typical of me, this whining self-pity! I can do something free from intellectual pressure—drive a taxi, for example—and be happier for it. The way to see my inability to work here is release from something wrong for me, not to whine about "another day's defeat."

My big mistake was not buckling down to my research immediately, in September. No, it was choosing the wrong subject. I'm trying to work on municipal government: the daily functions of city soviets. But I'm not permitted to observe their sessions, see their agendas, lay eyes on archives about meetings ten—or fifty—years ago. I've begged to attend five minutes of a single conference—a discussion, say, about revising a bus schedule—in order to sample Soviet democracy in action. I'm answered that this is unnecessary and even foolish. Soviet self-government, the freest and most open in the world, has been exhaustively described by Soviet professors. Why attend meetings, my academic overseers reply, when the material for my dissertation has already been painstakingly prepared? Unfamiliar procedures may mislead a foreigner at any given session, whereas skilled Soviet scholars provide a complete picture of the whole. For analysis of municipal institutions in action, they say, go to the books—the most reliable sources. And read Lenin. Study and restudy Vladimir Ilich—"this is the duty of a scholar examining a Leninist society."

But the books are impossible. Like wartime save-paper editions, these tomes from the State Publishing Houses of Juridical and Political Literature have warping covers and marginless pages, and chapter after chapter of text so dense that the pages make me seasick. And all of them, all the millions of words I'm supposed to be digesting, are arid elaborations of a defunct illusion:

In our country, an all-peoples' state has come into existence —a crucial landmark on the road to Communist self-government. In Communist self-government, into which socialist statehood is growing, the soviets, trade unions, cooperatives and other mass organizations will merge into a single, unified structure. . . .

As well as in the policy and practices of all state organs and officials, the strict safeguarding of citizens' rights is organically inherent in the Soviet state. V. I. Lenin devoted enormous attention to socialist legality. V. I. Lenin summoned the toilers to unflinchingly observe all laws and regulations of Soviet rule, and to keep vigilant watch so that everyone observes them. . . .

The soviets' strength lies in their indissoluble ties to the masses, to the people. V. I. Lenin called the toilers' enlistment into the administration of the state a "marvellous means" capable of "immediately, at a single stroke, multiplying our state apparatus *ten-fold*. . . ."

Socialism and Communism, Marxist-Leninist theory teaches, are products of the creative work of a people who are organized, tightly united and striving toward a single goal. Therefore, the further growth of workers' mass organizations and of the masses' unification constitutes an objective, inevitable development of the Soviet state and Soviet society. . . .

Enhancing the role of local soviets is one of the natural, inevitable phenomena of the Soviet state's development at the present stage of the full-scale building of Communist society. Basing himself on Leninist propositions, L. I. Brezhnev pointed out that "the genuine character of Soviet democracy is also evidenced by this fact: that in our country an ever-greater role in the State's administration and direction is being assumed by local governmental organs and communal organizations. . . ."

The Communist Party teaches that an essential condition for the soviets' successful accomplishment of its tasks is the further deepening of socialist democracy in all their activities. In carrying out their mass-organizational work, the local soviets participate more and more actively in attaining the course plotted by the Communist Party toward gradually transferring the functions now fulfilled by paid state officials to mass organizations of workers.

For whom is this gibberish written? Only a handful of foreigners—saddled graduate students, like me—ever see it, while the dimmest Russian student isn't taken in. He may be a vigorous patriot, may even feel personally committed to socialism; but the ritual constructions about socialist legality, Soviet democracy and workers' participation have long ceased to mean a thing. Yet new editions pour forth in hundreds of thousands of copies every year, with the key Lenin quotations rearranged in keeping with the latest nuances of the line: pamphlets, brochures, booklets, fat volumes . . . an ocean of pulp flooding a country where—despite immeasurable timber resources—paper is rationed for most useful applications.

Every book in the standard typeface; each a plodding repetition of the same mumbo-jumbo fraud. There can't be another mass of literature so monumentally *tedious* in the world.

The humiliating thing is that other exchange students working on even stodgier, less relevant subjects keep to their duty, cramming five-by-eight cards with notes. But my paralysis grows; I can't read another page. I've never daydreamed so much before, sunk to such purposeless wandering. And although I can hardly believe I've washed out, the failure also confirms what I've always known about myself.

When I was in the third grade, I felt I'd never possibly reach the wise and giant kingdom of the eighth. In the eighth, I couldn't picture myself in high school; in high school, college seemed far beyond my abilities and reach. The difference between me and others who surely entertained these common-place thoughts was that I made too much of them because of a notion that something was wrong with me, which would reveal itself before I fully grew up. And to verify the infantile dread, this block materializes in ye olde Lenin Library, on the last step from student to grown man, bringing greater shame than a thousand abandoned dissertations could otherwise provoke.

What an idiot I am! My presumed brain finds it interesting to feature me in plotless, reasonless melodrama. Unemployable at my age, supposedly because nothing's good enough: *I'm* not good enough.

With a swallow, I clear my ears of the jeers of the rabble and return to reality. The thing is to take some kind of *action*—get up to peruse the morning's newspapers, for a start. A stack of the nationals lies on a table near the door, supplied daily, as in every public room: whatever else doesn't work, the Soviet people must "sharpen its political consciousness" by reading the Soviet press. For this hall's sophisticated public, Communist papers from abroad are also available, although *l'Humanité* and *The Morning Star* are missing when the issues contain a disapproved photograph or opinion.

For a change, I chose *Sovietskaya Rossiya*. The feature article is about the current intensification of the ideological struggle.

The Soviet people are prepared. They know that increased trade and other contacts with capitalist representatives demand heightened vigilance under Our Party's guidance. For *ideological* coexistence cannot exist. The present historical era is characterized by a sharp intensification of the struggle of ideas, as capitalism thrashes about trying vainly to delay Marxism-Leninism's inevitable triumph.

It surprises no one that the West keeps braying about "intellectual freedom"—which is nothing more than a cloak for anti-Soviet propaganda. As V. I. Lenin taught, there can be no creative freedom without freedom from bourgeois-exploitative ideology and relations, which bind the artist's will and distort his talent.

The hypocritical farce conducted under the slogan "intellectual freedom" is actually a last-ditch attempt to somehow stem socialism's triumphant development. This too proves there can be no talk of even "ideological armistice," an attempted trick to slow socialism's march to its complete and final world victory.

The next piece is about bauxite workers mobilizing all resources for the productivity battle in this decisive second year of the historic Five-Year Plan. Then a progress report about scientists working to improve the sound quality of records that preserve Lenin's voice. Chemists, physicists, acoustical and computer engineers—all disciplines toiling together to restore dear Vladimir Ilich's inflections.

I keep wading through—about battles on the Ukrainian preplowing front (only four months left to prepare) and victories over Siberian rivers; socialist morality sermons and denunciations of "nihilistic" West German poets—because I tell myself that this is another form of work, more digestible than my academic stuff, thanks to the comic relief. Still, ten minutes is the limit. I long to telephone Anastasia, but it will do no good, for the same reason that it's too late to start again and make up for the lost months of work. If only I hadn't ruined that; if only I had her again! I know we wouldn't be blissful in the old way, but at least I'd be finished with these dreary self-doubts.

But my broken record is worse than Lenin's. If I leave the library now, I can't even pretend to have tried. What next?

Maya's alone at the counter now, again staring into space. She seems to be planning the life of the child in her bubble-belly. This is the quiet hour; the morning stragglers have arrived, her supervisor is out for tea. I go up for the briefest heart-to-heart. "We'll stay with his mother for a while," she whispers, an eye peeled for anyone observing our chat. "She's been terribly good to me. She'll sleep in the kitchen and give us the room."

Maya's tears are pearls of suffering, as the Russian saying goes. As a young Tadzhik actress, she was brought to Moscow from Leninabad (formerly Stalinabad, formerly Dushambe) and given a coveted place for "outstanding representatives of the nationalities" in a theatrical academy. Months later, a train crash impaired her voice and badly scarred her Hiawathan face. While she was in bandages, her mother burned to death in a factory accident. Unwilling to return to the Leninabad she had left triumphantly a year before, she enrolled in a librarians' institute.

After graduation, she was found a good job in the Lenin Library—comfort to her lonely years, for she was certain her disfigurement would keep her unmarried. It did until last winter.

During the previous year, a studious Englishman named Ian doing research in Hall Number One had chatted with her once or twice about the weather. His good-bye in June was as reserved as these earlier exchanges, but back in the University of Manchester, memories of her, perhaps colored by comparisons with his more frivolous students, took command of him. Without so much as a letter, he returned to Moscow during the Christmas vacation last December. He asked the Intourist car waiting at the airport to take him to the library, raced up the stairs and proposed to her at the counter.

Maya knew this was her Chance. Ian was gentle and honest; whatever Britain was like, they would raise children and be happy. Having applied with her for permission to marry, Ian went home to Manchester, planning to return for the wedding at the end of the month-long waiting period. Days after his departure, Maya was summoned to an office.

"Why do you want to marry that English fool?"

"Because I love him." Aware that the purpose of the interview was to terrorize her, Maya fought back her tears.

The officer slapped her on the face. "Do you still love him?"

"Yes, I do."

The second slap made her scars burn. "You hardly know him. You want to exhibit your" (sneer) "physiognomy in the" (smirk) "United Kingdom?" He raised a fist. "Do you still love him?"

"I do. More than *you* will ever understand."

"Leave my sight before I lose control. And start praying."

None of Maya's fears materialized. She continued working—and with foreigners!—at the library. The marriage was prevented simply by refusing Ian an entry visa. The coming and going of their wedding date deepened Maya's love even more than the KGB interview. Ian was educated, refined, kind; he wanted to take her to a world of cultivation. This quiet Englishman who had made his glorious gesture for her became a knight representing, as well as a polar opposite to the KGB's hands, the good luck that had been intended to compensate her for her bad.

During her ensuing grief, her sole interest was England. Within the limits of available materials, she became an expert on Manchester daily life. She had spent so little time with Ian that she was able to relive every moment; able to remember his every copper-colored freckle. Then a workman came to mend the telephone in her apartment, and her thoughts about England and the Round Table, even about intellectual life, ceased as suddenly as they had begun. Her letter breaking the engagement asked him not to write again. She had come to feel that marriage to a foreigner was distasteful *per se;* that Ian was trying to drag her to unhappiness. In this, at least, the attitude of the KGB interviewer was now her own. A Soviet girl can never be home abroad. Heartache is a crushing price for cars and suburban cottages. True happiness can only be achieved with one's own people—even an unambitious telephone repairman.

"My mother-in-law will be a great help when the baby comes. She was a nurse during the war."

"Boy or girl? They can tell you in advance now."

"We don't know. My husband wants a boy, of course. . . . And don't you marry a Russian girl."

I'm about to ask something about the vague husband when, for the first time, I decipher her expression of the last months. *It doesn't matter now. Nothing matters. I have my baby.*

Back at my desk, I smile at the irony of Maya's "Don't marry a Russian girl" in the context of Anastasia. Then I force myself to have another go at a page of text. But it doesn't work: torpor puts me in a trance again, like autumn mud paralyzing the countryside. I cup my hands over my forehead to pretend I'm reading; better the other graduate students not know. I let a film form over my eyes and float over this building toward the demoralization of failure . . . which is accompanied by spiritual bliss.

I pry open my eyes. A pretty girl with a broad Russian bottom is standing at the lending desk. A bottom that's already mine: I'm certain she will turn, smile at me, give the magic sign. The sensuousness of my next dream is accompanied by sunlight streaming through a chapel's stained glass. When Joe Sourian wakes me, my watch reads twelve o'clock.

Joe and I sometimes have lunch together when we're both at the library. He likes to eat at noon—likes to eat, come to think of it, at most times of the day (he always reckons it's just before or just after the rush), and his room is the only place for a satisfying snack when you're starved at night. He lives two floors below me in the dormitory, in a room crammed with jazz records, antihistamines, saucepans, vitamins, stacks of letters, heating pads, travel guides, boxes of soap powder, back issues of *Time*, back issues of *Playboy*, as well as Sugar Pops, Right Guard sprays and a substantial supply of canned chow mein from the American Embassy and other sources. Joe is as big and friendly as the stereotypical fat boy in any movie of fraternity life. He always wears a tie because his mother raised him to be a good Armenian boy; and because liquids drip down his stubby chin, the tie is always soiled. He's an exchange student like me, but this is his second full year; he likes it so much that he "extended" after the first. There are two kinds of Americans in Moscow, he likes to say: those who hate it here and "Joey-boy" Sourian.

"Let's chow down," he says, hand on his buckle. The belt is pushed so low by his stomach that his blue buttondown fails to reach it, revealing a triangle of T-shirt. "We gotta get a move on if we're gonna beat the crowd. Grab something quick so we can get back to the books."

In and out of the University, Joe has a hundred friends, and all have sucked him into their schemes. Russians, Frenchmen, Georgians, the two Dutch girls who pretend to want nothing to do with uncouth Russian men, and the entire English and American contingents are his pals. People who otherwise might have little to say to one another—East and West Germans, Pakistanis and Bengalese—squeeze together on his bed as a member of the Armenian community shifts to make room for them: every Soviet Armenian considers himself a blood brother of the easygoing American who always has a gift, if only an old *Esquire* or the chance to hear The Original Dixieland Band on four-track Sony, for everyone who enters the room.

When he leaves his room, it is rarely without items to deliver to friends, friends of friends and supplicants. Wrapped in newspaper, stuffed in a cellophane bag and stashed under his overcoat in the manner of Harpo Marx, the daily booty represents a small fortune in rubles—and otherwise unobtainable happiness—to the recipients. Joe's dark eyes goggle slightly, for it is not certain whether any one of the items or their aggregate can get him arrested as a "speculator." But he laughs at himself and waddles on, hoping his bulk conceals his cargo.

A pair of West German scissors for his barber, woollen knee socks for the daughter of last year's biddy, nylon ties and tights for the world of Moscow taxi drivers and waitresses. Even a tattered prayer book, passed in a cubicle of a park toilet, for an Orthodox Jew so frightened that he requested it from an American rather than his own people, who are Jewish but Soviet. Because he takes seriously the unwanted obligation of a Westerner to supply Soviet friends with what he alone can obtain for them—and because his ability to catalogue and find each person's need somewhere in the Western community is extraordinary—he is a phenomenon of procurement and supply. He can't say no to a request. They pour in like airline reservations. If he went into business he'd have an overnight trading empire.

The Armenian merchant: some would say it's in his blood. Some *do* say he loves the middleman sweat and intrigue, and that his complaints are like an executive proudly beefing about too much work. His truth, however, is that he does it only out of the class fat boy's sense of obligation, which he would happily shed if he could. "*You* try playing Santa for twelve months," he sighs. His acumen notwithstanding, he is nowhere as rich as Soviet students imagine: he takes just enough "turnover tax" on each item to keep his trade going. Nor, despite his chuckle to one and all, is he happy-go-lucky; keeping up this role is an even greater burden. "It costs plenty to be good for laughs," he told me on the night we played Russian and bought a bottle specifically to get drunk. On the other hand, his popularity and Russia's jumble have helped him break free of mama's inhibitions.

Even more than mine, his childhood is a case study of immigrant Americans stumbling in the tug of war between tradition and striving. His father, an A & P butcher, lost his job and died. Fed on starchy *lavash* and sweet *telmash*, pampered by aunts, Joe grew up a mother's boy—and mother's man, hope and idol. By fifteen, he harbored a self-fulfilling prophecy that his moist flabbiness would repel any girl he desired. But the sadness of this was softened by the general pattern of his adolescence. *All* interests, sexual and other, were subordinated to the goal of becoming a professor at Cincinnati University, whose library was visible from their house. He wore a white shirt to class every day. He had to succeed.

This is the background he is now bravely deserting: for the first time, he's up to his ears in wheeling-dealing and *life*. But it's less his Moscow goings-on that have freed him than the adventures of last summer. Instead of joining the other Westerners scurrying, on their first day of vacation, like baby gulls toward water to refresh their spirits in Europe, he decided to remain in the country between his two academic years. Convincing his sponsors that the travel was essential to his studies—his dissertation concerns prerevolutionary Russian attitudes toward Tamerlane —he wrested a subsidized tour for himself to Soviet Central Asia, seat of this branch of the Mongol conquerors. It was to start in the Uzbek capital of Tashkent and culminate, predictably, in a sentimental detour to Yerevan, where advance parties of Armenians home on vacation from studies in Moscow were already preparing the sumptuous welcome he would never receive. . . .

Joe once more urges a "quick nip" to the cafeteria in order to avoid the dinner crush, but I so enjoy the story of his Central Asian voyage that I persuade him to join me on the double seat and tell it anew. Wary of the authorities, he has whispered the whole tale only to Chingiz and me. But he seems to recognize my need for diversion today and starts at the beginning.

The trip began in the desert heat of July, after the usual false starts because of extra documents required at the last minute and hard-won reservations abruptly canceled when Swiss and Swedish delegations appeared to monopolize planes and hotels. On the first leg, his companions—if he could help it, gregarious Joe did not journey alone—were a young French couple on a fling south from the University before summering in Menton. The Parisian girl changed costume before and after every meal. Under a sun that fried feet through sandal-leather, her suitor followed in her footsteps, lugging trunks on their peregrinations from one Tashkent hotel to another. (Intourist had bungled their arrangements.) Entering a lobby where the porters were having a smoke, he tripped, tore a tendon, and could not move. His darling cursed him and walked on.

Joe couldn't help: he was busy ministering to a lady of his own. A resident of Akron named Mrs. Betty Vogl, she was on his plane coming down, and invited him to a nightcap in her room. She answered his knock in a spangled bikini.

"It's so hot in here and no air-conditioning—can you imagine?"

Although never facile with words, Joe perceived some things so clearly that they formed near aphorisms in his thoughts. This Vogl floozy, he mused, is as ignorant as lustful, as vulgar as forward. Until now, her American Express trip had not been a success. "I couldn't care less, Big Boy," the voyager's twang proclaimed, "whether this is Tashkent or Timbuktu. Long as I got you." Nevertheless, he succumbed to her patent tricks. He was mesmerized by her boldness and, when his shirt was unbuttoned, by her obviously unfeigned attraction to the growth on his chest. Here was a woman who *wanted* him.

Tashkent seemed as worlds-apart from Moscow as Moscow from Cincinnati, but Joe could only guess: he hardly saw more than the skyline from Mrs. Vogl's balcony, whose view was partially blocked by a Lenin monument. Here he was in the Central Asia of his five years' study and research, and spending his entire stay within four walls with pretensions to enclose a

Statler room. After each bang, he resolved to say good-bye to this thin-faced Betty with the hunger exceeding his own but could not leave her in the lurch. She liked meals in the room and was delighted with his ability to arrange this by actually *talking* that gobbledegook on the telephone. On the last morning, she promised to return via Moscow rather than Hawaii after the tour's India circuit.

From Tashkent to Samarkand, the second leg of his journey, Joe's companion was a gangling young "scholar" who introduced himself as Pavel, then groped for his surname. The circumstances of their meeting were quite enough to unmask his function: before fully arranging his limbs at Joe's side in the airport, the stranger with the genial smile but edgy eyes instantly had begun marveling about all they had in common—muffing, however, some of his lines. Quaintness can soften crudeness, thought Joe aphoristically. In such things, clumsy obviousness can add an element of Old World charm.

As Pavel had it, their main mutual interest was Ulug-Beg, a nephew of Tamerlane and the subject of his graduate research. What luck! They could spend time together in Samarkand! With nothing to hide and a year's experience of how to conduct himself with student narks, Joe did not mind that someone had been assigned to him for the trip, or even that Pavel knew almost nothing about Mongols and the fourteenth century. It was summer, after all, and understandably difficult to recruit someone of his own specialized background at short notice. Young Pavel's compulsion to point out every new cinema and row of trees as a Soviet Achievement in the former Asian badlands was disconcerting, but this very clumsiness was reassurance that he, Joe, was not taken seriously as a threat to Soviet security. This was routine surveillance, and all things considered—including Samarkand's evening dullness—he was grateful for the company.

Because it was the holiday season, Joe found few of the professors he wanted to interview. But he did spend time exploring minarets and glorious azure mosques—in which Pavel, to his own delight, developed an interest. And although thorough Sovietization had transformed the city from a fabled oasis lying across the world's most important spice route to a tackier version of modern Moscow, the new construction made Tamerlane's

tomb and other surviving Islamic treasures all the more important. Joe thought his way back to the dusty days of Marco Polo,
Ghenghis Khan and his own Tamerlane.

Soon it was time to fly to Bukhara, former oasis, ancient rival
of Samarkand, rich prize of warring Arabs and rapacious Turks.
Joe was much looking forward to this: Bukhara was said to be far
less spoiled, still a city of mud battlements and tapestries. His
fluency in Russian—and Pavel's mistake—resulted in their
placement on an ordinary milk-run flight, rather than one of the
better ones onto which foreigners were usually herded. The plane
for the hundred-and-fifty-mile journey was a two-engined propeller job modeled on the old, workhorse DC-3. Fine—but why
was it skimming so low over the baking scrub and sand?

"And why are you, my friend, so often nervous?" answered
Pavel from the aisle seat, taking this cue to provide a mini-
lecture about Aeroflot, the world's safest airline.

Joe reasoned that Pavel might be apprehensive for having
delivered him to this crate's din and dirt in violation of his brief.
But accepting that he, Joe, often did fret unnecessarily, he
opened his guide book. Because concentration was difficult
(despite their seemingly perilous altitude, the nose seemed to be
pointed down instead of up) he switched to memories of the best
moments—that is, the wordless ones—with Mrs. Vogl. But if
broken seats and a metal floor with cigarette butts didn't
necessarily reflect safety procedures, why were the engines
whining so? The scarlet-haired stewardess preferred not to
interrupt her bickering with a swarthy passenger to reply. Their
yells had begun over his right to keep a sack of slaughtered
chickens under his seat, but the question of whether they stank or
merely smelled led to mutual observations about the fragrances
exuded by the disputants themselves. Oh well, sighed Joe, if she's
not worrying, why should I?

Turning to the window after a shuddering wobble, he saw a
lick of blue flame dance out from the engine. A moment later,
the propeller was feathered. He pushed past Pavel's knees,
seizing the stewardess to inform her of the fiery substance to his
suspicions. Returning from the pilot's cabin to which Joe had
virtually pushed her, she assured him that everything was
absolutely fine, Comrade. The pilot had said that the plane was

in its normal pattern, and the sun's glare on the wings often played tricks on people unaccustomed to flying.

She went forward again, snapping an oily curtain behind her. Through a rip, Joe saw her examining a pair of new pumps with her dumpy colleague. They giggled into each other's ears. The shoes had obviously been procured in some machination "on the left."

The following fall—that is, last September—Joe asked the British air attaché why he thought no announcement had been made about the crippled engine.

"Not in the pilots' manual," the Britisher replied. "The blighters feel they must *deny* any and all malfunctions, even when lives are at stake. You know the revolutionary instinct: refute all imputations of shortcomings as anti-Soviet slurs."

Joe agreed that keeping the passengers in ignorance conformed to the country's spirit. They were only ordinary prols, after all; their fate in the air was entrusted to the pilots, just as their lives on the ground to the wisdom of Lenin's Party. And the Party not only knew what was best for, but also when to tell what to the masses it led.

But that was when he had the leisure and composure to analyze the episode. Now, as it approached an obvious climax— either a dramatic escape or a dramatic something else—the crew's silence seemed surrealistic. Believing *he* wasn't crazy, he assumed *they* must be.

His agitation alerted Pavel, who became one of the few to surmise that something was seriously wrong. His efforts to conceal this prompted a tenderness in Joe for all human beings forced by a code of something, usually gibberish, to violate their most basic instincts. Instead of fearing for his life, poor Pavel had to feign ardor for socialism. The engine on the opposite wing was now so straining that Joe felt a certain sympathy for it too. He remembered a morbid story about the copilot jerking off told him by the class wise guy the first time he flew.

Involuntarily, he also remembered a series of recent *New York Times* articles about Aeroflot. The line's first fifty years passed in almost total ignorance about its safety record, during which the Soviet authorities claimed to have eliminated human failure and many foreigners took them at their word. (Until the late 1960s, it somehow seemed natural to picture Soviet mechanics working to the highest possible standards, just as Soviet kitchens were always clean in the imagination and Soviet trains ran on time; certain sorts of slovenliness had no schematic place under socialism.) But when Westerners began traveling in the country, rumors of horrendous human *and* mechanical mishaps reached them; and now the newspaper series was giving details of no less than ten major crashes, taking some twelve hundred lives, in the last nineteen months. And these were only the planes in which Westerners were flying, or which fell at or near airports open to Westerners: an old kite like this—which Joe wasn't supposed to be on—wouldn't have qualified. He regretted having spent so much breath in so many offices and bureaus wangling permission to have his daily *Times* delivered (fifteen days late, on average) to his dormitory room. He regretted reading it so diligently. But both activities derived directly from his character, like those that kept his room stuffed with his drugstore assortment. Stacks of newspapers, magazines, Kleenex boxes . . . what good would they do him now?

On the other hand, he was proud of his self-control. He sensed that disaster was imminent and somewhere was violently afraid; yet also recognized there was nothing he could do about anything and kept his composure. He had not expected so comforting an answer to his old question of how he would behave in a crisis. He, Joe Sourian, could think first of the effect of his death on his professors and poor mother. He could be brave!

It was impossible to determine whether his fellow voyagers could be too, since they were still unaware of the trouble. The cabin was pungent with a human odor, but it was the normal bouquet of forty unwashed bodies in this land of black shawls and mules, not the smell of fear. The other passengers—a typical selection of small dark men in dusty suits and busty women with large moisture stains under the arms of their print dresses—continued to swig from bottles, gesticulate in prosecution of heated card games and fan themselves with limp sheets of *Uzbekistan Pravda*. Except for a lingering agitation after their characteristically frenetic Soviet shoving into the plane to make sure they weren't left behind or removed at the last minute, they might have been the lower-middle-class population of some Macedonian town. But given Soviet roadlessness and intensive use of civil aviation, surely they'd flown before? Then why on earth (if, in the circumstances, that figure of speech was permissible) did none of them notice that the plane was now down to almost rooftop level? And in this stretch of emptiness broken only by an occasional one-story abode, rooftops were probably lower than sea level—which was the way it came to Joe to say that the craft was insanely depressed.

Suddenly another native characteristic revealed itself as new, rather than the psychological key to everything in the cabin which Joe hadn't found until this moment. It was that no one, least of all the stewardesses, cared about anything not directly and manifestly bearing on his individual well-being. Not only his neighbors' welfare, but also all larger questions were of no concern to any of the good citizens aboard. The condition of the plane? Aeroflot's business. The way they'd been snarled at in the airport and kept on the approach to the runway for fifty-five minutes (in that heat! and without even a door being opened in the absence of an air-conditioning system!) with no explanation? Well, what the hell could they, ordinary Soviet citizens, do about it except shut themselves off from thoughts that could bring only frustration. In this political, let alone meteorological, climate, only *personal* grievances mattered. Each for himself and only himself (the converse, naturally enough, of the endlessly repeated "one for all and all for one" of newspaper language); it was quite enough to claim, fight for and guard one's own, without worrying about anything that was officially the responsibility of someone else. As if to illustrate that everyone cared only about his private interests, another client–crew fracas was in progress. A livid woman near the tail was screaming at the fatter of the two stewardesses about the ten unoccupied seats near the front of the cabin. Told at check-in that the flight was fully booked, she had to leave behind her husband and brother in Samarkand, where they might have to wait days for another flight. The irony wasn't lost on Joe: in this case, the usual practice of turning customers away, even when empty seats existed, had saved the victims. Deaf to the woman's woe, a conspiratorial-looking man seated beside her got up to trade a melon in his valise for a bottle of someone's homemade wine. Other men were singing in groups;

some in celebration of a legendary Uzbek princess, others in anticipation of the family reunion planned for that evening.

Neither the cacophony nor the temperature (not flames here, but the plane's heaters were on) disturbed yet other passengers from dozing on each others' shoulders. What a bunch to die with, Joe said to himself. It's as if my family came to America by mistake, and now I'm back. Pavel had stopped talking. Joe looked out of the window and, from some reading years ago, recognized the scrub as camel's thorn. Thank God this steppe can't support trees (for smacking into), he thought, feeling better immediately for his combination of observation and wit. Perhaps he could have been a parachutist or a frogman. In the past ten minutes he'd learned to take for granted his coolness under pressure. But to be on the safe side, he removed his glasses.

The instant he put them on again to check the window, the wing on his side grazed a high-tension wire. (Leading to a secret military communications center? Joe wondered. Just my luck! In the middle of this desert, what other use could there be for so much electricity?) Although there seemed no room for the maneuver, the plane performed a cartwheel. All but the few passengers who had actually seen the wing touch the wire *still* appeared oblivious to any danger. As if to confirm that negotiating the Kara Kum Desert upside down was a splendid demonstration of socialist progress, Pavel recovered from his trance and started to say something about the exhaustiveness of Soviet pilot training—or was it a statement about the dialectical incompatibility of crashes under a social system of and for The People? How sad, thought Joe again: even now, the poor fellow was trying to dream up a Save Soviet Face story for him. Wouldn't it be better if he could devote these last seconds to his own reflections, or to coming to terms with his Maker?

Joe wished he could think of something to say to *his* Maker. For it was clear that these were his last seconds too; only some James Bond feat would enable him to survive. And *he* was spending them in second-rate speculation about a man who meant nothing to him. On the other hand, perhaps this was a message about the importance of literally loving your neighbor, since you never knew who he would be or what you might go through together. Or a sign that he, Joe, was not a selfish slob because—although his lifelong pattern of rushing around doing favors for everyone was a phony pose—here he was, at the finish, more concerned about Pavel's peace of mind than his own.

But in general, Joe was not disposed to philosophizing, despite all he'd read about men facing death. It comforted him more to settle some little things. It was a mistake to have risked it with those glasses, he realized, pulling bits of shattered lenses from his cheeks. The sickening sound of crunching metal offended, rather than terrorized him. He realized the plane was crashing and crumpling. Then blackness descended for an indeterminate interval. He had an extremely peaceful sleep although, despite the seeming contradiction, it was also filled with profoundly disturbing dreams. He awoke to a midday sun mercilessly searing his face and a ghoulish chorus of grunts and moans from the dying, somewhere out there, on his right.

Weeks later, he learned that half of the forty-eight passengers and crew were killed on impact or expired before nightfall. He was saved by being thrown clear and landing, on the cushion of his fat, in a sizable ditch of water and mud. You mean it actually rained in this Sahara sometime during the last six months? he heard himself wondering. No, Joey-boy, this is some irrigation scheme to make the socialist desert bloom. It had better be that: Mama would be destroyed to learn I expired in a pile of camel shit.

He passed out again. The afternoon hours were an alternation of blessed unconsciousness and the awfulness of the others' wails and moans. The wall of the irrigation ditch shaded his forehead; his body told him not to move. A man in an Aeroflot uniform, only relatively more crumpled than the average one, was wandering about, cursing his luck and lazy mechanics. Evening was evidently approaching, but the sun did not relent. Joe wondered whether he would join the passengers who had stopped making pitiful sounds.

Once when he awoke, a rescue party was there, apparently from a local collective farm. So . . . the high-tension wire had led somewhere real. He could raise his legs from the ground, but not his head or trunk. More vehicles arrived; by the late-evening dusk, all wounded had traveled the road to the nearest hospital in the outpost town of Karshi. Each rut wrung a whimper through Joe's teeth, but at last he was between clean sheets and falling asleep. What a day!

In marched a delegation of local government officials to wake him and announce that he would be driven to better facilities in Tashkent. Joe begged to be left with the other wounded. Were they trying to give the grim reaper a second chance? Finish him off with another, much longer ride? He implored them to give him at least one night's sleep. Determined above all to relieve themselves of responsibility for the foreigner, the bumbling town fathers packed him into a vehicle, volubly assuring him that their handsome gesture was for his precious health alone.

It was not a vintage Packard but an ambulance. It narrowly missed being demolished by an oil truck when stopped on the road to repair a ruptured fanbelt with tape. Tashkent was attained well after midnight. During a further half hour, the driver was lost on its streets. It was Joe's longest, most action-packed day; whatever else was wrong with his body, it was pounds lighter.

Despite everything, part of him looked forward to recuperation in Tashkent. He was now placed to observe far more interesting sights than all he'd missed here under Mrs. Vogl's deodorized wing. To start with, there were a few things he wanted to record about Aeroflot's crack-up debut. The collective farmers who first arrived on the scene hesitating to comfort the parched, groaning wounded with bottles of mineral water still intact in the plane's tail—for fear they be charged with stealing state property. The failure to direct even that seat belts be buckled as the plane held its doom course. (The loudspeaker system was broken, as well as many belts, but the stewardesses could have shouted over the engine noise as they had to announce the takeoff, giggling like children on a summer camp stage.) The Karshi Party man's assurance that the plane had made a "forced landing" because of electrical storms, resulting in a number of broken bones. . . . His hospital stay might provide material to deepen these observations with more generalized sociological analysis. The insights into daily life and human relations here would make a fascinating comparison to Solzhenitsyn's panorama of the cancer ward of a similar hospital—perhaps this very one, although he hesitated to ask. He might put it all on paper: Tashkent ward, twenty years later. Break into print with it faster than with his unfocusable dissertation.

Joe's ruminations provided the silver lining required by the human psyche as compensation for tragedy. The hospital had other ideas. Another dead-of-night hour was consumed transferring a bewildered patient from his isolated private room so that the American could be moved in. Examined and given a sedative, he at last had his sleep.

He awoke the following evening to a delicious vision: Eva Marie Saint playing nurse at his bedside. She seemed Slavic, but with finer features than most Russian girls; and she was murmuring comfort tinged with adoration. "You mustn't worry; there is nothing further to fear." (Was this a dreamed improvement of Mrs. Vogl? Was it in fact "Big Boy" and not "My Large One" she was whispering—if the apparition was whispering at all?) "I am here; you will be well again."

Joe continued to doubt the latter assertion: he still could not move his neck, and the bandages on his hands suggested severe burns. "What you've endured, my bravest." (Now he imagined cool fingers on his brow.) "Sleep, I will restore you."

When he awoke again, the light was on, his neck pains were horrendous, and the fair whisperer was washing her hands in a corner basin: curious behavior for the angel of a semidelirious dream. Her name was Barbara. A Polish name because she was in fact a Pole: the daughter of a well-to-do Lublin mother, whose family had been uprooted and exiled to Kazakhstan after the 1939 Soviet occupation, and of a Polish prisoner of the same invasion who was also not allowed home after the Second World War. Her mother's first husband had been a cavalry Major who was executed in a massacre carried out by Soviet soldiers on the same day as the notorious one in the Katyn Forest. In a show of something, Barbara chose to bear his surname rather than her father's. Although her legs were largish and her face wasn't Polish-princess white—none remained so under that desert sun—a small mole on her cheek was a very model for an aristocratic mark. Altogether, she was the loveliest creature ever to cradle Joe's head, let alone sponge-bathe his hairy—and now sweaty and itchy—arms and legs.

How to explain her instant infatuation for him? Barbara's

uncommonly romantic nature showed even in the blonde braids she wore upswept on her head, like a Turgenev maiden in her family's summer estate. Her background also contributed. All her life, she had dreamed of being rescued from Tashkent. Borne away to Poland or some other gentle land—not that this had prevented two marriages to local bulldozer operators. Nor that she had made any effort to save herself, even when free (after the Khrushchev reforms) to resettle, say, in Tula or Kiev. She waited. And Joe arrived.

"I will return your strength, my pathfinder."

It was Barbara who told Joe about the deaths of twenty-four of his fellow passengers. Freakishly, however, most of the survivors were not seriously hurt, if the word-of-mouth information from Karshi was reliable. (Needless to say, the press mentioned nothing about them, nor the crash itself.) When Joe asked several representatives of the Tashkent City Soviet's Committee of Friendship and Hospitality, as the men who came to call on him identified themselves, about poor Pavel, their quick answer was that no such person had been on the plane.

"What?" Surviving the accident had given Joe a flush of courage. Moreover, he knew that the authorities' concern over the potentially damaging publicity of an American witnessing such an affair gave him a weak hold on them. "Look here, I've been in your country a full year. That boy was no archaeology student, but *he* got us on that flight."

Startled by this boldness, anxious about where it might lead, the officials agreed a mistake was possible. On the next visit, only two of the group appeared, of whom the talkative one was obviously a local KGB chief. He said that the passenger list had been studied, no one of that description was on it and Meester Sourian must continue to rest, since delirium was an indication of a continuing condition of shock. Thus did Pavel pass from Joe's existence, for he decided not to press the issue—nor to argue with the Aeroflot representative who appeared to investigate the value of his valises. Joe's lost suits alone could not have been replaced for a thousand rubles but, beset by a slight relapse, he felt too tired to itemize and suggested five hundred. Outraged, the man offered fifty, together with a declamation about the inconvenience of "this whole episode" to Aeroflot, and the danger, in a collectivist state, of concocting fraudulent claims.

Barbara's reappearance after each visit was beauty after the beasts. Because she had been warned to tell her patient nothing ("You *understand*," the hospital chief had said sternly, "that unpleasant news might retard his recovery") she put herself at some risk by mentioning the fatalities. By that time, however, she was up to her graceful neck in even greater dangers. For one thing, her hours with him were largely stolen from other duties. Twenty times a day, she slipped through the door and into the room's heavy atmosphere—it was Tashkent's most murderous summer in years, with an unbroken month of hundred-degree days—to fan, stroke and talc his corpulent form to the accompaniment of a Polish ballad popular during the Second World War called *"Przeminęło y Wiatrem"*: "Gone With the Wind."

Although his neck was still badly sprained, there was no malfunction of his central nervous system. Even if Barbara hadn't been a thousand times more enchanting than Betty, this second demonstration of his body inspiring affection in a grown woman—Barbara was twenty-three, and had "vaguely" lived with men before her marriages—understandably provoked an even firmer reaction than the first. As Barbara murmured and caressed, an area of sheet rose between his belly and knees, like a low, local tent. Since its stubby upright alone was a source of ecstasy, he could not find a word for the pleasure it afforded under Barbara's ministrations.

Yet the dreamy nurse's busy hands and mouth seemed detached from her romantic aura, as Bach was separate from his glorious cantatas. "Oh yes, I've noticed that," she said one afternoon when, while mechanically smoothing the sheet, her palm bumped the upright. "My poor darling. And your hands all dressed."

She opened the door wider to any approaching footsteps in the corridor. Joe quivered with thoughts of her intention and of discovery's terrible peril. "Don't be embarrassed," she said, pulling the sheet one way and his gauzy hospital gown the other. She fondled his testicles, occasionally drawing her hand up the pole like an archer pulling his bow. She moistened him with saliva, sustaining the rhythm. Joe supposed he would faint. He tried to control his panting: even before his recent inactivity, he had been short of breath. Relief came quickly. In the setting of the spare but friendly hospital, the afterglow was indescribably delicious and bizarre. He searched for something to say.

"I want to thank you," he mumbled, touching her hair with the tips of his bandages.

"It's such a pressure for a bedridden person to live with," she answered blandly. "They taught us a little about massages."

The following morning, the therapy was repeated. Then it was Barbara's day off, and she decided not to provoke the inevitable suspicions by appearing. The next day she relieved him twice, which would be average for the coming week. Each finger was like a machined piston ring; together they moved up and down him as if he were as long as an arm. Her mouth encircled him wholesomely, as if puckering for a Life Savers ad. He came like a whale blowing. She cleaned up, stood up, smiled.

When she took him to the bath, she washed his parts twice, first and last. Weak in the knees and unable to grip the railing through his bandages, he was supported by one of Barbara's hands in the small of his back, while the other laid on the soapy strokes. Masturbation was exultation!

Barbara now went directly to it with no exchange of words. It was understood that the silence was to help avoid detection: Joe's room surely had KGB "ears." This inhibition also made them accept that intercourse was impossible. With Joe's neck, she would have to mount him, and would require too long to get down if there was an alarming sound in the corridor. The one time he reached his forearm inside her long uniform skirt, she was moist but hesitant.

"Not here. Soon you will be well again." She went to her other duties and Joe sniffed the heat-heightened genital scent lingering on his skin.

But Barbara's disinclination to talk seemed to derive too from the dispassionateness of her attendance: the same professionalism, or whatever, that prompted her immediate attention to his erection whenever she entered the room alone, and her unhurried yet undallying relief of it. In any case, the only sounds were Radio Tashkent in the patients' common room one floor below and a medicine trolley's occasional squish over linoleum. The muteness of the room itself during these breathtaking acts imparted a dreamlike aesthetic obscenity to Joe's pleasure, which the fear of exposure heightened still further. Venery was ecstasy!

In contrast to Barbara, Joe beheld the sex as integral to something larger; the artistry of her hands intensified his worship for the whole of her. Ever since reading *A Farewell to Arms*, he'd had a fantasy of being wounded in a daring enterprise—the crash served perfectly well—and being nursed (true, on some cooler shore, with November sun and wistfulness) by a Grace Kelly in whites. Whereas beautiful girls had no reason to give him a chance in ordinary circumstances, the extended contact of recuperation would allow the woman of his reveries to truly know him. He and Barbara were following this scenario faithfully. His lust was only the icing, or confirmation, of a heavenly relationship whose coincidental elements were stronger even than the fanciful: how many lived to see so many elements of their sexy-angel fantasy come true? As if the two substances were trying to fuse permanently the interlocking of dream and reality, the old-fashioned starch of Barbara's uniform smelled much like his semen, which she swallowed to avoid staining the towel.

Still severely sprained, his neck was now in a cast. There were a thousand things to worry about, beginning with being held incommunicado these twenty-three days. His doctors seemed capable, but the Tashkent officials clearly hadn't informed the Embassy in Moscow, despite all promises. They were probably investigating him furiously to determine his connection to the crash. His whole Central Asian trip would be the subject of some Colonel's report about motivation and likelihood of espionage. Meanwhile, no one in the world who had known him before could guess his whereabouts. His Armenian student friends, waiting with their abortive banquets, no doubt presumed he'd been arrested and were planning how to downplay their friendship. His own family, to whom his letters were surely not getting through, might think him dead or be hoping for a miracle like Hemingway's after his African crash. (*A Farewell to Arms* was constantly on his mind. The hospital librarian brought him a copy and he read the Russian translation with infinitely more enjoyment than he had the American original.)

But his only *real* worries were the heat and fear of discovery. Nothing else mattered: not the boredom nor the food (they made special efforts for him); surely not the American Embassy. In this haven from pressures and neuroses, he began to realize he was a grown man, mature enough to accept Barbara's attention to his manhood and her respectful devotion. Only she could have done this for him.

Only she too could have made him think of disappointing his mother's *most important* expectation of him: to marry a nice Armenian girl. He ruminated and sweated, trying to weigh the apples of his upbringing against the oranges of this tumultuous love, all the harder to measure because of the suspected microphone and Barbara's untalkativeness. For example, he couldn't determine whether she was quiet-dumb or quiet-intelligent. But in the end, he was relieved of the decision. The romance terminated with much less originality than it had begun.

When he was well enough to walk for exercise, Barbara vanished from the hospital. Like Pavel, she might not have existed.

Joe had to be careful when asking about her, even though he felt more ill than after the crash. That the other nurses claimed to know nothing about her disappearance increased his dread. And indeed: the man "from the city soviet committee" who had continued visiting him after the others dropped off appeared in his room after three tormenting Barbara-less days. In tones of hurt, anger and menace, he accused Joe of violating Soviet hospitality and the "honor of young Soviet womanhood."

He handed him a piece of notepaper. On it was Barbara's confession, ostensibly to the hospital directorate. "I cringe when I think of what I have done to myself and to the reputation of Soviet women. I am tortured by thoughts of my violation of the People's trust. I sold everything I'd been given in life—all Soviet society's material support and moral development—for a foreigner's glad-rag promises. Oh why did I do this humiliating thing to me and my Motherland? Defile the sacred name of Nurse, even spoil hospital sheets with my vileness? These questions will haunt me the rest of my life. . . . I beg that my career not be ruined nor behavior publicized in the press. Please allow me to return to Tashkent and, in the spirit of Soviet humanitarianism, atone for my guilt by doing the bedpans—anything connected with my profession."

When it was all over and he was back in the University for this, his second year, Joe pondered two small puzzles. Had the entrapment been planned from Moscow, or at the initiative of local agents? And what purpose did it serve—unless to recoup Aeroflot's fifty miserable rubles—to make him pay for the "polluted" sheets? (When the KGB man left, hospital officials said they could not "impose" such linen on innocent Soviet patients, and a pile was produced for Joe to examine before—as they claimed—its feeding to the incinerator. If they were indeed his dirty dozen, this indicated surveillance from the very beginning.) Why the operation had been undertaken at all seemed less mysterious. He had seen too much and was behaving too cockily. In case his sickened deflation at the news of Barbara's fate were not enough, he was warned that any "exaggerations" he might spread would only "lengthen Comrade-Nurse Kowalska's social rehabilitation." The men in charge obviously reckoned that expelling him from the country directly from Tashkent would have increased the chances of his publicizing the summer's adventures. Instead, he was returned to his Tamerlane research in Moscow, where they had a hold on him.

The stiffness of his neck muscles persisted into late fall, causing back pains and eyestrain. His heartache, manifested first in total apathy, then in overwhelming self-condemnation for his selfish incaution and finally in a longing for Barbara's hair and eyes, lasted longer. Surely it wasn't possible he'd never see her again. On the other hand, the "Summer of the Two," as Chingiz called the five weeks in Tashkent, was a turning point; and when Mrs. Vogl turned up in Moscow and traced him to the University, he did not go to her hotel. The body for which he had lusted and thanked his lucky stars only last July had utterly no attraction for him; didn't that show remarkable growth?

Just before the deep freeze in November, the University organized a trip for English-speaking history students to Borodino, site of the great battle between Napoleon's and Kutuzov's armies. Puffing on the hills and, as always, visualizing Barbara, Joe lagged behind and got lost. His asking directions of three girls picnicking on an old breastwork sparked a conversation. Yes, he was American, he said wearily; and they were . . . *nurses from Tashkent!* His next question twitched on his lips. Two of the three answered yes. One had even studied with Barbara!

She knew more than the others. While Joe was still in the hospital awaiting his examination for release, poor Barbarinka was exiled to a village in Kirgizia. It had no medical facilities; she was put to work looking after pigs. But her mother collapsed almost immediately and she was permitted to return home. Now she worked as a floor-mopper and toilet-cleaner in Tashkent's ice-cream factory.

Devastated, Joe had to sit down. The pain in his neck felt just as it had in the irrigation ditch. But either because they genuinely knew or wanted to calm him, the girls said that Barbara wasn't unhappy. She blamed no one; indeed, felt nothing called for blame. "And we're not just saying this." The girls had seen her in cafés and strolling the main street, and nothing in her conversation or behavior suggested bitterness or even surprise. . . . Yes, for a month or so, she did talk of Joe returning to rescue her from Tashkent. But now she was planning to be married. To a half-Tartar boy who made deliveries to the factory.

Weeping about this, it seemed to Joe that the tragedy's added dimensions reached to new lows and new heights. Something transcendental was afoot; nothing else could explain his encounter with the nurses two thousand miles from Tashkent, in a Napoleonic battlefield's forest of monuments to slaughtered divisions. Would the summer's weirdness never end? The enormity of meaning behind the chain of events made him giddy with life's infinite mysteries and possibilities. He, a Cincinnati teacher's pet, living through this! But the multi-adventure's very quirks made it a kind of religious experience, so personal that no third party could sense its mystical effects, any more than they could know what Barbara would always mean to him.

So she wasn't crushed, but peacefully accepted her fate. But this new twist—the ultimate injustice of her goodness in the face of calamity—produced the greatest hurt. No, she was not just a shallow beauty; this had been no summer romance. But marriage to a Tashkent truckdriver? Surely she had the same commitment as he to the memory of their idyll? With new puzzlement and fresh areas of pain, the affair recaptured control of him for the winter season of brooding.

Time has held its breath during Joe's narrative. In a polite request for confidentiality, he reminds me that only Chingiz and I know the whole of it, then sits still for a long moment. I cup my hand on his shoulder as my lieutenant on a nonbelligerent street gang used to on mine. Slowly we return from Central Asia to the reading room's high ceiling and imposing four walls.

"You gonna check your books in?" he asks in his hoarse whisper. Despite the season, an oily film coats his cheeks. If only he knew how much everyone, from Arabs to Cambodians, likes him. How much everyone needs to relax with him in his café of a room, especially when bored or depressed.

"Might as well."

Yes, I've had enough for the day. If I leave now, I can make a fresh start tomorrow.

Depositing my five volumes with Maya in return for my canceled check-out slip, I follow Joe's bulk out of our dissertation works. Although he recuperated relatively rapidly from the Borodino blow, he turned to food for solace, growing larger than ever. We walk down the main, marble stairway, then through a series of wire-encased passageways and back steps to the cafeteria, with its mess hall smell. Like ten thousand eateries in Moscow basements, it is a steamy room with dishwatery smears on the walls, but with a much smarter clientele than average. We pick up our metal trays and cutlery, twisted aluminum pieces that might belong to some post-atomic holocaust survival kit. In the absence of knives—a favorite item of pilferage, rarely replaced—some diners are ripping off mouthfuls of meat from their chunks with bared teeth, while others try to cleave them into bite size with two soup spoons. At the counter, we choose the hearty borscht, a main course of scrawny chicken, and the dried-prune-and-apricot compote for dessert. But it's a mere seventy kopeks and, as Joe predicted, the line is insignificant at this hour.

In quest of air, we sit at a table near the door. His mouth full of food, Joe nods toward the steam table. During a pause for refilling the soup caldrons there, two teen-age ladlers in white smocks and caps have grasped each other around the waist.

"See what I mean?" he says. "This fantastic physical contact, it's everywhere. Where else would you see *that* scene?"

"That scene" is repeated severally in the stuffy cellar: girls holding hands, linking arms, touching. Pairs sharing seats, like kindergarten children. Before the summer, Joe used to position himself in metro cars, elevators and other packed places to explore breasts with his elbows. The ease of it amazed him. Either because Russian women were too healthy-minded to suspect his tricks or, he theorized, because a lifetime of crowded quarters had rendered them oblivious, none noticed even minutes of persistent kneading. After Betty and Barbara, he no longer needed this—nor did he feel his former awkwardness with girls: he even managed to take several dormitory neighbors to bed. But he slept only a few times with each; what interested him more was the Russian female as a genus, their attitudes and habits. What did it mean that in the library's other reading rooms, all less commodious than Scholarly-Scientific Hall Number One, females were always in each other's laps? That they seemed to enjoy rather than resent the squashing, as if the reassurance of a warm body touching one's own was better than sitting alone and tackling independent work?

He considered writing an essay that would trace some of the stable elements in Russian life through delineation of the girls' attitudes: the uncomplicated goodness, exemplified by the unself-conscious physical contact that comforts and fortifies the beleaguered nation. In this time of women's lib, his contribution would be as relevant as his stillborn chronicle of Tashkent. But he got bogged down deciding whether to make it a sociological study or an account of his personal observations. Too detached to capture Russian girls' beguiling informality, a scholarly treatise would mislead more than enlighten; too frivolous-sounding to be taken seriously, a first-person sketch might damage his academic career. This project too was abandoned.

But not thoughts about it. "I think I'll pack it in with you for the day," he says as we leave the cafeteria. "Wait for me in the main hall? I'll show you something."

I do wait while he pulls himself up the stairs to the reading room and hands in his books. The lines at the cloakroom counters have almost disappeared, and one of the attendants is displaying his dental work to a female colleague. When Joe comes down again, past the check-out matron and the police-woman, we put on our overcoats and step into the momentarily refreshing cold. He leads me over a bus and trolley route, grinning when I press him for our destination. I spent one afternoon with him searching for Ray-O-Vac batteries for a gadget fanatic, and a full day trying to establish whether a 1921 one-hundred-dollar bill, which a prerevolutionary publishing family had fearfully hid in an attic these fifty years, is still legal currency in America. But he'll only say that I'm in for "something completely different" in a moment.

We turn a corner to an impressive new physical culture institute that trains sports coaches and "amateur" athletes. One of the few Americans willing to risk bluffing his way past the pass-checkers at gates, Joe takes the lead today by talking to me in Russian about weight lifting loudly enough for the guard to overhear. Our final steps lead to the balcony of a huge gymnasium, below which a class of girl gymnasts is training, the cheeky sexiness of their tight boobs and behinds protruding from wash-shrunken leotards. I whistle to myself thinking of my best friend Alyosha—who has probably screwed half the class; and for the other half, if he'd only see them as I am now, he would swing down to the floor mats by overhead ropes, like Tarzan.

For a half hour, we stare explicitly at their darling parts, but this fails to penetrate their concentration on splits, twirls and headstands, just as old Joe's probing elbow went unnoticed in metro crowds. The blondie I find myself following most is almost my mind's eye image of Barbara. As the afternoon wanes, I suddenly realize something about my friend.

"You come here often, Professor?"

"Pipe down. There's research and research. Does it beat the Lenin Library?"

IV Alyosha

Seven o'clock one February morning: the gauntest hour I've seen on land. Cold so prodigious that the continent seems paralyzed, squeezing a chant from my depths to the cosmic forces. Wind moaning as if through Arctic forests and snow reflecting the stars' phantom gleam while a specter probes the eastern horizon: not yet dawn, but promise of an end to the deathly night. Frost on my eyebrows and the mittened hand of a girl called Alla clutching mine as we pick our way through drifts and debris toward the road, two tire tracks meandering along the horizon. (When we reach it, will we see the top of the world?) My head throbs with fatigue, my senses pound with the eerie beauty—and with a premonition of danger: my activities here would anger the American authorities as well as the Soviet.

We are somewhere in the western outskirts of the city, in a new housing development with the look of a Siberian industrial site cut from the forest. Finished now, as construction here is finished, with pipes unconnected and unopenable doors, the raw buildings are fully inhabited by grateful tenants, although a tangle of dirty paths over the ice must serve for sidewalks, haphazard in the Russian manner and strewn with bottles and broken bricks. But in the tundra-like vastness swallowing the twelve-story structures, what significance has disorder as petty as this?

Around us, mute figures in black overcoats are setting out to work, feeling their way over the paths and through the hoary mist as if moved by radio signals from some Orwellian Ministry of Labor. Like us, they are making obliquely for the distant road. At the closest curve, a battered construction truck bounces along it, lights on, groaning and rattling, trailing a banner cloud of frozen exhaust and the night's new snow. The pedestrians trudging along the shoulder disperse mechanically at the sound, unwilling to raise their faces from the sanctuary of their collars. In the distance, a group has clustered at the lone streetcar stop, bunching together like peasants fleeing the Nazi advance at a railroad crossing.

Alla and I have said nothing since leaving the apartment; we are silenced by the shock of moving directly from that world to this. She strides along the path ahead of me now, head down and teeth chattering. Ruled by my feeling for her, an unaccountable combination of comradeship and prurience, incest and pastoral innocence, I follow in her intrepid footsteps. Or is my awe of the natural forces aggrandizing my conception of her? I know the adventure I'm living inclines me to rhapsodize, but even the plodding part of me I keep in reserve can't separate the effects of a universe of numbing cold from the instincts of self-preservation that drive us through it. Of the mute whiteness that subdues everything beneath it to the body heat of Alla's loins and legs. If I idealize her flesh, it is through the same perception that senses something exalted in this climate's cruelty; the exhilaration of being tested and surviving. This is the link—the zoological instincts of sex and life—between yesterday's lust and the morning's forward motion.

The crunching of snow crust under her boots gradually quickens. She is a physiotherapist at a clinic near St. Basil's and must be there, in uniform, by eight o'clock. I'm going back to my room to sleep. We have just come from another orgy during which we made so much love, so freely and furiously, that Alyosha's thick morning coffee has made me slightly sick.

Last night we were five: Alla and I, Alyosha Aksyonov and two girls recruited earlier in the evening, en route to the "fete"—counter girls in a dingy dairy whose last names were neither asked for nor offered, although they gave body and soul to the paganism. Essential virgins (except for a cellar episode or two with tanked Russian boys) who went speechless when Alla suddenly gulped the last of her wine and stripped to her panties.

Again, it was the girls' reaction that most fascinated me. So many new pairs repeating the pattern, yet confounding me each time with whether to believe what I see. Since I knew what to expect from them, the other characters in the small cast, although more extraordinary, surprised me less. "Efficient" Alla, the stewardess-like twenty-three-year-old whom Alyosha has been seeing for weeks, and who had to stay home yesterday—bringing the party to her apartment—for the expected call from her traveling husband. Older and higher-class than the average participant, she is also more laconic and outwardly self-contained. And Alexei Aksyonov, the fabulous, notorious, adored and much-imitated Alyosha who lives the charmed life of a playboy and universal fixer and has become, after too long without one, my best friend. My tutor, protector and indulgent provider—everything summed up in muchacho, his nickname for me, pronounced as if I'm a newly discovered nephew.

When Alyosha first approached the girls on Kirov Street, flustered blushes showed through the glow of their cheeks in the cold. Two tallish, robust lasses in worn overcoats and clodhopper boots, who caught his lynx eye amid a shopping street's thinning evening crowd. Arm in arm, unlipsticked lips pressed close to thick ear muffs for transmission of girlish chitchat, they were wending home after work with the telltale look of having nothing to do, no money to spend, too few memories—certainly of good times with gallant suitors—to reminisce about. Offspring of the Moscow proletariat and dreamers of romance, having read Pushkin and Lermontov last year in school, who had begun to perccive that their lives would be spent behind cheese counters or with husbands, when hooked, who preferred vodka.

A strand of neon painted their faces as they crossed the otherwise shadowy street. Spying them from the driver's seat, Alyosha braked, parked and leaped out in a single motion. Of all I love in him, the great constant is the contrast he represents to everything surrounding him: his agility in unrelievedly ponderous streets, deftness in the homeland of the stolid and slow-moving, spontaneous wit where solemnity is a national institution. Alyosha the graying leprechaun in the country of hulk and drudge. His charm begins with his movements, whose fluidity predisposes even weary bystanders to smile, recalling carefree childhood moments. When I caught up, he had already introduced himself to the girls—"Please forgive me, ladies, may I stop you for just a moment?"—and induced the first laugh.

"Some consider 'lady' a nasty bourgeois slur. In which case, I take it all back, Comrades. What's a little solecism among friends?"

Mockery of his own eagerness as well as of the human and Soviet condition showed through his ever-so-earnest imploring. Swiftly drawing new women to his confidence and bed, the act of recruitment also prompts old chums to shake their heads in affection. "There's Alyosha for you. Still the naughty boy at fifty; he'll never change."

This particular pursuit took its fated course. While girlish modesty kept the "devoted friends" walking vaguely in their former direction, contending they couldn't consider a stranger's invitation, toothy grins showed that Alyosha's disarming one had done its work. Even when his humor is at their expense, new girls sense that good feeling underlies the mischievous enticements, and that sexual danger will leave them otherwise unharmed.

"Surely no one reared with our humanitarian precepts can be so heartless. *Why* won't you say where you're going? Will you 'fess up if I guess?"

Like a silent movie stock figure, the taller girl tried to mask her delight with a frown of proper affront. Convinced they had protested enough, the other betrayed apprehension that Alyosha might become discouraged. He did not.

"You're en route to an engagement? The conservatory, perhaps? You are—let's think—contrabassoonists? . . . *I* know: you're late for the evening plane to Cameroon. The country's going to pot: Black Africa gobbles up all our best exports. In you go, I'll rush you to the airport."

Giggling openly now—in response to the flattery of his attentions rather than appreciation of the patter: neither had heard of Cameroon or bassoons, let alone the understood triple entendre about "pot"—the girls allowed themselves to be guided into the car. Under a layer of refrigerated air, their overcoats smelled of years of use. Because we knew what was coming, Alyosha and I sensed in their breath, the residue of a cheap brand of bologna on which they had lunched, a fragrance of sex. He stretched a hand toward the back seat to squeeze the girls' in a clinching gesture of welcome, then stopped the car to rearrange the blanket over the bare springs on which they were riding, apologizing for the inconvenience in Fernandel-style profusion. In that one moment he had given them more courtly affection and entertainment than they had seen in real life.

But certain as it was, the lovemaking would come only after preliminary rituals. Alla's apartment, available while her husband was inspecting provincial factories, is near the center of the unfinished development with the sidewalks of bottles and broken bricks. When we arrived, she was frying the potatoes and cubing Alyosha's find of tender beef for Stroganoff. The girls wore the limp skirts and sweaters of my high school's poor twenty years ago. Welcoming them as old friends, although she'd been expecting only Alyosha and me, Alla offered them a bath and ran their water.

Emerging pink and chatty, they experimented with Alla's black market cosmetics, a treat followed by examination of her new *Amerika* magazine while we three completed the meal's preparations. Alyosha occasionally leaped from the kitchen to attend to their uncertainly held cigarettes with a French butane lighter whose shininess alone flattered their self-esteem. In between, he entertained us all with commentary about why native scientists led the international field in the study of mathematical probabilities and deviation, ending with a home-made punchline blending innuendo and burlesque to suggest it was all sublimation, since no one could deviate in real Soviet life. Then he donned his dark glasses in aid of his theory that human beings can fool themselves about anything—in this case, that Moscow was Sun City.

It was an evening like a hundred others. A table laden with Alyosha's provisions of vodka, wine and hors d'oeuvres. Toasts that appeared to grow funnier; laughs that got unmistakably louder; an outpouring of random talk to match the consumption of food and to enhance a sense of stolen well-being that waxed into sensuousness. Old tapes, transcribed from black market records, of the Cream and Diana Ross on a straining, throbbing recorder. Free-for-all dancing with energy and endurance in inverse proportion to its lack of refinement. And Alyosha pulling us up again for one more fling, tipping the bottle for one more drink, remembering one more joke—about the Bible salesman posing as a Serbian philologist—to fit that moment's theme.

Beyond the extravagance of the occasion, the girls understood little. Heads already spinning from the Hungarian salami and Revlon lipstick, even from their joyride in Alyosha's car, they succumbed to their lucky destiny, with only a pro forma contempt for vodka in the usual platitudes. Savoring their individual chocolate bars and sipping the last of their wine, they spoke of their preferences for film stars and summer plans.

The lovemaking followed in its turn, after the brief shock of Alla's undressing and the girls' mandatory declaration of unwillingness. "Individualistic" at first (while Alla patiently waited), we were soon five bodies entwined together, laughing, grunting, exchanging, teasing a tattered stuffed panda. Liberated from everything but astonishment about themselves, the new girls thrust their loins proudly in our faces. The more sophisticated Alla—who was also more experienced in group evenings, having known Alyosha for weeks—used a leaf of the rubber plant to invent an anatomical quiz.

In the morning, the girls begged Alyosha to concoct an excuse to free them from work. "Alyoshka, please Alyoshinka—can't we spend just today with you?"

Behind the surface of ice and prudery, irritability and drabness, this hedonism flourishes like jungle foliage. I've often seen such lust before, but never this surrender to it: sex to the limit of human appetite, as in the legendary—and real—Russian capacity for food and drink.

The memory of my first evening with Alyosha stands out from the jumble of all later ones. Although he knew me only as Anastasia's new lover, with whom he'd barely exchanged a few jesting hellos when lending us his apartment for trysts, he invited me to a party and regaled me with caviar and anecdotes. More poised and elegant than almost all who would follow, the girls were an aspiring actress and two models sporting trouser suits acquired from tourists. I hadn't seen false eyelashes in Moscow before, or that degree of female chic.

The celebration was in honor of the actress's November birthday, and of Alyosha's attachment to her, for they had once had an absorbing affair. During supper at an expensive Intourist restaurant, his hands stayed busy refilling glasses and adding food to heaping plates; his table was a refuge from every care in the world—including my first friction with Anastasia—except the stretching of stomachs and bladders. At midnight, we returned to his apartment for nightcaps and an hour's dancing.

One girl said she was tired and another remarked it was warm in the room—and suddenly, but nonchalantly, the three were taking off their clothes. Neither exhibiting themselves nor covering up, saying nothing in particular to me—as they hadn't all evening—they removed their underwear, ran a hand over their flat stomachs and reached for cigarettes, while I loved, feared, envied, *wanted* them.

Like a memory of my favorite sexy film, my mind's eye had already begun to rerun the miracle of their undressing. Brassieres cast off like gloves and breasts springing to life in slow motion as they were freed—with not a flicker of surprise, let alone of shame, on the three Slavic faces. Breasts so sylphlike that I remembered my adolescent doubt that I'd touch even one of that perfection in my life. Blood of astonishment flushed in my eyes as well as surging to my groin. Three white-skinned, long-limbed visions, as glorious as I'd ever seen, standing before me at the mirror, taking turns brushing their hair. Their nipples puckered. They were persimmon and pink. I had met these Aphrodites hours before.

Apprehension of the unknown topped off my astonishment. Thoughts of perversion, of my performance, of provocation and related dangers alone in a Russian apartment. I tried to imagine what Alyosha was planning for us and these exquisite *three*. And why this lavish generosity for me, a much younger, less interesting stranger? He was in the kitchen, washing glasses for tea. At a loss for what to do alone with them, I brought him some dirty dishes.

"My God, are they serious? What happens next?"

He cut me a fat slice of cake. "Orthodox custom stipulates rest after dinner, it's become something of a ritual. But maybe you're militantly anticlerical, *muchacho?* Shall we compromise on a nap?"

The models sashayed into the kitchen, two narrow-waisted cousins with Veruschka's cheekbones. Waiting with me for Alyosha to complete the tray, they put their arms on my hips as if we were at the rails of a skating rink. (With a lightning flick of the wrist, Alyosha drew the kitchen curtains. Whatever other danger was only in my imagination, that of neighbors seeing such a sight was wholly real.) I yearned, and feared, to kiss their lips—on the face first and then the others, with their russet covering. I hoped they didn't hear the boom-boom in my chest. I'd still not dared to make a move when the actress shouted to her friends, now flanking the refrigerator. "Not fair jumping the line out there, it's *my* birthday," she protested from the bed. A minute later, we were entangled together on it, the models chortling and moaning.

I woke up a dozen times before dawn, giving and taking what I wanted from the silky arms and legs. The warmth beneath the quilt smelled of cologne and sex. Thoughts about a provocation still lingered near me, to my annoyance; but if these were to be my last hours before a KGB arrest, I could only be grateful for the bargain. After many siren calls and echoes, a sweet soreness developed at the place of my passion, but like the Russian song, I reached for the taller model "one last time," while the younger one snuggled against us, cooing in semislumber. Then—final wonder!—the actress thanked one and all for her "yummy" night of love.

"No one can count the uncountable," goes the old Russian saying. Although it is impossible to speak of Alyosha without starting with his girls, it's no less possible to convey their numbers without resorting to a dry tally or some mechanical image. (Years ago, he himself attempted a count in order to parry stories he considered exaggerated. A nymphet's mother had caught him in the act, and before he could pacify her, there was a threat of prosecution and a need, in case things went to court, for facts. But after days of making lists on bits of napkin and notepaper, he gave up, estimating three thousand.) It can only be said that his conquests—a misleadingly mechanical image too, depriving the encounters of their shared communication through recklessness and laughter, not to mention the "victim's" own assertive pride—are a sea of Slavic flesh. A biblical multitude of rustic faces and springy bodies on the pattern of Masha's in the dormitory. Rarely do I return to his car after five minutes buying a bottle or picking up some tickets without a new one, or pair, bashfully waiting on the back seat to be driven to the place of their entertainment and seduction.

Although no Kremlinologist will ever hear of him, he is better known to the city's working class teen-agers than Podgorny or Suslov. Fully a quarter of those he approaches recognize the name "Aksyonov" from Moscow gossip, reacting to it with eager anticipation. Even factory girls in back-street areas know him by reputation: friends or friends of friends have enjoyed a few days with him themselves or have had him pointed out in a movie lobby or on a beach.

They are surprised, however, when Alyosha claims the name for himself. Although he is a boyish fifty with soft hair and a handsome plane of cheek, his nose, as he puts it, "isn't a faultless fit." Too large, it also tends to redden. In general, the young audience had associated his notoriety with a taller, more dashing appearance.

"You're Aksyonov? I don't believe you."

He sighs. "As well you shouldn't. Moscow's teeming with you-know-who dying to impersonate the proletariat. Whisper your telephone number and I promise not to believe *you.*"

Not noticeably cleverer than average, the statuesque brunette with the large, appealing mouth can only think to answer with a stubborn repetition of her doubt. The exchange is taking place in a fish store into which Alyosha has dashed for the makings of "luncheon" for another recruit, a Nordic-looking blonde strenuously coaxed from a minibus ten minutes earlier. With only a short lunch break from her office, the blonde is waiting restively in the car.

Not the least of Alyosha's urgent preoccupations is how to please her with a fresh carp without standing on the quarter-hour line which has formed for them. Because he is trying to hold the brunette's attention without leaving the store with her—in which case the self-respecting blonde, beholding his game, would instantly abandon him to his high jinks—Alyosha cannot spare more than ten-second dashes to charm the stout counterwoman weighing and wrapping the carp at the rear of the premises. At the same time, while we mentally calculate prices and count our money (behind fleetingly turned backs, so as not to "offend our new friend's dignity computing raw cash," as Alyosha explains) to see if the change will suffice for beer, a purchasing ticket must be punched at the head of a *separate* line to the cashier's booth, this time near the entrance. Trying to tiptoe into this second queue, Alyosha spies a People's Judge in the person of a square-jawed, box-bodied matron in whose court, a room of echoing pronouncements about the duties and moral obligations of Soviet citizenship, he sometimes appears. "Oh . . . er . . . top of the morning to you, Comrade," he singsongs, backing away from his line-butting and simultaneously trying to hide— but still not lose—the puzzled brunette. "It's a wonderful invention, don't you agree?" he continues, pointing to the cashier's abacus in an attempt to explain his behavior to the dour magistrate, and smooth his way free. "I'm always inspired by the skill of Soviet hands."

Having juggled brunette, counterwoman, judge, cashier and a former girl friend who appears in the shop at the last, disconcerting moment—Alyosha wants nothing at all from the latter except not to offend her with the sight of his new love—he will rush back to the car just as the impatient blonde is leaving and drive her to his apartment for a quick meal. No time to do justice to the carp. Then she must run; *her* turn will come after work tomorrow. But the brunette, who thought she came to the store for salted herring, is free for later this afternoon—and, with precious seconds ticking away, must be enticed on this final try.

"Can you meet me at two? You won't consider it? I respect your principles, of course. Shall we then say . . . three?"

Alyosha knows that she will indeed meet him that afternoon unless prevented by an unusual exigency, and be spread-eagled on his bed within an hour or two. He is no less certain that unless exceptional in some way—as in the case of the blonde, who boasts a fey sense of humor—she will disappear from his life, in a sexual sense, by the weekend. Without analyzing his problem in any depth—although the driest of his sarcasm is reserved for self-commentary, he is not given to introspection—he recognizes that his Don Juan drive is an expression of a fundamental disturbance. "In case you haven't noticed, the symptoms are a preference for pairs, youth and brief encounters," he once said. "Quantity bewitches, quality unnerves. I give them all a bath, and myself a shifty laugh."

When he related how he first noticed his obsession, self-disparagement thinned his normally whimsical voice. "Libidinally speaking" he had a normal youth and adolescence, he said; he was even faithful to one girl friend throughout the war—which now seemed inexplicable. But one night several weeks after his marriage, he was in bed with his darling bride—divorced from him a quarter century ago, although their friendship is still the comfort of their lives—when he realized that she played no part in the animation of his erection. "It stood," he explained in the Russian vernacular, "but *not for her.*"

He feigned sleep at her side for another dismaying month, almost bursting with a hardness she could not relieve. Although it quickly led him into his compulsive search for fresh bodies, his first brief session with a teen-age pickup gave him a kind of peace. Soon he needed daily fixes.

"I'm genuinely sorry to interrupt your private thoughts, but might you spare me a moment? Dare we break the senseless barrier of nonacquaintance estranging us?"

Countless repetition has so smoothed his patter that you'd expect the lines to be stale. You would assume he is weary, perhaps even resentful, of the compulsion to recruit. In fact, however, each time the pursuit is set in motion—be it the third time that morning and twentieth that week, be he fagged after days of furious activity and nights with little sleep—a surge of fresh energy rejuvenates him. Each new lass is a challenge, a prize, a bewitching new world; never mind the thousands of identical worlds previously explored. Besides, despite his inability to go deeper, he genuinely *likes* the girls at sight, and they sense this affection even before the signals of sexual appetite. The curious combination of predatory hunger and paternal fondness expresses itself in his round vowels and Clark Gable smile.

A certain percentage of his sweethearts last weeks. Others, like Efficient Alla, are returned to occasionally when husbands are away or other circumstances make them temporarily available. A few special friends are "joined with," as he likes to put it, for months and, in the rarest cases, a full year; and under the duress of hurt vanity, Alyosha can sometimes "congress"—as he also says; like writers, he avoids repeating a word, in this case the lusty Russian for "fuck," in consecutive sentences—with dear old friends of many years. But in most cases, he loses interest, and therefore can't perform, after three or four times. "A played card," he says with some sadness. An "old card," by contrast, refers to girls over twenty-five, whom he ordinarily avoids.

The girl wore imported ski pants and a bemused expression that enhanced her charm on this frosty afternoon. But a shade of something odd piqued her relationship with Alyosha from the moment of their meeting two hours ago in the gay skating rink adjoining Lenin Stadium. Demurely accepting his invitation to the apartment, sipping a thawing measure of vodka and nibbling at his *shashlik,* she sustained her knowing-something-significant detachment. Her secret is revealed only when Alyosha is bearing down between her up-pointed legs.

"You don't remember me," she says coolly from beneath him. "Four years ago, here on the couch. I was a silly high-school kid."

Surprise, worry and perverse delight widen Alyosha's eyes, but his reply is pure deadpan. "Of course I remember, darling. How could I ever forget that unique, unforgettable night?"

But the knowledge of previous possession turns him soft. When she leaves the car, he turns to me for comfort. "Honest to God, I wish women wouldn't *talk* so much. . . . And what about me? Age is the scourge of memory cells."

Alyosha's need for new partners keeps him in a state of perpetual quest, adding a relentless burden to his otherwise remarkably busy day. If only the energy expended coping with his self-imposed tasks had been channeled into some constructive pursuit, his artistic friends sometimes lament. Such a man!—who can converse with German tourists on the basis of a year's two-hours-a-week course in a slum high school thirty-five years ago; who steals the show at any table or party of Moscow wags. What a tragedy that all this, with nowhere creative to go, is dissipated in his fetes.

His discourse, say these friends, is by itself evidence of unusual mental gifts. Russian is a keener measure of intelligence than many other languages because its complexity and inflection force grammatical errors even from educated natives; yet it is supremely rich and flexible in the service of imaginative and exacting minds. Alyosha's everyday idiom is like an Irish diplomat's English: even when the substance is nonsense, the flow itself provides aesthetic pleasure. Sometimes too slick and cute, his conversation, however, is never commonplace, but full of vivid original allusions and intentionally obsolescent, as well as the newest, turns of phrase. In his personal campaign to keep the language fertile and precise, he spars with literary acquaintances about the meanings, declensions and conjugations of obscure nouns and irregular verbs. Does "to miss" in the sense of "to feel the absence of" *always* demand the prepositional case, or in certain circumstances can it take the instrumental with inanimate objects? Can a thing as well as a person be *odyevat* (dressed), or is *nadyevat* alone correct? After a stiff debate, the proof is sought in one or another of his dictionaries of Russian and foreign words, a collection dominated by the classic twelve-volume Dahl which stands at the ready, often under a pair or two of panties, on a trunk alongside his bed.

Although other friends deny that he has any remarkable creative potential—Alyosha is best, they say, at what he now devotes himself to: playing to impressionable female audiences— most acknowledge that the makings of excellence are *somewhere* in him, atrophying daily. Yet each day is also testimony to his baffling vigor. I've seen him rise at six; renail his splitting toilet seat; change the brake fluid and hammer a bit on his bashed fender (to avoid a penalty for operating an eyesore on Moscow's streets); run an iron over a shirt washed for his appearance in court; buy and prepare breakfast for four; deliver his three guests to various parts of the city and himself, frantically late, to his 10 A.M. trial; sit in his courtroom all day, composing and delivering a forceful—and futile—summation for a client heavily sentenced for buying up his own factory's ties to peddle them on the black market; use the lunch break to bribe the friend of a friend for a plane ticket to Odessa which would otherwise require hours of standing in line; cruise the early evening crowds for new pickups; hustle again among the shopping throngs for supper provisions; deliver a friend's television set to an "underground" repairman; buy a pair of hardly worn shoes from one ex-girl friend for another's birthday; return to the apartment and answer a half dozen telephone calls from legal colleagues and friends proposing evening plans while scaling two kilos of fresh pike on a cutting board; finish making supper while entertaining his new guests with "home-brew" anecdotes from the kitchen; look up a disputed interpretation in the commentaries to the Criminal Code while the others are feasting; dig out the requested tapes for the evening's music from under a tumble of junk in the corner; lead the dancing with his singular blend of jitterbug and frug; and finally, take his pleasure with the new girl, or girls, even if a part of him would have been happy to dispense with the sexual consummation.

(In my longing for Anastasia, I will question him about his time with her, and he will single out her delight in language as the icing of her appeal. Telling *The Seagull*'s Masha to "Close the window, *tebe naduyet*," one of the characters made an unintentional double entendre that could mean "you'll be knocked up" as well as "there's a draft on you." When in the whole of the Moscow Art Theater only they two laughed out loud, he knew he had to keep pursuing her.)

Having plopped prone after orgasm—which he can no longer reach easily, even when trying hard so that he can comply with his house rule, "Leave Naught Unfinished," and set out for an overdue appointment—he drags himself up again because he has remembered a final task. Donning a Finnish sheepskin jacket, one of the last surviving mementos of his gay blade days, over bare chest and underpants, he trudges into the 2 A.M. cold to drain his car radiator. Unable to find antifreeze for almost a month, unwilling to use alcohol because it would corrode the already suppurative hoses—replacement rubber is even harder to procure than antifreeze—he has been saddled with this before-bed imposition every night throughout the hardest part of the winter. It is a little touch of symbolism: little can be taken for granted here; nothing comes easy.

Ten years ago, he was a celebrity in Moscow's embryonic jet set of jazz musicians, beautiful women and car-owners: the several hundred hip personages who knew each other by sight or reputation, and whom certain doormen motioned to the head of the line, unbolting their portals. Although remarkably few for a city of this size, the sources of their status were, *mutatis mutandis,* those of the Chelsea set or swinging East Side. Good looks, rich parents, a collection of Beatles records, connections to the givers of good parties and to tipsters about where to find French perfume; it was often enough just to stand out, as Alyosha did most strikingly, in appearance, energy or savoir faire from Moscow's lackluster majority. The spice of every party and spinner of tomorrow-we-die illusions, he was beckoned to the tables of theatrical producers, underground icon suppliers and generals' sons. He also had his own supply of black market money for which, in addition to his vivacity, he was welcomed as a big spender in Moscow and on the Black Sea. And he was a dandy, dressing from socks to overcoats in then staggeringly expensive Western garments.

Even before his source of big wealth dried up, he began to retire from café society and operate as a loner. As his taste in women shifted from starlets to shopgirls, he tired of the pursuit of chic—sometimes more strident here, in proportion to the greater snob value of Italian boots—and grew increasingly fond of evenings with his anonymous brood. Still hailed on his occasional public flings to "in" places such as the Club for Cinema Personnel, he drifted to a simpler life, not bothering to replace his worn custom-made suits. Everything is homemade and makeshift, the freer to be of empty obligations.

For exercise he sometimes swims in the outdoor pool near the Kremlin or visits a *banya* for an hour of steam and birch besoms.

But netless badminton, improvised during a picnic in four feet of snow, is more his style. Once a month, a massive cleanup puts his apartment into a kind of order. Car-owning friends call him for advice about valve troubles and bribable mechanics. He also works occasionally as a volunteer legal counsel for a financial watchdog commission: possible "insurance," in the form of testimony to his "Soviet probity" in case he is one day prosecuted for his manifestly un-Soviet way of life.

His car deserves a separate annalist. No time can be spared for the major overhaul each part cries out for; the goal is to get it going *today*, which calls for a unique blend of knowledge, patience and touch. The twelve-year-old Volga with the hand-made clutch, ceiling lined with dress material and riding characteristics of a surplus tank has not a single original moving part. It hauls literally everything: last week, a new bathtub from a warehouse to his apartment. (A hole had been punched in the old one at a party.) Alyosha's driving on icy back streets—and in accordance with Moscow's unilluminated road signs and tomes of rules—matches the native "Yankee ingenuity" of his make-do repairs. Even after consuming great quantities of vodka, his reflexes remain keen enough to negotiate vicious potholes on dim streets without sharp swerving, and to fool policemen who stop drivers at random, arresting all who betray the slightest sign of drink. When he zooms into side streets to check whether a KGB car is tailing us, it is always just casually enough not to betray the maneuver.

With all this to cope with, his sexual quest, which seems fueled by an independent source of energy, illustrates the old adage about only busy men having time to take on something new. Keeping eyes peeled for comely faces is an unshakable habit, as is the procedure of "registering" for later enjoyment discoveries who will not accompany him on the spot. The vagaries of communication here—many girls without home telephones who can be reached only at work, others who have moved or make mistakes in giving their new addresses—require care in recording "coordinates." Alyosha performs this job with characteristically swift, and distinctly un-Russian, attention to detail, jotting down names, telephone numbers, addresses and—with girls who have troublesome husbands or parents—third-party contacts. In two weeks, a pocket notebook is filled from cover to cover with such information in a neatly compressed hand, supplemented by three-word descriptions of each subject, lest he forget—although this is rare; his memory of a thousand look-alike Natashas is phenomenal—as well as sketches of cabins and houses and, where needed, coded doorbell rings, nasty neighbors to avoid in communal apartments and diagrams of lanes too small for mention on the Moscow map.

To help with identification, the "cadres" are entered with nicknames. Compared to its richness of idiom, Russian is disproportionately hard up for contemporary common names: of ten teen-aged girls, seven are Galya, Natasha, Tanya or Svetlana. For us, therefore, there is "King-size" as well as "Angry-brother," "Cheeky-tits" and "Everest" Natasha; while "Efficient," "Toenails," "Two-at-once," and "Lickety-split" distinguish one Alla from the others. (All hell broke loose one evening—the rare exception to the rule of good fellowship in Alyosha's brood—when "Commissar" and "Left-wing" Galyas met on the same bed.)

Yet the life of these crammed notebooks is as limited as that of top-secret code sheets. When a new one is well started, the previous edition is casually discarded. Passing a trash basket, Alyosha will let drop a little black book without breaking stride and briskly walk on.

"Jeez, look what you've done," I lectured the first time I observed a register thus disposed of. "I'm glad I've got gloves." The little notebook that had disappeared into a post-office urn soggy with cigarette butts and spittle contained the "coordinates" of two or three dozen girls so lusty, friendly and willing that I was certain he'd made an unconscious mistake.

"Some people feel such collectanea should be burned," he pretended to explain the "error." "But this is a free country. All that Pentagon paranoia about staying eternally security-conscious, it's not needed here. We're secure enough just to throw old things out."

The disposition of these "encumbering" archives helps explain the poverty-amidst-plethora paradox of Alyosha occasionally finding himself without a soul to call. This usually happens after 7 P.M. on weekends, when the streets have largely emptied of likely pickings and many pretty girls, already out for the evening, are unavailable by telephone. The last such occasion found Alyosha and me stuffed in a forlorn telephone booth on a street desolate of buildings and trees. While the wind flayed us through its broken panes, he racked his memory for a promising candidate.

"For the love of God," I pleaded, pulling a fat register from his ancient sheepskin's pocket. "Let's be fussy *next* time. Just call one of these."

"Naw," he mumbled, "that's a superseded book." And he resumed retracing his recent movements to recall the *new* face that would make the evening.

It should be said that exceptional names in old books are usually transferred to the new one—and also that Alyosha's memory allows him to contact cadres recorded in books disposed of months ago. Nevertheless, it still represents a research loss equivalent to a graduate student destroying a month of dissertation notes. But Alyosha's analogy is quite different. "Old cards," he says, answering my persistent double take. "Are you hungry? Want something solid to eat?"

His address, by contrast, is the feature entry of a thousand otherwise blank-paged engagement books rattling in bare teenage pocketbooks; a steady troop of "Erstwhiles" use it as a guide to swinging Moscow, and more. Although most quickly accept the improbability of repeating their sexual festival with him, let alone developing a romantic attachment, they continue to bring him a domestic court variety of personal problems. Driven by his own compulsion, burdened by a dozen daily concerns ranging from where to find a camshaft to how to repay his oldest debts, he stoically adds others' delicate errands to his ever-growing list. One girl—whom he hasn't seen for three years—wonders how to retain squatter's rights to her dying mother's apartment; another has been caught stealing candy from her factory (she hid the chocolates in her hair) and is desperate to keep her job; a third has a boss who demands a kickback on her wages—and, incidentally, she is troubled by crabs. (When Alyosha's salve eliminates them, she brings two girl friends similarly afflicted— with whom he "joins" after checking the results with a magnifying glass kept specially for the purpose.) But the case of the girl trying to obtain support for her baby from a father whom a misled court officer wrongly freed of his alimony obligation takes first precedence. Alyosha is the man to turn to in such emergencies: if it is possible to place the bribe, pry loose the information from a congenitally secretive bureaucracy, procure an expensive medication not available to the general public, he can be counted on to accomplish the mission.

Other Erstwhiles come just to see him—to find a place somewhere in his living room–bedroom–dining room–cabaret, leaf through the alluring stack of dirty *Life*s and *Elle*s and enjoy the charged atmosphere his movements generate in any room: the fission of excitement and action in a city devoid of night life. Alyosha's attraction is more than the goodies of his kitchen and repertoire of jokes, larger than his whimsical-yet-supercharged commentary on the day's events. He provides nothing less than the "love of life" which every newspaper claims daily for the slogging Soviet people ("joyous and life-loving, we follow Lenin's path . . ."), but which is as absent on the evening streets as everything else for which propaganda is served up as a substitute.

Somewhere Alyosha too is very sad. On New Year's Eve, the only time I've seen him conspicuously drunk, he told me that aging libertines and clowns disgust even themselves. (This was the one time too when raw bitterness showed beneath his layers of political sophistication and sarcasm. "I hate these Kremlin bastards," he said. "Those stupid animals who've done this to all of us—I'd like to take a machine gun down there and do the world a favor.") Yet he revels in life, taking and giving delight with elements of Candide, Tom Jones and Puck. Only clichés— Western "zest for life" as well as Soviet "life-affirming"—can suggest his effect on others, for he's more like a jolly fictional hero than gravity-gripped flesh and blood. The more I try to fix the sources of his appeal, the farther I slip from the elusive buoyancy, for all that is most lovable about him—the impromptu repartee, happy-go-lucky saunter, eyes screwed up with the full range of human emotion—is the least describable. His audience is kept in smiles even between stories, convinced that they too can love life and be happy.

This is what prompts girls to spend their evenings "out" simply sitting as onlookers in his heroically cluttered room. In twos and threes, they beat a path to his out-of-the-way apartment house and find their way, uninvited, to his tumbledown door, sometimes years after he had spent his few hours with them. One evening, five separate pairs arrived on their own between 7 P.M. and midnight. When business has delayed him in town, he returns home some evenings to find small gatherings encamped on the log bench which has been cleared of snow in the village-like courtyard.

To pass their waiting hours, the shivering Erstwhiles make each other's acquaintance and drift into gossip, a practice that has led to the formation, independently of Alyosha, of half a dozen pairs of best friends. Bouncing home with bottle-stuffed pockets and an accumulation of newspaper-wrapped provisions miraculously balanced on both arms, Alyosha introduces the waiting girls to the new ones accompanying him, and all mount the stairs in quiet single file. He runs back down to the car for his briefcases, which vie with his nose as his best-known trademark. The battered skins are so outrageously packed with jars, cans, bottles and hunks of soup bones—never office papers, which are crammed into pockets—that many girls can't lift them. After the food and dancing, which is for everyone, the old girls watch television or skim magazines while Alyosha, several feet away in the small, undarkened room, "joins with" the new.

Highly inventive in his lovemaking—although that image is somewhat imprecise, all possibilities of experimentation having been exhausted thousands of bodies ago—Alyosha fondles and kisses his new sweetheart's sex, often squatting beneath her as she straddles him on the weary bed. While the satisfaction of lust wafts lymphatic odors through the room, only the shyest of Erstwhiles remove themselves to the kitchen or bathroom. Most keep to their magazines and small talk, neither staring nor averting their eyes, protesting nor offering to leave. So many Russian girls—or are they only Alyosha's devoted?—blushed scarlet when he first stopped them on their aimless strolls, but now watch their counterparts copulating as if they were vacuuming a rug.

Whatever the explanation of this, I've never seen Alyosha turn a visitor away. "Christ, it's cold out there," he'll say, as if apologizing to me for opening up to yet another unannounced caller. "Poor things probably came on an unheated bus. Let's give them something to munch. . . ." Very occasionally—during the final moments of "plumbing" a new girl, for example—he will refuse to answer any but the current version (cha cha cha-cha-cha) of the code knock for his closest insiders. But once the door is opened, his face creases deeply with tickled surprise, welcoming the guest more warmly with it than by his sometimes inflated salutations.

Inside, food is the first concern. A psychiatrist might offer several explanations for his determination to feed all guests fully and well. Was he himself hungry as a child? (Not exactly, according to my understanding of his hardest early years.) Despite his merry insistence that sex has as much emotional significance as eating a grape, does he feel guilty about his vineyards of conquests? (Of the stupendous Niagara of socialist-Bolshevik-Marxist-Leninist social theory, only Alexandra Kollantai's famous dictum—subsequently repudiated by Lenin—that "in Communist society the satisfaction of sexual desires will be as simple and unimportant as drinking a glass of water" appeals to him.) Or, as one old friend insists, is his inordinate libido sublimated maternalism: does Alyosha want to be mother to the world's girls? Whatever the inner truth, he is so solicitous of his guests' appetites that when evening newcomers arrive to a refrigerator already emptied by earlier hospitality, he scoots off for new supplies—even though much of the day has been given to acquiring provisions for and preparing meals already consumed. He is a recognized customer at the city's five or six best peasant markets: grudging little concessions to private enterprise where vigilantly watched, vindictively taxed growers are permitted to sell a portion of their personally tended produce—always far superior to the stunted offerings of ordinary, state-run groceries—at stunning prices. Thanks to his steady emoluments—and that rarest of phenomena in public places: his good-natured smile—Alyosha is also known by the managers and tenders of strategic counters in a handful of the best-supplied meat, fish, salami and cheese departments. If there is any chance of parting these public servants from some of the latest shipment of rump steak or perch, much of it automatically reserved for their families and friends, it is Alyosha's.

These daily extravagances have something in common with the progressively steeper borrowing of certain Russian aristocrats to finance brilliant balls to obliterate thoughts of their debts. Especially in winter, when four greenhouse tomatoes cost an engineer's daily wage and a pound of veal is a conversation piece, Alyosha leaves behind what the Russians call "a heap" on each dash into a market or shop. Where he gets his income is a separate story, not all of which I know. How he sustains the perseverance for his shopping forays—attracting the attention of besieged counter girls, darting from their lines to those stretching from the cashiers' booths, surveying a dozen stores, packed from wall to wall with gawking, babbling, pushing, waiting-for-a-miracle shoppers, as at noon in a Moroccan souk—is yet another matter. In ten minutes, he is in and jauntily out of such sea-of-downtrodden-humanity establishments, briefcases bulging with acquisitions that many would consider an afternoon's work.

Again, sheer physical energy—a rumba through the crowd to flirt with the counter girl, a deft backpedal to the entrance to smile to the dumpy cashier, a sprint to the nearest telephone, then to one that works (to call Gay Galya, as arranged, at precisely three o'clock) while the halvah is being wrapped—allows him to wriggle through and stretch over Muscovites' catalogue of obstacles to securing the perquisites for daily life. Occasionally he sighs that he's growing old fast, and old means ill; a shell of his former self, he is infected by a strange lassitude (but driven on by habit). Once he made this sound more than his usual self-mocking banter and spoke of visiting a clinic. But no doctor has laid eyes on him in almost thirty years, since his last haphazard checkup in the army. He has not been sick since—has not allowed himself to be: when he caught infectious hepatitis several years ago, he swallowed several aspirin, temporarily forsook vodka and returned to what for him was normal life after three days in bed.

Like poverty and the British royal family, illness and Alyosha are wholly unrelated aspects of life. My mind's eye image has him tanned, smooth-skinned and in quintessential health. Easygoing muscles, a slight sleekness of winter weight, a body that is not large, cared for or visibly powerful, but endowed with a charmed indestructibility that protects him even from the colds and influenza that lay low much of vitamin-starved Russia from October to May. He's the only adult I know who dispenses with a hat on all but the worst cold snaps, his shaggy pepper-and-salt hair presenting a quaint spectacle, since the other uncovered heads belong to teen-age boys demonstrating their toughness. And if his youthful endurance is in fact waning, he still requires only four to five hours of sleep a night, even after the craziest of his overloaded days.

For the self-invited guests who arrive late in the evening, finding food is distinctly more difficult. After 9 P.M., Alyosha must drive to one of the handful of late-closing shops, the location, staples and incidental specialties of which he knows better than most Moscowcityretailgrocerytrust officials. Up a murky street, through some deserted back alleys (in one of which live three teen-age sisters, consecutive Erstwhiles of a torrid week last summer), on foot across a final shortcut to a store whose principal objective is apparently to conceal itself from the public. "Of course it's hard to find," he sighs, setting up his favorite comment about Soviet rule's guiding precept. "Otherwise life might be marginally easier for people."

This particular Gastronomia, as it modestly calls itself, is a prewar relic with a sputtering sign and snarling counter women in soiled smocks. But its monumental obscurity provides a reverse advantage. Alyosha knows that even if its edible cheeses and occasional cans of crabmeat are exhausted at this hour, some chewable beef might be left, which could be nicely turned out with his dill sauce. Besides, the manageress of a smaller store only five minutes away can sometimes be persuaded to part with a few of the items pilfered for her just-married son.

If the last of these late-hour establishments is closed, Alyosha races to the one with the most bribable cleaning woman. Pounding on the bolted door, brandishing a handful of rubles— yet concealing them from police and public view—sustaining an attention-attracting jig and a stream of enticing patter punctuated by under-the-breath laughs at himself for submitting yet again to this ludicrous posture, he calls upon his most artful flattery to plead for delivery of a few items from a crone wielding a handleless mop. This having failed, he drives to the nearest restaurant and advances into the kitchen during the clanging moments before closing. Actually, this is not a restaurant but a relatively new café whose aluminium moldings have already begun warping away from steamy plate glass: a refuge—for proletarian curses, drunken bellylaughs and winter release—which few members of Moscow's intelligentsia, let alone foreigners, would have reason to enter. To discourage this, the scenes at the tables and in the toilet are quite enough, while the exchange of abuse and ultimatums in the kitchen, together with the utter disorganization of equipment and staff, make the establishment's reopening tomorrow, if ever, seem impossible. Only the Russian masses, unconscious of mere earthly comfort, could enjoy themselves in such squalidness; I want to both laugh and cry for them in their merry oblivion.

Alyosha is simultaneously at home here and totally alien, like a missionary with his loving natives. Amidst the cook's bellows, outraged shrieks of peasant dishwashers and mutterings of a drunken diner trying to reattach a sleeve onto his jacket, Alyosha does a deal with a venal waiter and the duty manager. (Years ago, when director of a better restaurant that foreigners are encouraged to visit, this manager used to transact a substantial volume of back-door trade with Alyosha, who himself then traveled in correspondingly higher circles. The restaurateur was dismissed for masterminding the theft of a relatively modest truckload of vinegar.) For a slight premium over the inflated menu prices, Alyosha's fallen friend supplies him with several portions of leftover chicken stew and a sufficient volume of (watered) wine. Successful at last, he gingerly sidesteps tables heaped with leavings and runny pools on the floor, and quickly drives home his catch to the waiting mouths. Then he watches them feed, washes, woos and wangs them to exhaustion.

The story of Suede Svetlana. Met on Sunday, in the ticket niche of the Metropole Cinema. (Though signally inadequate for the weather, her suede coat is too treasured not to be displayed.) Reluctant to join us because she has a ticket for the next showing, she comes to the apartment on Tuesday, drinks half a bottle of dessert wine and undresses. Her dimensions match her calling: she's a construction worker. On Wednesday, she is waiting impatiently at the door when Alyosha and I return in the car.

Thursday, she suggests dirty photographs, poses energetically, but leaves in offense when other girls arrive. On Friday, I recognize her under a thick quilt jacket: *she* is the cement mixer for the new University building on the way to the metro—the one I happened to notice weeks ago, while passing with Masha from the dormitory. This time she is one floor higher on the building's shell, whither I yell.

"Hello there, Svetlana! Come to the cafeteria for some lunch with me."

"Can't just now; have to get on with this."

Monday, she is not on the site, and I never see her again.

It is not enough for Alyosha to supply food—even good or varied food which, for Russians without foreign currency or Intourist coupons, is so scarce that Westerners would regard details of the shortages and deteriorating quality as crude anti-Communist propaganda. "Naturally, caviar's too rich for Russian blood," he sighs. "But we used to get sturgeon, smoked salmon—at a pinch, bream or eel. Twenty piscatory varieties worthy of a guest. Now you're lucky—and understand me, I'm offering my thanks—to find a salted herring with enough fat to keep its bones moist." Nevertheless, he drives miles for the prize purchase that will make the meal. He judges meat quickly by color, texture and smell, and distinguishes Bulgarian from Polish frozen chickens at a glance. Rushing home, he finds a place to transfer the coffee grinder's components—it has been waiting weeks for repair—and plunges into work, plucking the chicken, scaling the fish or trimming the roast with his butcher's cleaver.

His dishpan hands are as resourceful in such operations as in repairing electric motors and—because of the abysmal professional service—effecting his own plumbing. He will try anything: carp baked in sour cream, chicken *tabak* in homemade hot sauce, raw scallops with his house dressing of lemon mayonnaise, mustard and dill. Fresh herbs, as rare and expensive in winter as copies of *Penthouse*, play a principal part in his specialties. Like a juggler, he clears a space to serve them, hunting for the last meal's cutlery to wash for the next.

Alyosha also likes catering to his visitor's whims. Even in late evening—when ninety-nine Russians in every hundred instinctively suppress their hunger in the knowledge that any foraging for soup and bread would be futile—he takes orders. When, in the city's midnight muteness, a sad-eyed provincial textile worker just recruited in a railroad station hints at a fondness for eggs, he changes direction for a hibernating village north of town, wakes the occupant of a ramshackle cottage and bargains for all the angry hens will relinquish at that moment. (Because of a periodic slump in Moscow's supply, we ourselves haven't had eggs for weeks.) Twenty minutes later, the hungry waif is spooning down a half dozen, fried in butter, and sprinkled lightly with *petrushka,* a spicy parsley. Probably because she knows few gentlemen among swilling foremen and muzhiks—not, incidentally, that she has often enjoyed eggs *sur le plat* in a lifetime of bread, kasha and potatoes—she rummages for a pail and rags to express her gratitude by washing the turbid foyer floor.

"Tomorrow's another day, Evgeniya darling," Alyosha gently reproves, setting her on the bed to remove her shoes.

When a stock girl in an inferior department store mentions she's never tasted voblya, the dried, salted little Volga fish exalted by Russian palates (and, like many traditional delicacies, disappearing even from the daily vocabulary), he scouts about among his warehouse contacts and manages to have a bucketful for her—with fresh, Zhigulovskoye beer, the brand we love to pronounce—the next time she appears.

"What the hell, let the child taste something exceptional before we import Coke," he explains en route to fetch his allotment of voblya (and simultaneously quickening his pace to intercept a brunette with superbly pouting lips). "What can she look forward to, macaroni day in the cafeteria? And when our Leninist Party, in its wisdom, buys pasta, it's reject stuff the Sicilians or Syrians were tickled to unload."

This is the standard explanation for his intense commitment to the notion that everyone should secure maximum enjoyment from his nourishment. But the longer I know him, the more I perceive—unwillingly, because I do not want to know about his sadness—the deeper causes of his preoccupation. The devotion to indulging the appetite is also part of a hedonist's blind to convince himself that life is short and senseless, and that any striving for larger social or intellectual good is doomed from the start. This, in turn, is used to prove that pursuit of artistic or humanistic values is grandiloquent self-deception: the farther people stray from animal needs, the greater their emotional disturbance and potential for causing do-gooder's damage. How much more honest and constructive, he argues, to find and prepare a leg of lamb than to improve the mind by composing odes to collective-farm shepherds or a new panegyric about the happiness of socialist sheep. "The country's real, operative rules are nasty and brutal," he says; "nothing significant in the sources of oppression will change in our lifetime. Trying to achieve something honest and worthwhile might deliver some good, but would probably also increase the pain to living people. The more mature responsibility is alleviating a few friends' blues." Filling his day with a thousand market errands, Alyosha simultaneously demonstrates his theory's partial truth and his need to believe it is the sum and substance of life.

The flaw in his cynicism is his own love of rationalism—and poetry—which peeks out when his guard is down. Whatever it also says about Russia's fate and the hardships of his youth, his compulsion to keep his hands busy and his mind occupied with chores is surely a diversion from an unconscious recognition of the dissipation of his gifts. In this sense, food joins sex as an escape from grievous truths about wasted energy and talent: his personal contribution to the country's tragedy and folly of the human condition.

But such speculation wholly misrepresents the gaiety of our days and genuineness of his generosity. Clanging his iron pots in the kitchen with the sink reachable only by stretching across the refrigerator and the forever faulty gas water heater, he bones his fish and salts his roast because it delights him to feast friends amid gastronomic famine. I've never known such happy giving, and his underlying wistfulness only sharpens its joy. The sad element is that he himself is largely indifferent to food except for new tastes—he yearns to sample artichokes and oysters—or on special occasions. Despite his promiscuous drinking ("Water can never quench a thirst /Once when broke, I tried it first") he often goes a full day without nourishment, a cook untempted by his own sauces. Or he'll have an early breakfast of bread and coffee and nothing further until a supper of boiled frankfurters. If hunger does come, he's content with leftovers. Sometimes I awaken to a sound at night and, peering over young female shoulders slumbering between our places on the bed, I see him at the bottle-strewn table, spooning down some cold casserole lying between picked bones on someone's plate.

When we pick her up in her school-uniform pinafore with the chaste white collar, Nadya says she's seventeen, but admits she may have "added a year or so." A Norman Rockwell sapling with bony knees and batting eyes, she devours a quarter-kilo chunk of apple tart held to her mouth like a chipmunk, then performs a surprisingly witty striptease, bowing to our applause. Legs extended, she examines herself in the mirror, delighting in our assurance that she looks fine down there.

Suddenly she jumps out of bed, throws on her clothes and glissades over the ice to a telephone booth. (Alyosha's phone is dead again, probably until the recording tape is changed on the morning shift.) Returning with Winesap cheeks, she announces that she's invited her best friend. "Verochka mustn't miss this . . . and she might not believe me if I just told her, with no proof."

Something in her very innocent enthusiasm prompts a wincing suspicion that it was not at all a friend she called, but her parents—or the police. She's an unpredictable child, after all. But Vera does arrive within the hour: a prettier girl with a snub nose and more developed curves. The two share a double desk in their homeroom class.

Naked again, Nadya greets Vera as if they'd met on some corner to stroll to school. Vera undresses in the bathroom and appears in a towel. In response to appreciation of her breasts, she reveals that she and Nadya are fifteen. Before they grow sleepy, they alternate between sharing giggling discoveries and friendly competition to restore erections. "No, it's my turn now. . . . Do it to me like she just tried it. . . . Verochka, lie over here and let them show you *this*."

When Alyosha is attending to the car in the morning, I ask the classmates, for want of more enlightening conversation, whether they've been together like this before. No, this is their very first time. Then how have they managed the new, er, games with such aplomb?

"Oh, we're not so young as you think. We've been hoping to meet some interesting men. Hoping and waiting . . ."

Alyosha owes his handsome, although irregular, income and much more cherished command of his own time to a partial exception to Soviet economic rules. He is one of thirty lawyers in a cooperative called a Juridical Consultation Office—which, despite the political and professional restrictions of state control, Western eyes would recognize as a law office. Schedules of permitted fees and heavy taxes notwithstanding, the members of this legitimate sanctuary of semiprivate enterprise work largely for themselves, running their own practices and working lives— and, if unusually energetic and capable, earning a schoolteacher's weekly salary in a matter of hours. Besides, knowing defendants slip twice the maximum official fees under the table to all established law counselors, hoping for more conscientious briefs and better luck at their trials. Thus Alyosha's relative riches.

Thus too his intimate familiarity with the meshed operations of state and self-interest. The information and experience of years in court, access to confidential whispers and trusting relationships with speculators and other former clients supplement a powerful native practicality, finely attuned to beating the system through bribes and inside intelligence. And he protects himself through his meticulous understanding of bureaucratic, legal and political dangers, allowing him maximum area of maneuver with minimum risk.

Yet the gaps in his knowledge are as instructive as his operator's expertise. As privy as he is to the secrets of whom to see for assignment of a new apartment in a railroad workers' building, which black market duke can supply a Parker pen or Yugoslav refrigerator, how much to shell out for a Moscow residence permit, he knows almost nothing of the sociopolitical stuff of New York—or even sophisticated Moscow—dinner party conversation. This ignorance too is a deliberate good-time Charlie's blind. "Why work myself up about the persecution of this errant intellectual or which mental asylum that dissenter is languishing in?" Beyond learning the names of the new martyrs —Fainberg today, Gorbanyevskaya tomorrow—such details, he says, reveal nothing new about the nature of Soviet rule or his place under it, both learned long ago. Nor do newspapers, which he pretends are sold for wrapping contraband and for patching walls. "What do a thousand *Pravda*s contain that we don't know? That has the slightest bearing on our lives, on what concerns *us*?"

What concerns us is exclusively the fixing that affords comfort and pleasure to our daily lives. The ceaseless barrage of hosannas, production figures and political indoctrination has no more relevance to our hunt for lemons, Alyosha says, than to insects boring through bark. The whole of the official world is a giant exercise in lies and fantasy—better to be consciously blocked out than simply ignored. Since the Soviet version of foreign events makes them farcical irrelevancies, Alyosha also knows and cares almost nothing about them. Only occasionally does he put a question, assuming my Western sources will provide an easy answer. Have Arab terrorists killed neutral civilians at European airports? Are peasant refugees fleeing the Vietcong? Did America react violently to the Soviet "education tax" imposed on would-be Jewish emigrants? In these queries, he wants to confirm hunches about certain sequences of events, deduced from the Soviet presentation's very fallaciousness.

But such interest is incidental; and he usually avoids more than the political aspect of social thought. "Heavy" films, plays, novels and conversations—anything smacking of "culture" and meaning-of-life rumination—are equally shunned. "Has it got a Hollywood ending?" he asks when I suggest a play. "A good cancan somewhere? . . . Splash and flash, a bit of leg—you know what the likes of *us* need." He insists that *And God Created Woman*—seen at a special, closed showing for cinema personnel— has done more for mankind than *Hamlet*; that Peter Ustinov is more humanitarian, because he offers more relief to the masses, than Dostoyevsky; and declares people unbalanced who spend money, let alone their precious free time, subjecting themselves to gloomy theater. The novelist's and dramatist's obligation is to give the psyche two hours' rest from the injustice, hardship and tragic futility that are the stuff of Soviet life.

"We don't need art to stimulate morbid meditation; good old life takes care of that. No sir, *escape*'s the thing: a good beat in the sound track, frolics on the screen."

But of all his attempts at self-deception, this is the most obvious. The sham preference for "gladden-the-heart" entertainment is a dead giveaway to the depth of his feeling about art's true function. It is to avoid Soviet drama's half-truths and falsifications—which deprive a wounded people even of catharsis for their inexplicable sufferings—that he fakes disdain for "the theater of masochism" and pretends, when handing me yellowed volumes of his favorite novels and prose poems, that he's happy to rid himself of old junk.

This has a more intimate meaning too. "Escape's the thing" draws me to him and absolves me from heeding ordinary rules and norms. The distinction between us in our private passageways to subterranean chambers and the outer world through which we conspiratorially burrow is as real as a child's make-believe. But although we lose ourselves wholly in our diversions and levity, our very escapism makes keener and more personal the conditions and thoughts we banish from conversation. Unhappiness is a step away, held back by our self-made timbers.

Cruising noonday Moscow in the trusty Volga, worrying about the effect of trenchlike winter potholes on its busted shock absorber, and about nothing else in the world. Puddles from my boots on the car's bare steel floor—the rubber mats are long departed and substitute linoleum was stolen last week—and my window cracked open to the sweet wet air. Alyosha's gloveless left hand gripping the top of the wheel cowboy-style, the right coaxing Czechoslovak jazz from the newly patched radio. . . . I am in my soothing semitrance, gazing lazily at whatever passes my eyes. I hear no calls to scholarship, conscience or duty to get ahead in the world—not even to focus my vision on significant buildings. Aware that no Russian is as free to wander as Alyosha nor as savvy about Moscow's hurly-burly, I feel myself exceptional as his companion, but without the means or desire to advertise this to a third party. The city's labyrinths and sprawl, encrusted façades and clumping crowds still exude enough exoticism—and Alyosha's command of time enough sense of purpose—that I need only be here, luxuriating in passivity as in my childhood fantasy of surveying the Casbah from a magic bed.

It is a warmish Wednesday that is turning ice to slush. Alyosha has fetched me outside the University to accompany him on his rounds, a standard agenda of appointments and errands. The first stop is to leave an antique samovar with a metalworker for polishing. Bought during his latest redecorating crusade, it will doubtless soon be sold to pay for a rainy day's fete.

(At the moment, however, we are filthy rich, thanks to a lucky professional coup. Two months ago, the wealthy parents of a swaggering Georgian convicted of rape approached Alyosha for help. Knowing his reputation in such cases, they could not, however, have hoped for the coincidence that saved their son: the victim happened to be a well-liked Erstwhile. Persuading her that the parents' cold cash would be more useful than her abuser's imprisonment, coaching her in a story attributing the assault to nightmares, arranging the payment of the bribes—involving great amounts, since the prodigal was already in a labor camp—Alyosha managed to spring the prisoner last week, pocketing a handsome commission on all the transactions.)

For ten minutes we ride in silence, something easier with Alyosha than anyone I know. The memory of my discomfort on our first outings—my habitual awkwardness in response to unearned generosity—only enhances my present sense of well-being. I used to wonder what animated his affection. Girls were one thing, but why did a man of his years and standing dash to the market for fresh greens for *my* supper? What, in fact, prompted him to invite me to that first party for the actress—and beam when I agreed to drive to a nearby village with him the following morning? But precisely his fondness has shown me that such questions need not always be asked. I've come to accept that he simply likes me with him, above all cruising in the car, and that I need do nothing in return. Certainly not provide the intellectual stimulation—the seeking of common ground through earnest discussions of The Youth Problem or Developments in Western Art—required by many Russians and foreigners reconnoitering toward a relationship; it was weeks before Alyosha and

I first mentioned politics or literature. For some reason, he took to me at sight, and showed it freely and openly, like the uncle I liked best, who died at Alyosha's age off Anzio. . . .

The first stop. With the potbellied samovar, we jog down crumbling back stairs to the metalworker's place, a basement room straight from a mad-scientist movie. A refugee from a nineteenth-century ghetto, the old Jew who hears each outside sound as a pogrom's starting signal peers through an inch of opening in the bolted door of his illegal shop. At the sight of Alyosha, the exception to his rule of not trafficking with gentiles, his face relaxes from suspicion and terror to mere tragedy and hypercaution; doom has been postponed until the next knock.

The business is concluded in a minute: the samovar will be ready next week and Alyosha will pay then; from *him*, no deposit is needed. As we leave, "Pops" manages a glance up into our eyes and a smile, as if we three have entered an alliance against maurauding mankind.

In the car again, Alyosha turns talkative. "It's no accident," he says in parody of Marxist historians, "that I fell for a Yank *and* a child of Israel." I take this as a new way of tossing me a compliment, but in fact it is an introduction for musing about his relationship to Jews. In black market affairs, his preference for them is practical. "With Jewish traders, a deal's a deal. They're sober and responsible—mature enough to trust." With Russians, by contrast, even the minority who know their craft or trade, vodka or indolence usually queers the arrangements. The promised article is not delivered; its supplier turns stoolie, disappears, or curses *you* for bothering him. "A Russian with money in his pocket thinks first of spending it, usually on a fling. About doing a job well, even protecting his reputation, he rarely cares."

But what of Alyosha's affinity for Jews as company? Here there is no sound sociological explanation; he simply feels less kinship to Russians, even those of his own cosmopolitan instinct. This puzzles him, and he wonders whether his never-seen father—a university student whom the family banished after the seduction that sired him—was Jewish.

The next stop is a nearby foodshop's spirits department, to return the unbroken wine and vodka bottles among the sixty-odd that have been chinking and smashing in the trunk. On to a secondhand bookstore where an old Erstwhile has promised to keep a lookout for a prerevolutionary dictionary I can sell at Harvard for a small fortune. Then to a secondhand clothing store that, under Alyosha's name, has taken a pair of my old boots on consignment. When the sale is made—not yet, as Alyosha is informed in the office—we'll split the twenty rubles: a concession to ritual, since money changes hand between us as if from the same pocket. Next, a women's shop, all plate glass and fluorescent lights, where a tip has it that mohair scarves are on sale to mark the grand opening. No luck: the goods were either never there, as the assistant manager assures us, or, as a salesgirl insists, were whisked from the counter to prevent damage to the new fixtures. Then to a private shirtmaker who is sewing ten pairs of underpants for Alyosha on the pattern of mine from Macy's. He is enthused about this because domestic models are made without openings.

"After fifty-five years of Soviet rule, we're on the way to engineering a fly in our drawers. Life's important things, as they say, take time. Meanwhile, when nature calls, a hundred million Russians try to work their he-man fingers around five hundred million buttons—zippers, presumably, are a nasty bourgeois trick—or reach in *like this* to dig out their dings through a leghole. Jesus Christ, *pissing* in this country is a trauma . . . Oops!" (He points to the Volga's roof, where a KGB microphone may be hidden. Although less certain that "ears" have been planted in the car than in the apartment, we try to confine all incriminating talk to the open.) "Oops, but *we* don't lynch blacks, do we, or bomb Asians. All progressive mankind is grateful for the inspired leadership of the USSR. And you and I, *muchacho*, must pledge yet again to intensify our fight against the dirty imperialist war in Vietnam."

Down Lenin Prospekt, with its growing busyness of cars and lights and back toward the center of town. As always, Alyosha's coat is open and his thin Soviet shoes soaked with slush; immune to winter, he rejects boots as offhandedly as headgear. I can't remember Moscow before these rides, although this one has not been typical: we've spied but two girls, both unreachable in the traffic. Even the conversation about them has been limited to

Alyosha's casual question of what I have in mind for the evening. I wouldn't mind inviting Marya the Muff, I answer, referring to a sloe-eyed teen-ager who has provided us with exceptional pleasure.

"But you had her *yesterday,*" Alyosha sighs in mock puzzlement over my "perversity"—and, I think, in a gentle campaign to make me sexually more like him. We're already so close; why not be brothers?

A snack of greasy *cheburekhi* sold from a booth. A quick stop at the Supreme Court of the Russian Republic: Alyosha must peruse a new directive, available to legal personnel but not to the public, in the revived campaign against state embezzlement. A longer call to a new enterprise equivalent to an advertising agency, where Alyosha is trying to get a secretary's job, through an acquaintance there, for an ex-girl. Then a visit to his own Juridical Consultation Office.

During the past few weeks, I've lost my apprehension about following him inside; this time, I have a good look while he collects his messages and confers with a colleague. For offices, the lawyers share nine toilet-sized cubicles in shifts throughout the day and evening. Each has a tiny desk and two chairs, one for the client; they all reek of urine because soused devotees of the beer hall next door piss nightly on the outside wall. For the thirty attorneys, two telephones are available in the corridor; in grave crises, a third, in the chairman's room, can also be used. Some clients dial literally all day without getting through, and energetic lawyers with urgent calls usually run a few hundred meters down the street, to the nearest pay phone.

How can they, who are among Moscow's best, work in such conditions? Reappearing in the corridor, Alyosha laughs. "Faith and dedication—we're a heroic lot. And inspired: Lenin's portrait in every room."

On the Bowery-like sidewalk outside the office, he briefly questions a witness about a forthcoming case. Then we're off on a considerable ride to a huge taxi garage in an industrial sector of the city. Alyosha scampers in and has word passed of his arrival to his current mechanic. When the towheaded youngster appears outside, we drive to a field of deep, wet snow several hundred yards behind the depot. Here, as if in battlefield emergency, a new shock absorber is to be installed. The cheerful lad is soon soaked through, but does the job quickly and well, happily accepting Alyosha's generous payment and obligatory bottle-of-vodka tip. Dropping him off, we're on our way again, and it occurs to me to ask why not do the repairs in the garage itself. Because if caught, he explains, the use of state premises to make a profit on stolen parts would compound the charge under the law. As it is, the mechanic's labor is "tolerably" illegal.

Setting off in our "brand-new conveyance," Alyosha swings the jalopy through side streets and shortcuts, pointing out historical curiosities as we pass: the site where the Mongols assembled their annual booty of virgins, the office building that collapsed during construction in the thirties, the execution of a dozen architects and engineers; the sagging house of a Tanya and prefabricated apartment of a Galya he drove home once and thought he'd forgotten. In this steppe of a city whose rambling mazes anger taxi drivers, he has an instinct for direction that derives from more than memory and knowledge; he loves Moscow with a curious proprietary solicitude. His favorite places are the few remaining haunts from the days when the streets were full of character: a beer bar, the least spoiled of the city's handful, jammed from door to counter with fierce and bedraggled types; a slop house of a restaurant on a river barge, frequented by bosses of minor speculation rings. An apartment in one of the Stalinesque skyscrapers where a game of poker can be joined at most times of the day and night.

Least of all, he likes the Sovietization that continues to blanch these remnants of local color, to smother the wheeling-dealing of urban life, to homogenize everything into a single stretch of prefabricated apartment blocks. And relentlessly rename tradition-laden streets: each new sign announcing the appearance of yet one more "Redproletarian," "Lenin," "Leninist," or "Marx" in place of a descriptive or old Slavic appellation is a personal wound.

"Splendid news: Kaluzhskaya Square becomes dear 'October.' Naturally, measures *had* to be taken: 'Kaluzhskaya' stood for something in the life of old Moscow, and had a comforting ring.

Besides, millions of people knew where it was and didn't waste hours getting lost or trekking to one of the thirty *other* Octobers. Too pleasant, too convenient . . ."

On his personal count, eleven Moscow streets are now called "Leningrad," and he suspects he's missed a few. Like everyone else, he says, street-namers prefer a safe bet—that is, anything with Lenin in it—to risking Oak Tree Lane or something similarly untried. And every time we pass the famous open-air swimming pool a mile east of the Kremlin, a biting quip reminds me that before Lazar Kaganovich and Stalin stuffed it with dynamite, this was the site of the third largest church in Christendom, built to commemorate the victory over Napoleon. Only in the renaming of academies and institutes from "Stalin" to "Lenin" does he milk some satisfaction, for the former derives from "steel" while the latter, "appropriately," has the same root as the Russian word for "laziness."

Two more minor errands involving French swimming trunks and an old debt. Then a quick foray into a speciality food shop to inquire about grouse while we are waiting outside a metro station for Fantastic Natasha—who doesn't show up.

"Well lad?" he asks as the pallid street lamps go on.

"Let's take in a movie."

During the gung-ho film about Soviet counterespionage heroes he falls dead asleep, reviving as we emerge for a quick check on the señoritas at the Central Post Office on Gorky Street; but on the way there, we notice we are almost out of gas. Instead, we go directly to an old section of town, full of log houses and trolley rails. One of the city's three gas stations that stay open evenings is located here, opposite a former monastery shorn of its bells.

It is only eleven-thirty, but apart from the station nothing is lit and nothing moves: we are immersed in the haunted village atmosphere I so love, with the moon casting long shadows on the snow and the wind's whine through electricity wires suggesting the old houses are deserted. The station itself is a decrepit affair with a single pump like that of an old Maine farm. It is also clean out of gas. This is announced, with gleeful spite, by its night manager, a powerful woman in boots and a greasy quilt jacket. Spitting her sunflower seeds almost in our faces, she grunts that the delivery to replenish her tanks may come by one o'clock—and, heh heh, may not.

Rather than wait, Alyosha decides to hail a passing truck and do his usual deal with its driver: a ruble for ten liters of the State's gas. The third truck stops and follows us into a dark side street, where Alyosha removes his trusty siphoning tube from its permanent place in the truck.

I have just read a *Newsweek* article warning against this very practice. ("Anyone who tries to siphon gasoline by sucking it through a single rubber tube is taking a tremendous risk. Four ounces, if swallowed, can be fatal, but even much smaller amounts can cause dangerous symptoms. If the siphoner should vomit after swallowing gasoline, he is likely to inhale some of it, and this can lead to chemical pneumonia, with a severe risk that the lungs will abruptly stop functioning due to the effect on the central nervous system. . . .") Although pleased by my plea for caution, Alyosha treats it like an alcoholic reminded that whiskey can impair clear thinking. He's done it a thousand times before, taken a thousand greater risks to maintain his life-style. And indeed, he completes the siphoning with such dispatch that the cheap, domestic gas causes only one grimace. Then he gives the country-boy driver a bonus of fifty kopeks for being so "alert." Both are happy to have done business so well.

When we emerge from the side street, the station's harsh light is shining upon two girls walking briskly past. Alyosha emits his parody of a war cry while speeding up for a closer look, but is cut short before deciding. "Allooo . . . , look who's here," cries the nearer one in gleeful surprise. An Erstwhile of three years ago, she is returning home with a girl friend after the circus, where both perform. Home is the peeling former monastery opposite the station, which is not the wartime billet it looks like in the midnight darkness but a dormitory for circus personnel.

The girls chat about rising prices and their disappointing pay, but can't come home with us because their troupe is going on tour early in the morning. Soon we drive off on a roundabout circuit of old wooden Moscow, then along the river. It's the dead of night now; even the heavily traveled quay is empty except for an occasional construction truck.

Although we've been in the car since morning, we set out to burn our new gas. Roaming roads at random, we discuss this and that, including, of course, the night life at this hour in the West. "Paris?" says Alyosha, mocking his inability to thrust his nose close to the Soviet border. "We'll need another ten liters. Paris is"—pointing to Bolshaya Serpukhovskaya Street—"just down there and to the left."

Returning to the center, we park in front of the Bolshoi Theater's columns. Perhaps because we're the only car in sight, a policeman approaches us and, having scrutinized Alyosha's license and the Volga's ownership papers, salutes politely: the exception to the rule of boorish traffic cops. As we're about to push off again, we spy a well-dressed man teetering across Sverdlov Square whom, through the mist, Alyosha recognizes as an old friend. The son of an impresario who founded an important Moscow theater, he is filthy drunk and searching for more vodka. While we drive him home, he tries to tell a story about his weekend in an artists' retreat, as if he and Alyosha had met last week rather than a year ago.

For some reason, the new dormitory for Aeroflot crews we pass on our way back reminds me of the Newark hamburger joint where, acting out my teen-age bum fantasies by living in the YMCA, I first groped for the courage to pick up girls. Then I think of my new confidence, of all the barriers Alyosha has guided me through. Learning the inner workings of Moscow life has somehow opened me up to larger discoveries about life in general and about myself. For the moment, there are a dozen questions I need not ask, a hundred worries that need not be worried. Anastasia and I will ultimately have a happy ending. Meanwhile, Marya the Muff will come around tomorrow, perhaps with her much-touted friend. Everything's in place.

Pleasantly exhausted, I savor my nightcap of Alyosha's stories about inventive embezzlers he has defended. The strange thing is that although our talk and pursuits skim the surface of life, it is the substance of his personality underneath, about which almost nothing is said, that makes me at home with him.

"Zonks," he says. "We forgot."

"What?"

"To borrow a reel from my friend. Want to go ice-fishing when the sun comes up?"

It has been a beautiful day on my magic carpet.

The fetes take place roughly every third evening. In addition to Alyosha's apartment, friends' quarters are occasionally used: the basement studio of a dandyish photographer; an important mathematician's luxurious apartment borrowed by his son while his father is away; the mildewed room of a recently divorced actor in the Theater of the Leninist Komsomol. The setting shifts; the props and scenario hardly vary.

The principal feature is a bountiful supper, enjoyed for itself in the spirit of Russian feasting as well as to prepare the guests. (Many are more impressed by chocolate bars and my contribution of Kents than Alyosha's chicken soup or lucky find of smoked sprats. For factory girls, the old cheese and bologna hors d'oeuvres, not to mention Alyosha's supply of leftover Western cosmetics and magazines, would be seductive enough.) The drink matches the food: an assortment of vodka or cognac, wine or beer in their dirty-lipped bottles, all drunk in sequence as haphazard as the use of knives, spoons and hands. The jokes are as motley—crude scatological humor mixed with choice selections from the vast repertoire of political satire. The music, last year's pop hits taped from Voice of America broadcasts or black market records, plays over and over, again and again, to the point of hypnotic effect, the provocatively un-Soviet sound of throbbing electric guitars casting a stronger spell than in its native setting, and prompting associations with the birth of jazz as a vehicle of black liberation. We are immersed in noise, gluttony and food-alcohol-stuffy-room smells. But although Moscovskaya osobaya vodka, oranges and the new rock make the parties exciting, it is even more true that the parties enhance the deliciousness of the treats.

Alyosha is occasionally bored and faintly dissatisfied with himself for returning yet again to this ritual entertainment, and I'm sometimes slightly nervous at the start. But vodka speeds our transformation to the spirit of celebration and languid indulgence infusing the hot, hutlike room. Although a detached observer might specify vulgarity as the parties' dominant trait, something simultaneously uplifting is at work, releasing the participants from the heaviness of the national environment. Eating, laughing, dancing, watching an ice-skating competition in Budapest on television, dancing again—free of any thought of how foolishly ragged we look—making love, changing girls immediately to make it again, holding on to the last glasses of wine because not a square inch for them remains free on the table, spitting sunflower seeds onto the floor, cramming into the bathtub for a mass wash, playing Ray Charles's "What I Say" one last time and then a last-last time. . . . We are here to do what we want—nothing more, nothing less. No sober discussion of the national condition or the cultural scene; never an attempt to impress with what we do, how much money we make, how intelligently we can converse. For neither pretension or rationalization are needed to justify our surrender to gratification.

That we have met the girls only that afternoon does not seem strange, even to them. Each new group is bound together by the sacred obligation to spend *this* evening in the present company as happily as possible. After the first hour, even the most reserved are steeped in this camaraderie, behaving as if they, or their ancestors, have enjoyed such revels ("orgies" somehow implies a greater element of self-consciousness and planning) since the beginning of time. Fate has brought us together; life is short and hard. These few hours, this auspicious opportunity, can never be repeated. We must honor them by putting aside all other thoughts.

But in the morning, we take pains to appear irreproachably respectable as we descend the stairs and step outdoors with all the decorum required by Soviet public standards. Like all others, Alyosha's apartment block is the preserve of a censorious state. Neighbors are watching; the police may be called. Nothing must be done—seem to be done!—that might offend a dutiful citizen in the form of a puffy cashier, schoolmarm or self-righteous housewife; or the scrawny pensioner whiling away his golden years at a window overlooking the courtyard. To a pillbox of a woman there whose black pupils follow us like eyeballs in an observation slot, Alyosha tips an imaginary fedora. His flouting of the winter-hat convention is enough to arouse her suspicions!

We take our ladies' arms to help them over the ice—anything more might appear to violate socialist behavioral norms—and deliver them to their jobs or convenient metro stations. The night's activities are not mentioned; they have ended, and sex talk in the cold light of day is dirty-minded. Again the curtain is drawn on our private pursuits. With the smell of snow in our nostrils and the worry that the Volga will further delay our late start, the lingering images of our paganism seem wholesome.

And I remain entranced by the miracle of the girls. Taller and shorter, brunette and dusty blonde; yet all deriving from one model in my mind's eye: of Olga, my summer camp swimming instructor, whose incredible naked body I spied through the showerhouse knothole when I was fourteen. The city teems with this leggy loveliness, squeezing through crowds, pushing into buses, fighting into stores and onward toward the counters. They often travel in twos and threes, maintaining their reassuring physical contact. Linking arms, holding hands, grasping waists— and chattering, humming, giggling with an air of buttery healthiness, as if they'd carried water from the river that morning, then come home to try out their first lipsticks.

They have made outwardly austere Moscow endlessly provocative. I remember July evenings in New York, when the sultriness screamed of the sex I hadn't had for weeks. I'd prowl Third Avenue, my nerve endings pleading for the smart women in hot pants and halters. Anyone of a hundred from Forty-eighth to Fifty-ninth streets would do—or all of them together; their names and faces were irrelevant. Here, this fantasy is real. Make your choice. Pluck her away for an ice cream or a pastry; envision her fully revealed before midnight. With this secret knowledge, just to loiter on Mayakovsky Square is a forbidden pleasure, your body warm under your overcoat.

From the sea of silent shufflers that floods the downtown streets, a limitless stream, effortlessly tapped and funneled, flows to our tables and our embraces. Only one sweetheart in a dozen stays with us long enough for us to remember her last name; yet collectively, I seem to know them better than any of the New York girls with whom I've spent a thousand more earnest and less revealing hours. I've been given a glimpse of the Russians' spirit and secret, something mysterious and profound in their very anonymity—for this is truly a country of the masses, an immense reservoir of sorrow and strength. This Nero's roll call of Galyas, Svetlanas and Natashas has a meaning I can almost grasp, something even more elemental than the lust they provoke and satiate. Something related to the attitude of Russian mothers, perhaps: the breast is here and full; take it when you will.

But when I try to probe this meaning, it wriggles from my grasp or drifts into patronizing clichés. I can only record the images, so strong that they must be symbolic. Ill-cut, loose-fitting skirts dyed dark brown as if, as among nuns, to discourage any thought of what lies underneath. (Or, in the shortage of dry-cleaning facilities and money, to conceal a winter's dirt?) Pink rayon brassieres stained by underarm sweat: supremely functional, wholly ungainly articles smacking of women war workers in Detroit. An odor of open pores and physical exertion, as outside the girls' gym in high school. Sometimes lurking under a sickly sweet eau de cologne, usually sharpened by the effects of the same garments worn daily, the scent is often spiced by the unexpectedly "southern" accent of garlic and onions. And the vodka goes down easily after the usual protests.

Faces that speak of peasant hardiness, refined but not smothered by city living: an intriguing combination of sensuousness and innocence. Bodies muscled by walking and work, protected against the cold by a coating of fat, yet surprisingly supple and lithe. A light growth of leg and body hair; rarely the stout squatness of the popular Western image of Russian women. Most will turn quickly to that after marriage and children, but in their youth the stereotype of Olympic gymnasts is closer to the truth. "Fresh, sturdy, comely, smiling"—just as Tolstoy wrote of the peasant girls of his prurient youth.

Unhappy about their brassieres and the clumsy bloomers of discoloring wool, the girls insist on undressing themselves, resentfully rebuffing any encroachment by us on a button or a zip. "That's my concern, I'll do it myself." Even many who have invited themselves for a second fete protest when a man's hand reaches for their skirts. But undressing effects a transformation: the girls have a startling lack of modesty about their naked bodies, especially their breasts (which are smallish compared to their hips and thighs). Within minutes of meeting, they are persuaded to expose them—to cup them out of their own blouses themselves—for appreciation and caresses.

The contradictions go further. Unashamed of their bodies in the presence of girls as well as of men, many of our guests reach out to one another. Kissing her mouth, adjusting the hair, fondling her breasts while murmuring their language's tender endearments, one helps prepare another—a stranger until the second rang Alyosha's bell forty-five minutes ago—for the mating she herself has just enjoyed. This seems no indication of homosexuality as such, but an expression of Russian "togetherness," always strongest among tight, private groups convened for pleasure. Often the sex itself is secondary to the larger satisfaction of sharing—especially, in the general gloom, the sharing of frivolity and flourish. I wonder whether this is the same instinct that moves Russian prisoners to divide their food parcels; or whether, as my University friend Leonid suggests, it is a hidden sense of shame, rather than good fortune, that they want to apportion.

But this lack of inhibition is wholly unrelated to the sophistication it may suggest. Ignorant of deodorants and contraceptive techniques, many girls also know little about the danger days of their cycles and blush fiercely when we ask. They would rather not be put through this shame than insure that the evening will be safe. And few use their hands, let alone fingers, before or during "bed-love" as they stiltedly call it; even those who groan lie almost still, scarcely moving themselves. Supposing orgasm to be a male pleasure, many consent to strive for their own only in the general spirit of accommodation. From deep in their upbringing, they sense that women should not be too active.

Free of complexes, modest of expectation—above all, they are complacent, seemingly in the spirit of the Russian masses' patient acquiescence. Scanning old literature, I repeatedly find the explanation of last night's revel in the serf mentality. "I motioned to something pink that looked very nice from a distance," Tolstoy confessed to his diary. "I opened the back door. She came in."

Seven of ten girls enter the car immediately on the strength of a genial invitation; one sends us packing and the other two promise to meet us later, with barely any compunction about cheating a new husband or skipping work. Guilt and superego being as absent as the pill and boutiques, many girls spend the next forty-eight hours lazily pottering around in Alyosha's apartment, insulated from the outdoor cold. The paradox—or law of nature?—is that in this rigid society, they are so personally free.

But what do I care about sociological paradoxes? I need not apologize for my plenitude, nor placate my professors with dispassionate analysis. I adore the darlings not for their artlessness or innocence, but because they are *mine*. Lips like avocados, beings as simple to penetrate as warming to hug, they are my comfort and joy. Each one whispering "my closest sweetest precious" as she surrenders is dear; each shapely overcoat a searing temptation because it can be taken directly to Alyosha's to touch what makes it bulge from underneath. I become excited in the most unlikely places: spying a pretty face in a museum, pressed up against a young body in a creaking bus. "Excuse me, miss. May I trouble you for just a moment?" Surfeited on this vast harem, my appetite grows.

She is in the Central Post Office when I mail a letter one evening, and leaves with me as a matter of course, knowing she'll sleep wherever I arrange. Eighteen years old, just arrived from Irkutsk, she had nowhere to stay in Moscow, and didn't know where she'd go when the post office would close several hours hence. The look of her in the taxi so arouses me that my hands are inside her dress the moment Alyosha locks the door. Happy for this, she nevertheless questions my haste: can't we stay here the full night? Before morning, she has found the romance she wanted. Alyosha and I are "my darlings," "my dearest dear ones" and "my soulmates."

Hearing that we lack permanent attachments, she pleads that we come live with her in Irkutsk. She has a room of her own there; we will love Siberia. She'll cook and clean for us, wash our clothes—

"I'm a foreigner," I say to nip the false hope. "I can't go fifty kilometers from Moscow without permission, let alone five thousand."

"But no one has to know where you're from," she bubbles. "Just get on a train—I'll buy the ticket. We'll say you're my fiancé."

For two days, Sweet Svetlana lives at Alyosha's, washing curtains and singing, tempting us with promises of Siberian freedom and fun. Then she disappears and we get a postcard from Irkutsk. Three weeks later, she knocks on the door. Since we wouldn't come to her, she says, she returned to us. But she met a handsome engineer on the plane and is living with him. This is just a sentimental visit—and can we help her get a residence permit?

Alyosha leaves Moscow for a week to appear at a trial in distant Alma-Ata. (He will defend two Armenians accused of peddling marijuana, one of the rare drug cases I've heard of here, although he predicts considerable growth in its use and severe tightening of the laws penalizing it within a few years.) While he is gone, a suspicion that I have exaggerated his flair and significance works on me, fusing a sense of cheapness to my loneliness. In his absence, my musings about our flings make them seem synthetic, like the bragging of for-the-asking sex in magazine articles about Swedish girls' mythical delights. To test my memory and feelings, I decide to record the first fete after Alyosha's return.

He returns, in fact, a day earlier than expected, calls me gaily from the airport and suggests a "homecoming fiesta" to celebrate our reunion and Aeroflot's skill in wafting him both ways without mishap. (He is genuinely relieved to be home: Alma-Ata's judges make Moscow's appear enlightened by comparison; the hotel had bedbugs; the city was short of meat.) At the University gate, he greets me with a bear hug and suggests we invite Ira, who must be called before leaving work because she has no home telephone. Have I any objections?

Ira offers to make her own way to Alyosha's but has not arrived a full hour after the agreed seven o'clock. In the interval, I contemplate the apartment's natural state.

A one-room "Khrushch-slum" apartment with attached kitchen and bath, it is decorated in a grease-stained burgundy wallpaper that Alyosha hung himself, seemingly after removing it from a Barcelona bordello. Of the furniture, only a bookcase surviving from his salad days rises above the nondescript. On top of it, held in place by a threadbare tire and a stack of disused pots, teeters a coffee table with broken legs. This sets the pattern for the chaos at floor level, five feet below.

Tattered stuffed toys and an assortment of wooden Russian dolls covered in dust. A row of pistons and connecting rods dappled with candle wax. The well-known flower-child poster—equivalent in rarity value to a Picasso lithograph on Park Avenue—of the nude blonde and pony in a field of high grass. A set of medical syringes—for treating girls' venereal diseases—laid out in a cigar box balancing on an old cauldron. Stacks of paint cans; a whole old overcoat turned cleaning rag; an ancient enlarger for picnic and pornographic photography; a large supply of the best toilet paper—he's fussy about this. And sprinkled in the general jumble, a hundred jars, bottles, books, butcher's tools and artifacts lying where they were dropped on the divan, television set and cigarette-burned rug. The gaping disrepair of the apartment building itself is most noticeable in the steps missing on the staircases. I first thought Alyosha was joking when he said it was erected only eight years ago—and by a construction trust as housing for the very workers who slapped it together.

The knock sounds well after eight. It is not Ira, however, but a thin neighbor who has come for her weekly injection of vitamin B-11, prescribed by Alyosha as a winter cure. He quickly sterilizes the needle and gets her over her embarrassment to let me see where she will be jabbed. Her shyly pirouetted behind makes me plump for her to pinch-hit for the evening, but she is far too familiar to interest Alyosha. Besides, she's late for a sewing class.

By eight-thirty, we agree it's time to call a substitute. *Moskvichki* disregard appointments as casually as they make them: having arranged a rendezvous, many first-timers fail to keep it and are never seen again—or turn up at the apartment after months. Alyosha's latest address book is already in our hands when we hear Ira's saucy knock.

An ambitious girl with aspirations to marry a scientist or diplomat, she is better groomed than average and carries traces of good breeding. (Her father is a Polish officer who was detained in Russia long after the war.) Although her job in a laboratory for evaluating clothing affronts her pride, she hangs on for its opportunities to meet young chemists.

Ira is a womanly nineteen; Maya, whom she has brought with her, a year younger: a shorter, pudgier colleague—whom we've never seen before—with large eyes and Clara Bow lips. She remains on the threshold stammering that she shouldn't have come, that Ira *dragged* her—until Alyosha happily whisks her in.

He coaxes the bashful Maya to name her preference for drink, hides his wince when she designates the syrupy substance called port and hurries to the nearest café while the guests start on the salami. Between mouthfuls, they describe a futile trip from their lab to a distant store supposedly selling East German tights— which has put them in a mood to be, well, feted. Returning before they've thawed, Alyosha pronounces a toast that wends from tardiness (Ira's) to tartness to tarts, but which flatters rather than offends. Overcoming Maya's eye-blinking protest, he sets down her glass and persuades her to show us "the source of your *own* honeyed wine, milk of—God grant it—a clutch of providential infants." Remonstrating feebly, Maya undoes her buttons, liberating a Renoir breast. Aroused by Alyosha's tongue on it, or by rivalry, Ira strides to the bathroom and emerges naked except for her boots. A lithe figure despite her fullness, she assumes a position on the bed favored during her previous visit, her temptress's wink so superfluous that I chuckle to myself. And I adore Maya's inevitable "Must you really do that?" as she makes room for my hand in her panties.

I touch her wonderful bush. The lovemaking begins with a rush. Maya changes partners affably, then back again, assuring us redundantly that she doesn't quite know where to go in this unusual "hoofing" for her supper. The tape recorder has picked up Ray Charles's faithful beat, filling the air with nostalgia and ritual, transforming the room into our private cabaret. Telephone rings go unanswered but the television set is still documenting a Czech delegation touring a steel works. I catch a glimpse of Alyosha's head deferentially lowered between Ira's legs—as curious a spectacle as the Bessemer furnaces on the flickering screen. In place of the revulsion I'd have for another man, I feel as if I'm taking a bath with the family. I know his smooth, clean body as well as my own, and in some way I suspect that this moment of hardness together is more an expression of our companionship than of lechery. Yet I love Maya too, clenching her chubby fists beneath me. Sweet Maya, who is giving me this trust of her body at first sight. My cup runneth over again. Jesus.

Alyosha's rolling on his back, finished. Ira transfers her attention to Maya and me, encouraging us—"Harder!"—somewhat condescendingly. When she tongues our nipples, I respond with a surge for her, still inside Maya. Now the dizzy joy of pure carnality takes hold of me. I hold still in the pungency of Maya while kissing Ira's mouth, then switch. This is what I was born for. My head spinning, I hate the voice that says I should try to record this. Through pumping and whirling, I make out a pile of cookbooks I've never noticed before. "Oh my handsome one," says someone—but our swish-sloshing is the only sound I fully hear. I come. Trade to start again almost immediately. The second release gives me a moment's slumber.

"Yeah, some wop ship went aground," I hear Alyosha from the kitchen. "The Ministry of Foreign Trade keeps shifting our underground rocks."

This is his commentary on two bottles of Italian vermouth I spied in a downtown store this afternoon—which also set the theme for his supper stories. Early one morning, he begins when we're all at table, the manager of a food store steps outside to tell all Jews in the line to leave. He tailors the message throughout the day to Kalmyks, Kirgizians and other minority groups, locking the door behind him on each return inside. As evening approaches, he tells the remaining Russians to go home too: the store is closed for inventory and will not open.

"See that?" says Kolya to Tolya, who has also waited all day. "The dirty Jews always get special treatment."

The meal is like an after-dinner cigarette. The brandy is Zhenya, a chic "older" woman who arrives to talk to Alyosha about her failing marriage. Vexed at the sight of Ira and Maya—who is in an ancient bathrobe that she herself used to wear—she is distracted, however, by Alyosha's new Rolling Stones tape, and demonstrates her frug. After she allows the younger girls to admire her underwear too, we are suddenly in heat again, three pairs of thighs pointed toward the ceiling.

The sweet joy of dumb potency washes over me while Zhenya insists she has no time for this, I must first finish with her. I am aware that Alyosha has got up to answer another knock and that Lev Davidovich, a timid colleague, has entered, but I can't follow their corridor conversation. All I hear is that he wants to buy a barely used Volga from some speculator on the cheap but fears a new car might antagonize the Party overseer at the Juridical Consultation Office. He leaves without a peek at our balling.

I've had one drink too many. Or there's one woman too many; something is confusing. Tight in one with my fingers up the other two—but why am I laughing like a clown? The first time I saw Zhenya in the Journalists' Club, I thought she was a snob. She's trying to tell me something interesting about her husband, or that she *will* tell me later. I think she'll like it the back way. Maya and Ira want big-deal husbands too. Meanwhile, they decide to hold hands while sampling simultaneous fellatio with Alyosha and me. My hard-on is my head. Somebody's trying to thread a new tape. The recorder falls, smashing glasses on the floor. Zhenya suggests a screw for the road. C'mere baby: I'm shouting in English. I come and sprawl on my back, my stomach all wet.

I revive to Zhenya ordering Alyosha not to get up from her to answer the new knock. He's trying like hell to come but the sounds of an argument in the adjoining apartment—wife raging at drunken husband, he coaxing her to drink herself—make him laugh and slip out. Glasses of fresh tea are served, with Bulgarian cherry jam spooned from the jar. Searching for Ira's necklace, we improvise a game of sexual chain on the floor, with pats and licks, but no desire. Dressed again, we waltz to the Dr. Zhivago theme, rendered in our own la-la-la-la. Outside, a wind is driving thick new snow against the windows. We leave only when Zhenya *really* can't stay any longer.

During the following weeks, I'm like a scientist afraid that his new discovery will reveal itself to be a hoax. But the pattern repeats itself like a telephone weather report. Recruiting a bakery girl who has only an hour for adultery because she must hurry to the boy she married last week. Watching two nymphets, fellow-workers in a printing shop, racing to undress themselves: Alyosha has told them—"Socialist competition in all things, Comrades!"—that the first will win "a certain corporal prize." Stepping into the apartment the next afternoon to find three new teen-agers improvising a nude ballet. (One helps me with my overcoat while the other two dive for cover.) The arrival of a girl from Murmansk whom Alyosha met on the Black Sea last summer, and her lying down for me as if it were integral to entering the room. Above all, the meeting, celebrating, mating and return of the innocents—who, despite this, will somehow remain lifelong friends—to Moscow's multitude. Strangest of all is the strength I sense in this submissiveness, as if our easy conquests have something in common with the sucking of French and German armies into the Russian heartland for destruction.

Mornings, the girls sedately make up in the wavy mirror, as if we've known each other forever. Although the adventure started with Alyosha's traditional stop-you-for-*a-minute* ploy, some will stay days here, their new home. No one at their old homes is informed; no adjustment time is needed. Although meeting an American in these circumstances is as unlikely for them as coming across a snake charmer in Gorky Park, most accept my attendance as casually as everything destiny tosses them. We all belong to the big human family.

Sometimes I leave alone, making my way to a trolley that passes near the University. Hollowed by dissipation, pleased and disgusted with myself, feeling the after-tingle and dried secretions on my skin, I wait with old grandmothers at a stop outside crumbling yellow houses, knowing I am as close as I can be to the purifying mystical visions claimed by certain advocates of voluminous sex. What is commonplace elsewhere, perhaps even debased, here contains an element of the miraculous. I know why primitive man worshiped fertility symbols.

"To seduce all the girls in Moscow is impossible. But" . . . (heavy pause) . . . "toward this goal one must strive." Alyosha has compressed his girl-knowledge into such maxims, pronounced at appropriately incongruous moments in the oratorical tone of a radio announcer citing old Russian proverbs in substantiation of production claims. "A certain number of darlings resent granting their favors immediately," he also likes to exposit. "Roughly eleven per cent. I understand them; it's a matter of principle. 'No matter how much I like a man,' they say, 'I just won't succumb the first time.' To which I reply, 'Of course, honey, I'll drive you home. I guess it's good-bye for us—until tomorrow.'"

At happy moments behind the wheel, he breaks into song, blessing the Motherland for its gift of orgasms and orifices instead of "organic unity" and the "orchestra of social sounds." And traditional limericks and verses are resurrected from obscurity to illustrate, with an altered word or phrase, salient points. The abundance of instant, anonymous sex, for example, is conveyed by slightly modifying a typically cloying Soviet ballad:

> Lilac's blooming in our native fields as if glad,
> Sweet Spring, she's always the same;
> A brigade leader's fucking a maiden like mad—
> And wants to know her name.

Passing a secondhand bookshop, we see the famous poster of cloth-capped Lenin in a gingerbread countryside, with verses implying that the Father of the Communist Party, born in April, caused the buds to open and birds to sing. Alyosha reads it all—

> The snow of the fields is melting,
> Warm winds caress our ears;
> Flocks of birds without counting,
> Frolic in the sun without fears.

> Brooks babble in their fullness,
> Slim birch trees, again all alive,
> Remind us of our heartfelt gladness,
> LENIN'S BIRTHDAY means Spring's arrived.

—changing only the final line: "LENIN'S BIRTHDAY—enjoy an alfresco jive."

His story for illustrating female submissiveness starts with Vanka, the sometimes sober village handyman, spying a pretty milkmaid in a barn.

"Hey, Mashka, c'mon up into the hayloft, we'll have some you-know-what."

"Fresh. I certainly will not."

"Why not?"

"Because I said so."

"Aw gee, Mashinka. C'mon."

Masha's sigh expresses the full futility of further resistance. "Oh all right. Bully, you wore me down."

The bread and butter of his expertise is knowledge of the richest pickup grounds: the exits to certain metro stations for tarts, several bustling shopping streets for counter girls, the telephone booths of certain major buildings for secretaries planning their evening. And throughout the day, the Central Post Office on Gorky Street, where local girls are telephoning friends to announce their purchases, and visiting lasses—who are even happier to find a bed—are calling Sverdlovsk and Kharkov to ask their parents to telegram thirty rubles. We sometimes drop by at five o'clock just to stand in earshot of the booths, keeping our fingers on the nation's pulse.

Operating procedures are equally important. One of the most fundamental axioms is that Russian girls require a gentle push—coaxing, teasing, plying with vodka or laughs. Eighty per cent return for more, says Alyosha. But *you* must guide them through *their* little barriers.

Another canon is never to be without a supply of two-kopek coins. Calls sometimes must be made on the dot—when a girl has access to an office telephone—or from a suburb; and since the "deucer" is as scarce as evening taxis, not having one in your pocket for the nearest booth can lose you the ball game.

Other injunctions are to ask girls to repeat aloud all arrangements for future meetings before leaving them, and never to let a just-stopped lovely who won't join you immediately move on until her coordinates are recorded. If she has no telephone, a girl friend's who will serve as intermediary must be elicited, or an address for telegrams to fix rendezvous. Since *her* promise to call *you* is worth little, leaving your number is never enough. Not inhibition, Alyosha tutors, but Russian nonchalance is the great enemy. Girls lose slips of paper, become distracted, forget.

Boredom, on the other hand, is the great ally: the cosmic variety implied by the Russian *skuka*. Once I pushed for a serious explanation of the permissiveness. Was it the free-love propaganda of certain early Bolsheviks? Had the Orthodox church's social attitudes prepared the way? Without denying the relevance of traditional Russian tolerance of carnal sin, Alyosha's explanation was rooted in more immediate influences, especially the girls' great emptiness of routine. "It's a monotony of monotoneness: no entertainment, no excitement. On seventy rubles a month, they can afford either a movie or two a week or their daily sugared bun. On a larger scale, our social system has them dragging on in dreary poverty, with no 'bourgeois' escapes. Understand why Jaguar-driving playboys in sane countries are so much poorer than you and me?"

Without having set foot abroad (except as a soldier), Alyosha senses that he could not hope for a tenth of his popularity in the West. Like easygoing social relationships, he's convinced, quick sex is one of the reverse benefits of Soviet suppression, which leaves young women in a state of *skuka*. Where restaurants are few and primitive, people are concerned with their stomachs rather than a proper selection of knife and fork: hence the inelegant—but lusty—scenes at Russian tables. Where wages are depressed, television abysmal and pop groups banned, Alyosha's fetes are royal divertissements. But precisely this is what enlarges his burden. A compulsion to sleep with every attractive girl is one thing, but "the knowledge that you can do it," he sighs in mock complaint, "gives a man no peace. I keep telling you, bureaucratic error begat me in the wrong motherland."

But by now, I realize that Alyosha's ratio of conquests is not a wholly accurate measure of Moscow attitudes, not only because of his uncanny talent for disarming even the inhibited minority (he would make a superb sexual therapist) but also because most girls he stops have given indication of just this cosmic ennui. Like a predator selecting prey from a herd, he judges women by their posture and walk. Those slouching at a bus stop or trailing toward nowhere are the most grateful for attention, and register like off-guard gazelles in his peripheral vision.

As if to illustrate the point, we notice a sweet thing outside the TASS office. Yes, she'll come to the apartment now, but can we "put it off" for just a while? If we "do it" this afternoon, what will happen to her in the evening?

Desperately late for crucial appointments first thing this morning—mine with my faculty supervisor, a Stalinist hack threatening to inform the Embassy unless I produce some work; Alyosha's with a police captain, to quash a license-losing charge of drunken driving after a cop stopped us at midnight—we fly down Alyosha's stairs and into the courtyard, gorging our breakfast of leftover cake. Shoes still untied, laughing at the sun and a mangy neighborhood cat who greets us for scraps, we dash through the snow to the workhorse Volga. After last night's fete, the prospect of serious business in the outside world strikes us as diverting before we meet again for lunch.

Suddenly we remember, and jolt back in minor shock. The car won't start. Precious minutes must be wasted. Alyosha forgot to refill the radiator first thing this morning.

Counting every second, he sprints back up the stairs three at a time, fills cauldrons and kettles with hot water and, the faster to revive the frozen motor, heats them further on the stove's blackened burners. On ordinary mornings he submits uncomplainingly to this tedious routine, as to the thousand everyday frustrations that a lifetime of obstacles has trained him to endure cheerfully. But today, his hands are coarsened by the cold and the grease; and he badly stains his single respectable suit crawling under the battered car to reseal the stopcock. And we are now impossibly late.

His inspired driving recovers several minutes. While taxis crawl and private drivers stop to spread ashes, he plows, churns, spins and slides over the ice of an artful route of back streets. Although his appointment is minutes before mine, he insists on delivering me first. Skidding between a parked car and a towering snow bank, we turn a corner to cross the last of the main streets. There my heart sinks.

Head tilted, smiling to herself, the girl is swinging a briefcase as she saunters. Like a hound sighting the hare, Alyosha chortles and swings to the curb.

"Good God, no," I plead. "Not now. Any time but now. We don't *need* her."

I might have said more. The police captain has warned that Alyosha's case is very serious—a strident new anti-alcohol campaign is in progress—and that he will be available only before nine o'clock. We've made crazy detours before when rushing to a trial or to beat a Bolshoi Theater curtain; in fact, it's a rare drive that is not interrupted. But this delay is suicidal. Alyosha without a license would be like a postman without legs; and there is a real danger that my academic bankruptcy will get me expelled, especially if I make my self-admiring supervisor wait.

"I'll get you Elizabeth Taylor when she comes. Forget this one and *let's get going.*"

Then I desist. More from me can only protract the inevitable. Before leaping out, Alyosha looks at me tenderly, explaining with his eyes that it can't be helped.

"Have a Chesterfield, I'll only be a minute."

In fact, he is three minutes. As they tick by, a wave of affection washes away my exasperation. Winning a wide smile in spite of the startled girl's effort to be prim, gesturing grandly toward the jalopy, trying to avoid the unseemliness of rushing her—he is inimitable, the Peck's Bad Boy of our time.

When the girl has settled warily on the back seat and Alyosha has introduced me with his customary fanfare ("Meet my buddy *muchacho* visiting from New York and Miami Beach—you know, next to Cuba . . ."), we speed off again—miraculously without penalty, for my supervisor arrives later than I, and although Alyosha must waste most of the morning in a corridor filled with worried petitioners, he manages to see the blustery police captain and prevail by offering free legal services in a suit against him by his angry ex-wife. Having waited uncomplainingly in the car, the girl spends the day playing house in the apartment.

The following day we are dashing toward an important meeting only to stop dead in our tracks and zoom with equal speed in the opposite direction, in pursuit of some blonde hair and fetching calves. And two days after that, we are hoping against hope that we'll still be on time to catch a man who claims to have a fifteenth-century icon, but Alyosha stomps the brakes before we've covered five hundred yards.

"In the bakery doorway—look! Hallelujah! have you ever seen such a darling?"

"Not since noon, I haven't." In fact, we've spent the morning frolicking with two waitresses, but Alyosha ignores my allusion to this ancient episode—or pretends I'm agreeing that the new lass with the hand-knitted cap is indeed more fetching than the pair who departed four minutes ago.

"You're not suggesting we should let her get away?"

"We're holding up traffic. Some citizens might be—uh, *late for important appointments.*"

"You're probably aware that thousands of icons were painted in the fifteenth century. How many living things, by your guess, are made like that work of art?"

Cap allows that she fancies visiting a girl friend in a distant district. Snow banks and one-lane traffic make us fifty minutes late for the appointment with the mysterious icon man, who, if he showed up at all, has undoubtedly left. "How did *I* know what was outside that bakery?" sighs Alyosha.

And so on. Rushing Efficient Alla to the airport for a flight to join her husband, we see a fair face framed by a bus window. In violation of two dozen road rules and with flagrant disregard for the cops on every other corner, Alyosha risks a spinning U-turn, then threads the traffic like a car-chase film to stay parallel with the vehicle transporting such loveliness. One hand rotates the wheel for these reckless maneuvers; the other is performing a repertoire of feverish waves, first to catch the beauty's lofty eye, then to cajole her into disembarking at the next stop—and then the *next* one as we follow our mile of detour despite Alla's moans about the disaster of trying to rebook an Aeroflot flight.

Hurrying to a compulsory foreign-policy lecture for lawyers one day, Alyosha is smitten by a trolleybus *driver,* who proves much easier to lure out than yesterday's passenger. The vivacious lass stops her vehicle, emerges in her overalls and, pretending to adjust the trolley's leads to the overhead wires, delightedly announces the telephone number where she can be reached at four o'clock.

But the missed prizes cause him corresponding pain. "Vanished!" he yelps of a girl who has disappeared into a metro entrance or around a crowded corner. His voice is full of puppy hurt and genuine distress as the old self-parody wells up in his eyes. "A fine person, a distinct *individual,* and we may never see her again. . . ."

When they first met years ago, Alyosha knew her as the wife of a prodigious drinker and philanderer nicely suited to his actor's job in Moscow's worst theater. She refused him. Later, the husband crashed his tinny Zaporozhets, beheading that night's darling and so rupturing his internal organs that his doctors predicted a single drink would kill. He never had that one—nor ever slept with any other woman except his wife. Smashing his face, the accident also totally changed his character.

His new appearance precluding any work on the stage, he turned to writing, quickly winning fame and fortune with screenplays and television scripts. With no time for anything else, he began to hate restaurants and carousing as he had once loved them, often turning acrimonious when distracted from his typewriter. His asceticism was too much for his wife, whose normal interest in occasionally seeing the town developed, under the pressure of his severity, into an appetite for affairs. She comes to the apartment to offer herself and curses—but also laughs—when Alyosha declines, turning the tables.

This is the evening we've put off for weeks, like schoolboys with term projects. Alyosha is home alone and I'm in the dormitory, each attending to neglected chores. Although my studies are past the point of salvaging, I must stay at my desk at least long enough to answer disquieted letters from my sponsors, a committee of high-principled scholars representing America's Soviet-studies establishment. Its letterhead and language stare at me like emissaries from another galaxy. Citing my failure to correspond with Harvard, the executive secretary has hinted at my recall in the absence of a satisfactory reply. To this task, I settle down at last, surprised and relieved at the tales of my nonexistent research that flow from my imagination to the letter paper—like the atmospheric hallucinations that prompted Gogol's fantasy?—and hopeful that ignorance, mysteriousness and the distance to Cambridge will keep secret my intellectual collapse.

His suspicion piqued by seeing me home at this hour, roommate Viktor peers at my table. In nothing is he so clumsy as trying to appear casual while scouting for "information"; but perceiving that I am writing in English, he desists with a grunt. Having exercised with his weights just long enough to spice the air with pungent sweat, he retires at his customary ten o'clock.

An hour later, Kemal summons me importantly to the telephone. It is Alyosha, protesting he is lonely, claiming he has something vital to tell me—and in a rush of enthusiasm, as if struck by a startling new idea, suggesting we find company for the "budding eventide." Although my emergency letters are unfinished, I agree to meet him outside my gate. Hearing his voice, I realize that the whole of my purpose in Russia has somehow come to simply spending time with him. More than spread legs or rompish escape, the lure is his boundless impulse to go somewhere, explore something, sniff out what's happening. Forgo this for books? Never has the distinction between life and graduate school learning been more clear-cut.

It is nearly midnight when the Volga pads toward me over the snow like an old mascot; we must go, therefore, to one of the main railway stations, the only public places alive at this hour. Alyosha steers seemingly by memory and instinct over a route of muffled streets, in defiance of the windshield's near obliteration by pelting flakes. (The wipers were stolen again yesterday afternoon while the car was parked outside a courthouse.) Soon we are approaching Young Communist Square, a huge former marketplace where three major stations serving trains to the vast steppes of the north, northeast and northwest, stand almost shoulder to shoulder.

From dawn to dusk, the square swarms with provincial visitors come to Moscow to change trains, search for warm underwear or a new tablecloth, make a deal for their home-raised ducks or gawk in reverence at Lenin's mausoleum. From the sidewalks around the stations, the throng spills into the even larger roadway, cardboard suitcases and sacks of provisions clutched in burly hands, rag-wrapped rations stuffed into pockets, prize purchases—mattresses, armchairs and bolts of carpet—balanced on their heads. Searching, soliciting, gesticulating, glowering, haggling, conspiratorially whispering ("Psst—where'd you come into them boots?"), the army of workers and peasants clamors and claws about its business: craving a bargain, yet morbidly suspicious of being cheated; knowing their only rest is on their own haunches—not one in ten thousand wastes time even looking for a cot in a hotel—and that this year's trip must cover everything, since next year they might not be lucky enough to return.

But at night, this rousing multitude is gone without a trace, leaving the Colosseum-like expanse almost deserted. Now the very emptiness exerts a grip, tightened by silent mist. Only haphazard clusters of taxis loiter outside exits, their exhausts rising in thick clouds past Yaroslav Station's Russian fairytale façade and Kazan Station's Tartar tower. In this air, the unmistakable presence of illicit transactions drifts like Claudius's ghost. The quilt-jacketed taxi drivers refuse ordinary passengers with a sneer: their game is pimping or peddling vodka from under their seats, and for this, they are willing to wait hours, ignoring their passenger-mile norms as well as the iron cold. A handful of prostitutes has also assembled at this outpost of night life: a hag in an open coat near the metro entrance, foully abusing a man who has declined her advances; others in the relative comfort of clammy underground passages linking the stations and metro. A scattering of drunks and hangers-on completes the roster of outdoor personages: remnants of Moscow's prewar underworld to which Alyosha is drawn by nostalgia and a penchant for the colorful. (I used to wonder why the police don't simply clean up the square once and for all. The answer seems to be that disreputable elements are rooted out less vigorously than political dissidents. For all the drunks, prostitutes, "parasites" and petty criminals exiled from Moscow and foreigners' eyes, a small devoted band—"Shrunken," laments Alyosha, "but no more than everything else in the economy"—remains, to steal nightly to one of the stations.)

At the fortress-like doors of the Leningrad Station, a policeman stands watch from within his tent of a sheepskin greatcoat, turning away (one important measure of a new drive to cut hooliganism and crime by controlling the waiting rooms' vagrant population) everyone without a train ticket valid for tomorrow. His face purplish with cold and ill temper, the officer observes the traditions of his service by snarling, "That's prohibited!" at anything that moves. While Alyosha waits—my face is more innocent than his, he insists—I sidle up to the law's bulk and initiate a conversation by commenting sympathetically about night duty in this weather. Soon he is telling me about his two-year-old daughter, the same flatulent face radiating fatherly love and sentimental humor. Even with this bellowing bully, the standard stratagem of establishing *personal* contact quickly transforms his public surliness into an open-hearted comradeship that has him sharing his misery with you, as he would his last ruble for a bottle if he could. Happy to have met "friends," grinning at his new pack of Camels, he opens the door for us, hinting a warning about plainclothesmen in the waiting room.

In the murkiness of the hall itself, however, detectives—if they are in fact there—cannot be distinguished from the rest of the depot-of-the-homeless assemblage. Foul-smelling peasants are asleep on the benches, faces cradled by their dusty bundles—which are also tied to their wrists to prevent theft. Impassive, submissive, ragged to their bones, they have been waiting days for a place on a train. Lacking friends to take them in and contacts among hotel personnel, less disheveled provincial town-dwellers too have settled in for the night. At the decrepit snack counter, a red-faced woman is dispensing the last of the pasty bologna together with a liquid called coffee. A child sighs in its sleep, another sucks noisily at a fierce-looking gypsy. Picking our way among this sampling of mostly non-Muscovite masses, we are transported back fifty years.

But the lure of vagabond adventure hangs in the air. Long rail journeys, as Koestler noticed, are Russia's social equivalent of transatlantic boat crossings. Dots of light and life in the roadless, oceanic land mass, trains are therefore the setting for much "shipboard" literature of strangers exposing secrets. And stations are only marginally less rich in dramatic possibilities. The time-machine holds a promise of unusual tales.

The female pickings themselves, our excuse for coming, are slimmer than average this evening. A handful of tawdry prostitutes with drunken gazes, cheeks smeared in lipstick and a layer of Vaseline—to simulate the Russian maiden's healthy flush. Certain disease. A sprinkling of teen-age saplings who would obviously be happier barefoot in their villages, together with several less bucolic provincial lasses—students waiting for telegrams with fare money—whose sleep we haven't the heart to disturb. Peasant wives too dumpy to merit this, even were their men not snoring on their boots. . . . Our choice—although it seems that she, not we, have made · it—is a thirtyish woman whose eyes have been following us hopefully while the rest of her remained slumped on a bench in the far corner.

"Hello, may we trouble you for a moment?"

"Please don't look at me like that. You must think I'm used to this, that I make a practice of using waiting rooms."

Her clothes are soiled and she needs—and craves—a bath. But back in the apartment, when Alyosha runs one for her with a heap of East German salts, she demurs. Are we laughing at her? Taking her for what she's not?

Locking the door, she remains in the bathroom almost an hour. After she has eaten and arranged her underwear on the radiator to dry, we make love—with half the passion and twice the conversation customary with railway recruits. Recalling old photographs of Colette, her rounded shoulders and globular bottom confirm that she is a survivor of an earlier era. Ample thighs resting, quiet joy on lips, Aksyona gives herself as if this were a respite between migraines. When she tells her story, we understand why.

Her mother was a survivor of a noble family destroyed by Revolution, Civil War and purges; her father, a Kiev baritone who recorded surging war songs, and whose need for drink, as colossal as his size, kept the family near starvation despite his handsome earnings. Aksyona was seven when her self-sacrificing mother died of cancer and her father, after stupendous bouts with vodka, disappeared in grief and rage, bearing away the last of his wife's heirlooms. The upbringing of the bewildered child was taken over by a sister who had turned sixteen and supported them both, largely on bread and drippings, by leaving school for a job in a shoe factory. For reasons of her own, the sister refused to ask for police help in tracing her father, or for a kopek of state aid.

When Aksyona herself was sixteen, an elderly aunt wrote from out of the blue that their father was working on a collective farm north of Kazan. From that city, the daughters took a bus to the end of the line and thumbed a ride on the back of a truck. Falling out at a bend, the elder sister hit her head on a rock, suffered massive hemorrhaging and died, blood streaming from her mouth. The truck continued to the farm, but the former leading baritone, now a senile handyman with a speech impediment, did not recognize his younger daughter. After a shivering hour with him, she returned to Kiev alone.

And remained alone so long that she accepted spinsterhood and reclusion; she seemed made for schoolteaching. But after a dozen years of solitude she fell in love with a sixteen-year-old pupil in one of her classes. Their after-school trysts took place in her room—the same one, with the piano still smashed by her father's hand and cupboards peddled for his drink, where she had lived as a child. The strange, devoted couple were married when he was seventeen. Well before this, she had been disqualified from teaching.

When sexual drive subsided, shared comfort as pariahs held them together against callous attempts to pry them apart by police, Party supervisors and scandalized social workers. They lived carefully and quietly on the youth's salary as an apprentice librarian until a week ago, when he left her for a homosexual editor in Leningrad. In numb despair, she boarded a train for Moscow, not knowing what she was seeking there to save her. But the capital was frighteningly puzzling; she found herself bewildered by questions of why buses ran on streets and trains on tracks. From the Kiev Station where she arrived, she ventured out only to others, staying one night in each to avoid suspicion. When we met in the Leningrad Station, she had twenty-one kopeks in her handbag and nothing in her stomach for three days except scraps from a kindly counterwoman at one of the buffets. Aksyona recounts her searing misfortunes as if they belong to a distant past. She has a grip on herself now, she asserts. Her strange marriage could not reasonably have lasted much longer; she's still young enough to start a new, realistic life. Meeting us has broken her enervating depression.

"I'll only stay a few days if you'll have me. You won't turn me out?"

"Relax, Teach," says Alyosha. "This is like the army, we don't bump nobody. Certainly not pedigreed ladies. . . . We seem to be clean out of handkerchiefs, so just use the sheet."

To soothe her, Alyosha muses about the etymology of "linen." Aksyona is in fact using the pillowcase for her tears, but soon reaches to us for more affection. Happy all night, she turns positively cheerful during morning ablutions. For a better breakfast, Alyosha and I go to the bakery—and return in ten minutes to an empty apartment! Aksyona has left no note; ten rubles from my jacket and Alyosha's new cigarette lighter are missing.

Alyosha is inured to girls stealing sweaters and toilet water from his room, just as he cleans up overindulgent young ones' vomit with the mien of a mother attending to diapers. Although such inconveniences are ordinarily part of the price, Aksyona's betrayal hurts. Was she a vagabond thief, like many waiting-room pickups? A novice prostitute who lost her nerve to ask for a fee? Alyosha, who has heard a thousand equally moving stories from con girls, as well as from genuine unfortunates, at first insists it is one or the other, and that we waste no time thinking about a clever little trick who can well look after herself. But the morning fails to erase thoughts of her possible suicide.

We spend the afternoon and two successive evenings searching Moscow's dozen stations. At the same time, Alyosha asks the chief prosecutor of a city district—whom he tells that Aksyona has been left an inheritance, to save her trouble in case she's found—to inquire whether news of her has reached the police. That no one has seen her allows us to reckon she's found a man or made her way home to Kiev. Although this is not our first encounter with such tragedy, we feel depressed, and have no wish for railroad action for some time.

Tuesday afternoon with one of Alyosha's old friends, a stolid engineer called Edik. The apartment belongs to Edik's father, a mathematician engaged in high defense work. (Edik's ease in skipping work every third afternoon is attributed variously to the protection afforded by his important sire and the poverty of his own efforts at the drafting table.) A hundred yards from the Supreme Court of the Russian Republic, the quarters are suitably grand for a man of his stature; four large rooms in a high-ceilinged building that could pass in a residéntial district of nineteenth-century Prague. From the living-room window, a tip of the Kremlin is visible, its fortress wall impinging on our lives like a prison on the outskirts of a college town.

The apartment is a museum of low-grade Victoriana, so quintessentially shabby-genteel that the very concept might have originated here. All the rooms like this I've seen and the spirit they represent flood my memory. Tasseled lampshades, age stains and light-bulb browns dappling the sallow silk. Sagging arm-chairs that discharge heavy puffs at a touch, a broken grand-father clock, and threadbare oriental rugs, long dead of dust and thirst. All this and more—including the inevitable aspidistra, as if transferred from some defunct ministry—pressing in on the oversized, overstuffed divan where we are taking our pleasure with Voluptuous Valya, and Lyuba, her thinner, harder friend. Lyuba (from *lyubov*—"love") is one of the few girls I've met who can be called sexually voracious, but our nakedness is so cartoon-like in contrast to the bedizened room that we can't take her more seriously than ourselves.

A week's dirty dishes and leavings are stacked in every corner: Edik's housekeeper is sick and his father away on a project. (I suspect rockets but, of course, do not ask.) His tape recorder has been lent to a friend and the shortwave bands on his radio need new tubes; *faute de mieux*, therefore, Radio Moscow provides the background noise. While we squirm, pant and change partners, the announcer soars on in his go-team-go voice about a cement factory that has voluntarily raised its own quotas for this, the crucial second year of the historic new Five-Year Plan. But no one laughs at the program's wild incongruity: no one else has heard it. Nor would they notice even a declaration of war announced in those tones and these circumstances.

We are drinking ,a cocktail of gluey apricot nectar and medicinal spirit, which is almost pure alcohol. Although Edik swallows his straight from the jar, he takes no part in the communal sport, for he is wrestling with an individual problem: headlights he left on all night have irreversibly finished the battery of his father's car. From the edge of a chair facing the divan, he telephones one hot tip after another in search of a replacement—*any* battery, new or used, for trucks, buses or cars. Absorption in his quest blinds him to Valya's vulva wriggling ten inches from his nose.

"Edik, old pal, drop that a minute and give us, as they say, a hand."

"Are you kidding? My father's back tomorrow. Christ, Alexei —help me juice up that vehicle."

Lyuba borrows the telephone for a quick call to a girl friend. From the lend-lease gasoline canister in which the spirit is stored, Alyosha pours another round of drinks. Voluptuous Valya plants her six feet of Amazon flesh directly over Edik, the warmth of her parted legs—or his anxiety about the car—steaming his spectacles. He gulps his fifth inch of straight spirit and racks his brain for another contact to telephone. Wolfing a slice of bologna, Lyuba pulls us back onto the divan. The Kremlin bells record the passage of another hour in our under-their-noses hideout.

At five o'clock, the festivities end as if a factory whistle has sounded. Hurry-scurry, we dress and dash from the apartment, each to attend to his own, suddenly urgent business. Having clinched a deal for his battery, Edik searches anxiously for a taxi to claim possession of the used twelve-volter before a bigger bribe takes it elsewhere. After two consecutive days with us, Valya must rush home to make supper for her "jealous" husband. (But he's going to a Komsomol meeting afterwards, and she suggests we all meet again at nine o'clock.) Lyuba—who, it seems, is moody when clothed—is already late for her factory's second shift.

"Who says we're not a work-disciplined people with higher goals?" chirps Alyosha, enjoying our jerky haste after the squandered day. While he delivers the girls to their destinations, I hurry to the National Hotel for talk of Soviet legal trends with a visiting Columbia professor.

"Do svidaniya, gents. Stay healthy."

"So long, *privet.*"

"You'll stay in touch?"

"Of course! What's on for Sunday?"

We disperse into the afternoon darkness, then the slogging rush-hour crush. At this hour, the city center swarms with dark-coated robots with shopping bags, bunching up at traffic lights, crisscrossing in and out of shops, pushing to their destinations like beetles in a box. The sounds are trolleys whining and ten thousand booted feet tramping in the slush.

My own route takes me down the Twenty-fifth of October Street, past GUM's dingy posterior to the top of Red Square. In this homey district of once-thriving retail trade, the restrictions on commercial activity have left a hollow melancholy, matching the weather's. Above the unsmiling crowds, buzzing strands of neon starkly announce "Milk" and "Bread." Plaster busts of Lenin guard every office-entrance, like the motionless sentries at His mausoleum. Everything is submerged in the gloom I felt when my friends and I could think of nothing to do with ourselves on winter afternoons after school.

Several minutes early for my appointment, I linger outside the Historical Museum, wondering what connection might possibly exist between this bleakness and the lush hours we relished in Edik's apartment. Outdoors, not so much as an advertisement dresses the stores; not a single bikinied form enlivens kiosks plastered with political magazines and Central Committee brochures. The whole of the puritanical public setting seems like camouflage for our dissipation.

Walking the somber streets, shivering in the blank cold, I'm struck again and again by this paradox of nature. How did these Tahitian attitudes take root here?"

The next time we meet Lyuba, it is in her family's musty room in a communal apartment where they all live, as if in a fourth-class *pensione.* (Both parents work until late afternoon.) Edik has joined us again, but this time I'm the one who is taking no part, except for holding Lyuba's breasts. Prohibition from anything more is my "measure of social correction" for making us a girl short by allowing Blondie Bella to wander away from the car while the others were shopping for provisions on the way to Lyuba's. More excited than ever by my enforced frustration, Lyuba takes wholly seriously someone's playful proposal that I be pardoned after an hour.

The next time we meet Voluptuous Valya, it is the afternoon when Alyosha is the duty lawyer in his Juridical Consultation Office. At last the enterprise has moved to its new quarters in a sloppily renovated apartment house, of which the pride of office fashion and convenience are half a dozen consulting rooms instead of the old premises' toilet-sized cubicles. Here counselors can meet their clients in private—even, should they desire, behind a locked door. Checking in at the office, Alyosha takes the key to one of these tiny new chambers from the matronly secretary, and with a flourish, invites Valya and me inside. The key is turned, a bottle swigged at, a moment taken to recount recent events. Then Valya undresses and climbs on the desk.

Fucking in a Soviet office? With telephones ringing, clients arriving and the Chairman—a Party man of course—giving advice in the corridor outside? Yes, but it's with Alyosha, who knows when to practice the unheard-of. On this quiet afternoon, he judges, our room won't be needed, we'll remain undisturbed.

It's not for nothing that he served on the committee to expedite the three-year renovation. The chambers are smaller than he wanted, and positioning is tricky on the cheap little desk. But Valya is experienced, having first favored him precisely here, after he stopped her on the sidewalk outside. In any case, she will not tolerate the "indignity" of using the floor.

I wonder whether his elderly secretary knows why Alyosha asks for the key. Surely his reputation suggests why young ladies flocked to him for private consultations after the move to the new office. When we leave she wears a knowing expression. Yet her fondness for Alexei Evgenievich, Alyosha's office name, helps protect him. He is the man who arranged for her husband's admission to an excellent cancer clinic—which cured him—and whose gifts of chocolates on holidays and occasional daffodils brighten her life.

The next morning, we meet when the sun has finally established full-fledged day and are joined by an old friend of

Edik's who, on rake-offs from the dental laboratory he supervises, dresses like a Midwestern college professor. (Alyosha claims he has perfected another first for Soviet dentistry: extracting bad teeth through the anus. "It's a great new technique for people who can't open their mouths.") The entire day lies before us to fritter away, and despite our failure to accomplish anything in life—despite everything that keeps us down enough to be grateful for small favors—we are wrapped in an idler's sense of luxury. Lolling in this, Edik's friend says it first: *"Kovo ebat budyem?"*—not "Whaddya wanna do tonight, Marty?" but "Who are we going to fuck?"

It is always said with an element of parody, this private motto: a mocking of the girls who will submit after feeble excuses; of ourselves for our self-indulgence and abdication from more constructive interests; of the system that demeans values and trivializes existence, reducing us to this childishness. *Kovo ebat budyem?* expresses the futility of striving for noble goals—and our relief from the need for such exertion.

We saunter to the car and drive around, searching for a leash for the new boxer of Edik's friend. (Although there is apparently a pet shop somewhere that sells them, he will not humiliate his animal by making her wear an item of Soviet manufacture, and is willing to pay the outrageous price for a secondhand Western one.) But when he repeats the motto after lunch, it has a more straightforward ring: unable to get free every day, he's concerned lest this afternoon not produce the planned consummation. Reassuring him playfully, Alyosha makes some calls and we pick up our girls as they leave work in the Ministry of Light Industry. Somehow the day was richer before they appeared.

Her body is the socialist-realist statue of "Woman Exercising" in every park; her face, a film poster of a kerchiefed milkmaid. In fact, she is the daughter of Moscow factory hands who herself worked for a year in a rubber plant after high school. Then she studied theatrical makeup and was expelled for truancy. At a second institute, she tried industrial design, quickly leaving of her own will. Next was a language school, where she hung on long enough to acquire a household serf's command of French. She applied for a job with Aeroflot.

A smitten personnel man gave her the job despite her repulse in a taxi. Soon she was earning as much as her parents.

When promoted to international service, she started, according to custom, with the "democratic" countries. It was a nice break: raincoats bought in Prague and sweaters in Warsaw considerably enhanced her style—and her income, when items were re-peddled to eager friends. Now she aspired to work Western routes. On capitalist territory, Embassy and KGB officers watched their own almost as closely as enemy agents; during the two-hour London turnaround, she had heard, no one could leave the plane alone. But there was always the occasional bad-weather layover with its openings for shopping and sightseeing. The prestige alone of Western travel warranted the added straight-and-narrow demands, and although her looks militated against her now—to lower the possibility of defection, Aeroflot assigned its least prepossessing staff for capitalist routes—her proletarian background was strong recommendation. She was careful to dress plainly and talk "patriotic" with the political types.

But her best friend, also a stewardess, married a Frenchman and settled in Paris; and she was soon summoned by the KGB. "We're not *prohibiting* you from writing to her, but not recommending it. Don't ruin your career. You know what we mean."

She did, of course, but decided to answer through a third stewardess whom she thought she could trust. A week later, she was back on domestic routes, where a pretext was found to cut her salary. Thus began her sharp decline in mental energy as well as in work. Now she is a substitute stewardess, called on principally in emergencies. Her wardrobe is ragged; she spends her afternoons at the movies or eating ice cream with girl friends.

Underlying everything is her placid resignation. She tells her story without a trace of resentment toward Aeroflot or the KGB—or, of course, her lucky friend in Paris. Blows of state are like the acts of nature her parents and grandparents endured.

But to bed again. She gives her plastercast body with good-humored warmth—but why get overly worked up about *this* either? When she leaves, it is to meet her former husband, who divorced her for a girl who flies to Cuba.

Alyosha and I grow fonder of wandering at night, when the whole sleeping city is ours, providing as much stimulation as Cannes or Nice for our game of playing tourist. We are silent for hours, conscious of something scratching in our relationship, like chicks inside shells. We will not be able to separate easily after my year will be up. What began as a good-time lark has developed according to its own laws.

"Gimme a cigarette," he says, informing me with his inflection that he too is thinking these thoughts.

"Gimme a left turn on Petrovka Street, and easy past the you-know-what."

Turning the corner, we almost hit two cars that have apparently crashed into each other minutes before. One contains a small boy with a gory face and a woman wailing about what had possessed her to drive him home at this hour. Because the damaged cars must not be moved until the police arrive, we rush mother and son to a nearby clinic, then cruise for another hour, hardly talking.

But the boy's wounds have somehow introduced yet another element to our relationship, and Alyosha begins reminiscing about his military service, the period that has long intrigued me. The link is blood, but I press him to begin at the beginning. . . .

He was first inducted during the shock of the Finnish campaign in 1939. A foul-mouthed orphan of seventeen whose world was poker, fistfights and occasional errands for shysters on Moscow's toughest streets, he half-welcomed his induction as a break with this aimlessness and as a possible opportunity to acquire the profession he already sensed he needed. Together with the last of his innocence, this notion disappeared within a week.

Basic training was brief, penal and brutish. And insanely inadequate; although cursed by bellowing officers, whose opacity he could hardly believe after the slyness of his card-playing mentors, Private Aksyonov did not fire a single round of live ammunition during his training. Thus prepared—and similarly equipped: one of his two changes of underwear was reclaimed as the camp's shortages grew more severe—the new infantryman was shipped directly to the Karelian Front, an army group assigned to cut Finland in half at its waist. He arrived in early January, 1940, the nadir of the war.

Only the enormity of Russian disasters preceding and following the Winter War can explain why its suffering has been largely forgotten. The few soldiers who survived both the northern Finnish slaughter and Stalingrad actually preferred the latter: less hunger and irreversible chaos; more hope, at least, for survival. The day after arriving, Alyosha, who still knew ludicrously little about his rifle, understood that something was horrendously wrong. Compared to the fighting army's confusion, mindlessness and paralysis (fostered by decimation of the general staff and field officer ranks in purges completed the previous year), basic training seemed almost quaint in retrospect. In the field, muzhiks with nothing but fatalism and dumb political faith—the backbone of the new Stalinist army—wore the boots of Russia's executed officers. And they were frightened rigid as well as ignorant: after the purges, guessing wrong on the simplest decision might lead to unmasking as a saboteur. Initiative was more feared than the Finns; staff and field officers cringed in mutual suspicion; on the front line, even tactical withdrawals—another quick route to a firing squad for "defeatism"—were beyond consideration. "In a sense, muddle is endemic to this country and has a comic element, but this one was beyond description and very sad. No one knew anything; nothing worked."

The fighting took place three hundred miles below the Arctic Circle, in the coldest winter ever recorded there. Alyosha's unit was woefully undersupplied, even with winter overcoats. Their opposites in almost everything, the Finns had superb snow parkas and rifles with German telescopic sights. From steel pillboxes and skillfully camouflaged positions in the overlooking hills, they methodically picked off their targets; it was documented that one rifleman dispatched over a thousand individual Soviet troops. Khaki bull's-eyes against the snow, the Russians crouched as ordered, awaiting bullets in their stomachs. In the first five days, two thirds of Alyosha's company, including the uncomplaining lads to his left and right, got theirs. Clutching their wounds, they sank quietly to their knees as if commanded by higher will.

"This was literally a massacre of the innocents; few of the boys had had enough knowledge or joy from life to feel sorry for themselves about leaving it. Their problem was limited to whether to take an overcoat from a dead body, which would help with the cold but also make them cleaner targets. Most simply waited their turn, wondering only whether a canteen might appear so there'd be some hot soup first."

Before his own turn could come, Alyosha was dispatched on a reconnaissance patrol. A pair of binoculars was found and reluctantly entrusted to his sergeant. When he was shot an hour later, the glasses passed to one of the two other privates sharing the mission. When they were both killed, Alyosha snatched them and ran. A sudden, violent snowstorm engulfed him; profoundly exhausted and hopelessly lost in the white vastness—divisional headquarters had refused to give the sergeant a proper map of the region because he was not entitled to such security information—he was grateful to the numbing cold for helping prepare a peaceful death. At dawn the following morning, he was still alive. The snowfall having eased, he was able to use the binoculars, and put them to his eyes to amuse himself in his final hours. There was no point walking, even if he had had the strength. Without a map, one mute hill was like all the others, and a small valley in the distance might as well have been on the moon.

(Hearing how the humble sergeant had entreated for a map, I suddenly understand Alyosha's fixation for always knowing his precise location. Of everything for which he mocks Soviet rule, only his grievance over the perpetual shortage of road maps crosses the line from irony into rancor. Even the few available, he curses, are deliberately falsified: roads, bridges, and railways are moved out of true position; university cartographists are among those denied the "secret information" of accurate data. The purpose is to confuse enemy rockets and bombers—futile nonsense, he says, in the age of satellite mapping, whereas the dupe's real victims, as always, are the Russian people. "A million ditch diggers tunneling a few yards off, twenty million drivers taking wrong turns—or getting run over as they get out of their cabs and stand on the asphalt scratching their heads over the puzzle of some heterotypic road. . . . Fishing boats have been lost, hikers actually *frozen to death* because a stream meanders right instead of left. That sums it up, *muchacho:* the Pentagon knows every hayshed's position while we all grope around, trying to dope out what belongs where in our brave new world." But despite this, Alyosha saves every map he sees; the apartment is full of them.)

The fading private played aimlessly with the binoculars. Suddenly he held his breath. Through the frosty lenses, he distinguished a large Soviet force, seemingly an armored division, straddling the road of that distant valley. Before his system could fully respond to the joy of rescue, he made out several figures. Incredulous, he dragged himself closer. Hundreds of soldiers were frozen literally stiff beside tanks and field guns. The scene's ghoulishness was doubled by his beholding it alone in the whole white world. Rifles clutched by arms frozen outstretched; mouths opened in shouts and snorts, even conversational grins, as if flesh had instantaneously turned to stone. (Like monuments too, the black faces were heavily dusted with last night's snow.) Dozens of men had been praying; one officer held his cap in his teeth. But most were on their backs with limbs stretched skyward, like horses in rigor mortis. Shrieking, seventeen-year-old Alyosha established that nothing moved.

He ran again. Instinct ordered him not to die like this. But even if it weren't starting to snow again, even if he could do no more without snowshoes than thrash about like a doomed man, he had no more idea of which direction to take than of whether last year was a good one for Burgundy. It was remarkable that his wobbly circling led anywhere at all. Somehow it did; and extracting the last calorie of his extraordinary endurance, he stumbled back to his camp.

Somehow too, he remembered that it was to reconnoiter that he had been sent out the day before, and he conjured up a few more minutes of strength to report the spectacle of the lost division to his lieutenant—who led him to headquarters to repeat the story. A major with a beetle's face listened without comment, and told Alyosha that for one more word about his "subversive rumor" to anyone, he would be shot.

Suddenly everything was clear about his obligations to himself and to society. In those thirty-three hours, he shed his tough-guy affectations and became not just an adult, but roughly the kind he was to remain: cynical and cunning, a master manipulator of the system. Deciding that he wanted to live, he simultaneously recognized that the principles of Soviet rule made this synonymous with living cunningly and *well*. Honest men were peons or cannon fodder; there was no third choice.

The following morning, he launched his *personal* war of survival. By evening he'd wangled the job of headquarters messenger, a few hundred splendorous yards from the front. An intelligence perceived as exceptional in comparison to his fellow peasant-soldiers won him rapid advancement to divisional postman: opportunity to inch farther away from the carnage. Here too his ability to memorize names (training for the girls?) and to remember a few consecutive sentences—above all, his facility with pencil and paper—made itself known, and his next promotion was to divisional clerk. But his recognition of the obtuseness and rigidity of men in command was more important than all his quick learning of army forms and procedures. Because divisional officers struggled to formulate simple sentences without errors, he was increasingly called upon to draft their dispatches. His own disillusionment and cynicism now absolute, he made the stunning discovery that his superiors still thought in the language of patriotism, duty, belief in authority. His salvation lay in that very obtuseness, which would keep them from suspecting his scheming.

The next promotion made him ghost-writer of the divisional wall-newspaper for the Party commissar: as the soldiers continued to slog forward to be chopped down, Alyosha composed the necessary paeans to the Marxist-Leninist-Stalinist leadership inspiring their glorious victories. (In the end, twelve of his company's one hundred and eighty enlisted men survived, four without permanent injury.) When the political commissar was killed, Alyosha was temporarily entrusted with the additional duty of censor, one of the lapses—since Alyosha was non-Party— for which the officer responsible was subsequently executed.

Although relatively safe from snipers' bullets and entitled to hope that his wits might see him through, Alyosha's single interest was to get as far away from Finland as fast as he could. "War and obligations to History, defending the sacred Motherland and world Communist cause—such noble instincts can impair your health." Although he wanted nothing less on earth—except to remain near the front—than to become an officer of the Army of Workers and Peasants, this, he discovered through his access to secret circulars in headquarters, was his sole escape. He applied for officer's training, was quickly accepted, and feigned modesty at his commanders' gratification that a local boy should hear the call to higher duty—simultaneously pretending to be full of regret over leaving the front while socialism's treacherous enemies still breathed life.

It was now late February. Packed with limbless and lice-ridden soldiers, Alyosha's railroad car resembled tsarist convict wagons before Alexander II's nineteenth-century reforms; but as it struggled—south!—down the single track, he kissed its clammy wall.

The officers' training school was located in a dismal base in the western Ukraine. His arrival there having served its purpose, his goals altered accordingly: at all costs, he now had to *avoid* becoming an officer—that disastrous prospect, with years of obligatory service—and, if possible, part company forever with army life. His plan was to demonstrate himself as manifestly unfit for a commission: as incompetent as zealous. This seemingly sensible scheme was foiled by an underestimation of the army's sorry condition and extreme need. Desperate for recruits, the school accepted for training "everyone who had four limbs and could remember his birthday."

"Once in, you didn't get out. Each new body was a prize; only outright spastics were rejected. Even the hack doctors were surprised at some of the types. And you had to be a genius to flunk the so-called entrance tests."

Industrious and conscientious as in no school exam, Alyosha worked two dozen eye-popping grammatical errors into the single-page composition designed to test knowledge of the Russian language. The unreadable narrative was marked "B." During the ensuing physical exam, he managed to fall over a chair and to collide with the senior doctor—Act One in his mime of appearing virtually blind. Under his breath, he admitted to a medical corpsman that his vision was blurry beyond ten meters and headaches had tormented him since childhood. He was pronounced fit for combat.

When the course began, Alyosha became anxious. Rejecting a

plan to stutter in favor of continuing the eye gambit, he was unable, however, to attract anyone's interest in his seeming disability, even though it kept him from properly making up his cot. "So help me, I couldn't stand out. Some of my colleagues couldn't cope with the *principle* of bed-making." Only after weeks of scrupulous and sometimes painful melodrama—crashing into doors, plummeting into trenches—was he given his chance to botch a re-examination of his eyes one afternoon while a painful sprain was being dressed. Finally, grudgingly, he was pronounced unfit, and during weeks of cleaning horrendous latrines, impatiently awaited his orders. Would he be assigned to clerical duty? Discharged from the Army entirely? Good God no, he was ordered to return to his unit—back, that is, to the Karelian front.

"Finland, by Jesus. *Back to the slaughter!* I had to puncture the ploy, of course. I waylaid the doctor and told him a wondrous whack on the head by my drill corporal's rifle had restored me to perfect vision. Oozing compliments about my patriotism, he considered that the circumstances excused this transparent lie: I'd flunked the eye test so badly that there was no sense even trying me again. Do you know the Russian saying about wit generating woe?"

As the train rolled north this time, Alyosha brooded while earnest green soldiers in his wagon broke into song about Stalin's wisdom providing fearlessness in battle. By now, his old divisional commanders were probably killed or executed; he'd have to start as a foot soldier at the front again, a lamb awaiting sacrifice at the altars of officers' incompetence and terror. When the train approached Moscow, where he was to change, it occurred to him to write a last postcard to the aunt who had helped raise him.

Stepping from the Kiev Station into Moscow's now dear streets, he thought better of his idea: why not visit auntie in person? Indeed, why not take a short holiday in the capital of world socialism before proceeding north to die for the great cause itself? Living hand-to-mouth among his Damon Runyon friends, he stayed two months in the relatively-undisturbed-by-war city. By this time, the spring flowers were in full bloom and a peace treaty had been signed. Wangling his way onto a train, he returned to his unit, which was now guarding the newly expanded frontier. Six weeks later, he was demobilized. As he had foreseen, his papers were lost in the bureaucratic farrago and never arrived from the officers' training school; traveling alone, he was lost cargo. No one knew or cared about his Moscow detour.

A civilian again, he was back in the capital by June—to become, while pondering possible professions, a poker player, school janitor, truck driver and warehouse watchman. He had discovered literature and was reading widely in the Russian classics, but his musings about writing himself were always quashed by the recollection that nothing about the Moscow he knew and loved—and cherished more than ever after his experience of Karelia—could be penned; like everyone else's, his material would have to be hosannas to socialism and Stalin. Recognizing the agility of his hands, he considered training for surgery. Meanwhile, the eighteen-year-old continued to drift and observe, not hurrying to make up his mind.

The resumption of war made it up for him. Six weeks after the German invasion, Alyosha was called up again—but his bones balked. The accumulation of agitprop lectures about "Finnish aggression" which he had endured as a soldier generated a suspicion that the current line about the treacherous Nazi invader was similar propagandistic perversion. The more strident the broadcasts about "everyone's sacred duty to battle the fascist foe with his bare teeth," the stronger his conviction that Stalin and Hitler were somehow in league, and that this war—perhaps any war—was not his.

Among his reprobate acquaintances was a certain Abram Aronberg, known to friends as Abrasha Abramchik and celebrated by them as one of Moscow's cleverest raconteurs and most adroit cardsharps. An "underground" tailor of great girth, undersized hands and an appearance decades older than his thirty-odd years, he was in a relatively jovial mood that summer because a host of physical impairments, from severe boils on his neck to feet painfully inadequate to cope with his weight, had earned him one of the highest categories of unfitness for military service. The lucky man—who was to die of food poisoning that autumn—tried to lift Alyosha from his draft-notice depression by agreeing to present himself as Aksyonov at the latter's induction physical. Both surmised that the disastrous military situation had aggravated the Army's bureaucratic muddle. Abrasha Abramchik's shrewd gambling sense assessed their ruse an odds-on bet to work.

But Alyosha again ran afoul of the Army's unpredictable standards. Although Aronberg was indeed accepted as Aksyonov—no one questioned the hastily forged identity papers they'd bought—the physical wreck was pronounced fit for combat and ordered to report for induction almost immediately.

"To his own horror, he flunked for me—that is to say, he actually *passed*. Poor Abrasha couldn't hold his cards steady. He wouldn't even eat. He was terrified he'd pass muster on his own examination next time around."

When sober the following morning, Alyosha dispatched an irate letter to his examining board, protesting that a deplorable error by the induction clinic had confused him with another draftee. It was a venture that few Russians would have risked, even if genuine victims of such a mistake. But Alyosha had guessed shrewdly again. And when directed to report for a second physical, he fell back on his tried success with eyes, this time choosing a weasel of a pickpocket for his surrogate—who, when his heavily besmudged eyeglasses were removed, had to be told that the chalky blur on the wall was the chart. This fine fellow failed admirably for Alyosha, affording him respite until the next call.

Meanwhile, the Wehrmacht was closing in fast on Moscow, whose bomb damage and ominous rumors—radio sets having been confiscated—"rather less than compensated for panic and food shortages." In early November, Alyosha joined thousands of citizens similarly impressed, digging antitank trenches on the city's western approaches. That evening, he visited a library to contemplate a map of his native land; he had decided on a quick self-evacuation. "Was it Lenin who coined the phrase about discretion and valor? Besides, there was talk that Stalin himself had snaked out of town. I chose not to insinuate I was braver than he."

Since only the south promised both distance from the advancing Germans and a hospitable climate, Alyosha's choice of haven seemed to make itself. Walking, hitchhiking and riding the rails of guarded, war-packed trains, he made his way to the Black Sea coast, settling, for no particular reason, in the sleepy Georgian town of Sukhumi, where asses outnumbered cars on the packed-dirt streets. Although hardly a gay resort even by Soviet standards, Sukhumi enchanted Alyosha even beyond a venturous young man's first discovery of the seaside. He fell in love with the sun, palms and evening air's scent of dissipation; he learned to swim great distances and to carry himself among the clannish Georgians. For work, he was hired as a handyman by the local dramatic theater, a pretentious palace on the central promenade with more columns on its façade than productions in its repertoire. As the theater's personnel were drafted one by one, he was propelled up the slender hierarchy, becoming an actor and ending with appearances in major supporting roles. By this time he was also a star in the town's scanty society, to which he brought energy as an organizer of parties as well as linguistic amusement. The summer heat seemed to swell rather than deplete his strength. He had always been unusually robust; now he became the very picture of tropical health. He had a quiet love affair with a tender Russian girl who sewed him shirts and trousers. It was the best year of his life.

But by the end of it, the Germans had reached the Caucasus, from which they threatened the entire coast. Knowing he'd be drafted again sooner or later, Alyosha staged a week of parties and "gave myself up." Although this was less an expression of patriotism than restlessness, he had begun to believe that fascism must really be stopped. For some reason (he did not yet suspect that his never-seen father might have been Jewish), Russian anti-Semitism disgusted him, and by this measure, the Germans were probably that much worse.

Although he spent two years at the front, the record of his service itself was less interesting, because more commonplace, than his long avoidance of it. He spurned the commission his Sukhumi friends offered to arrange, preferring a soldier's dismal rations and serflike treatment to an officer's obligatory hypocrisy and troubled conscience. First a cavalryman, later a mechanic, he was finally transferred to tanks, in which he fought in the great battle at Kursk—which weakened the Wehrmacht more than Stalingrad had—and across the Ukraine, through Poland

and into central Germany: a thousand-mile, village-by-village slog including some of the hardest fighting in the history of warfare. "Our invincible-armed-might-of-the-Soviet-Motherland films have it right—except that those prebattle 'hurrahs' from us were actually for an issue of a few grams of vodka or a lick of jam. Believe me, we were too scared, exhausted and wary of our own officers for any unauthorized exuberance."

(His early months in the cavalry reinforced his obsession with cartography. When he overheard staff officers ordering company commanders to capture Wehrmacht maps as the first step in counterattacks, the symbolism of Russia's condition which this suggested now stung him less than the universal acceptance of absurdity as a guide to action. Apologizing for nothing, leaders behaved—with officers whose lives were at stake—as if the need to steal information about one's own country from the enemy were utterly normal. "No one questioned it. Even mentioned it in passing. Communism hasn't turned this land of ours surrealistic; it's the monkeyshine of a whole, mute people pretending—or believing!—that black is white.")

Although wounded twice by enemy fire and once, severely, by the crash of a Soviet fighter beside his tank, he was never again subjected to the stark horror of the Finnish campaign. Indeed, the war ended with an episode which Alyosha saw as a kind of reversal of the first satanic weeks in Karelia. In the euphoric days after the Allies' historic meeting at the Elbe, a contingent of American soldiers crossed the Soviet lines for celebrations with hand-picked politically rock-solid Russians who would uphold the Party line while making merry. From a safe distance behind a row of potato sacks, Alyosha stared at the first Westerners he could remember seeing in person. More than their informality—open-necked uniforms, jokes and drinks swapped with officers—he was fascinated by what their gestures revealed about their state of mind. The GIs were loose, happy, *unafraid.* One glance established that they knew nothing of commissars and Marxist-Leninist chants, witch-doctor myths and inexplicable prohibitions—of everything that, in trying to account for and remedy clumpish hardships, only made them worse. These were children of the land where he belonged!

Overcome by a divination that the calling for which he had

been waiting had arrived, Alyosha began to sweat. He knew he must escape. The vision of himself sprinting to the Americans (somehow expanding on "the man I love . . . kiss me again, my darling . . . Pennsylvania, five, five thousand"—the sum and substance of his English vocabulary) repeated itself so vividly in his mind that his fingernails pierced the muddy potatoes. And remained there well after the Americans were led away to the entertainment.

Aware that he had cheated his destiny, he returned to the sacks the next morning as though on a voyage to his birthplace. The mistake of his citizenship *could* have been rectified; he *should* have shifted to the world suited to his reflexes and temperament, where he'd have devoted himself to son.ething real.

"I was twenty-three then," Alyosha says quietly. "I had energy. Do you think I'd have made a go of it in the West?"

"How on earth did you expect to get out?" I play the straight man. "The GIs would have handed you straight back to your officers. They understood nothing. Anyway, they'd have had no choice."

Alyosha's expression reveals that he has always known this, and hoped not to. "Do you think I'd have made a life for myself in America? I always wanted to see the Rio Grande. . . . I might have been able to do something in films."

"Mother Volga beats the Rio Grande, in case you still want to go romantic. No, I see you a bit further north in California. A playboy-producer of television trash—filthy rich and despicable. You virtuous types turn shamefully crass on exposure to real action."

Pleased at my image, Alyosha grins and takes a moment to contemplate himself driving a convertible in the Hollywood he knows by way of Hollywood. "Yeah—but over there you have to work. All those plush-office millionaires, and so pressurized, so nervous. It's true, isn't it, *muchacho?* You and I together, we've got more of what they're really scrambling for than the lot combined. . . . I'd have flopped in America: no ambition, no real drive."

I do not state the obvious: that Alyosha's enormous drive would surely have been channeled and he could not have helped but make something unusual of himself. Nor do I say that I shall never visit anywhere beautiful or exciting in the West without thinking of him. Two years ago, his application for a holiday tour on the Bulgarian Black Sea coast was rejected; now he's working on a scheme to visit Prague, but his friendship with me has probably killed forever all chances of any foreign travel. About a trip to America, we do not even fantasize.

"That's what I like about you, Yank," he drawls to dispel the melancholy. "The moment I laid eyes on you, I knew *you* were no millionaire. With an extra ten years you could pass for one of those Elbe GIs with . . . er, the common physiognomical touch."

He throws his arm around me and laughs the laugh of our friendship. He has driven me home during his narrative, parking outside the deserted University. We get out together and walk to the gate. But as always, we make our way back to the car, then stroll up and back around the iron fence, aimlessly turning over tomorrow's avowedly important plans. The real reason for not parting goes unmentioned.

Did the Army damage him? Surely this is too simple—like the notion that he is damaged at all. I, who know him best, understand that in his way he is righteous. Arm tight in arm, we continue to pace the fence's vast perimeter, totally alone except for shawl-swaddled watchkeepers at the gates, an autocratic sky and the silent University skyscraper. We are in step, and happier with ourselves than ever. If our relationship includes a homosexual element—the anonymous girls serving as a vehicle for our vicarious contact—I'm glad it is with him. I yearn to do something grand to repay his love—no, to sustain it, for somehow I constantly fear that such generosity can't last. It's not enough to be the "Yank" who brings back lost illusions. If I could invite him for a visit to the West, I'd spend my last penny to show him the best. We'd go to the smartest "21" places, the kind for which I have no taste on my own. Acapulco, Capri, Cannes—anything he wanted would be his, and he, who makes a holiday of a walk along the Moscow River, would revel in it like the whole of a cruiser's crew on leave in Hong Kong. For one glorious month, *I'd* be the guide.

A haunting moon is rising over Lenin Hills, barely illuminating the dome of a disused church. In its wan light and my surge of tenderness for him, his shaggy head suddenly seems frail; more than ever, I perceive the hide-and-seek child inside the clever operator. The unreality of my fantasy about giving him one dazzling fling squeezes my chest. I know that he senses my affection and sorrow. With comic grandiloquence, he is composing a courtly complaint about my recent snapshots of him in which his teeth appear bad and his nose "more protusile" than usual. From a satirical discourse on the ethical implications of "photographs don't lie" he moves to an exposition—simultaneously twitting his own vanity and Socialist Realism, while reminding me of my life's vastly greater opportunities—of the artist's duty to illuminate mankind's "progressive" nobility rather than irrelevant individual defects. Nonsense phrases— "the aesthetic prophylaxis of the creator's proboscis perception, in a society underpinning vigilant development"—are sprinkled among the pseudo-philosophical contemplation, and my inability to stifle belly laughter intensifies my heartache. Steaming like dry ice, the moon tries to burn brighter. A passing police car slows to inspect us. When we finally kiss good-bye, I like myself too for feeling what I do behind the previously taboo gesture.

"Amber teeth, lad, mean meat in the larder. It's an old Russian saying."

"For God's sake, don't take a detour on the way home. Amateur bards need sleep."

But having coaxed the engine back to life, he jumps out again and runs back to the gate for our *n*th rehearsal of tomorrow's rendezvous arrangements. Parting is such bumblingly protracted sorrow.

The tidal wave of depression that submerges me the next day is as strong as any before I met him. Only his exhortation extracts me from bed. Convinced at last that something is wrong with me, he parks the car where we happen to be: alongside Lubyanka.

"What's the point of feeling blue? What's there to be blue about? The sun's shining; *you* don't have to kill the day in the shadow of a bar—of justice, I mean. But I'm listening, go ahead."

How to tell him what troubles me? His problems—the Finnish front, everything symbolized by the dreaded yellow structure whose shadow darkens the car at this moment—are real; mine a silly collection of New York neuroses. Lack of parental affection, ha ha? The breakdown of my career; loss of Anastasia? Blessed with everything denied to him, I can't explain the subconscious mess that lays me low at these times, nor that my life will never be rich the way he assumes. For all our closeness, we're sometimes strangers; but another lesson I learn now is that best friends need not be psychic twins.

Our long drive ends in a village whose single street is a cortege of battered trucks spewing noxious gases. During a stroll through the dreary village to escape the Volga's ears, Alyosha is talking about B.B., our code for the scheme that increasingly preoccupies him. Big Business. He will obtain some superb icons suitable for smuggling to the West; two or three will make us both rich.

It is a hazardous plan which can easily bring the KGB on us, but he's determined. If I'm discovered with the goods, I'm to say that I bought them from an unknown street pusher. If the smuggling succeeds but *he* is caught with the dollar profits, he'll concoct an explanation that avoids implicating me. No matter how strong the circumstantial evidence and pressure to confess, his trial experience tells him that conviction for conspiracy is unlikely if we stick, stick, stick to our stories. And although he might get ten years, they'd probably limit themselves to permanent expulsion for me.

"Listen, *muchacho*, I trust no one on this tricky earth. Only you. Because . . . well, I know you. And if you're worried about this end, I'm going to make a speech. They can do what they want to me. Hack me up in little pieces, I'll never rat on my Yank."

I know this is true, and that Alyosha has said it with an intention broader than just to reassure me about the operation. He and I against the world through icons; and I *won't* disappoint him, despite my dread. With this danger to cope with, my depression subsides, his words thumping in my ears. "They can hack me to shreds, I'll never sell out on you."

The climax of the next day's errands is an urgent consultation with two friends from Alyosha's smart-set days. Painters rich on book illustrations and "underground" canvases flogged to Westerners, they dashed off an erotic drawing one drunken night, which found its way to splash publication in a recent edition of a

Hamburg magazine. The Union of Artists' answer was to end their careers by depriving them of their studios.

Forsaking their customary finery, the wives join the despairing conference about how to avoid ruin of their swank life-style. Cross-examining the doomed about the Union's disciplinary procedures and about their own movements on the fatal night, Alyosha advises them to beg for mercy but also to explain that the woman depicted in a lewd position was intended as Stalin's daughter. The revanchist magazine, they should say, foully distorted a patriotic, if tasteless, sketch by removing the "Svetlana Alliluyeva" on her forehead, together with "bourgeois press" and "monopoly-capitalism," the labels on the penises inserted in her, and the drawing's title: "Traitress to the Motherland, Prostitute for Dirty Dollars." At first irritated by what they take for untimely wisecracking, the painters are persuaded of Alyosha's serious intent and, lacking a better plan, agree to consider his.

We are far away, shopping for a coffee-grinder, when Alyosha mentions he once had an affair with the more elegant of the wives. For the rest of the day, I can't suppress the sad question of whether I'll ever feel as casual about Anastasia as Alyosha about the tense woman on the couch. Once again, I ask him how he and Anastasia met, but he adds nothing to the story, saying he still doesn't understand what went wrong with us, nor why I don't claim her instead of pining.

"With your looks, *muchacho*, you can rouse Sleeping Beauty. Two slim meters you are, suave from head to toe . . . she's the lucky party in this suit."

I can't explain why I still love Anastasia so after our split, but his cool conviction that she'll be mine if I truly want her brightens my longing. With a thump, I realize that if I'd satisfied myself vagabonding with him before I'd met Anastasia, we might be married now. But I knew her first; the paradox is that she led me to Alyosha. I suppose that's life, and I'm not complaining, but my happiness would be complete if there were somewhere a place for Anastasia in all this.

Desperately late again for the usual reason—a blue-eyed pedestrian—Alyosha pushes the Volga past trucks hogging an icy road. When the bald tires lose their grip, he whoops at the skid's challenge, lets the wheel find itself and stomps the accelerator again. We are rushing to visit King-size Natasha who, we've just heard, had an abortion this morning.

The hospital is a modern building in an outlying district. Our risks on the road were in vain, for we arrive after visiting hours, and Alyosha's cheeriest song and dance about being a Ministry of Health sanitary engineer cuts no ice with a sour Chief Nurse at the desk. Contemplating the purse of her lips, Alyosha decides this is not an instance for pushing his luck, but he thinks fast as we leave. From a telephone booth outside the grounds, he calls on cheek, flair and practiced skill to cut through the obstacles separating us from Natasha. The first trick is eliciting the hospital's number from waspish operators; the last, flirting with a ward nurse until she summons the convalescent in her charge. Soon the large-boned girl is waving to us from a third-floor window.

We plod through a field of unbroken snow until we're directly below her, and she tosses down a roll of cotton cord, whose end Alyosha ties to a shopping net filled with the sausage, biscuits and chocolate we bought on the way. Natasha hauls up the booty and blows us a chortling kiss. We shout plans to taxi her home tomorrow evening, and start back toward the road.

Then it begins. A dozen bored girls in uniform bathrobes appear at the adjoining windows of the abortion ward, teasing us to shimmy up for a visit. Suddenly two at separate windows recognize Alyosha and squeal. "Alyoshka, come rescue me." "Alyoshik, be a knight!" Inviting one and all to a recovery celebration, Alyosha calls up his telephone numbers "in case anyone has an emergency requisition." The commotion alerts the authorities in the persons of a stout nurse appearing in a window and an angry watchman struggling through the knee-deep snow toward us. As he blusters, we race for the car.

"Jesus, did you see that beauty next to King-size?" sings Alyosha over the motor. "I've been a tax-paying citizen of this burg for forty years; how the hell have I never met *her* before?"

She is loitering in the corridor of a People's Court into which Alyosha has dashed, a tall girl with a tasteful scarf. Yes she'll come with us, she says after our introduction—but can we be patient? Unfortunately, she must wait for a certain verdict. Twenty minutes later, a judge stands up in a musty little courtroom to announce his court's finding. The young defendant, probably dark and handsome before his capture, has been reduced to a pitiable creature. Crushed by defeat, prison-shaved skull hanging like lead on his powerful chest, he cannot raise his eyes above his filthy boots. The judge sentences him to seven years in labor camps for robbery. It is the graceful girl's husband.

"But won't you even write to him?" I persist as Alyosha opens a bottle of Bull's Blood at the apartment. "You say he has no one. He stole for you. His life is ruined."

"Mine's not."

About Alyosha's postwar life, I learn in snatches. Demobilized in late 1945, he returned to his personal status quo ante bellum—specifically, the need to acquire a vocation. Acting no longer appealed to him, and although he had an impulse to try movies as a cameraman or director, it was soon suppressed. Fashioning the obligatory panegyrics to factory and collective farm of Stalin's postwar cinema—"or to the great victories in 'defense' against the Finns"—directors had less chance of personal satisfaction and lived under greater risk of labor camp or execution than dealers in black market penicillin. Black market penicillin was precisely what an old friend of Abrasha Abramchik offered to cut him in on, but although it would have made him a millionaire, Alyosha declined.

Returning to odd jobs in warehouses, he weighed alternative careers while coping with the memory of his day on the Elbe. In postwar Russia, where one's own sense of humor provided the only vapor of gaiety, the fifty yards which had separated him from the Stars and Stripes seemed alternately infinitesimal and infinite. Yes, everyone knew it was impossible to cross that mine field; but everyone was usually wrong. Ending his youthful illusions that he would somehow grow up rich and happy, the war, however, had changed nothing for the better in the country. Whether or not Russia was psychologically and morally sicker than in 1939—as it clearly was physically—Alyosha perceived it as such. The stupendous edifice of strain, isolation and ideologi-

cal perversity—the chants to the takers and cripplers of lives—
seemed to him less hypocritical than insane. Yet even intelligent
people pretended not to notice. To keep themselves in power, the
authorities had created a centralized system of permanent terror
and depression. An entire population was toiling to make life
harder for themselves under a Kafkaesque antiphilosophy based
on forcing society as far from possible from what was *normal.* By
comparison, even the devastated Germany through which his
tank had clambered seemed a haven of enlightenment and
comfort. It was now clear that a lifetime of odd man out awaited
him in this ocean of sullen poverty. Yet when his chance to
escape peeped out, he hadn't dashed for it. *For such stakes, why
hadn't he taken the risk?* . . .

In 1946, he worked on the wall newspaper of a Moscow
subway line under construction, using the Glorious Victory
lessons he'd learned during the war to achieve the proper prose
bombast. Then he was briefly a darkroom assistant. For all his
pondering, it was an accident that made him a lawyer. The
ambitious girl he married in 1947—she already had a foot in the
door of the capital's tiny upper class of wheelers and dealers—
was a Jewish student in the Moscow Juridical Institute, where he
too enrolled. It was she with whom he was soon to lay in bed at
night, bursting with hardness for others.

In keeping with its role in Marxist-Leninist theory and in
Soviet governmental practice, law had become the least intellectual of disciplines. Studying in his spare time, Alyosha finished
the three-year course in less than two. The curriculum was
designed for the solidly proletarian lads who (like roommate
Viktor) would quickly take their places as the nation's judges,
prosecutors and Ministry of Justice officers. Less backward than
provincial army officers, many were nevertheless unequal even to
the primers that reduced all legal theory to easily memorizable
formulas, applicable to any case without thought.

"Lecturers recited the bold print, we intoned the answers. No
music: it was a recitative Mass."

Alyosha was again reminded that underestimating the stupidity in official places prejudiced one's survival and well-being as
much as insufficient caution. The course taught the smattering of
cosmopolitan youths who were to be Moscow's successful advo-

cates that one gets ahead by exploiting the pervading apathy and ignorance.

For these reasons, law provided a happy choice. In half the time it took most of his colleagues—a fifth of the average Soviet work week—Alyosha earned a relatively handsome income: enough from his first month as a practicing lawyer to enjoy restaurant meals and presents for sweethearts. Within a year, he had met Georgian speculators and other "businessmen," the cream of the criminal lawyer's clientele. His long affair with Moscow's café society was beginning.

As with almost all his prosperous colleagues, Alyosha solicited under-the-table payments from criminal defendants or their relatives. But unlike some, he kept his private fees reasonable, which is why brothers and uncles of robbers and embezzlers he'd once defended sought him out when they too came a cropper. This was true even when these robbers and embezzlers had been convicted and shot, for Alyosha's best arguments sometimes came to nothing, even in the rare cases when he believed his clients innocent.

In a non-Soviet court, his agility of mind and precision of expression would have made him brilliantly successful; here, he was careful to use a goodly part of his powers to control the other parts from exercising their natural abilities. Beyond certain limits, defense of a "criminal" in the dock was not merely unseemly, but anti-Soviet. Thus Alyosha walked a narrow line not only between prosperity and greed with relation to his clients, but also between integrity and discretion vis-à-vis judges. Since a vigorous defense, especially one that punched holes in the indictment, might anger the judiciary, he had to disguise his thrusts, even when the indictment was full of blunt contradictions or where evidence of police mistakes or prosecution wrongdoing might have mitigated the sentence. Quite calculatingly, he repressed his briefs almost to the level of his former fellow students, now the plodding representatives of Soviet jurisprudence on the bench.

Nevertheless, Alyosha's clients trusted him to adapt his tactics to the circumstances. He became known as a connoisseur of which judge would stand for what amount of "legalism" (read "introduction of previously unnoticed, exculpating facts") in the defense case, or of "unhealthy oppositionism" in general to a prosecution conducted in the service of the Party and the Soviet people. Sometimes suspected but never disliked, the young lawyer with the easy smile learned that sensitivity to moods and character on the bench—and to Party-organized campaigns against this or that public abuse—was as important to his craft as knowledge of the law.

Of all his rewards as a lawyer, Alyosha most cherished the uncommon luxury of being almost his own boss. Apart from court appearances and the occasional volunteer stint for the sake of his record as a good citizen, his involvement with the system that monopolized ninety-nine of every hundred lives was minimal. Taking the cases—and vacations—he wanted, he worked an average of ten hours a week: just enough for food, drink and gasoline.

Over the years, he handled every kind of case, from bank robbery and murder to wrangles over square inches of floor space between estranged husbands and wives forced by housing conditions to continue sharing the same room. But commercial considerations prompted a preference for criminal rather than civil trials; the highest-paying clients remained embezzlers and captains of speculation, which shortages nourished like ragweed. Despite the narrow limits of his ambition, his reputation grew, especially within the sparse ranks of the Moscow advocacy. Trusted to split fees honestly as well as never to betray a venal colleague, he was referred choice cases that others were too busy to accept.

The making of his name in a specific area of the criminal code was as accidental as his choice of law itself. One day, a former client asked him to represent a nephew charged with rape. The accused was no less than the center forward of Moscow Dynamo, one of the country's most popular soccer teams. But instead of having his indiscretion hushed up, the usual practice with athletic and other celebrities, he was apparently in for a severe sentence, as demanded by *Evening Moscow*'s squib about the crime. Rumor had it that the stadium hero had earlier taken liberties with a niece of a Central Committee member, and that this was the moment for a drastic lesson.

Titillating talk about the case swelled greatly when it came to trial and the heavy sentence was approvingly publicized. As a side effect, the newspaper's incidental mention of Alyosha provided him with more popular publicity than a Soviet lawyer could attract in a lifetime of squatting on a flagpole. From Murmansk to the Urals, requests streamed to "Defense Counsel A. Aksyonov," as he had been identified, from relatives of young men accused of sex crimes. When the parents were of the upper middle class or the black market bourgeoisie, they paid handsomely. Alyosha discreetly left unmentioned the curious circumstance of his professional expertise now running dead parallel with his personal.

"Not so curious at all," he said when I put it this way. "Not when you know what's happened to others. Whose fate do you know that isn't erratic in our happy land?"

Although his reputation as a sex crimes specialist slowly diminished over the years, Alyosha still handled many more sexual cases than the average lawyer, and continued to be visited by an improbable assortment of clients, from schoolteachers to generals, seeking confidential advice about conjugal duties and rights. Alyosha gave it objectively. With his adroit use of humor and of matter-of-fact tolerance to human diversity, he also tried to soften the vindictiveness of narrow-minded judges but, even within possible limits, never actually advocated sexual liberation. His attitude toward obtaining satisfaction was summed up in a ditty he liked to quote: "Kolya's fucking someone/Someone's fucking Kolya/And what's it to you, Tolya?" But although this was intended to satirize the whole panoply of Soviet intrusion on private lives—the idiocy of armies of inspectors, investigating "what The People think when they pee"—he felt it wiser to affect professional detachment on all larger issues.

Nor did his occupation either strengthen or ease his own satyriasis. Work and play were kept prudently apart (except behind a locked consulting room door in the new Juridical Consultation Office); trials were one thing, fetes another. And so it goes to this day. Fifty yards from a courthouse where he has defended a man charged with unnatural practices, he recruits new girls for an evening that will include many of the same sodomitic acts.

Only the sheer number of his former darlings effects an occasional meeting between business and pleasure. One client,

for example, raped an old friend of Alyosha's on his first charge
six years ago, then a second Erstwhile soon after his release. One
pretty victim, the former typist of a minor official, got her boss
indicted for "Compelling an Economically Dependent Woman
to Enter into Sexual Intercourse" but confessed, when Alyosha
interviewed her as defense counsel, that she was willing to drop
the charges out of consideration for the happy week her mother
had spent with him, Alyosha, after the war. A Young Communist
representative of a shoe factory appealed, in the name of her
"entire collective" and in phrases of the highest socialist morality, for a severe sentence against one of its workers accused of
rape—not disclosing, of course, that weeks before she, the
representative, had brought along two teen-age gluers from the
same factory to share Alyosha's bed. . . . Alyosha's explanation
of these coincidences is that Moscow, by which he means the
circles who are active and *alive*, is incongruously small. To me,
they are illustrations of the stranger-than-fiction eccentricity that
flourishes in its daily life, and the qualities in him which
consistently bring them out.

We move our skull session to Edik's, out of earshot of the
apartment's microphone. A mother has heard of a "filthy
debauch" involving her seventeen-year-old daughter, and is
threatening to "ruin" Alyosha. He immediately summoned the
evening's other participants and, like a prosecutor preparing a
show trial, drills the wide-eyed teen-agers about what to say if
the police make inquiries. Totally trusting, they accept their
obligation to dissemble for his protection without a second's
hesitation. He knows that three eyewitnesses with the same story
of innocently passing the evening in question will invalidate one
mother claiming perversion—but also that a single deviation
from the common alibi will disastrously weaken the defense.
Hence a hard afternoon of memorization and quizzing.

That very evening, we leave the Peking Restaurant at closing
time with two bonny language students. Although we're all
groggy from too much food and drink, we wander in and out of
side streets in the cold before going home. Tipsy as he is, Alyosha
senses plainclothesmen are stationed in the lobby and feels it
unwise to be seen entering a car in our condition. The Volga

may be followed or its license recorded, all the more because our girls had been practicing their French with two foreign business-men at the adjoining table.

Wherever we are, the sixth sense he has developed to gauge how far to go in any criminal defense also screens him in his potentially perilous sexual adventures and his meetings with me. Beneath the jauntiness, his reflexes are constantly alert, periph-eral vision cast as wide for policemen as for girls. And when driving me to the American Embassy for an errand, he's like a Captain approaching shifting underwater hazards. While he's waiting for me two prudent blocks away one day, a policeman opens the door to demand to know who it was who just left the car and why he entered the Embassy. Alyosha replies that I'm *The Worker* correspondent come to investigate the number of Negroes lynched this year—and when I reappear, vigorously shakes his head "No!" to my move toward a beautiful girl in sight of the same glowering cop.

"Wowing her here might have been less than entirely dis-creet," he apologizes as we drive off—and although this emerges as Peter Sellers burlesquing a spy, his purpose is deadly serious. He even senses when he had better speak for me on the telephone because my accent might provoke the suspicion of a girl's parent, neighbor or office colleague.

Only someone so skilled in precaution can afford to be so cavalier.

The procession continues. Will anyone believe how ridicu-lously easy it is? (Under Alyosha's guidance, that is. With girls I pick up alone, I can't direct the progression from opening banter to bed with his touch or speed.) By now, it's less the numbers than the variety of stories that baffles me. The curious and coincidental cases that spice the progression of anonymous girls seem teasingly implausible.

There is Chekhov Tanya, the picture of one of his innocent heroines in a wide-brimmed hat—although at sixteen, she's had literally twice as many lovers as years. And Anomaly, a blushing thirty-year-old who has sought out Alyosha to "become a woman" but flees into the corridor at the last minute. (Alyosha calls Lev Davidovich, who will take her to a concert.) Later, a former convict girl whose breasts release a thin flow of milk when touched: she gave birth ten days ago.

A smattering of celebrities also appears in curious new lights. A young visitor to Moscow casually mentions that she's the niece of the celebrated Alexander Stakhanov—the first of the "Stakhanovites"—and that when she last saw the old man he was swilling his inflated pension and kicking the neighbors' cats. A quiet graduate student remarks that her best friend, a girl of twenty-five, is a favorite of Rudenko, the feared Procurator-General who made his name at the Nuremberg Trials. The intriguing offspring of a Russian father and Georgian mother claims that the former was once Khrushchev's driver—and that she couldn't care less. Nor do the wives of actors, colonels and Honored Artists of the Russian Republic show an interest in their husbands' achievements. We represent an afternoon's diversion to them, during which talk of their status would be out of place. But they all seem to live a story. Changing jobs like lovers, drifting with the currents of emotion and the breakers of social upheaval, they are the plankton of the country's land mass, totally independent from the ship of state on top.

The Chip off the Old Block. She strongly resembles him, the corpulent chest of medals in the second rank behind the Politburo, taking the salute in Red Square; a veteran with porcine eyes and the reputation of a die-hard Stalinist. Through her pudgy prettiness, the family resemblance shows in the mouth, wide shoulders and faintly muscular chest. To her mother's dismay and father's fury, she has run away from home, abandoning the restricted luxury shops, government-staffed villas and grand stables on closed state preserves. Sickened of Party bosses and playboy sons' unearned wealth, she dropped out several weeks ago and plans to join Uzbek shepherds in the spring: a hippie in a land where very few can afford or get away with it.

Meanwhile, she will not take advice, put on her brassiere or leave the flat. She sits cross-legged and bare-breasted in a corner for days, drinking cocktails of sweet wine and vodka, taking on one after another of Alyosha's friends who drop in. Convinced that her father the General has ordered a search, Alyosha begs her to move the dynamite of her presence elsewhere.

"Alyoshik, there's nothing to worry about, *I* can assure you. You must learn to say 'screw you' to Papa. If people understood this, the world would be a better place."

The Scholar. A handsome woman of twenty-eight ("Ye gods, I'll be running an old-age home next," moans Alyosha) in a well-tailored suit, she has come to Moscow from Sverdlovsk to obtain a black market copy of something by Freud. Any Freud, it hardly matters which, so long as it "you know . . . explains about sex." Scholarly ignorance and popular indifference in this field are a Russian plain of darkness. What are we to make of our chance meeting with this provincial belle of maverick interests?

"Actually, I'm not a sexologist yet; that's what I want to be. I'm a psychology student in Sverdlovsk University. But sex is *so* important, don't you think? I want to make it my life's study."

"In theory or practice?" Alyosha chimes in, wriggling his ears. "You know Lunacharsky's admonition about book learning estranged from the people's daily life."

"Oh, practice is valuable too. I never realized Lunacharsky was involved with it."

While Alyosha is searching for the telephone number of an old friend likely to own a prerevolutionary copy of Freud's treatise on dreams, she undresses, placing one finger in her mouth and another in her sex. . . . Two hours later, she asks for the names of other potential "fellow-students."

"I only have a couple of days left in Moscow, and I have to find a book by Avid *[sic!]* too."

The Volunteer. Again and again, she promises to return for "whatever you want" next week; but she simply can't let us "have it" tonight.

"No I *won't* stay over; I've already stayed too long. Where's my coat, I'm leaving this minute." She has something *terribly important* to attend to early tomorrow morning and *must* not be late.

"Eight o'clock on a Sunday morning?" Alyosha's inquiry is a polka of skepticism and cheery confidence that the new prize, a fornicator's dream of lewdly beckoning breasts and buttocks, is on the verge of abandoning her improbable excuse. His experience of ten thousand fibs and feints have honed a sixth sense about genuine and invented appointments. To help recruits keep the former, he will drive any distance in any weather; but he is correspondingly deft at dismantling spurious defenses.

"You're a Catholic then, my darling? Tomorrow's your holy confirmation? Nothing to worry about. We'll fix you up with a peccadillo for confession; everyone will feel finer for it." The incongruity of this—not one practicing Catholic in ten million girls her age—is lost on the amateur acrobat, who laughs because "confirmation" is something naughty boys do, and you can't call *that* "holy." With her lemon hair and tarty makeup, she seems unlikely not only to attend church but to have anything but monkey business planned for a Sunday morning.

But when she rises early and returns to last night's plea, Alyosha becomes convinced. Rushing with breakfast, he repairs the toilet for her use and cranks the Volga alive. Relieved at being sped toward her required address at last, she reveals the nature of her business. Today is election day and she's an agitprop volunteer for turning out the vote.

I jump on the chance to learn something about the infamous agitprop, terror's repellent henchman in my textbooks on totalitarianism. No, she replies thickly, of course she didn't offer to do it. As her wallpaper factory's newest hand, she was *instructed* to volunteer, *told* where to report. No, she couldn't say what the work would be. Something about ringing doorbells and reminding the Comrades of their socialist duty to vote. The candidate? What *candidate?* Oh, the one she'll be canvassing for. Well, what about him?

"Who is he for a start?"

"How am *I* supposed to know, they didn't tell me. Anyway, what difference does it make? . . . Shall I come back this afternoon?"

The Star. We spy her in a new record store, this winner of Cannes prizes and most internationally celebrated of Soviet actresses who, in Moscow, is as well known for her visits to mental hospitals and persistent nymphomania. A shrill mockery of herself in her immensely popular movies, she reviles us from the moment of entering the car.

"You want to fuck me? Okay, you can fuck me. All studs want to fuck me. But get out and hail a taxi. A decent one, a limousine. You cunt-lappers think I'm going to ride in this shit-heap?"

On television last month, my third viewing of the film that made her a public idol again moved me as deeply as the first and second. She played a girl of haunting purity who loses her lover to war. Now, en route to Alyosha's, she demands cigarettes and vodka—"Western fags, goddam it. And my own bottle."

"You can fuck me up my asshole, that's what you scum want. But bring me Stolichnaya, not coffin varnish, you cheap bastards."

His aplomb slightly frayed, Alyosha buys two bottles of the best vodka, serving them in the apartment on a tray with gleaming glasses. She shatters hers against the wall and drinks straight from *her* bottle. Glugging noisily, she lowers it to her other lips and inserts the neck, groaning with forced pleasure like a has-been diva. Later she snorts like a laughing record, vomits into the sink, curses us for palming off rotgut on her. Still retching, she demands champagne.

Smacking of a Hamburg cabaret, the sex has been so degraded that Alyosha and I need a tramp through the snow after she has sobered up enough to leave. Staggering from the Volga toward her entryway in an apartment building for Party and cultural big shots, she warns that she'll set the police on us for seducing her.

"You dirty bastards, I'll send you to a labor camp. You won't get away with trying those tricks on me."

Having met his match, Alyosha drives off like a bank robber on the getaway.

"I *told* you we take in too many movies," he mutters. "Makes us too starry-eyed to handle real life's challenges."

After a rest come two post-office file clerks wooed from an ice cream parlor on Saturday afternoon, who mention that they must testify at a trial on Monday. Alyosha too will be in court the day after tomorrow. Because his case seems a nasty one—the defendant and his Georgian friends apparently robbed as well as raped two Russian girls slow to submit to them—the parents have promised him a whopping six hundred rubles under the table. But such matters are far from our minds as, during leisurely preparations for a fete, we explore our guests' ungrudgingly presented charms. The table gradually acquires its customary clutter while the two eighteen-year-olds nibble on olives and toy with Alyosha's stuffed monkey.

"I'm not hungry," says Alla feebly, in response to the aroma of roasting meat.

"Got any good records?" asks Olya. "I know a boy who was in France and saw the Rolling Stones."

"The trial's early," muses Alla, returning to their Monday-morning devoir. "If it's over in a couple of hours like they said, will we have to go to work in the afternoon?"

Alyosha and I quickly gulp the rest of our beer in order to shout our double-take *"Whoops!"* together. Like news of a bounced check, it dawns on us simultaneously that our callers are none other than the rape victims he is due to meet across the courtroom two days hence. The fete must be canceled: even a hundred rubles is too much to sacrifice for the favors of two pleasant but wholly ordinary postal clerks—precisely the kind who might kiss and tell on the stand. Sleeping with the prosecution's principal witnesses on the eve of a trial could cause permanent disbarment.

Like a clown in sorrow, Alyosha gazes adoringly at his unattainable prizes who, still unsuspecting, are distributing herring morsels on large cuts of bread. Even my homily that all is not lost forever—after all, we can safely reinvite them after the trial a not unendurable forty-eight hours hence—does nothing to dispel the hammy pain from his eyes. Squeezing Alla on his one side and Olya on the other, he pronounces a melancholy discourse on modern life's killing pressures, wherein invidious business is "always" smothering pleasure.

Then submits to the logic of his own self-lampoon. "What the hell, some say you're only young once," he intones happily, freeing a hand to propose a toast. "Temptation's evil, it's our duty to fight it—in the form of filthy lucre, I mean. . . . Anyway, divide by two"—he pats each girl lovingly between her legs—"and it's a mere three hundred rubles each, *si, muchacho?*"

This is his way of saying that he wants to sacrifice the extraordinary fee for Alla and Olya's favors. The thought of this wild extravagance—six hundred rubles is a worker's income for half a year—transforms the otherwise ordinary fete into a luxurious revel and gives our companions an aura of exceptional allure, as if they were fabulously costly call girls. I know Alyosha has made the gesture partly to provide something extra for my weekend. Nothing—especially such outrageously expensive pleasure—is now for himself. All discoveries and disappointments, every tale told by every new girl, is nourishment for our friendship. And offerings to appease omniscient *skuka,* god of Overpowering Boredom.

We spend the weekend together in feasting and brief outings. Monday morning, we drive to the courthouse, Alla and Olya to report as required, Alyosha to disqualify himself from the case on the grounds—which he must argue ardently to overcome the judge's so-whats?—that having dined at the adjoining table in the restaurant where the rape was planned, he felt personally involved.

By the somber light of Monday afternoon, Alyosha decides to sell the new samovar to pay off pressing debts for which the Georgian bonanza had been budgeted. But he has no regrets about the weekend, not even now that it's over.

On the Sunday when Agitprop Tanya is helping turn out the vote, Alyosha too performs his civic duty. To lose the taste from his mouth "before it spoils the Sabbath," he likes to vote early. In a school corridor near the apartment, he turns from the officials' table where he has been handed his premarked ballot and, in the same motion, drops it into the box without having given it a glance.

I leave quickly because I assume I'm not supposed to witness this spectacle and am afraid my expression might give me away. The very ordinariness of the ten-second ritual of totalitarian control makes it deadlier than I had expected, and Alyosha's smirk hides neither his humiliation nor disgust.

"An informed electorate makes its choice with dispatch and resolution," he says on the school steps. "Rest in Peace, the election results will be gratifying. And what else is new? *Kovo ebat budyem?"*

Rest in Peace, our code for the propaganda's inane edge, comes from the story of the eulogist's farewell as his factory director is lowered into the ground: "Rest in Peace, dear Comrade; the plan will be fulfilled." A spoof on the standard description of Soviet leaders' firm final words to his "comrades-in-arms" about strengthening the Party's unshakable unity and raising productivity, it reminds us of Edik's influential father, and we call the prodigal son from a booth. He asks to meet us tomorrow. Alyosha often gets his pickups excused from work by obtaining a chit certifying they appeared as trial witnesses; now Edik needs this proof for a schoolteacher who missed two days of classes last week for a spree with him.

The clinic where an Erstwhile of Alyosha's supplies medical excuses from work if his favorite court secretaries are unavailable happens to be our next stop. It is part of a huge complex for oncology and internal medicine, but Alyosha doesn't reveal his business here and even says I'd better not come in with him.

"Happily, *hombre*. What's the attraction of a cancer clinic on Sunday?"

"Chief doctors are away, comrade nurses like to play. The heater's on, I'll be a minute."

But he is gone an hour, looks wan when he reappears—from a different building—and apologizes with uncharacteristic formality.

"You're not sick, señor?" I quip.

"Sick of winter. Let's home it for a bit. I'll do soup."

A broth made from dried, wild mushrooms, it is my favorite. We have just started spooning when a knock sounds. I open it to a woman wearing a pasted smile and a dirty coat I seem to recognize. It is Aksyona, our disappeared railroad friend.

"I know. It took all my courage to face you. But I'll explain everything, may I come in?"

She finishes the leftovers together with the soup, explains nothing but asks to borrow twenty-five rubles. After sharp chastisement for stealing from individuals when there's a whole huge State around, Alyosha gives her thirteen in single bills. Aksyona takes a long bath, but perceiving no great demand for her favors, leaves with a promise to return "when I feel I can tell."

We stretch out together for a rest on the bed. Folders containing Alyosha's current cases crown piles of less important papers scattered everywhere, and as always, we talk in whispers because half our topics—exchanging dollars for rubles, my obtaining Pall Malls and a Sinyavsky book for acquaintances of Alyosha, the Palestine and girl situations—are taboo or illegal. These conspiracies are part of nature now. The strange peace I feel, despite the underlying dread, in succumbing to the limbo of being Tonto to his Lone Ranger is strongest on Sundays. Abandoning the last pretence of library work has been a relief. The possibility of my expulsion because of this or for some convenience to the authorities is all the more reason to spend my rationed hours here.

I flip on the radio to a selection of oh-so-Russian folk songs in a superpatriotic arrangement of a provincial choir. "Music to vote by," comments Alyosha dryly, threading the Ray Charles tape "for jamming" on this Election Day.

Our plan is to spend the rest of it enjoying the easier weather—wind tasting of oozing earth beneath the snow—with a walk in the countryside, but first Alyosha wants to consult a colleague about a truck driver he defended who was sentenced to eight years for manslaughter in a highway accident. Ordinarily resigned to miscarriages of justice, he is distressed for the doomed man, who was not only blameless but also accepted ruin by hanging judges without a word of protest. For months, Alyosha has been pursuing every avenue of appeal and pardon, all on his own initiative since the convict's wife cannot spare a kopek from the meager income she scratches together to support their children. The final hope lies with the Supreme Court, and since all previous rulings have ignored his mass of technical evidence, he wants advice—not to be trusted to the telephone—about whether to approach one of its members.

The aged lawyer welcomes us to his apartment. After the consultation, we drive to a peasant market, where Alyosha buys a chicken for today, lamb for tomorrow and, despite my protests, a handful of murderously expensive tomatoes. "Enough bravado. I know how fast Yanks run down without fresh vegetables and chewing gum." It is three o'clock and we haven't talked of women for the evening. A counter girl in a white smock—normally perfect prey—goes unnoticed.

We climb into the car, then out immediately because we

haven't discussed B.B.—the icons. Keeping voices low and distance safe from alien ears, we pace the old fence that conceals the eyesore of the market, apprehension making me excited yet weak. Estimating our wealth, plotting and double-checking our moves, we rehearse the entire operation, as we did yesterday and the day before.

". . . yeah, but real masterpieces, okay? . . . more fakes than informers . . ."

". . . knows monastery sources. He's a vodka priest; once defended him . . ."

". . . still the one crucial step. *Got* to get into that diplomatic pouch . . ."

". . . not more than three trips . . . something safer than a tourist; they've really started to check . . . fetch fifty thousand dollars—or pounds?—in London . . ."

I will smuggle Alyosha's cut back to Moscow—the more on the first go, the better chance of buying museum pieces for "reorder" and the greater our eventual wealth. But if I can't return, at least one of us will be rich.

"The right one, *muchacho*. It's anomalous to live under capitalism without capital. . . . Besides, Rockefeller's pile can't change my style or, er, domicile. You're the new generation, you need the stake."

A voice in me gloats at the prospect of these crooked riches. When I return home—without Alyosha, prospects, even interests, fit only for nostalgia about this, my great adventure—I'll be alone. *Different* from everyone. This lump sum will be my compensation. I'll invest well and live the life of an Alyosha in New York. . . .

Yet the dream only increases my foreboding about the future. In my heart of hearts I know that something will go wrong—and anyway, how can we raise ten thousand rubles for a museum piece when we must sell some rag for tomorrow's food and drink? B.B. is sheer escapism—not even proper wishful thinking, for at bottom neither Alyosha nor I want to be rich. What we do want is to do something princely for one another; and to court danger together along the way. His riches and mine will be our only link when I'm home and he's here, a world apart. Meanwhile, we try to lift the conspiracy to this charitable objective.

"Take your time selling. Maybe a private collector instead of the auctions, that's where your judgment counts. . . . Remember, they count on panic and confession. If anything flubs, we stick to our stories."

"Right, and stay with those art books. It's hot air until you find the right goods. What about the museum right now?—No, better not be seen there together. . . ."

Provisions safely in the trunk, we proceed with a reduced agenda of Sunday errands. A stop at a dry cleaning outlet so that Alyosha will have his suit in the morning. An in-and-out visit to admire Volodya Z's new boxer pup.

But we skip the rest, and Alyosha is not going to attend his lecture about the highway code, a spiteful cop's punishment for crossing a lane line last week. For the sky has suddenly cleared to an early spring sun, and we drop everything in the usual rush to the great outdoors. Fresh air is at least as important as fresh cadres.

In our early weeks, when I was still making appearances at the library, Alyosha lamented the "pessimism" that kept me inside the somber building irrespective of whether the sun was shining. "It's a common-law *crime* to waste such an *opportunity*," he pleaded at the first sniff of mildness. And I'd chuckle at this childish order of priorities, until I adopted his sense of values and began to cherish each bright hour like a personal gift.

"When the sun appears, heed the call of duty. To the countryside, quick!"

After our late start, we choose the nearest park reasonably free of Sunday crowds. There the sun is glinting in a million drops of melted snow. Despite the slush sloshing into Alyosha's shoes, we stroll for hours along rambling paths, talking about an Erstwhile chosen for a screen role and another whose indiscreet remarks to a Dutch journalist has landed her in an asylum; and about our plan to marry two sisters who work in the powerplant so that I can invite him—as my relative—to New York. Full of admiration for my "feat," Alyosha questions me about my wandering through Europe without guides or fixed routes on a college summer vacation. We have started toward the car when a shout rings out.

"Aksyonov! Hey, Aksyonov—my God, you're a sight!"

A sight herself, the woman is chasing us like a goose on the run. Forty pounds and a quarter of a century ago, she was Alyosha's favorite for a winter. Now she's a grandmother: *this*—she exposes the bundled face of the infant in her arms—is her daughter's son. Did anyone suspect life would pass so fast?

"How wonderful to see you," Alyosha interjects. "Tanechka darling, you haven't changed a bit."

Beaming at his recognition, Tanya, which is indeed her name, says she's been following Alyosha's amatory progress by word of mouth, and warns she's considering a "refresher" visit herself. Pleased with herself, she waddles her pram away.

The evening chill and our appetite for the market chicken make us eager for the apartment. But approaching the Volga, we notice a black car parked twenty yards behind: one of the KGB teams that follow us occasionally, in conformance with no pattern we can decipher. This pair is drowsy, no doubt because their heater is on full blast, and Alyosha simulates clumsiness to sound his horn while settling into the driver's seat.

"Hello darlings, it's the good guys—no, I mean the suspicious elements," he mimes to the beefy men. To me—between phrases of a patriotic song, anesthetizing the microphone—he whispers that if we leave unobserved, the apartment will be patrolled for a week.

"Our sleuths' dislike for being outsmarted contributes handsomely to the common interest. Learning to play dumber than them, the brains of the nation are sharpened."

When we stop to telephone Fawn Galya, he holds open the booth door with his foot, the more visible to make the exaggerated cooing and wooing expressions that demonstrate to the detectives he is surely talking to a girl, not enemy agents. Galya isn't home but her younger sister has answered. "What's that again?" gasps Alyosha, who senses his flattering banter is about to bear new fruit. "But maybe you *feel* sixteen, what's a year between old friends? Mistakes are made in birth certificates, you know. . . . What can we do, then, Natashinka? I'll wait for you."

Watching him at work, knowing that when fifteen-year-old Natasha attains the age of consent next year, a hundred beloveds and a thousand errands from now, Alyosha will remember to call her, I think of his inimitable qualities. The impulsive generosity on borrowed rubles and self-parody that makes him a metaphor for humanity trekking its eternal route; the mascot nose and the slightly undersized physique—which, despite everything, makes his philandering funny. "Mother Nature didn't *want* everything perfect," he sighs when contemplating his defects in the mirror. "Even the sun has spots."

I also question myself because I don't want to fool myself concerning him. Would I be as moved by his taking me in were it not that few Russians dare invite me even overnight? Is it *his* acceptance, in fact, that I'm grateful for—or through it, my open sesame to the back doors of Russian life? Would this friendship have happened, or Alyosha himself have been spawned, in another land, or only where gloom and fatalism weigh the air, giving us day after day to ourselves and our private pursuits? In other words, is Alexei Aksyonov a straightforward freak of nature or the kind that reveals more about ordinary life than a hundred average types?

Is it odd or logical that my best friend is Russian; that five thousand miles and a political eon from New York, I feel that I'm home? I wonder. And can't decide whether the cave-in of my plans explains my need for him as the personification of health and dynamism; or whether he prompted the academic collapse. He who makes me feel I'm watching a nature film about the miracle of creation and of life-energy.

Everything is jumbled together: his qualities, the ones in me that respond to protective openheartedness, the relationship of these personal questions to what Russia gives and takes. When I'm an old-timer looking back, I'll complete the equations. Meanwhile, with him near, I needn't worry about what I'm going to be or do. I know that when I'm blue, he will drop everything to be there outside the University gate. Never mind that his standard remedy of an afternoon fete is becoming less effective; he'll even endure a television documentary if mindless distraction is what I want. That if I ask him to make inquiries about some state secret tonight or to drive me to Siberia tomorrow, he'll fill up with gas and set off. (He's already made plans to microfilm certain Revolutionary legal brochures in a closed archive—the material, he insists, for a quick dissertation, which I must finish, even though I'll be icon-rich.) That when I perform some task, he'll make a great fuss over my ability to cope with Russian life: watching me complete a telephone call or fight my way to a spirits counter before closing, he beams with pride and affection—just as he laughs delightedly at my weakest witticism. Whatever else is incomplete about him, his central trait of unqualified, unconditional affection is what was missing from my modern education: the commitment not to what I do or know, but to me.

Yes I love him, in the end, for his loving me. The other attributes, even his trace of Chaplinesque genius, are bonuses. We are not going to Siberia tomorrow, of course, but will cruise around on our permanent junket. Our limitations and self-delusions will ride inside us, yet we'll feel as footloose as Dos Passos' heroic bums. If a supply of the first spring crayfish has arrived at a certain specialty store, he'll boil me a potful to be wolfed down by the dozen with the best beer. A hubcap filled with unobtainable oranges will sit on the table because once, in the throes of a bad cold, I mentioned a craving for citrus. After supplying the medical chit for Edik's "fiancée," he'll drive me to a funeral—of a Party official, for extra pomp—simply because I'm curious.

I'll give him the Japanese turtleneck I bought in a hard currency shop and he'll put it on immediately, according to custom, and wear nothing else until it has holes. (After a washing, he'll don it again before it's fully dry, but remain impervious to cold and to the flu epidemic.) When he spurts forward on a new lovely's trail, I'll try to distract him—not because I don't want her too, or because the current pocket notebook is full of telephone numbers we haven't had time to call, but because the accommodations necessary for any third person will pull us that fraction apart. But if the girl prefers an hour with me alone, or if I want privacy with her, he will make an excuse to leave the apartment, mentioning what's most tempting in the refrigerator and apologizing for the unironed sheets.

Waiting for a bus that passes near the apartment, images of what awaits me often irradiate the dusk. I will be welcomed, fed, entertained with code expressions—"Rest in peace, Comrade, the plan will be fulfilled!"—and new stories. Girls who look like bit players in a spy film will be impressed by my un-Russian height and haberdashery and will come to bed without effort. That this may be the evening of the KGB raid will add to my tingle; that Anastasia might hear of our goings-on heightens the excitement even more, although I no longer know whether this is good or bad. The next day, I'll have the deliciousness of doing nothing in a state of total depletion. . . . The air at the bus stop is frosty clean, but when I take a deep breath at the sight of the bus, I go dizzy with anticipation, as if my lungs were filling with incense.

But despite the wonder of this, I'll be just as happy if no girl has appeared and we go for our late-night drive alone. I've only a few months left in Moscow. Who would have guessed that a supply of time—for wasting together—is as luscious as willing breasts and thighs? What crazy luck I had to meet him!

V Anastasia

It was three weeks after I'd arrived in Moscow that I caught sight
of her for the first time. She was in the rear of a bus that had
stopped on Lenin Prospekt, and I was waiting to get on. It was
just after nine in the morning, and the bus was packed like a
stockyard runway—as are many, for that matter, at any hour.
And in the herd of solemn countenances surrounding hers, faces
worn by weather and hard times, by too many potatoes and a
lack of them, hers was a jonquil. This sounded all the odder in
the pressing Russian fall, but jonquil is what crossed my mind the
first instant. It was a face related to things blooming in spring:
white, gold, soft, clean. And it had a wide-eyed, slightly startled
look, as if discovery of womanhood had made it keen to uncover
similar delights in the stolid boulevard.

I happened to be holding a slim volume of lyric poetry, bought
not to enjoy the verses—my Russian was too shaky for such
pleasures then—but in imitation of my more purposeful

colleagues who were busy accumulating personal libraries of classic literature. When the bus slithered to a halt and its doors creaked opened, the pressure of overcrowding evicted several bodies; only two of the dozen people waiting ahead of me managed to fight their way aboard. As the girl turned toward their grunts, a photograph of the beloved young Esenin on my dust jacket caught her eye. She glanced at it, then up at me, and made a teasing motion hinting, "Throw me your love poems if you dare."

As the doors thumped closed, I tossed the book over shaggy hats and heads. She raised both arms above the crush and caught it, laughing at her success. As the motor groaned for takeoff, she placed her eyes on mine again and smiled. The almond paste of sweetness and provocation sent a surge of happiness through me, tempered only by a need to recall where I had felt its source before. To my further elation, I remembered. "And suddenly," went the Bulgakov line I'd read on the plane about the Master's first sight of Margarita in a Moscow crowd, "completely unexpectedly, I understood that all my life I had loved precisely that woman. Some joke, eh? You'll say I'm crazy, of course."

All my life, I'd dreamed of meeting my stranger and being equal to the occasion. She had performed exactly according to my scenario.

The Embassy warnings of female perils only served to enhance my exhilaration. If I were being followed during my first weeks here, would such behavior be dangerous in my dossier? Had I broken some municipal law? Long lists of rules for using public transport were posted here and there, and duty policemen sometimes led unwitting offenders from the metro. But no police gray was in sight, and a teen-ager in the lighter hue of a school uniform gave me a companionable nod. No one else in the somber bus-stop cluster allowed my triumph to penetrate his weekday morning cares.

Fighting my way into the next bus with a veteran's callousness, I defended my position next to the door. I'd already observed the custom several times: when Russians are separated by a crowd or a spiteful driver, the one who has boarded waits at the next stop for the friend who hasn't. This next stop was the usual half a mile away, toward, which my coughing conveyance strained at its maddening pace. I was not in a trance; not too overwhelmed to regret not having worn a better shirt. But the rush of pure instinct still gripped me, dissolving almost all doubt about who I was and what I was doing at this longitude and latitude. To have spied her at last, my age-old picture of the fair yet natural woman, was sufficient to explain my determination, previously curious even to me, to come to Russia. My tenderness extended to every passenger on the bus. Squeezed together into a continuum of flesh, breathing air damp with old clothing and exhalation, they bore themselves with Russian forbearance and dignity. I loved them all, my fellow travelers.

But my joy was not waiting at the next stop. She was nowhere in the swarms for various trolleys and buses there, nor in a little square facing the metro entrance. It was a warm September morning; I remember underarm sweat stains on calico blouses as I searched lines at stalls selling postcards, grapes and crude jars of cold cream. A massive lady peddling kvass from a tanker truck said she'd seen no one like that; a man with one leg was too drunk to respond. I looked in a bakery and a smelly fish store across the square, then sprinted back to the metro's cool marble foyer to recheck the people waiting for rendezvous beneath an overpainted mosaic of Stalin. Maybe this was a game of hers. Of Russian girls in general. But if I'd imagined her gesture, why had she taken the book?

Then I understood. Clever girl, she'd returned to the stop of our meeting. It was faster to run back than to wait for yet another bus. But I was too late. When I gave up searching at the original stop, almost an hour had elapsed after our moment of sighting. Another passed riding to the end of the line and hunting in the courtyards of the old University and the entrances to Red Square. I sat on a bench and visualized the prism of her cheek.

The next week, I was at our stop at nine o'clock. But no glowing face, no spring stalk of a figure. I'd seen only enough to know my woman actually existed. The one whose scarf could be either peasant kerchief or chic silk square; whose beauty was so artless that we'd never be stuck in intellectualism or pretense. Who, like me, was different, and would have helped me to be special while ending my loneliness.

*Her name was Anastasia. Or Nastya, Nastenka or
Nastyusha, depending on place and mood. But she was the only
Russian girl I was to know whose full name suited her more than
any diminutive.*

"I must pee," she declares, lashing her fingers around my wrist
like a skier his pole. Irritation, desperation, even accusation are
in her voice. Announcing her need is not enough; she must also
complain of it. Someone is surely at fault for the affront of
inconvenience.

"In here, hurry up. Stand in front in case someone comes."

She tugs me into the courtyard of an apartment building just
off Arbat, a densely crowded shopping street. The surflike rumble
of afternoon throngs trudging through slush is only yards away,
and I'm nervous: Anastasia has relieved herself in improbable
places before, but this one is *too* public. Wriggling with impatience, she interrupts my objections.

"Not worth the worry, my bronco. I'll only be a minute."

And in fact, she carries it off before anyone appears in the busy
courtyard. Crouching behind a toolshed, she descants a trill to
accompany the hiss and stands to adjust herself—all in twenty
seconds. Then she gives the yield a proprietary glance: a lemon
stain, still steaming in the snow.

We continue up Arbat and I sense her exhilaration. She has
triumphed again: felt an urge, proclaimed and satisfied it on the
spot. And got away with something, defied the world and its
dreary conventions. Smiling her I'm-*me* smile, she leans on my
arm and examines the shop windows, alert for dabs of color in
the gray.

This is the quality I love most about her and fear correspondingly. She's never really known guilt and needs no one else's
approval; it is enough for her to express her truly free spirit—and
to be loved by me. She is a cliché only because her rareness has
prompted so many to imagine her: a female animal who is what
she looks like.

On the average, Anastasia must relieve herself hourly outdoors
and at every intermission at the theater. The need becomes
urgent within a minute or two of first being felt and her
fastidiousness exacerbates the problem; gagging at the sight of an

inevitably foul public toilet, she refuses to go in. Once she dashed into a well-known municipal building, found an empty corridor on an upper story and used a dark corner. It's impossible to know in what proportion her drive is due to purely physical need, as opposed to embellisment of instincts she esteems. This is the image of herself she likes and cultivates: a child of nature, harassed by powerful natural needs and society's preposterous obstacles—lack of cafés, Fellini films, goose liver—to satisfy them. However real the whims, she's acutely sensitive to the effect they produce. "The cold makes you pee," she declares, simultaneously explaining her behavior to me, underlining her approval of it, and inviting me to join in making even this a source of amusing self-expression. Or: "I purposely peed before I went out. *Twice.* Ye gods, can you imagine if I didn't?"

Yet the urges *are* genuine. Hypocrisy, false modesty and bureaucratic stupidity make her literally ill. Her body is litmus paper for registering the health and sanity of social arrangements. In her unqualified trust of it, she is convinced that discomfort to her proves stupidity by "them." To hell with all sociological-philosophical-ideological mumbo-jumbo proclaiming higher or lower criteria: a proper society is one in which her natural functions are easily gratified.

Her appetite for food is the most eccentric and tyrannical of the urges. Suddenly she is ravenously hungry, and nothing can be said, no other thought or occupation pursued, until her stomach is appeased. She hunts the meal—or prepares it, or spurs on others who are preparing it—with intense impatience and concern. Her ration must be delicious or unusual: this opportunity for pleasure will never return, and never mind that a similar one—but not the same—was seized hours earlier. As a schoolgirl, problems such as "Sunflower seeds give 50 per cent oil and peanuts 40 per cent; if a collective farm plants 100 hectares of the former . . ." consistently stumped her. She could not fight free of her reverie about the yummy nuts to set up the equations.

Moscow is a conspiracy against her appetite. She can't bear either the cheap cafeterias with the twenty-minute lines nor the hour's wait at tolerable places. When hunger stabs, she will lie, sham sickness, incur any wrath of those waiting in line to get into a restaurant quickly. And when the café we've dropped everything to race to turns out to be locked—a third of Moscow's sprinkling of eateries are closed for repairs, inventory and "sanitary operations" on any given day—she succumbs to wrath. Her challenges to doormen can wax shrill enough to attract a crowd—and sometimes policemen.

"I'm *not* being unreasonable, pantherkins, I'm *appealing* to reason. It's time for a civilized restaurant where people can eat in peace." Then she suggests sneaking into the Union of Journalists club to cop a steak reserved for members.

It's tricky to be with her when the great hunger, or even some lesser whim, comes on. We've lost hours to futile wandering in the cold because, in the middle of a sentence about antique furniture, she was suddenly *dying* for a cup of black coffee. Our quest for the vital fluid would take us hiking from one café to another a quarter of a mile distant. In vain: here an espresso machine is broken, there the ration of beans has given out, the staff of a third counter is "resting"; and most places offer milky mud alone. (No amount of hectoring will get it for you black: the menu of the Moscow City Soviet's Restaurant Trust stipulates coffee with milk, 150 grams, eight kopeks.) Where the right coffee is available, the line is impenetrable, and Anastasia threatens to turn nasty. One morning she jumped on a trolley and rode off, without saying good-bye and never mentioning the incident again, let alone where or why she had gone. When we met that evening, the irritation had long been replaced by enthusiasm for a just-bought book about monastery frescoes.

But the converse of her impatience is a heightened sense of enjoyment. When set before her at last, food gives her extraordinary pleasure. She eats with total concentration, swallowing with noises of gratification and self-congratulation. (A television nature film we saw showing a lioness seemingly caressing a just-killed zebra with great tenderness before devouring it turned her sentimental about all creatures' profound debt to their food.) Odd things at strange hours: a chunk of tough beef and fried potatoes the moment she wakes up, cold fried cod and dill pickles in the dead of night. Restaurant diners set down their knives and forks to watch her cleaning the bones of a cut of salmon; her performance with her portion is more interesting than ingestion of their own. Frequency of intake—five healthy snacks a day, on the average—accounts for the total volume, rather than bulk at any single sitting. She wolfs down the last morsel, savors her triumph for a time and is ravenous again two hours later.

And so with sleep; the same with sex. Every impulse of her nerves or libido is an expression of nature's will, any hindrance to which constitutes a moral wrong as well as a source of discomfort.

Physical frailness, she likes to say, is so fundamental to the human condition that philosophers overlook its implications. "First a person's hungry—and he eats. Then he needs to make love, and he's sleepy. Next there's a different call of nature—and he's hungry all over again. He has to drink, must take a walk, can't do without rest—it's always *something* manipulating him, which he doesn't even acknowledge in his fumblings to explain 'bigger' things. Respite is illusory: before you've finished relieving one urge, the next one is gathering force for an internal ambush. And this leaves out religious needs, which are acute in this country because the physical ones are so hard to satisfy. For example, I now require a lemonade."

These thoughts come in a tone suggesting she's saddened by the tyranny of appetites. But her eyes are sparkling.

"Then, of course, the teeth need brushing after eating, the dishes need washing. . . . What's left for *us*?"

I can only answer in terms of why she finds all this important. Although resentment of foolish convention and dreary routine accounts for some of her concern, the opposite is also true: she is trying to inject an element of conscious enjoyment, even of creativity, into what she calls "the dead half of life."

Two or three times a week, we whet "the live half" with a concert or play. Eager to be lifted into the realms of art and fairy tale, Anastasia comes prepared to contribute to her own treat—at least until the curtain rises.

When it does, she often galls everyone near us. She will not control her reactions. When the performances are good, she comments audibly, laughs in midline, anticipating its conclusion, and claps at will—not so much applauding as encouraging, asking for more. When they are very good, she becomes rigid, squeezing her hands together until they whiten, while a characteristic gurgling of pleasure gathers in her throat. But these are the exceptions. When the standard provincial bathos of most Russian theater is being dished up, Anastasia suffers real physical distress, squirming and groaning at the moral offense of the artistic failure.

"*Will* you behave, young lady?" hiss voices front and back. "This is a *theater.*"

The rebuke is utterly serious. Despite the wide Russian nature, many theatergoers display a petit bourgeois stuffiness that survives only in Vienna if anywhere in the West. Theater is a place of sedate manners and Reverence for (pickled) Art; the mainstay of the audience is the churchgoing type, seeking moral and cultural enlightenment. When the house lights come on, the incongruity gives them a second shock: *her* face made *those* rude noises?

Her critical reactions too slight the general public's. As she is the only customer in a long store line to complain that the cashiers are doubling everyone's wait by relieving one another instead of working in pairs as intended, she is often the sole dissenter among the spectators. Crowd-captivating pomposity, the lure of so many productions, makes her shudder. While the audience cheered an elderly matinee darling named Evgeny Samoilov—father of Tatyana Samoilova, the famous film star—making Hamlet ludicrous with hair-rending poses, Anastasia writhed.

"Can *that* be Hamlet? I'm going home." She had never read the play—but knew.

Weeks later, the touring New York City Ballet disappointed a huge audience in the Palace of Congresses. Accustomed to Bolshoi pageantry—a hundred sumptuously costumed dancers on stage, executing a De Mille-like extravaganza—the Moscow public resented Balanchine's sparse, avant-garde sketches. But Anastasia sensed the performance's brilliance, and her bravos elicited a final curtain call. Afterward, she was ecstatic: she'd discovered a new kind of art.

The theater is where she reveals herself publicly as a creature of instinct, attuned not to education, imitation or cultural training but to her own reflexes; reacting instantly to what is genuine and what spurious in any work. Not actual but *artistic* truth moves her; some of her favorite stories begin, "Once upon a time," and the twentieth reading of a Lermontov tale can give her joy. When *Boris Godunov*'s beggar wails his sorrowful aria, tears wash mascara over her milky cheeks. That aria, she gasps, is her people's suffering. I treasure her for this.

Yet the theater is also where she's at her worst. The performances begin at six-thirty, and our standing agreement is to meet at the entrance fifteen minutes beforehand. I pace around columns, making my way through the forest of black overcoats and searching the frost-flushed faces, or, when the cold is too painful, stand in the vestibule scanning the incoming concourse. She's sworn solemnly that this time she won't be late. I try to keep this in the context of general Russian nonchalance about appointments. "So what?" say people who have failed to show up. "It was cold out there. I knew you wouldn't wait forever." But even measured by this, her disdain for the first rule of social intercourse is exasperating.

The remaining minutes evaporate, the second bell sounds, a hundred normal couples greet each other and hurry to their seats—and my resentment soars. The festive crowd is gone, leaving me with the half-dozen unfortunates who can't attend for some reason and must sell their tickets. Will she stand me up again? At best, we've missed the first scene. Why does she put me in this humiliating position? Never think of others, never show any consideration. But the penchant to be late for everything is also integral to her personality. And a portion of her critical sense applauds the Noble Savage pose.

I'm angry because it was she herself who first expressed interest in the play, after which I dropped everything to spend the day spieling, bribing, pleading to get us in. Fighting through a chaos of telephone calls to a belligerent box office and rude assistant manager, flirting with secretaries and traveling to an Intourist hotel's entertainment desk or the theater itself when the telephone turns useless. I've blustered my way past the woman guarding the entrance, outlasted denials that "the bosses" are in their offices, and obtained the tickets from the manager himself through shameless supplication, spiced by the white lie that I'm leaving Moscow tomorrow, this is my last chance to see his vital work. (I know as well as he that he's keeping a block of the best seats in reserve on the off chance some Party nabob telephones a last-minute order.) Despite this time-consuming, nerve-frazzling procedure, the foreigner's advantage in procuring everything of any value in the country extends to attending the theater; on her own, Anastasia would have had no chance.

But my umbrage also derives from the advantage her tardiness gives her over me. Her nonchalant treatment of the tickets demonstrates that whereas I have nothing important to do all day—the truth is that I dropped *nothing* for the hustling—her life is crowded with work, enthusiasms and optimism. And the deeper reason, which I do not want to act on, is her free spirit. She has precisely the independence of convention that my talk has long claimed for me. Waste the tickets for an important performance? Lose the money? (My money almost always, but she's equally negligent of her own.) I can never make the gesture without bourgeois qualms; she truly doesn't care.

Envy of this abandon, which rides tandem with my hurt pride when she doesn't appear, is the weak flank of our relationship. I resent the silly halfway position she leaves me in. Among my friends, *I'm* known as the man of impulses who wanders far from graduate-school convention. I too propagandize instant gratification: making love with Anastasia at the planetarium and skipping the second act of *Prince Igor* for a glass of mango juice. But she knows my stronger inhibitions will make me withdraw first from the truly outrageous. I'm forced into the role of the sensible adult. The very freedom I laud to others puts me on the defensive, acting on me not only as a token of her charm, but also of the discrepancy between myself and my self-image.

Each time holds the promise of a new start. I telephone her triumphantly.

"We're in! The manager said 'inconceivable,' but I got them in the fourth row."

"Wonderful. I'm dying for some real entertainment."

"What time will you be there?"

"Quarter after six." Pause. "I promise."

"You always promise."

"I don't always have something to tell you. Let's make it six."

I come at ten to six with a sprig of snowdrops and eagerness for her news. The third bell rings at six-thirty, hurrying the last stragglers inside. Like witnesses to a cleared accident, hopefuls for last-minute tickets disperse, leaving me with my resentment. I've spent the entire day preparing to please her with these tickets. All I ask is that she be on time—and show me some appreciation.

I try to look unruffled as I wait. I envy not only the ticket-holders already inside but also the evening passersby. Yes, they're down and out; but they have dignity. They are preoccupied with mature pursuit of caloric and intellectual nourishment, not with what others think of them because a date is late. Strong Russian faces: I admire even the solemnity.

She arrives at last, one hand clutching her gloves, the other a cellophane bag with her theater shoes. Her handbag is wide open and she is breathless, having rushed frenziedly from her dormitory but several minutes ago—when she was already late.

"Hurry up, let's *dash*. We'll just make the curtain. I . . . couldn't get a cab."

If I persuade the usher to admit us, the first act—usually ninety minutes long, in good Russian tradition—and the satisfaction of her beauty at my side drain my irritation. During the intermission, she mentions the real reason for her delay. She was in her bath, and the water was so warm, the peacefulness so delicious, that she couldn't force herself out. (With twenty girls sharing it, how does *she* get the tub at peak time every evening? Most Russian girls share cheerfully by instinct, but with her classmates as with me, Anastasia takes for granted that she deserves the cream.) Or she was listening to a Bach prelude on the radio—such a rare joy that she couldn't tear herself away. I boast of these fetching replies to friends, but also feel misused.

Her excuse can be barer. When the moment for dressing came, she felt "dreamy." Somehow, she wasn't "craving" to go out as she'd expected. Or it was storming outside and she was "blissfully snug" in her room. She relates this information matter-of-factly, as if her mood constitutes an incontestable explanation. Far from censure, she deserves recognition for her keen sense of responsibility. For in these difficult cases, didn't willpower vanquish her languor, that awesome force of nature, in the end? Naturally, the battle put her several minutes behind schedule, which is as nothing compared to the obstacles overcome.

On the evening after our first hours of truly abandoned

lovemaking she did not appear at all. We were in a traveling sculptor's studio that she had secured through the owner's lover. Later we fell asleep in the room's afternoon darkness, but I woke to thoughts of our evening plans. Slipping from under the quilt, I dressed quietly and left to make the clinching arrangements for the tickets, Anastasia mumbling she'd meet me outside the theater. It wasn't cold there, but my humiliation stung more than ever. I could only wait there: the studio had no telephone and I'd forgotten its address. After an hour I went inside for the second act, facing the ignominy of an entire audience registering the empty seat at my side. Public desertion by a girl just made love to.

I once asked a Radcliffe girl whether she preferred more bed for that evening or a concert. "Oh, the *concert*," she answered appreciatively—but Anastasia was just the opposite, and my training in a different culture made me miss her dozen hints. My leaving had insulted *her;* and she couldn't betray her instincts by sitting through a performance. But how could I have known then that our private pleasure transcended an evening out, which she usually relished? Later I learned that she slept there until morning, returning to her institute hungry and blue.

I am purposely raising the difficulties before confirming that she was indeed the girl I'd always wanted, for I want to fix her in my own mind as unsentimentally as I can. The queer coolness with which she accepted gifts, even items, such as a Swiss watch or an English trench coat, that she'd never dreamed of. (This too I understood *later.* It wasn't reserve but an outgrowth of our closeness. Of course she should receive goodies from me, just as she offered me everything she owned and knew. Giving and taking merited no fuss.) How she would suddenly look the peasant girl: with a Liberty silk square tied around her head, her too-large "shitwader" boots, as she called them, tapping her slender calves, and her lips in a pucker because she'd finished her ice cream—a creature of such uniqueness and animation that I kept hugging her. The pucker itself, a blend of spontaneous sentiment and instant play on it for dramatic possibilities— tinged, as always, with a hint of eye-batting innocence.

Her perverse refusal to jot down even the most essential

reminders in a pocket notebook, and the rage with which she ravaged her handbag and drawers for a crucial telephone number preserved on an old napkin. Again and again she repeated this Russian celebration of anarchy, turning even angrier when I entreated her, *for her own sake,* to be orderly at least in this. But no matter how often she was late and whom she kept waiting—even when she lost the card of the director who asked her to audition for a television play about medical students—she *would not submit* to dreary good sense.

The way she switched in the blink of an eye from a movie mogul's sophisticated Stockholm mistress to farmer's daughter with a yen for unpasteurized milk; these two aspects of her were like an optical illusion. The mole on her collar bone; the line of her back as she waited, lying on her stomach and cupping her mannequin's breasts. Her frail clearness one warmish day when, for the hell of it, we toured the All-Union Exhibition of Economic Achievement, and in those square miles of bulldozers and spaceship models, nostalgia for her enfolded me, as if I were seeing her from the perspective of twenty years hence.

This is what I want to remember: she as a sovereign being, independent of her involvement with me. I must keep the two separate: a likeness of Anastasia Serigina and the story of our bust.

Much happened in the month following our first encounter to make me accept that I'd never see her again. Then the second meeting, a coincidence too bizarre to illustrate anything—yet the kind that keeps overtaking me here. Ah—as Alyosha says with quite different inflection—if I could relive that sweet night!

In October, a busload of foreign students was treated to a trip out of Moscow—to Yaroslavl, proud township of ancient Rus. Seven rattling hours north and we entered its provincial hollowness and turn-of-the-century industrial gloom. A membrane of dirty ice coated Mother Volga; winter's gray subdued most movement by midafternoon. Touring the splendid six-teenth-century Kremlin, we retired to a restaurant on Freedom Street, its neon strand providing the urban centerpiece.

Leaving the hotel at midnight for fresh air, I was absorbed into an album of prerevolutionary photographs. Darkened log cabins, a pair of drunken workers stumbling in snow, a lone mongrel prowling a side street. . . . For something to drink, I made my way to the railroad station, where peasants blanketed the waiting room benches like battlefield corpses. My heart thumped in the oblivion of this outpost of civilization. A baby cried, then took the breast. Great sadness deepened the grip of provincial isolation.

I saw beer at the buffet and joined the line. The brownish shawl covering the back of the woman in front of me seemed as tacky as the waiting room, and as she began turning her face toward mine, I wondered absentmindedly what the hard-up stranger might want of me. Before the thought ended, those eyes were again on mine.

A current tingled my skin. The huge hall was airless. "You!" I said in a melodramatic bray. And was filled with a rush of happiness because her shining countenance was no less than I'd remembered. A modern icon framed by the shawl—and it was endearingly familiar, already mine.

The waltz of her laugh through the murkiness brought a second wave of pleasure. She bridled the words on her lips. When she said them at last, her voice was an octave lower than I had imagined.

"Clever to find me here. But do you think we should know each other's names? If we meet again, 'you' might be inadequate."

"I can't believe this."

"I almost can't, unless you've come for your book. . . . Do you read Bunin? Lucky people begin believing they embody special virtue."

I felt we were making the sweet small talk of beautiful people tipsy on champagne. Again I thought of *The Master and Margarita*. "Do you read Bulgakov?" I countered, but again waited before explaining.

We talked about chance and traveling. She took my foreignness as casually as my proffered glass of beer, asking neither why I was in Russia nor what I was doing in a back-country railroad station. It might have been our old custom to take a weekend drink there—in the dead of night when, except for the station, the city was long asleep.

"Are you tired?" I found it natural to ask.

"Not like last night. . . . Why are so many men sailing the world solo?" she said, gazing at the train departures. "Do you think people are trying to protect their fantasies against a universal commonwealth?"

"Are you a loner?" I asked in reply.

"Anything but. My panda attends me."

"But you protect your inner thoughts."

She examined my eyes again. "Less than you, serious one. Much less than you."

We shared more beer, then brandy for antifreeze. She led me through the gelid night to her uncle's room, half of a log cabin even more rustic than those I'd previously seen because it stood alone, in a village-like outskirt. Gulping the sweet wine for which Anastasia had hiked to the station, the old-timer stared into his oil lamp, cackling a monologue about a pilot incinerated in a Liberator that had crashed ferrying supplies to his unit during the war.

I wouldn't have believed that anything I'd see during the trip would be more remote from my world than Volga moonlight and the station's shadowy eeriness, but the hut and its dilapidation were farther into fairyland. Accusing me of not helping him with his chores last week, the scrawny uncle embraced me in forgiveness, repeating an old Russian aphorism about everyone being a sinner.

Anastasia guided me up a homemade ladder and into an attic containing a dresser and a bed. It was not a "night of love" because only hours remained before I had to answer our "guide's" roll call at the hotel; and also because I was too full of bewildered admiration—for the smoothness of her skin, suppleness of her limbs, provocative matter-of-factness. Too edgy at the strange surroundings, risk of detection, challenge of performance. She smelled of Seville oranges. Although her uncle slept days and brooded at night, she assured me he was deaf. Even during our first embrace with her long legs, I noticed that she accepted our adventure as it came, concentrating on its physical sensations, while my thoughts rebounded in compartments for *analyzing* unusual phenomena and appraising my reactions. What did it *mean* that I was with her in this incredible situation?

In the darkness before dawn, she walked me to the hotel and my day of group touring of monuments and a tire factory. At the weatherworn peasant market, we persuaded a woman to sell us her steaming *pirozhki* before opening hours, and I was introduced to her celebration of food. If it were in me, I'd have loved her as much as the knight—as she could already make me feel about myself for moments—who had stumbled on his Russian princess. But it was just these symbols, which the dramatic night and I had cast up, that prevented me from being real.

Despite associations with Romanov heraldry and the Winter Palace, hers is a peasant name; she is a country girl. Therefore, I wonder where her sprucelike individualism germinated. Her attitude toward religion, for example, typically centers about herself, rather than Church or State. Contemptuous of the Orthodox church in general and of its obscurantist subjugation of believers—the spectacle of ragged women's foreheads on a crumbling vestry floor makes her wince—she is nevertheless drawn to murky cathedrals: to the mystique of candles flickering on icons and choirs chanting their captivating dissonance; and she pulls me in with her, especially to a dark one near her dormitory, at every chance. Shuddering at the Gunga Din prostration, she simultaneously exults that primordial Russian forces have a hold on an unfathomable part of her.

The same ambiguity surrounds her own origins. She is appalled—and excited—by the mud and vodka of village life and often guides me on a walk from the last metro stop to absorb the countryside's psychic stimulation and strange grant of peace. We tramp for hours along meandering trails and eroded stream beds, saddened and gladdened at the rural backwardness and resistance to change. Even polluted ponds and dumps of old pipes heighten the haunting desolation.

About Russia itself, Anastasia's feelings shift sharply. Most days, she knows it as a coarse, dreary place best suited to proving Dostoyevsky's maxim about misery being as important as happiness to the human race. She scorns the superstitious, passive masses who acclaim their oppressors almost as acidly as the leadership's frauds. She can't remember Lenin's birthplace on the Volga or the cruiser *Aurora* of the first revolutionary shot—which are repeated a dozen times daily (in case someone missed the hundreds of school lectures) on every radio station.

Ordinarily she will not glance at a newspaper or popular magazine. Bored waiting for a train at a suburban station, she once picked up *Pravda* and tried to read, but the onward-to-Communism tone switched her off as emphatically as when she witnessed Samoilov's mutilation of Hamlet. Plowing through the leads of several articles, she pushed the paper back at me and closed her eyes to nap, her frown indicating she'd not repeat *that* mistake for another year.

Her reaction to such things derives not from any interest in politics, but from her intuition that the Soviet setup is "a big bother" because it prevents her from tasting the world's treats: the cup of espresso, a visit to Rome. "Bananas and cream?" I once answered her query about the phrase encountered in her reading. "That's an expression we know from childhood. Like corned beef and cabbage, or ham and eggs."

"Of course," she replied with sudden annoyance. "In Russia we too have an expression. Bread and lard." The real fault of the system, or curse of the country, is that it deprives her of so many delights of the stomach and eye. No French restaurant in Moscow or the entire country!

What's strange about such sentiments is their lodging in a born hick. Ordinarily, they'd be muttered by disaffected—and relatively rich—Moscow intellectuals, who give them a more political slant. As with her personal hygiene, so scrupulous that "that place" is always as fresh-smelling as her hair, she's the exception that proves the rule: a mutation from the village girl species.

But although she laments the country's condition, I must be careful not to "slander." Occasionally she erupts into Russian-earth ardor more fervent than a dozen Viktors. Once we were in a village and I was shaking my head—in commiseration, not disparagement—at the sight of a peasant whose frostbitten face and splayed earflaps spoke of a lifetime of draft-animal labor; whose cottage cried out with slovenliness. Her response was violent.

"I'm sick to death of people denigrating Russia. Smooth Westerners who'll never understand the truth of this country, who don't know its suffering, even its pleasures, because they're insulated from real life—even their own. By what measure do you suppose you are superior to that man?"

"What's this, Long Legs? I'm with you on the countryside— even the country. I've got nothing against him, and you know *I'm* not smooth like that."

She softened just as quickly. "I suppose not, but I've had too much of people criticizing everything. Russia is everybody's butt; it's humbled enough without your mockery."

To say that she was the one inclined to "criticize everything" would only have rekindled her pique. Besides, it would have been only literally correct, as I'd just been reminded. The larger truth is that while her spoken comments about Russia are consistently reproachful, what she leaves unsaid contains much affection. This was summed up in her observation that foreigners not only look much happier than Russians, but seem *trained* to look happy. And despite her aversion to propaganda, she weeps irrepressibly when viewing relentlessly repeated films of the Nazi invasion. I wonder what effect this will have when the crunch comes and she must think about leaving the country.

Yes, leave with me: a voice whispered the forbidden word "marriage" from the very beginning. I knew that if I ever took a wife, she must be Russian. Meanwhile she gave me far more than an introduction to the local ways, in accordance with the traditional prescription for a young man's best method of learning about a country. Going to the theater with my splendorous Russian companion was a triumph as well as an occasion. Acclaim for myself becluttered my thoughts of her. Ending my isolation—this was still November, when Alyosha was only a man who sometimes lent us his room—she also began my longed-for romance.

She returned from Yaroslavl on the day after me. Her long hours of classes, at Moscow's Second Medical Institute, often kept us apart, but her free time was a shared gift. We walked for hours, feeding on back-street scenes, sharpening our appetites to splurge on smoked salmon and shashlik in hard-currency dining rooms. I came to see my boyhood image of springtime Paris in the city's autumn glumness. Forsaken leaves clinging to slender trees made Volzhsky Boulevard as picturesque as any Latin Quarter postcard; fall wind and rain blew the last stalwarts onto our raincoats. The very banality of my associations made them surprising: who would have pictured Moscow a city for lovers?

But eyesores drew us together as tightly as the dapplings of charm, proving that our tenderness for each other tinted our perceptions rather than the other way round. Rehearsals for the November 7th parade in Red Square dragged on for weeks. One evening when snorting military equipment was learning its route, we found ourselves on the Krimsky Bridge above the river, its graceful cables etching the sky's darkening mauve while black vehicles, glistening in the drizzle, rumbled along the embankment underneath. United by the ugly beauty—the sinister splendor of the tanks, finest item of local manufacture—she turned her Lapland face to me at the instant I was seeking her lips. The river burbled below us, the sky turned pearly, tank after sleek tank roared on its way. As we clung to each other, our passion sent regards through my heavy trousers and her thick skirt. Only her eyes were made up. She smiled with them. I had never kissed like this.

We are on the streets so often partly because of the difficulty of finding refuge. Anastasia's Yaroslavl uncle, whom she visits twice a year, is her closest relative in the geographical sense; her immediate family is further north, on a swampy tract near the town of Vologda. She herself shares a dormitory room with three classmates. Even discounting an unusually strict entrance guard, the others' presence eliminates her bed for our use.

Although my room is easier to sneak into, she has rendered it unusable. The first time went according to plan. I gave her my pass; she negotiated the gate by flashing its cover while hurrying through; I joined her inside by persuading the guards I'd left mine in my room. The following weekend, a different shift— alerted, no doubt, by Anastasia's striking yet unfamiliar face— told her to open the pass. Before she could retreat, the ruse was exposed.

In this situation, Russians apologize grovelingly and implore a once-and-only, life-and-death exception to the rules to visit a sick brother or save a depressed friend from suicide. Had Anastasia

conformed, she might have been admitted, even though un-
masked. But she disdains "the sensible thing." It is a matter of
principle that officials must trust her, and when caught violating
precisely such trust she is outraged. True to form, she now
produced a scene instead of an excuse.

"This system. We're a socialist country, it's supposed to be *the
people's* university. Take those hands off me, I'm going through."

Angry now, the battle-axe biddies gripped her, chortling as if
they'd caught a pickpocket. Two beefy security men sprinted out
of their strategically placed office and led her away. Only after a
full hour of scary interrogation was she ejected. Still huffing that
she could sneak into Brezhnev's office if necessary, she did not,
however, return to the University for months.

Thus we stayed on the streets. If I were Russian, the
responsibility for finding an empty room, the crucial male
desideratum for courting in Moscow, would be mine. Anastasia
substitutes when she can by asking for the sculptor's keys or
taking me to Alyosha's. And by settling for makeshift. As winter
waxes, we explore the stairwells of mouldering apartment houses
near her institute. In their basements or on their top landings,
she makes herself available on the banister. Her panties are in
my pocket. Her body is immaculate after the latest languishing
in the bath. Against the background of staircase grime, the slight
lankiness of her limbs changes to sylphlike grace. With them, and
because of our unusual positions, she grips me hard, as proud of
her command of these muscles as of all her physical urges.

The stairwell's dank chill plates our cheeks. The building is a
Bronx tenement soon to join a black slum; the courtyard from
which we've entered is strewn with rotting timbers and junk.
Domestic sounds—from television movies, kettles, irritated vocal
chords—reach us through flimsy plaster, and steps sometimes
resound on the dusty stairs themselves—occasionally shuffling,
for tipplers straggle home at this hour of evening. When we stop
for a moment, our hearts beat with the Benzedrine of apprehension and passion; when we resume, we continue to hold our
breath. Then she arches her back and bears down. Her eyes are
open. The frankness of their desire gives my narcissism wings.

She turns around and thrusts herself upward. Later, to play it
safe, or to indulge our fancy for variety, we move to a staircase on

a parallel street. "*Again,* please," she urges. We're pushing our luck; our fear of discovery grows. To compensate for not being naked, she makes use of her fingers, bringing them up from time to time with her customary appetite for exotic tastes. "Now you sit down," she whispers. "Here, spread my coat. Don't you love exchanging roles?"

The freedom to act out our fantasies fills us with confidence that nothing important is beyond our grasp. "Oh what a love it was," said Zhivago. "Utterly free, unique, like nothing else on earth."

She loves jokes, especially about resistance to work, interpretations of social messages to justify embezzling, and bureaucratic malapropisms. One of her favorites is about the ailing factory worker told to produce a specimen of his feces. Abashed by the strange medical terminology, he brings his material in the customary match box, but cringing embarrassment prevents him from asking whom to give it to. Finally, he charges a nurse. "Where's the place for leaving your shit for the stool?"

It is the worker's endearing resort to his class's real language that delights her, but this joke in particular provides one of her rare conversational references to medicine.

Her perfunctory interest in her studies shows in her greater enthusiasm for almost everything else. The health of dumb animals concerns her distinctly more than that of human beings; the only time I saw her excited about anything faintly medical was during the birth of kittens to a tough stray she'd come to feed outside one of our stairways. During war films, the sight of wounded *horses* upsets her most. Convinced that "no species is crueler—lower" than *Homo sapiens,* she often accepts man's inhumanity to man but gnashes her teeth at his barbarity to beasts. Her mother and father wanted her to become an engineer, their image of social virtue and personal success. Medicine was an afterthought, but I doubt that any profession would stir her—certainly none requiring long "crazy boring" hours of study.

What does interest her is literature. In spurts, her reading is as voracious as the—misconceived—stereotype of the culture-hungry Russian. Rereading *The Idiot,* her eyes were riveted to the book from the moment she entered one metro station to her emergence at her destination—and then for the rest of the day and evening, for she skipped classes to finish it, murmuring constantly about Dostoyevsky's uncanny understanding of people *she knew.*

Classics unspoiled by force-fed learning and political vulgarization in school grip her, especially Lermontov's Byronesque tales. But her greater affection is for secondary, slightly offbeat masters—Alexander Green, Mikhail Saltyakov-Shchedrin, Alexei Konstantinovich Tolstoy, Andrei Platonov—whose recreation of the spirit of Russian life enchant her all the more for the authors' lack of world renown. The obscurer the writer, the chummier her patter to his pages.

"Exactly, and don't back down from it. . . ."

"You've no right to assume that, thank God you did. . . ."

"Yes, a hundred times *yes.* Clever man, you've omitted the main thing."

One mock-heroic tale delights her especially for its picture of daily routine. Entitled "Home Sweet Home," it is by a long-suppressed 1920s poet who called himself Sasha Chorny ("Sasha Black") in counterpoise to the great turn-of-the-century symbolist Andrei Bely ("Andrei White"). The scene is a communal apartment of screeching neighbors, dismal prospects and petty scores to settle; the images are of someone's child trying to give the cat an enema, the last drop of vodka that disappeared yesterday, a meditative cockroach perched on a plate like a large plum and a glum teen-age girl in a workjacket raping a piano that has a nasty cold.

Anastasia recites the sad-but-riotous lines with squinting eyes—to help, she says, visualize the Yaroslavl apartment where she and her mother once rented half a bedroom. But she loves the poem too for its playful use of the diminutives, colloquialisms, pen names, grammatical gaffes and peasant solecisms that enrich and personalize the language, conferring the same intimate candor to tête-à-tête communication as in all aspects of private Russian life. The sharp disparity between the outer, public world and the inner one of family and friends declares itself in the contrast between the two languages; sensitive, irreverent spirits show their affection for the unofficial one by savoring its subtleties and hints. Inventive argot heightens the sense of shared secrets, we-against-them loyalty—and even of sensual pleasure. Anastasia's flair for this—which is what Alyosha most loved—shows best in her vivacious appreciation of coined words.

For me, she begets hundreds in addition to the familiar ones—"my joy," "my dearest only own"—that would be inanely mawkish in English. One week, I am forms of "little bunny"—not just the usual *zaichik,* but half a dozen semantic varieties, all changing, but not interchangeable, in accordance with her mood. Or I'm ten variations of "kitten" or, lately, "kitten's paw," *lapuska, lapinka, lapunik, lapunya, lapusik* and *lapushka.*

"But *lapa* is any kind of paw," I pretend to protest. "How do I know I'm a kitten and not a tiger?"

"Can't you hear the way I say it, my *tigroynok* [fierce-and-gentle little tiger]?"

Or a nonsense word, changing daily, sometimes hourly, in play on the weather or the rhyme of a recently devoured delicacy. She is as much made for sweet nothings as for hedonism and passion.

We are in each other's arms on Alyosha's daybed, waiting for my renascence. Lit by a thinning afternoon whiteness through the window, the room I'll soon know so well seems suspended in space. Alyosha himself, who is still only Anastasia's somewhat mysterious older friend, has invented an urgent appointment somewhere to leave us alone, apologizing with elaborate pseudo-contrition that he can't return before evening. During a silence I ask Anastasia to tell me about her first lover.

Soon I shall give this up: something weak lurks under the cover of my contention that old adoration reinforces the new. But I sometimes feel tongue-tied during the wait, and to my secret hope that the girl's reminiscences will shorten it I have the added excuse here of investigating Russian ways. I half expect Anastasia to demur, but after a moment's hesitation, she answers matter-of-factly.

The first was a Czech engineer on assignment in Moscow. He was thirty-two; she—who was visiting the capital with her high-school class—had just turned fifteen. He spied her with her group on a street; she said she was eighteen and that night sneaked from the boarding school where the class was sleeping to meet him in the moonlit big city. Returning to her village the next evening, she found his telegram waiting. Throughout that year from Moscow and the next two from Prague, a stream of weekly gifts, photographs and letters arrived, pleading for marriage. . . .

Anastasia's pause becomes a full stop.

"That's all you have to say about him?"

"For now."

"What was his name?"

"Mirek."

"But what did you *feel*?"

Together with relief that he didn't get her, *I* can feel an odd attachment to this story—and masochism for liking its ending. How could she have been so blasé? Part of me is appalled by her teen-age heartlessness; another part recognizes that I protest too much and want to experience the same petty ruthlessness on myself, as when I rail against her being late.

"What was he like? *Why* did you answer only one letter?"

She says he was gentle and that she was flattered, then stops again. My jealousy stays bottled up because I think it is of her, not him; and for all the wrong reasons.

Later, we laugh together at Mirek's successors. Her high school's Young Communist secretary, who used to meet her, still underaged, in a coal room, satisfy himself in thirty seconds, and sneak out of the building first, like a burglar. The collective-farm driver who nearly died from a blade under the heart in the knife-hurling, Yul Brynner-imitating craze that followed the showing of *The Magnificent Seven* in the farm's Palace of Culture. But what I really want to hear about is her promiscuous period. The Moscow weekends during her final high-school year, when she allowed herself to be picked up in exchange for meals and her train fare back to the village. The nights with provincial factory directors or military officers. Once, two Georgian black marketeers half-abducted her, and after half-struggling, she joined their game. Together, they took her nine times in twelve hours. . . .

Again I'm full of sterile hurt, and of excitement. She ravished by Georgian lovers of Russian blondes—and I'm jealous of her, not enraged by them. All the more because she has remembered this incident with obvious satisfaction.

She and Alyosha behave with each other like fond old friends with an almost benign ghost in their past. Neither speaks about their relationship, but he did before he acknowledged the intensity of ours, and she occasionally makes a comment about an unmistakable "man I once knew." From this—and her homely dormitory roommate—I've pieced together the story of their affair.

They met during her first year in the institute, when her language and clothes screamed "village" and "her nose ran like a farm kid's"—yet she was tenaciously independent from the first moment. She found his recruitment talk charming but would not enter the car, having for some reason decided not to be swept off her feet.

Instead, her sass captivated *him*. Ignoring his "if at first you don't succeed, pass to the next" maxim, he called her twice a day. She replied only at whim; he parked outside her dormitory for hours, "like a poor man's Paolo to her Francesca, er, da Rimini." Again and again he swore not to waste another hour on the "demon-nymphet," but just this self-will is what made him happy—and grateful for the surprise that he could still be bewitched—when she did succumb, sitting chastely at his side for long drives.

He plied her with flowers. Eventually, she allowed him to take her to restaurants and exclusive film showings at the Union of Cinema Workers. Most of all, they argued—about everything. Sometimes they sat in the car until morning ruthlessly debating the talent of an actress or the declension of a noun. She demanded treatment as an equal, taking for granted nothing he said about the meaning of a movie, the implications of a war, the intention of one of his friends' remarks. Or he would open her books and coach her for the next day's classes, stopping for pseudo-medical commentary and laughs.

Her refusal to be touched "until you have an operation for satyrism" drove him to delight. According to his probes, her defense relied on physical nimbleness or quickness of repartee. He courted—and enjoyed—her more assiduously than a thousand of his standard prey.

When she came to the apartment at last, it was under agreed terms. She sat alone in the armchair, demurely sipping wine. It was insanely cold outside; he had fed her beautifully and put on a Frank Sinatra tape. Suddenly he was making love to her with his mouth. She realized he had planned everything to the last drop of Bull's Blood, but this no longer mattered. She looked down at the shaggy gray head that was doing such wonderful things and realized she adored him. His face between her legs became a symbol of something important, which she herself could not explain.

"How long did you love him?" I ask, lost in the image. Somewhere I'm jealous; somewhere glad. They are my older brother and sister. "How long did it last?"

"Three weeks."

"And then?"

"He couldn't go on."

It's very strange: neither of us want this conversation, but she is answering matter-of-factly, perhaps because she doesn't want to be asked again.

"Alyosha's made for good times and when you need help. You can't even suffer properly with him, if that's what you want from love. It's not what *I* want, *lapuska*."

I wonder why I continue with this. I know she's telling the truth, and it's a simple one that doesn't disturb me. I feel nothing much more than that I *should* feel more.

"Yet you kept seeing him."

Her sigh says this should finish more quickly. "There's only one Alyosha to go to when you're disgusted with everything or deep blue. Or"—she squeezes my waist—"when you need an empty apartment."

"You still love him. So witty, such a lover."

"Enough silliness, let's go wash our ears."

There's nothing more to it, except that I still feel there should be. Anastasia and Alyosha seem to represent two sides of me that otherwise were entirely separate. I wish we three could set up house together. I wish I were older. And that I understood why the story of the forty-six-year-old him courting the nineteen-year-old her is so important to me.

Today I have found a place. A girl named Evgeniya who picked me up last September saw me again crossing a street and offered me her "all-new pad." Evgeniya belongs to the growing caste of semiprostitutes to the foreign compounds, whose life consists of affecting Western manners to go with their imported clothes. But the gesture of handing me her keys—and drawing me a map—reminds me that even her kind of Russian is good at sharing.

A long ride by metro, another by trolley, a tramp to a tumbledown cottage and furtive sneaking over ancient floorboards into a dowdy room. Anastasia tears off her clothes as if resenting them for restricting her body. "Hurry, *hurry*," she says, gazing almost worshipfully at the part of me most straining for her. "Skorei, *skorei*, my dearest, my tiger."

My slightest touch of her nipples elicits shuddering and groans. I remember the scene in Koestler's *Age of Longing*, which I always felt rang false, where a man brings his mistress to a climax—also climaxing the novel—by manipulating her breasts. Something important must happen to us soon.

We fill the tiny room with our limbs and passion. She takes my face in her hands and sobs with joy, then falls back exhausted. As she lies there with eyes closed and locks adorning her breasts, I think of her as Slovene or Magyar—and remember what she said during our first restaurant feast, days after Yaroslavl. "Sex isn't like eating. You get what you give."

One day a nurse in an old age home will ask me if that was the best I ever had.

"No, but the most beautiful."

She adores: cheap garlic sausage; organ recitals in the Tchaikovsky Conservatory; sarcastic taxi drivers; Byron's most romantic poetry; buckwheat kasha swimming in butter; the circus; stripping to skinny-dip in half-frozen streams (she never goes in); a superb, almost unknown Soviet film entitled *Shadows of Our Forgotten Ancestors*, the down-and-out beer hall next door to Alyosha's old office on Collective Farm Square. . . . *She despises:* ballet on television; ice-skating on television (which the masses adore); Nikita Khrushchev—about whom she knows almost nothing, yet about whom she will not listen to a word; organized physical exercise; *Dr. Zhivago* (a copy of which I smuggled to her); Soviet films about children that win prizes in the West; American women in Intourist hotels. . . .

I also remember her shortness with her friends when she was annoyed with them. The memory of her temper, of her childishness—which I didn't protect because of my own—allows me to wonder whether I might be putting too much blame on myself for our failure. Besides—I assure myself—many of our misunderstandings were inherent in our circumstances.

For example, there was the incident that began with Evgeniya's telephone call, urging that we meet immediately. An hour later, we were outside the Metropole Hotel.

"It's only for your sake," she said. "Only to protect you from a danger you can't understand." Her information was dead certain because it came from a cousin high in "the organs."

"Well the long and short of it is that your Anastasia's on the KGB payroll."

Her last words curled up like a scorpion's tail. Never mind that she was showing herself a vile liar as well as a tart; she had managed to flick out and poison *us*. For even before I had time to reject her words, they had formed an image: *Anastasia an informer.* I crumpled with the bite's outrage and nausea.

The worst came when one feeble station on the shortwave band of my thoughts wondered whether the accusation might conceivably be true. I remembered that this very Metropole, almost the only hotel open to foreigners during Stalin's time, always crawled with informers. One evening when we were dancing in its rococo restaurant, Anastasia mused about what would have happened to her if she had dared to do the same "in the old days." Even then it struck me that this was an uncharacteristic remark.

Maybe she was one of those who "reported" irrelevancies and nonsense just to keep the KGB, paradoxically, as far as possible from their genuine lives and thoughts. Maybe she'd kept quiet in order to spare me. Still crumpled, I tried to think of what to do. Poor Anastasia, even—or especially—if a scrap of this were true.

When Alyosha's investigation was complete, the evidence confirmed envy as Evgeniya's motive. She had seen me with Anastasia in restaurants and was piqued that I hadn't called her after what she considered our opening night. Here was a chance for revenge—all the easier to play on the basis of her own unquestioned assumption that a beautiful Russian girl could not keep company with an American without KGB sanction. But before these facts emerged, I'd broached the matter to Anastasia; the evil was done. She wilted. My stomach turned as when I, an eight-year-old, accidentally poisoned our rabbit.

It was the mistake of the husband who confesses. For although I recognized no such hidden cruelty in my news—*I* hadn't ratted on her, after all; and wouldn't the silly business draw us closer?—she was stung by the scintilla of uncertainty that had prompted me to tell it. How could *I* believe *that* of *her,* even for an instant?

Like the wife who hears the unwanted breast-beating, she could no longer hold my hand in pristine trust. I was to encounter people far grander than Evgeniya, including some of the carefully rebellious intelligentsia, who trade on precisely such narks' gossip—but as in so much else, Anastasia's loathing of it was an exception. We both were innocent, both felt dishonored.

The injury was only to our illusions, but it had been just those illusions that had encouraged us to see a message in our bond. Our alliance had been bolstered by the uplift of two people born five thousand miles apart, and in antagonistic supercultures, reacting more similarly to stimuli than the kids we grew up with. After the accusation we talked less of this. Skipping the second act of a much-praised play because our behinds were asleep or "adopting" a tot to get us admitted to a children's zoo suddenly seemed less inspired. Formerly, we had invested our tricks with the belief we were illustrating something about necessary priorities, teaching the stuffed shirts of the world. Now we were two friends trying something clever.

The next week, I invited Chingiz to join us in a countryside tramp. Before meeting Anastasia, my rambles with him past pine trees and frozen streams were of much the same spirit. Liking them both, I was confident they would like each other.

Exchanging greetings at our rendezvous in a metro station, I was struck by the likeness in handsomeness and temperament between my two student friends. Chingiz saw a pamphlet about his beloved Mayakovsky at the station bookstall and excused himself to check. While we waited, Anastasia pronounced him a "shallow phony."

"Believe me, he cares nothing for Mayakovsky except to pass off self-boosting sentimentalism picked up from some university crowd. And that stuff about shepherds loving his Communist father—don't make me laugh."

About Chingiz's father, she knew only what I myself had told her over the weeks. About his feeling for Mayakovsky, she judged on the basis of one remark when he spied the pamphlet: that the tempestuous poet might have found reason to kill himself even if the Revolution hadn't soured. It was hardly an original comment, yet in no way offensive; she might have said something similar herself. Yet she took his departure to declare the whole of him, with his complex ways, a fraud.

"On what evidence?" I asked, hoping to keep my plans for the day from falling apart.

"Don't ride me. You're not my teacher."

After this, nothing Chingiz might have said all day could have cleared him: she was staying loyal to her intuition. For the first time, I realized how dismaying her keen artistic instinct could be in situations requiring objectivity. How easily she condemned not only actors that displeased her, but people. Embarrassed and ashamed for her, I changed the subject.

Chingiz returned and their antipathy flashed. But neither was willing to insult me—oh, this paradox!; if only they had!—by calling off the outing. We went to an undeveloped tract just outside the city limits, the vagueness of their dislike for each only increasing the tension.

Laconic on the best of days, Chingiz said almost nothing for the first hours, my efforts to draw him out only clamping tighter his jaw. It was a piercing morning of individual snow crystals and fir branches with sunlit icicles: as perfect a winter day as I'd ever seen. Its beauty deepened our aloneness. In the immense silence of a horizonful of unspoiled countryside, the squeaking of our six boots was as in a prison yard.

Again, I could blame circumstances. My contribution to the misery had been breaking the rule that foreigners should not introduce one Russian friend to another. For obvious reasons, of which Evgeniya's deceit should have made me fully conscious, the parties can only mistrust each other. I thought of this when I saw the darkness in both their faces, each trying to feel out whether the other's relationship with me, the American, was clean.

But I also remembered a wise man's warning. "In every triangle, there are two corners on the base. The third one is the lonely apex." Why had I really chosen to form this tight-lipped triangle? The hazy notion nagged that I had invited Chingiz out of some fear about my ability to entertain her: to spice up our relationship, which was already blander than the promise of our savory first meetings. Our respect for each other was also tarnishing: there was Anastasia, hiking up ahead—as usual, evading her responsibility to cope with unpleasantness. Whenever we landed in anything distasteful, even through her caprice, she solved the problem by walking away, leaving it to me.

"Nastinka, I've been telling Chingiz—remember the day when we saw the hare with the rear end?"

"No."

She marched on, pretending to be too absorbed in nature to notice us. I thought of what I'd have said to her if we were alone, as on our last outing to a country estate. "Let's not spend our money on a palace when we're rich and famous. Let's hire women to shell our sunflower seeds."

Suddenly a bird darted from a glorious aspen toward the incredible azure, the sun spangling the tips of its feathers.

"Chickadee," said Chingiz. "They're in pollution trouble."

Anastasia shouted back, without turning round. "In central Russia, a bluetit is usually recognized when seen." Her voice oozed sarcasm. "Maybe not literary scholars, but a poet's first obligation is to know wildlife."

A repugnant squabble flared, kept above the level of Anastasia's comment—her mention of central Russia to the half-Kalmyk Chingiz was barely disguised racism—by Chingiz's restraint. I'd seen the bird best and thought it a humble sparrow, but tried to make them laugh by swearing it was a pelican. The attempt fell wretchedly flat. I went home with Chingiz because Anastasia had stalked off, sparing me the choice.

If the presence of a third party diminishes every couple's special language, it was understandable that ours, based on the proposition that it expressed a rare compatibility of disparate backgrounds, suffered more than most. But this grim outing did worse. It lodged the vile suspicion in us that if Chingiz could reduce us to strangers, not only our sparkling language of shared observations and associations but our very rapport was a carnival souvenir.

Logically, our inability to sustain the happy freedom of our own company in Chingiz's presence should have made us prize it even more—but it didn't. Our sense of uniqueness in taking a rattling bus ride or taking in a bad movie on ancient plywood seats was further diminished.

Only with Alyosha could we be ourselves, although I still knew him only slightly. He would fry us a steak if we liked, then leave with a droll apology. His was the sole apartment in the city of eight million she liked, and where we felt no obligation.

We were there one evening when he returned, whistling a happy warning, with two girls. After some dancing, those three climbed into bed while Anastasia and I laid out the rubber mattress on the kitchen floor. Soon their room resounded with romping, and I sat up for a look through a crack in the door. These games were still new to me. Anastasia followed in time to see the prettier of the two girls beckon me to join—and to notice the gesture make me ready again, although we'd finished a moment before.

"Alyosha's busy and the hungry one's calling for help," she whispered. "Why are you snubbing her?"

"Are you serious?" I hoped she was. Or wasn't; most of all I wanted her to tell me clearly. But her smile was truly enigmatic. I thought it said what I was learning for myself from so many girls at Alyosha's: what does it matter if I move on to someone else for a quick screw?

"Why should I mind, she won't snap it off," she added. "Go on to her. But hurry back to me."

She urged me to my feet. A sudden memory of her tale of the two Georgians who took her *nine times* in twelve hours convinced me she was in earnest. After all, she herself had told me about her promiscuous streak. I went to the bed. The girl rolled over, opening her warm legs to me.

When I returned to the kitchen, Anastasia was asleep. Months later, when Alyosha told me she was feigning this after watching my performance in furious hurt and loathing, I realized I'd misinterpreted everything, even why she had been willing to talk of her earlier lovers. It was all done to observe my reaction: she already suspected I was going the way of Alyosha in bed.

"Apparently she loved you," said Alyosha to my plying. "I didn't know. She swallowed a pile of pride to stay after her test of you that night."

The incredible thing was not that I needed someone else to tell me I'd behaved like a pig, but that even then, when my insensitivity clinked in my ears, I pretended not to have known what I did to her while I was doing it. It was "just a screw."

She could not see me the rest of the week. On the weekend, we had our first row. Naturally it concerned trivia.

She had lost her "passport," the identification document Russians are supposed to carry at all times. It was her second loss of the vital folder since I knew her, but this could hardly explain my pique. She, not I, had to waste a Saturday afternoon on police lines for a replacement. I pressed the bills for the fine on her, silently contemptuous of her for her eternal carelessness, and of myself for my hypocrisy in playing the benefactor. My disgust for my own meanness shifted back to her negligence, without which my shoddy reactions wouldn't have been provoked.

The next day, she was caught on a bus without a ticket, the inspector adding a lecture to his fifty-kopek fine. Anastasia's temper snapped. "For God's sake stop the 'social responsibility' song, it grates." The inspector summoned a cop who led her to his precinct station, me trailing behind, wondering whether my presence would help or hinder. With lesser looks she might have spent fifteen days for hooliganism in a stinking jail.

We emerged impossibly late for a restaurant lunch to which I'd invited Alyosha. I bought two ice-cream sticks to celebrate her release and waited until our nerves had recovered.

"What was the point of that, scrumptious? You told me you'd paid the damn fare."

She strode on, not answering.

"Whatever were you trying to prove?"

"Oh stop," she snapped. "I didn't have the right change."

"Why didn't you ask me? You never pay when you do have change."

"Drop it, I don't want to have this discussion." The peremptory nastiness in her voice pulled me up. It struck me that she was *always* trying to prove something with her demonstrated uninhibitedness. With nowhere to go and no way to telephone Alyosha, we were just wandering—toward the Krimsky Bridge, I noticed, of our enchanted kiss. I realized my grievance would pull us down further from that seemingly distant exaltation, but could not suppress it.

"Sure I'll drop it—having bailed you out of the station. You can pretend you're above everything again."

My bitterness amazed me. The worst was not my anger at her *using* me—taking my help when needed but rejecting every word of accompanying advice—but shame, somewhere, for the shabbiness of my resentment; which of course amplified it. I was allowing a young girl to dominate me, even asking for it; and she scorned me, rightly, for my pettiness.

"Why are you beside yourself about five kopeks for a bus? Why can't you let me worry about what's fair for myself—about who does the real cheating around here?"

"I'm the first to agree that the way the system cheats you, you deserve a million free rides. But what's the advantage of striking back with these kind of 'victories'? The real reason is your infatuation with playing the naughty innocent."

She stepped off in another direction. When I caught up with her, she exploded; and the argument dredged up personal grudges that dismayed us. I spat up resentment, growing clearer by the minute, that beneath her captivating recklessness lay a spoiled child's heedlessness of others.

"You always want to be 'liberated' from the 'petty rules' binding 'less sensitive' people. Like paying your way, or coming on time for an appointment. Elevate cheating to a principle—a splendid way to demonstrate superiority."

She hissed back that bragging about helping her in the police station would have been far beneath Alyosha but was characteristic of me, since I was trying to ape him, with none of his maturity or generosity.

"You're often an imitator, *artificial.* You're not guided by your feelings, but by what you think they should be. That's why you always react first to the secondary things: theater tickets and bus fares, not people. Lacking real instincts, you try to act on the basis of—ugh!—of what you read."

Oh God, how right she was! How I yearned to be able to *laugh* with her about the police sergeant and passport fine. But I pretended that my stodginess was linked to some better part of me that tried, at least, to understand others" arguments. The proof of her perception about my being guided by what I *thought* I should feel was that I held myself back and tried to make peace, congratulating myself at not stalking off in her kind of fury.

Letting her have the last salvo, I took her arm, which she surprisingly hugged to her side. We were still walking aimlessly. One of her best qualities was the ability to make up almost instantly after an outburst. But I no longer felt I had to love her: I was beginning to see her as an ordinary person. And although she might help me get beneath my measly poses and defenses, the closer we approached our inner cores, the stronger I sensed our essential dissimilarities. We came to a river beach and she herself summarized one of the most important.

"The difference is that my ambition is only to see what happens to me. I could be happy sunning here for a whole summer. You'd be nervous because you weren't accomplishing something—which is why you will one day."

"The difference is that you've lain on fewer beaches. Naturally you want more of it."

But this was a half-truth, offered to avoid further debate. We *were* products of different societies. Growing up in hers, it was natural that she saw freedom as getting away with something, the good life as lazing on a beach. Instead of feeling constantly inferior, *I* had something to tell *her* about goals in life, but she didn't want to hear.

The twist of me urging her to be a better Soviet citizen was part of it. What I wanted to say was that not giving a damn about accomplishing anything wasn't the answer. And that my irritation over her bus caper was connected with the notion that true individualism demands more worthy expression.

"Look, Nastyusha," I kept saying—to myself. "When rebellion comes, it should be *useful* to mankind, not your mosquito bites." This pompousness provided the laugh at myself I was after, but Anastasia's fancy-free stance remained frayed. She was a little like Zelda, doing everything in her delicious power to keep Scott down. However insignificant I was compared to him, I sometimes longed to be myself, rather than the more dashing but less true variant affected in her presence.

We needed more walking. It was strangely asexual, as if revealing even as much as I did to her had bled away my potency. We came to an area of wooden cottages and suddenly I was thinking of the Brooklyn house where we lived until I was four. Whenever we returned from somewhere the sight of it brought a flush of comfort, but almost immediately the anxiety began and I was afraid to go inside. The roof would collapse, I sobbed; termites might be undermining the timbers this very minute. I could put no trust in this home where I hated myself for hoping my parents would go on screaming at each other instead of me; this seemingly sound structure that might crumble before my eyes. . . . How hard it was to come to terms with Anastasia's defects, already weakening our beams. How I wanted her strength to match her beauty!

We parted before supper and I went to Alyosha's alone. The comforts and distractions of *his* house were growing daily. He had a bottle of Polish vodka. The main thing to forget was why, those few days after witnessing my obscenity from the kitchen floor, she was in a mood to lash out at the bus inspector. The remark of hers that rasped loudest in my ears was the reference to "who does the real cheating around here."

Alyosha and I went to a movie. Anastasia continued to ignore the cash boxes of buses and trolleys. On principle.

The following weeks the weather was dismal. Days passed like a column of prison coats in a labor camp. A combination of normal cold and unusual damp pained fingers and toes, no matter how you dressed. The stuff in the air and on the sidewalks was Russian *slyakot* rather than ordinary "slush" or "slime." Little relief could be found indoors. The movies and plays were bad: we'd already seen almost everything of interest. Returning to the circus was a disaster. And the restaurants had turned depressing.

The same meals in the same handful of places had lost all their exhilaration. The objective reason was Russian gastronomy's winter decline. Even in The Berlin, our "Old World" favorite, the service wore at our nerves. Waiting the sweaty hour between courses, I occasionally had to choke down the bile of frustration that had been my prevailing taste in Intourist restaurants before meeting Anastasia. The music gave us headaches, the chairs cut into our thighs. We used to drop such evenings in the middle, but now we stayed, prolonging our unhappiness: the small things were working in reverse. We caught each other's eyes as they returned from observing other tables and shuddered with a common, unspoken vision of our relationship's flimsiness—based, as it was becoming, on the sham luxury of these socialist bordellos. Their link to real Russian life was providing three wretched hours of escape from its deeper wretchedness.

"If only we'd had our own apartment!" I entreated under my breath to the strangers sharing our table. Hers, mine, her uncle's; anywhere to be in bathrobes, alone with a book or a television movie. The artificiality of those long evenings out would evaporate; we'd be ourselves—which was still best friends, although our passion was subsiding. Meanwhile, we saw ourselves as victims of winter and Soviet circumstances, and waited to be nuzzled by spring.

Soon we were returning for second viewings of our favorite plays. Her spontaneity in the audience still sharpened my senses, and I had the added pleasure of being seen with her on my arm. Half the orchestra of the best houses is occupied by members of the Western colony who know only a handful of especially authorized Russians encountered in their work and value the most casual social contact with the least prepossessing nonofficial citizen as evidence of penetration into native life. Anastasia's obviously Russian loveliness produced gratifying whispers and stares. It was the same winter and same Soviet circumstances, but the same me—with my blocks to going deeper—enjoyed the shallow pleasure of flattery to my vanity.

One evening in late January, we went to three one-act ballets at the Bolshoi, the theater we loved more than all the others together, including the shinier new ones. From the outside, the building is smaller and less impressive than its name implies, and triumphant Russian disorder asserts itself even here to dent the roof and send streaks from rusty gutters down the yellow plaster. But the interior exudes other-worldly magic. Russians would trudge the snow barefoot to reach its lavishness.

It was the only place in Moscow that allowed me to forget I was there. The thick crimson velvet, friendly gilt, fusion of opulence and intimacy are more warming on a black winter night than the extravagant performance itself. We were lifted from seediness and sadness into the kingdom of illusion the moment we entered.

I loved Anastasia again in these surroundings. She wore a black jersey dress I'd bought from a French diplomat, which deepened the white of her skin and the sheen of her hair. She was fairer than ever, as ethereal as a fable. I walked down the aisle behind her to her seat with a premonition that something extraordinary was going to happen. The first ballet was Prokofiev's *Lieutenant Kije*. Unplayed through much of the Stalin era, the score, with its echoes of Kurt Weill's sardonic jazz, helped make it an "avant-garde" favorite when revived forty years later. Delighted with the respite from its *Swan Lake–Les Sylphides–Giselle* treadmill, the company enlivened its usual technical skill with verve. Anastasia gurgled.

I went for something to drink during the intermission. To my disappointment, she insisted on staying in her seat. When I returned, she was at the opposite end of our aisle, laughing with Joe Sourian.

"He's invited us after the theater," she said when resettled in her seat. "To an American correspondent's. They're having a party."

"How do you know Joe?"

She chuckled. "Who doesn't?"

Again my twinge of irritation. Or jealousy—but of Joe Sourian?

"What party? I don't think we should go."

"Why do you always assume you'll decide for us both? You still picture yourself dispensing goodies to native girls. Arranging their movements."

She was always wrong about content, feeling out my weak spots in order to belittle my advice; but right about me. Here we were trying to forget our last row, but starting another one— which might be our last.

"Please spare us an argument this evening. I just think it's foolish for you to be reported with other Americans. One's risky enough."

"Nonsense."

"You know it's good sense."

"But not the real reason. You have something against Joe. Maybe even that he's broken your 'monopoly' on Russian friends."

"Oh Nastya."

"I accepted. I haven't danced in ages. Some of your countrymen know how to have fun."

I didn't answer. Nor reply to her "last word" on the matter: that I was purposely playing up the danger of informers; she knew her own country, thank you. But she'd never been near a diplomatic compound, let alone had any idea of the surveillance.

I wanted to pull her out of her seat and take her . . . where? If only she weren't so beautiful tonight. Too splendid to lose, too exasperating to be with; full of unique qualities that only I could appreciate—and of lapses from what she should be. She was so close to what I needed; the perfection she *almost* gave me made me want it—and resent her—all the more.

The house lights went down. *Geologists*, the second ballet, was a hackneyed propaganda piece about steadfast prospectors discovering mineral deposits for the Motherland. Anastasia's squirms produced the usual indignation in the people near us, while her attitude toward me, indicated by an arched back and refusal to look, was the equivalent of a mild pout for being held back by some "sensible" restriction.

She came to the buffet with me during the second intermission and for the first time in my life I ordered champagne. If I'd thought about it, I might have done this to effect a reconciliation in style—to best my countrymen who "knew how to have fun." But I couldn't think. After the first glasses, I was already succumbing to an overpowering spell. Everything irrelevant faded into the background as I moved toward my true thoughts.

It was closer to a pot high than anything the champagne could have produced, for I was lifted to the miraculous state where time stretches without limit in both directions. Crammed with a psycheful of perceptions about myself, all the most honest and profound I could produce, each minute seemed a day.

Some of the reflections were so piercing that I felt touched by an oracular gift. Sitting at our table, I detected lines in Anastasia's hands and face I'd never noticed before. She wasn't simply more beautiful; she had attained a higher level of beauty, which I recognized through a new feeling of communion with her as a fellow being with her own links to the awesome source of universal life that was streaming into me. Walking back at my side, I saw a figure of sacred dignity taking her place, in the black gown, on the throne of the audience.

The third ballet plunged me deeper into visions. *Petrushka*'s first flute call haunted me as if I had never heard it before; the dancers in the motley crowd of its opening scene were like the first performers I'd seen on a stage. I immediately realized that what I had taken for fanciful episodes portrayed, on the contrary, the profoundest truths of national character; that I was about to see not a ballet but a revelation coming from the creators' deepest unconscious sources. Russia's history and art, everything that made it sad and great, were passing before my eyes. The sidewalk player lifted his concertina; I understood why man needs music and Passion plays. The gesture was boundlessly melancholy and hopeful, totally mystifying and revealing. Free of time and space, I floated toward ultimate causes.

Although most of the visions were forgotten in the same microsecond of their divulgence, some landmarks remained in my sight, as if after the illumination of some cosmic lightning. The old man—still in the first scene, before I caught my breath—beckoning passersby into the show booth where the puppets would perform explained why my grandfather left his Lvov ghetto in 1901, an event whose importance to me I had never acknowledged even to the extent of asking the question.

Next the hoi polloi milling in the Saint Petersburg street were showing me that I and my failures were part of humanity, somehow related to art's eternal concerns.

Snare drums beat out a foreboding tattoo: something fatal was going to happen in this tableau. An old juggler, the symbol of carnival magic, took command of the theater. Slowly I became aware that a titanic debate had started between my pro- and anti-Anastasia forces and was quickly building in the context of the larger apocalypse. The moment I understood what was going to happen to poor Petrushka and the light-headed Ballerina, I saw that Anastasia and I must not continue as we were. No compromise alternative was available for a Russian and a foreigner; the only remedy was . . . MARRIAGE.

Matrimony, holy wedlock, eternal union—I wanted their absolution. But would the cure be worse than our ailment?

The world was *there*, on the spell-struck stage. The juggler was toying with it; the sounds of his enchanted flute told me that was the decision of my life, and only the premonition that something I'd glean from his tricks would make it for me kept me from groaning with tension.

Recognizing that the verdict would determine whether I was to be a phony gay blade forever or a normal man, virulently antagonistic sides of me joined forces for the battle. That my leaning toward lifelong bachelorhood always derived from a suspicion that a girl like her could never love me—a dodge against admitting I was unable to love—had strengthened the fear of committing myself. I might conquer that now. But did this unorthodox creature merit sealing all escape routes?

The stakes were all or nothing. Not marrying was losing her forever; I couldn't pop over from New York for weekend visits. It wasn't a marriage but an irreversible break with the past—for her, too, since she'd be moving to a new world.

She might travel badly. Her capriciousness could be disastrous in the West: a child of nature who keeps losing her own passport might refuse to take telephone messages, throw away my notes, discover a principle for supermarket shoplifting. Wouldn't it be crazy for me, with my milksop's sense of loyalty, to assume this triple risk?

Yet only a marriage with some extraordinary challenge could

tempt me to take any risk at all. The attraction was precisely in the uncommonness. I'd backed away from a dozen arrangements with the Wellesley girls I was supposedly destined for. I'd never take a vow unless it promised the *total* commitment I needed.

The fight rages across my skull like a Hopalong saloon brawl. The anti- forces score a tremendous knockout. The notion of such a marriage is so preposterous that only I, in my goalless groping, could have entertained it. The temptation is finished forever; she's my best girl in the port of Moscow, but no more. The immense relief of this certainty lasts long enough for a street dancer's bounds across the stage. It is already being undermined by doubts, longing and sadness at my loss when shock troops strike a stunning blow for the pro- side. Suddenly I see incontestable signs that Anastasia is my one-and-only. To give her up would be my greatest possible act of self-destruction. Thank God I've seen the light in time; thank God the decision has been made for me! I savor my relief, while the next counterattack advances from my innards to my brain.

I must do something, must decide; I'm back in the panic of recognizing that being fit for nothing else, I'll also never be a professor. All hope for redemption turns on the right decision, while the wrong one will deprive me of her splendor, extinguishing every chance for what I've always yearned. Anastasia is unique; she's manifestly not good enough. She has an incomparable capacity to enjoy; she lacks intellect. She'll be a dazzling success in New York; she'll seem a second-rate hick. And the decision is crucial; I must have the best because . . . I don't know why, but in this crucial matter I'm special and deserve it—which, of course, is why I don't. . . .

I know I'll marry only once. But if I do it now I'll never have a chance at the others. Never Liv Ullmann, the librarian in the Frick Museum; not even the new Tanya on our dormitory floor, who gave me to know I wasn't fantasizing: I *can* have her. Committing myself to Anastasia is substituting real for visionary beauty, which is always more glorious, isn't it?

This battle in my head! And now my squalid stinginess sneaks in some lower blows. Will I have to support Anastasia in America? Maybe she won't want to study, but get a fat job as a model instead. Disgust for this selfishness pushes me to think of whether *she* can be happy away from Russia. Because *I'll* have the extra bonus of talking Russian all my life—her kind, with the instant plays on words. She'll be my movable Russian feast with the permanent taste of this year's adventure. And in Paris, Venice, Barbados, her sensitivity will heighten my own. Who else could respond to the cabman with the gypsy girls on the stage as she is responding now, with every cell of her being?

The deafening ding-dong quickens in pace, like a gargantuan metronome breaking its springs. Yes, no, relief, horror, grin of victory, moan of defeat. Concertina, balalaika, piccolo. Surely goodness and mercy shall follow me all my days—and the suspense will end. Yes, I'll beg for her hand. No, no, I MUST NOT; it can't work even for a single day. I want to swim clear of the tension but can't remember which way is up.

Yet I'm still transfixed by the performance, beholden for its unique aesthetic gift. The company plays and dances as if atoning for the forty-year unpersoning of Stravinsky, Diaghilev and Nijinsky, the geniuses of twentieth-century ballet. Each glittering dissonance of the score—truant clarinets, burlesque bassoons, tender-jazzy piano—tingles my imagination. The carnival bear romps on his leash; suddenly I understand the symbolic place of bears in the Russian consciousness. The old juggler brings Petrushka, Ballerina and Blackamoor to life with his magic flute, and the human sap animating their floppy limbs revitalizes my long desiccated emotions. I'm alive!

With my senses opened, I am discovering that the ballet is nothing more or less than *reportage* of Russian life, more piercing than a hundred heavy volumes. The tipsy muzhiks attending the carnival are *the* Russian muzhiks, whose brief jig reveals everything about cheerful peasant resignation, key to the country's moods. The fat merchants, fussy policemen, flashing gypsies . . . I am absorbing the last word—in music and movements!—on their classic types. And not only in Shrovetide Saint Petersburg of the 1830s, but this very afternoon on Gorky Street, Sretenka and the Arbat. Now I know what the Moscow throngs have always been trying to tell me.

The puppets break into a folk dance. I devour the daily Russian stew of gaiety and carefreeness, pettiness and melancholy. The infinity of gloom underlying the market's festiveness, the apparitions that rise up from the very humbleness of the jumbled street scenes. As Chagall perceived the spirit of a Russian village as figures drifting over mud and moon, *Petrushka*'s creators recognized the phantasmal strains—the puppets' inner world—in their outwardly ragged market. No explanation is required of how Petrushka, Ballerina and Blackamoor can be consumed by love and jealousy. In this theater more than any, such "absurdities" are ineffable truths; and with the woman who loves "Once upon a time" stories rigid at my side, they reveal their place in the country's—and her—temperament and outlook. How wrong I was to judge her on whether she forgets appointments—the criteria of petty rationalism. *She's* made of dreamier—Russian—stuff.

The lilt of "Down Peterskaya Street" draws up affection for Russia in me like the moon with the tides. But I must remember that her most exasperating traits, the I-don't-give-a-damn forgetfulness, are Russian, too. At last I'm on the verge of the real question. *Are we compatible?* I must know whether we will make each other better or worse. Will she understand that I have it in me to achieve something, that I *can* be less petty than I seem? And will I allow her to enjoy her individuality? All the niggling rest is trivial.

Bang! the door of Petrushka's room is flung open. Kicked out, he seeks solace in his love for Ballerina. I see, grieve, understand. Booted from my academic ambition and American assumptions, I too have sought comfort in love for a Princess. But Ballerina is indifferent, and humble Petrushka begins his famous lament. Weeping, agonizing, dying of despairing adoration. *To hell with compatibility;* I must be with Anastasia whatever the cost. Must defeat my tendency to bring Petrushka's heartbreak on myself. Look how he fills with gladness, trembles with joy, at one half-friendly glance from her.

If I don't settle this tonight, she'll go to the correspondent's party. My Anastasia must not be corrupted by that kind of American's flattery. I know this is jealousy, but it's also for her sake. I know it is superstitious to credit anything to the signs I see in Petrushka's suffering, yet I believe them because they confirm objective truths.

A fanfare stops me. An alarming tremolo of strings. Petrushka and Blackamoor are quarreling while Ballerina swoons. How much does my resentfully admiring perception exaggerate Anastasia's excesses of instinct? To what extent does she shine only in comparison to the steel teeth of the dumpy Russian masses? I must not judge by Russia's standards, where even I stand out as a member of a taller, handsomer race. I must stop judging at all and just do what's right.

I'm so utterly exhausted! How long can this blind festivity continue at the show booth? Petrushka rushes out of it, but is chased by Blackamoor who deals him death with his saber. The betrayed and beaten reacher for beauty who was so innocently good has had his head bashed in. The juggler picks up the puppet, pitifully lifeless without love, and returns to the booth while the crowd disperses as if nothing had taken place.

But suddenly Petrushka's ghost appears over the booth, shaking his fist in triumphant revenge. This is not the end!

Somewhere I see the audience statue-like for a moment, then surging forward with cheers. I reach for Anastasia's hand. She too has remained seated. Our fingers lock. We are the only two unwilling to profane the experience with clapping.

The emptying of the house leaves us serenely exalted. Cleaning details appear with homemade mops, sealing our bond to the theater. I know I must speak while we are still inside, but otherwise feel no need to rush; my decision took itself as the curtain fell.

Anastasia lingers in the empty foyer: I think she's even guessed. Her overcoat and red headscarf have returned her from elegant princess to peasant girl. I am thinking of how best to present my case, avoiding theatricality. At last I can *give*.

The black and white of the foyer floor is coming to an end. My submission is abrupt but quiet.

"Will you be my wife?"

Before I have time to gird for the suspense, even to hear the echo of the fateful phrases, she has answered.

"Yes, of course."

The three words emerge as one, and so lacking surprise and stress that I want to restate the question.

Of all I'm about to ponder, this moment will have pride of place. After the religious revelation that made my decision, the supreme matter-of-factness of her reaction seems to promise a lifetime of anticlimax. "Yes of course"—as if I'd asked whether she wants wafers with her ice cream. And I've been so careful not to ham up the dramatic element she should supply. We've been shortchanged.

Which is why I question her. At first, I swear it, I'm as certain as I was; my prodding is intended merely to elicit some indication that she appreciates this venture's importance. She once chided me for being too voluble about love: "If we know it's there, why must we pronounce it so?" But surely the emotion of forging this wonderful union should be seen as well as felt?

She knows what it means to me, I've often talked about remaining a bachelor. And I know she's pleased. Why doesn't she throw her arms around me, like the thrilled girl she should be? Why must I wait for her to be first?

We step outside; stand at the top of the steps for a moment spotlighted together with our columns; walk in the square across the street where we first met after Yaroslavl. She carries herself very straight, but with the faintest hint that she will follow my lead as my bride.

I'm careful to talk about her grave problems rather than my letdown. Of the uncertainty of an exit visa even after the wedding; of the possible prevention of the marriage itself. I think of Lenin Library Maya and Joe Sourian's Barbara, reminders that the worst possible outcome for her would be to apply to marry a foreigner but be refused. With all my heart, I swear never to fail her on my end. But is she absolutely certain she wants to take on these perils with *me*?

"Yes, pantherkin. A sailor who likes mango juice: all the omens are auspicious." With puffed rosy cheeks, she blows a fair wind.

"You can put up with my faults? You don't know half of them. I want to tell you that, for the sake of our future. And that I don't know what I'm going to do, where we'll live."

"Won't we live together?"

"Darling, be serious for a moment. For a start the institute will expel you. Do you care about your career?"

"I have to think about that. I am being serious; I'm bad at those questions."

"And what about leaving Russia?"

"These aren't the main things, you know."

"Of course not. But so many immigrants grieve. Can you be happy in the States?"

"That's not the main thing."

Although I know this and am determined to attain that main thing—of what has eluded me since Yaroslavl as well as of this conversation—we slip onto another tangent: my plans for tomorrow's first steps and her needed fortitude against KGB pressure. A homosexual eyeing us from the square's fountain moves us on; a dreary Aeroflot sign drags me into the realm of everyday. "Cheap, Fast, Comfortable"—and the anemic neon is flashing from stilts atop the Evgeniya-defiled Hotel Metropole. The gloomy, deserted streets are a darting image of our recent emptiness. As if to supply the eagerness I expected from her, I find myself pronouncing on the importance of marriage in general and the wonder of ours in particular. But I'm aware of how different this is from what I envisioned; how curious *this* form of role-reversal. And somewhere I know she is waiting for me to complete my proposal. Why can't I open up *plainly and simply and say I love* her, nothing else matters?

Suddenly she takes my head in her hands. Through her gloves I feel the awaited tenderness at last.

"This is an enormous step for you," she murmurs. "Are you certain you want to take on so much?"

The very predictability of my protest betrays its vulnerability. Questions I believe silenced forever are already drifting back, like Petrushka's ghost gone haywire.

"Don't be silly, it's you who's taking the giant step. . . . I've never been happier. I'm proud of having asked, proud of being accepted, proud of you."

The reward for this comes on her night-cold lips. I feel a tremble in her mouth. We want very much to have a place to ourselves now, but merely cross under Prospekt Marx to circumvent the Metropole, the clamminess of the underground passageway pulling us together, yet apart.

"If I weren't Russian," she says. "If I weren't Russian, would you have thought twice about me as your wife?"

I think twice now. "But thank God you are Russian, you'd
have been something different. You're you, the only one."

"All the same, there's an old Russian saying: 'Measure seven
times before cutting the cloth.' "

How odd this sounds on her impulsive lips! How I admire her
for giving me this escape, for considering my interests at this
crucial moment more than her own. What better proof that she
isn't heedless of others? It is the ultimate testament of her
goodness and the wisdom of my decision.

Yet strangest of all this evening's strangeness is the slight
ambiguity precisely this wise counsel leaves me in. I've broken
my emotional barrier. Asked and been accepted. Volunteered to
tackle the bureaucratic procedures tomorrow. Yet it's far less *final*
than I'd pictured; I am less changed.

Are we engaged? It is too raw to walk, too hard to get a taxi,
too late to wangle a restaurant table. How can we have a fitting
celebration?

Wary of Soviet feints, I sought preliminary counsel about
marriage applications in the American Embassy. The cultural
attaché, who doubled as exchange students' advisor, knew me
from the Harvard gym. My news swept away his chumminess; he
went straight to a warning tightly laminated of political gravity
and personal concern.

Marriage to a Soviet girl would make me suspect in America
forever. *Any* girl: the KGB had a lien on them all. As a favor to
him, might I "rethink the whole situation" for twenty-four
hours? Meanwhile he'd bend the rules for an old friend and
postpone informing Washington, in case I wanted to "contain"
my youthful impulse.

I wandered among pensioners in the zoo, trying to think of
what to say when Anastasia emerged from classes, feeling the
awkwardness of last night's anticlimax thicken in the January
day like leftovers in a refrigerator. Having agreed on our bold
venture—if that is what we did; it was still less than absolutely
clear—ordinary conversation with her seemed paltry. I wanted
to say something that would stave off the descent to our previous
imperfection.

The attaché's discouragement wouldn't do for this, of course—nor my response to it. Instead of blazing up at his cold-blooded Washingtonese, which I'd do one day when I needed to shunt the blame for my spinelessness, I agreed to his suggestion. Despising myself, I thanked him—even hoped, somewhere, that he would take over my responsibility.

The squeak of my boots pinched my nerves. Each hour apart from Anastasia increased the importance of producing tidings big enough for our new roles. I decided to wait until I could announce that at least my Embassy end was straightened out. I knew I wouldn't hear from her: she was giving me time to reconsider.

Next morning I shared the elevator with an older Embassy official who quipped about tying the knot to a Russian maid. I demanded to know how he'd heard.

"The outgoing Washington cables—isn't it official?"

I pushed the ground-floor button and left. The attaché's betrayal was so shaming, I told myself, that I couldn't see him, let alone tell Anastasia. Explaining my reaction in the Evgeniya affair, I used to say that a free country's respect for the individual had badly prepared me to cope with double-dealing. Far more than clothes or meals, it was this I wanted to give my bride; this promise the Embassy had smeared. The less certain I was of myself, the more my country mattered. I felt I could not introduce it to her by way of official guile.

Another day passed in limbo. More ebb after the Bolshoi crest; even stronger presentiment that the longer the silence, the more necessary to break it dramatically. Hoping her eyes would prompt the necessary words, I went to the institute. She descended from the building alone, wrapped in thoughts and scarves. The very need for me undisguised on her face unmanned me; calling out to her mentally, I backed away. If my most mellifluous voice were asked, it would say that I truly wanted her for my wife, but wasn't ready. If it were the most honest, the answer would be in terms of girls and goodies too yummy to sacrifice. But there was no such questionnaire; I simply sensed a distance between us—which is all I felt; the rest of me was desensitized. Her hair fell over her eyes. She was so lovely in her faint melancholy that I feared to disturb it.

I now left my room in early morning, and to kill thoughts of what to do, spent my waking hours with Alyosha. One day, I knew, Anastasia and I would laugh at the sorry functionary called a *cultural* representative. We'd thank him, too—for providing a background of his shabby sense of bureaucratic loyalty against which the importance and beauty of our own would more brightly shine. Meanwhile, I thought of how best to protect her from reprisals when we did go to the marriage office—which would be soon. And of how to make unimaginative me good enough not just for glittering theater evenings with her, but for a lifelong commitment of weekdays.

Soon I sensed that my absence itself was taking care of this. Our communion in such things was so strong that there was no need to say when I'd return, even why I was away. Her sense of dramatic timing would tell her how a temporary separation now could only increase the romantic tension, enhance our mutual dependence, make my heart even fonder.

And despite this self-deception put out to cover my mangy retreat, I'm foresighted at least in this: by the end of the week, I cherish her more than ever. I know her so intimately, am so certain of the affinity of our reactions, that I can feel her attachment growing in step with mine.

Evidence appears of precisely this: worried about my whereabouts, she discreetly telephones Alyosha. As I've asked, he says only that I'm well—and brooding.

She surely still feels I'm trying to copy him and that this is a mistake. More and more certain that we're sexual twins, Alyosha, by contrast, can't understand my "hypertensive" interest in her when "you'll only be bored soft in the end." The truth is that neither is right. I have long wanted two lives, one to dedicate to family and utter constancy, and the other for the opposite ultimate of abandon and debauch. Anastasia and Alyosha have been revealed as the two summits I must attain, but a beneficent god—which is what my guilt calls my duplicity —has arranged it that both can be squeezed into my single lifetime.

More—that one will prepare me for the other. For I'm hooked now on the intoxicating round of fetes and syllogize that far from spoiling me for my one true love, the profligacy is purifying me for it. When surfeited on the anonymous bodies, I'll be the better man she deserves, capable of unconditional faithfulness. Fit to achieve the sublime devotion I've always yearned to achieve.

The concern she transmits to Alyosha for my whereabouts strengthens everything I feel about us. Two weeks go by in swelling love for her, for the sweetness of my separation ache, for the comfort of knowing we'll be together again, more steadfastly than ever.

Cruising in districts I know would please her, I jump out of the Volga to call—and replace the receivers of half a dozen phone booths: I want to intensify the expectations yet more. Meanwhile, Alyosha's confidence and kindness with women expands me, also contributing to *us*. This is how I deal with images of her during the orgies.

Another week quickly passes. Although I love her for the way she misses me, my guilt for what I suspect of my self-deception is rising to the safety-valve level. I drink alone and go to the telephone booth across the street from her dormitory. My suspense is enrapturing after this long lapse; apprehension of her reaction to my cruelty is atomized in the alcohol. She can't have been offended; she trusts me to do what I had to. I hear my charming, witty, tender answers to her questions, all lavishing on her the devotion she deserves after her faithful wait. She will ask neither about my mysteriousness in disappearing nor my devotedness in calling now, as she always knew I would when my task was complete. For the first time, I'm totally fluent with her.

Her approach to the telephone pushes me higher toward ecstasy. *"You!"* she utters in response to my brief adoring greeting. I drink in the flaxen timbre with the trace of northern accent, its crowning glory.

"Do you think we should know each other's names?" I say, repeating her Yaroslavl pauses with her words. "When we meet again, 'you' might be inadequate."

She receives this like a hack performance at the theater. I rush to something even more trite. "I'll need that book of yours back—forgot to pen the dedication."

"Something about never forgetting old friends, no doubt."

"Something about eternal infatuation for a woman of instincts. I'll find a suitable line from one of the reverent verses."

She shifts to a lower octave. "You know the saying? 'When the barrel's empty, it's late to conserve the wine.' "

I don't know the saying and can't decipher its moral now. I am too frozen by the chilling new self-assurance and secrecy in her voice. Throughout the hiatus, I have pictured her wrapping her red scarf around her head and rushing gleefully to our reunion. It is midnight, the perfect time for this flourish. But she won't even talk about joining me.

"Someone said 'When we meet again' a whole five minutes ago. I've heard that prolonged waiting for your desideratum damages the heart."

She gives this the grunt it deserves, and stays put. She doesn't say she's just washed her hair or is tired; simply that she doesn't want to go out now. Her tone asserts that my gesture of appearing at this hour is puerile, not romantic. "Let's set a better time and place," she says.

As I try to continue bantering, maggots of doubt multiply in me as on the Eisenstein meat. *What have I done with my appalling absence?* Suddenly I realize I must raise the stakes.

"For God's sake, I love you, I've always loved you, I always—"

And she'll always love *me,* she interrupts, her inflection suggesting my feelings are melodramatically exaggerated and her "love" for me is a prima ballerina's for a reporter. The whole conversation is nauseatingly out of character.

"Please, I must see you for a minute. Otherwise something terrible will happen."

If I like we can meet after classes tomorrow. Sorry, she's busy in the evening, can't get free even for a ballet. A fellow student must use the telephone now; she's looking forward to tomorrow, five o'clock. . . .

Although I knew my punishment would start soon, I felt only stunned, as in the moments immediately following a blow to the face. The blood of an overwhelming desire shot to my head, then seeped down through my being, from the moment I accepted she actually wasn't coming. I *had* to look at her face. Put my arm in hers. Know that she loved me.

Everything after this was weighted by monumental banality. My reactions to the shock conformed to a story: "Whenever life is at its most dramatic, it is least able to escape the commonplace. . . . At the so-called great moments, we all behave like characters in a penny novelette." But recollection of this passage, written by Koestler about what he endured awaiting imminent execution in a Franco cell, provided no satisfaction. My pain controlled me no less, but I could take no pride in it. I had to live with the dreary reality that everything I felt was utterly hackneyed.

On the following day at five o'clock—she came on time!—her presence suspended my longing. While she was with me, I believed she had never left, or that my old attraction for her would quickly pull her back. Even when she *explained,* I was enlivened rather than depressed. It was we two together: better than old times because our discussion was more urgent. She wore the same green sweater, sipped the same tea without sugar. The workaday café took on an intriguing atmosphere. Her terrible news was from the same penny novelette which we'd soon laugh at, then forget.

On a very low day two weeks ago, she was trying to finish an experiment. A man from the institute's staff entered the laboratory and saw her weeping. She did not want his comfort but they talked—and talked again after completing the experiment. Walking to the dormitory with him, she felt each step separating her from *us,* but only now, warmed by his intelligence, did she realize how lonely she had been in my absence.

No, she did not love him. But she could not leave him. Their give-and-take was very different from ours but must not be trampled on.

I implored her to go away with me on the weekend. To Leningrad, Sochi, the country's best. I would use any trick, offer any bribe for permission to travel together. No; she would be with him in a scholarly retreat on a nearby lake. Now she must leave.

I spent the dismal January evening in the café's intense atmosphere of restless boredom, feeling I understood the despair of its bleary drunks. It was no longer a lark; I needed anesthesia.

Outside the institute the next morning, I met a bantam student named Alek who had sometimes accompanied Anastasia and me for a walk after classes to talk about American cars, his passion. He identified the man as a thrice-married professor of neurology who appealed to pretty students despite his scraggliness. He, Alek, wondered what they saw in him—especially Anastasia, who had loved me so.

This struck me so violently that I yearned to lie down. I loved her—like no one else on earth. The rest had been incidental, even my cruel games and emotional stinginess. The heart and soul of her was so close to my own—but better than my own—that I couldn't go on alone.

Two days passed; the thought of a *lifetime* without her was unbearable. If only I hadn't known her uninhibited tenderness, her support, her affection—which made me a hundred times finer than a purposeless screwer. I couldn't believe her handbag's frayed handle was no longer mine to toy with while she was in some restaurant toilet, from which she would wind her way through all other tables to *mine*. That her exhilarated whisper would not be in my ear as we walked down a street, turning me into a man I could admire.

I remembered a recent account of Moscow life by a good-natured Englishman who was depressed by the drabness and gloomy weather, but never felt so happy to feel so sad. How perceptive this seemed until the real sadness I'd brought on myself began taking me to the bottom.

The clichés sprouted so abundantly that I had to hack through the undergrowth of my own hackneyed thoughts. To my horror, I noticed that our old love talk of code words and private jokes embarrassed her, as if I were offering to doll her up in shoplifted clothes. Then I tried to blackmail her with my desire, which of course had returned. When she next saw me after her weekend at the lake, I brushed against her with the hardness that used to make her carol. She forced a chuckle, as if for an acquaintance who had told a boorish story.

To my desperate plying, she confirmed that our sex had been "good," but she couldn't turn it on like a faucet. "And I'm bad at dual allegiances. You have different notions about passion."

Unavailable, she became irreplaceable. In our previous state, which had so dissatisfied me, I came to see a richness I could never again hope to achieve, and prayed to exchange the rest of my days for a week of our former bliss. In short, I was the rejecting lover whose tactics had backfired and heart burst with self-pity. *Now that she was unobtainable:* how predictable it all was, how tasteless and self-serving! And how little this recognition helped!

And how I wished to make something grand of my misery. I reread the *Cancer Ward* scene where a former labor-camp prisoner tries to make sense of a department-store customer asking for silk shirts.

> Men were . . . being thrown into mass graves, into shallow pits in the permafrost; men were being taken into labor camps for the first, second, and third times, being jolted from station to station in prison trucks; men were wearing themselves to nothing with picks . . . and here was this neat little man who could remember the size not only of his shirt but also his collar!

This was the picture of niggling *me*, with no way to emulate Solzhenitsyn's stalwart victims.

I kept dreaming I'd been born when I'd have been forced to prove my guts instead of pampering my bourgeois neuroses. My wishy-washy generation experienced less suffering than any on earth and read more about it. I knew about the terrible sacrifices of the Spanish Civil War, the excruciating bestiality of the Nazis; in groups that I could cite were a million of the Continent's finest men and women whose reward for selfless dedication to mankind's betterment was unspeakable torture. Ludicrous as my hurt was in comparison, I grieved for myself.

For it was all I had. I knew literature, not life. Raised on middle-class melodrama, I wanted the heroism of suffering, which is why I despised myself while I cried—and why I missed all the more the only woman I'd known who had something heroic in her, from which I was "incomprehensibly" cut off.

The world had the pallor of a morning before a snowstorm. I lay on my cot for days, dreading the moment when I would have to move my limbs to make a cup of soup. Frightened by my moans, roommate Viktor summoned a doctor—who diagnosed the flu that had lain low half the University, and slapped me with mustard plasters. "Man has places in his heart which do not yet exist, and into them enters suffering in order that they may have existence." I quoted this in English. He checked me again for delirium.

When bed became tiresome, I swung into "action," keeping Anastasia in flowers and refining the mawkishness of the accompanying notes:

My Darling, I shouldn't send you these. For when they've withered, what will you then think of my love?

I bought a medical bag, entered her institute, lurked in corridors to watch her changing classes. It was her kind of exploit; she should have laughed. Chatting with fellow students, she passed me by with a chilly nod. Not even my skill in sneaking in drew acknowledgment from her.

I went to the cafeteria with bantam Alek, who had secretly adored her since their first day at the institute. Together we kept watch for a tender sign—as his size, my new acquaintance with pain told me, might make him wait for someone the rest of his life.

Challenged at the old building's entrance, I moved my vigil to her dormitory, maintaining surveillance on her window from the roof of an adjoining apartment house. A re-enactment of my teen-age capers—when I could prove my dauntlessness because the girl had already left—the stunts also answered my calling to explore Russian life. What other foreigner has not only loved but been rejected by a Russian Helen? My intrepidness in finding roses, hens' teeth in winter Moscow, also stirred my self-admiration. Anything for a gesture.

The roommate closest to her, a homely Svetlana, came to lunch and gave me the solace I begged for by predicting the quick separation of the incompatible couple. I invested further hope in the purgatory of sitting close to the gawky girl's bad breath. My buoyancy collapsed when our conversation was exhausted fifteen minutes later.

Shadowing the slow-gaited professor, I remarked to myself, was as close to undercover work as a Westerner wants to go in this country. A rumpled Galbraith, he led me lumberingly to his apartment house. The nights I spent outside it were surely as cold as Greenland, but I welcomed physical punishment as a shipmate to my psychic variety. Hiding in a blind inside the courtyard, I watched them pass on their way home—as un-reachable, I said to myself, as Alyosha's Yanks.

My frozen fingertips yearned for the touch of their old friend, the weave of her overcoat. She was shiny-eyed and incredibly alive, but also slightly uneasy with his remoteness, even when she took his arm. A slight darkness under her eyes—from nights of love?—was the finishing touch to my crushing.

I remembered Svetlana's comment after they didn't fall apart in her predicted week: "He's not for her—but Nastya has a way of falling for her lovers." The notion of her Swedish model's legs in his bed seemed farfetched then; now I had the sickening firsthand proof of a light going on, then off, in his fourth-floor window. A secret darkness, an invulnerable enemy. One day, I'd have a much more luxurious apartment. One day the creep would die. But strange as it still seemed, I was more jealous of her than of him.

I snuck into their entryway and inched up the mute staircase toward their door, imagining the miracle that would strike me on the *next* step and hesitating to take it. The frozen iron and stone held an aura of profound mystery, as if I'd stumbled on a residence of Trotsky's. It was crazy to be there at that witching hour, crazier still to know the old stairway's every ripple of paint, every word of instruction for a pay phone. My study of gouges in the landings was preparation for recapturing *her* on the other side of the massive wall. No building anywhere in the world was so intimately mine. Minute by unbearable minute, I relived the scene outside the institute when *she* was mine and I backed away. It was as if I had lost my birthright.

The trip down, away from my idol, was always worse. The streets were deserted except for rare night workers who might mistake me for the very plainclothesman I half hoped would arrest me—initiating the tearful reconciliation when she visited the jail. Like a soap-opera writer bawling at his own episodes, I took my own games seriously. When day came again, the masochism of throwing an occasional bouquet at her feet as she walked to her bus stop was all the cheaper because it cost nothing except further decline in her estimation. But nothing else filled the void.

There was only puppy-like wandering on the streets where she walked and wasting my precious moments with her pleading for more of them. Her very stressing that we would still see each other underlined how rationed my time with her was. When I persisted, she interrupted in a tone I'd never heard before.

"I'd prefer not to say this but I'm busy with exams. And frankly, others have first claim on my free time."

How could I win her back when she denied me the time to do it? How was she going to learn about my new chastised self? My Russian Sovereign Anastasia, resorting to censorship.

I kept walking. With its radiance extinguished, Moscow was as stark and remote as a moonscape, black holes replacing the bits of color she used to blink at. A sidewalk stall's fresh *cheburekhi* made me gag: together with the aroma, I tasted the memory of her delight in it. How could I have cheated enough to pretend the quickness of her "Yes, of course" came from anything but her certainty?

Only Anastasia knew about *us* and, therefore, the extent of my deprivation. But she wasn't here to comfort me, depriving me even of this satisfaction. Losing the one person needed to talk to about the tragedy of the loved one was beyond all bounds of reasonable unfairness.

Yet I also knew I was bearing not the "cruel injustice" of my plaints, but the just deserts of my personality. When *I* had abandoned *her*, she took the normal, healthy course instead of whining, proving even more conclusively that when the mess ended, this whole woman who stood on her own two feet was worthy to be my wife.

I also understood that my expectation of her to cheer the conquering hero on his return from the month-long disappearance was only the most absurd manifestation of the cold-heartedness that from the beginning had kept me from thinking of how *she* felt, what *she* wanted. This was somehow connected to my diminishing desire for her before the break, just because she was so loving and available. I was good enough at poses to attract an Anastasia, but too self-serving, too sadistic in "love play" to provide what she needed after the dazzling start.

But this too was a pose. For I worked to describe my contrition eloquently to myself—therefore to her—in the same cause of winning her back: "It's not that I wounded you; I don't deserve you." Yet I hoped the very confession would make her believe the contrary. I was on an old cycle that led me to mocking deception whenever I played at attaining the real, real truth about myself. Instead of fading away in accordance with my own knowledge of my unworthiness, I convinced myself that this recognition enabled me to make her happy now. This was me in a slicker disguise.

Meanwhile, I clung to my hurt, seeking wisdom even in radio ballads, elevating an amateur Bing Crosby's "I can't live without you" to the paragon of understanding. "Why did you leave me before I felt I could tell you the truth?" I strained for solace in every sloppy ditty, opening myself to the other broadcasting messages. Two hundred million tons of steel at the end of the Five-Year Plan? Splendid, Comrades; how can I help? I must do *something* to join the rest of honest hardworking humanity.

She was ignoring my telegrams now. Each ring of the telephone in the common room jolted me because it might be her returning one of my calls, then harder because it wasn't. I had to record my supplications on paper.

Notes from a Twelfth-Story Window

Dawn. I just noticed the pattern of the formal gardens at the
approach to the University complex. Kindly covered by snow,
the outline nevertheless reveals itself at this height, like old
trench lines seen from a plane. The garden is as stiff as a Central
Committee declaration, but I used to want the flowers to grow
well this spring to please Anastasia when she stood at my
window. So she'd have the aesthetic pleasure—and seeing her,
I'd have mine.
   The wind whistling out there; I think: I know that sound,
Anastasia listened to it with me. Anastasia's with me, she hears
the wind. The laundry grinds my buttons to powder—and I
catch her sweet, scolding "snip off, sew on, save sorrow."
   . . . And a line that keeps repeating: "Give us this day our daily
bread."
   I just want to say I'm here. And think of you.

But why didn't I tell you this? That I love you for your
shoulders in your "Monday" suit? Your one and only smell, your
biting into an apple as if it's the last on earth. For the cut of your
jib—which I've written in English because some day you'll
understand.
    Do you know it's Anastasia I need? The round warmth that
gives me beauty and peace; the woman who's so much more
human than anyone I've known.

    A radio program for children playing. "And don't forget, gang,
that LENIN *(sigh) loved Pushkin. Throughout his revolutionary*
life, Lenin found time to refresh himself with this greatest
Russian poet." Violins, followed by one-two-three, Comrades:
the usual morning exercises.
    Yet Shadows of Our Forgotten Ancestors *was what you said.*
Lyric, honest, perfect. I don't understand how inspired works like
this are shown while the censors grind far lesser unorthodoxies
into sausage meat. We must talk about this. About why these
rare films are released that probe life as few Western productions
can, implicitly demonstrating that no word the Party ever
uttered has any relevance to the important truths. Now I hear
there's a new one by your Vasily Shukshin about a
criminal—can you believe it?—who ends tragically for all the
wrong ideological reasons.
    Can it be we won't see it together? Here it is again, my burden.
I try to carry it silently, but the more I concentrate on a
"neutral" subject and approach its inner meaning, the closer I
veer toward you, my inner meaning. And one more plaint. You
promised you'd save the new Cherry Orchard *for me, but friends*
tell me you've seen it with someone else. Perhaps mine is a
feminine jealousy. But didn't you too like changing roles?

    You reminded me of my stupid remark to Chingiz while we
were crossing the stream, and it stung. I wanted to tell you that,
and why. But I fell into an old despair of mine that no one can
ever get to the full truth about anything. I tried to limit the
hundred background causes so that we could discuss the
principal ones of what had gone wrong on the walk—and with

us. But I kept being overwhelmed by the larger, philosophical problem of everything being interdependent, then gave up because of the impossibility of a truly honest explanation.

You asked me why I was silent. I answered that I couldn't tell you. Because I didn't want to lie, or play the hero with sham profundity. My very need for a completely truthful exchange with you was the undoing.

So my motives were okay in that case—unlike now, when I'm making precisely the kind of half-truth justification I avoided then. But no justification can possibly exist for my cursed month "away." Only an inadequate explanation: I was so certain of our perpetuity that it never occurred to me you might think it was the end. Why didn't I come to put my arms around you, tell you that you were dearer than ever? That's what I was thinking the entire month—and the paradox is, I was learning how from Anastasia. . . .

Roommate Viktor is actually reading The Kreutzer Sonata. He's not sure whether he's angry at himself for wasting the time, or proud for persevering; whether to be appalled at or applaud Tolstoy's prerevolutionary misogyny. The better I know him, the less there is to talk about because we can't agree on a single sentence. But he's wonderfully kind in his way. Seeing me up during the night, he worried. He thinks the winter's too much for me.

Have you any idea how wretchedly empty this building is without you? "Since you were gone/My barren thoughts have chilled me to the bone." And all the more because I imagine how I left you alone in your dormitory.

The things we did in bed, those things, were beautiful because honest. Hemingway was wrong: it happens only once in a man's life. Dear Anastasia, "love" evokes your image.

Now the Pravda summary on the radio, the editorial ending with the line about "continuing and intensifying the struggle," which I interpret in my own way with respect to Citizen Anastasia Serigina. I haven't told you how my thoughts of you consume me. The important thing wasn't love but trust. And opening up to the true and beautiful in life. That's what you gave me and what mustn't die. If you believe I exaggerate it may be

because you're younger, you haven't had time to see the
dreariness of everything else.

But whatever happens, I thank God for your beauty. He must
make you happy with me if possible, without if not.

Incidentally, I still haven't told you that story about the
emigré who first taught me Russian.

The white lies were minimal. Despite the spontaneity affected,
I rewrote a dozen times, hoping the prose would evoke our best
days. The hint about putting it down after a sleepless night was
also misleading: I worked on it an entire day, adding the first
paragraph as an afterthought. But in the sense that earlier
sleepless nights in my room and outside her dormitory were the
equivalent, this was poetic licence.

I merely omitted the central truths: that the real reason for my
disappearing act was cowardice, plus greed for the girls at
Alyosha's. In that sense, it had the elegance of simplicity.

I took the occasion to enter a library for the first time in
months, borrowing a Russian style book from there. My other
loan was of a typewriter for the final draft, partly to give myself
something to do the following day too: a clean Russian page took
an hour. And to preserve my heartbreak in carbon. I hadn't
written anything for ages. I liked the embellishment of my
anguish.

Time imposed its humdrum relief. True to the platitudinous
pattern, part of me continued to resent my reconversion from
tragic hero to old me, even drearier without my princess. But I
also resisted rehabilitation because the thought that life might
become tolerable without Anastasia was itself intolerable: the
recovery of an amputee reconciling himself to a legless future. At
this stage too, my impulse to dramatize my sense of loss did not
prevent me from genuinely feeling it. Everything was true.

I'd started spending every day with Alyosha. And I *did* forget,
sometimes even gloated. Other times I went down a different pit
and could no more feed a line to, let alone sleep with, some
salesgirl than eat coal. This polarity extended to Anastasia. Some
mornings in bed, I choked with desire for her as a purely carnal
object. My tongue licked the air where I visualized her body's

shapes and smells. But usually my respect for her soared above lust; I limited my longing to becoming her buddy again. With that comfort, I could survive, simultaneously proving my purity.

Daydreaming of six months hence, I sometimes saw myself as a daring gambler who had stoically lost on his highest card. But in the hours when my sorrow filled me with tenderness for every living creature, I felt that this new capacity to feel could not be for nothing. My trial had been imposed to temper me for a truly holy union—perhaps not even with Anastasia, although I tried to suppress the blasphemous thought.

The relapses were like muscle cramps. I am on an old shopping street sanctified by our strolls. I pass the flower shop into which I dashed one afternoon having asked her mysteriously to wait and returned to delight her with a bunch of lilies. The sight of the same window causes a spasm, and I push through crowds searching for a telephone booth like an asthmatic seeking oxygen.

Temples pounding, I dial her dormitory. Blessedly, she comes to the telephone. I try not to overdramatize, simply stating, as if she is already a doctor, that her absence is suffocating me. Amazingly, she says she will see me this evening. My relief is instantaneous.

The rest of the day is a thicket of joyful chores. Alyosha gives me the apartment to entertain her "at home." But I buy the food, grateful for this project, at last, worthy of my time. An obliging American correspondent helps me get steaks and tomatoes from the Western colony's sources and I pick out an embroidered tablecloth from the best folk-crafts store. The final hour goes to folding napkins, polishing glasses, much trivia I'm good at. This is the kind of giving—like supplying Revlon nail polish and theater tickets—I always puffed up because I somehow tried to make it substitute for the more important things I held back. But I admit these failures now.

The table gleams; she'll be pleased. Forty-five minutes after the time, I begin to plead. *Please* come Nastenka, even if you're three hours late. To my dismay, my anxiousness swirls over the line to the old resentment when she made me wait.

I've started the steak. It won't be rare, as she loves it. She never let me perform at my best—even for her.

I remember my vexation over her favorite irrationalisms. Her willingness to let food rot—remains of the treats Alyosha set out for us—because putting it back in the refrigerator was boring. I'm a fool to have spent a frantic day on this lavish meal she'll spoil. When all is said and done, it was instinctive wisdom that saved me from the trap of her impetuousness.

But she's knocking! My heart leaps to answer, my profane resentment burning out like a defective match. She has responded to my plea and is framed in the doorway, her face as glorious as I remembered.

A new lemon blouse, the old amber necklace: she has dressed up for me. Her eyes focus on the foie gras, then rise to me. Once again she is high on delicacies, seasoning each dish with a graceful compliment. And perhaps my brief anger has helped loosen it, my tongue is equal to my table. I do not mention today's telephone-booth crisis, let alone The Subject. She sits in her straight-backed way, cocking her head in amusement during my story of a Christmas spent in Dallas. Through the chatter, I attend to her wine glass with an Alyosha-like deftness as host.

I switch from Vivaldi to Rachmaninov on the record player. The concerto's lilt transforms the room, and she has a new nickname for me, playing on *kulik* and *kulinar*: woodcock and culinarian. It's going so well that the measly part of me hopes it ends soon, before I run out of entertaining jabber. Partly to make things more exciting, but also because I already feel the withdrawal pangs of when she'll go, I relax my control and begin questioning.

"But how could this have happened to us? This impossible separation."

"I don't know. I'm sometimes appalled myself."

Her voice has a new wisdom that will teach me, I swear, how to sustain romance forever. At last we're going to have our heart-to-heart talk. I suspect I have engineered everything, even the break, just for this.

"We're so much better than others," I say. "Even this evening."

She straightens her new pleated skirt. I visualize the old one, which made her plainer but more obtainable. I want them both, the superior woman and the collective-farm maid; want to dominate *and* submit to a female being of disdainful grace.

"I want to tell you in the spirit of our friendship," I say gravely. "You mustn't throw away devotion of this magnitude; you may never find it again."

She blinks. I rush ahead because I'm afraid she may laugh.

"Ours was opening up to possibilities in ourselves that few people have. Believe me, I'm older."

"You've already pointed that out. Tell me something new. What are you and Alyosha up to?"

Ignoring this, I cautiously ask about her "friend." She says only that to leave him now would tear her in half. I curse my amorphous age.

"But logically you're mine. My feeling for you is as strong as the survival instinct."

I can't quite believe that at just this moment she has to excuse herself. Walking out like an office secretary, she closes the bathroom door instead of inviting me, as of old, to the celebration of her peeing. Confronted with our lost intimacy, I have to start from the beginning when she returns.

"I'm deeply grateful to you, but you still don't know why. I'm grateful for introducing me to love and its colors. In my ignorance, I always dismissed fairy tales, poetry, romantic novels as fakery. Now I understand: how Paris stole Helen, why Tristan will never forget Isolde, what motivates the families in this very building. The real and allegorical meanings in life and litera-ture—that's what you've given me."

She puts a finger to her lips, but again her eyes permit me to continue. The emergence of my literary allusions without conscious thought reinforces the dependence they proclaim, like prayer strengthening faith. But I can't tell what she's thinking beyond wanting more wine. The professor has obviously taught her to drink a lot.

"You're the most beautiful woman I'll ever see—but did you know you're plump? Not slim like strangers see you, but round and radiating like . . . like a New York artist who paints the sun and moon as concentric circles: the warmth of day and holy light of night. . . . Wait, he was Russian! Doesn't that prove I'm right?"

If only we could go on in this euphoria forever, hearing my *in vino veritas* adoration of her that stills all skeptical voices. While I implore her shamelessly to return, she strokes my hands, saying she understands, it's hard for me. She is my best friend again, helping me through a bad patch.

"I'm fond of you," she says. "I don't enjoy seeing you wriggle."

"The suffering's not the main thing now. It's . . . I'm a stray dog without you."

"You're what you always were. A fine young man."

I wonder whether it is her praise or devastating put-down that is swelling my lump. Her "fine" was for describing chicken broth.

"Look at my face," I murmur. "Listen to my heart. I've lied before, but—"

I go to my knees, pressing hers with my forehead. But I believe enough of our fellowship has returned to make ourselves comfortable with one another, even in this preposterous situation. I also sense I am making progress, which must be consummated in physical union. I can break all barriers and finish the professor by crushing my mouth on hers, lifting her into bed.

I drink a full glass of cognac and let my tongue wag.

"Did you know that breasts can be off-putting? Embarrassing when inadequate, deadening when too large. . . . I've never seen perfection like yours. Your nipples are symbols of you; instantly sensitive to the touch."

With reverence for her godlike femininity, I raise my fingertips to the edge of her rising. Breasts in her homemade lemon blouse, like Aztec shrines.

"Take your hand away."

Only the transformation of her expression convinces me her rebuff isn't banter. Nothing has changed, she says; why must I spoil the evening?

"I come to have a meal with a friend and he dishes himself up as Tristan and Paris. I wish you'd stop moaning. I wonder whether you know how much it detracts from you."

While I'm still speechless, she tries to soften the blow. "When you find the goal you need, you won't imagine you love me so much. Your limbo makes you exaggerate my importance."

While I wait for an answer to this truth, the futility of knowing

I've become a bore and a burden undermines my will to fight. But I plod on.

"If you won't accept my feelings, teach me how to smother them. I can't by myself."

"When will you understand I'm with someone else?"

"And can't come back to me now."

"I don't *want* to."

This can't be true. I must win something back. But I'm too drained to try; my hot air is exhausted.

She says good-bye, insisting I not take her home. I feel I am sealing my own doom by not overriding her objections and going with her; that to obey now would be the same fatal flaw of failing to prove my affection when we were together. But I'm too unsure of myself for an all-or-nothing bid. Despising my meekness, I kiss the hem of her overcoat.

"For the last time, Nastenka. Are you bluffing?" Like a subordinate asking permission to rebel, my question claims the worst of both worlds. She need not answer it. Long after the ground-floor door has slapped behind her and the gust of night air splashed my face, I remain on the dark landing of the stairwell, reproaching myself for being not quite submerged enough in my disorientation to ignore the cabbage smell.

The emptied apartment asks what disguise I'll now assume. The chair cushion still holds her shape. Tenderly, I wash our dishes, seeking nobility in defeat.

The following weeks, I cut a comic figure scheming new treats for her. But I am young and eventually will go the way I swore I wouldn't. Alyosha takes me ice-skating while the rinks are still well-frozen, and his orgies are more fun than my Wertherisms. In most ways, life is much easier with him as my buddy instead of her.

The first smell of spring arrives when he is trying his drugs case in Alma-Ata, and I decide to celebrate with a symphonic concert. Riding the bus from the University, the one in which the jonquil first showed itself, puts me deeper in the mood of regret and nostalgia for Anastasia than in many weeks. Oddly, she never said where she was going that September morning, but one day I'll see her again just to ask her. I want to hallow the experience, raise it through knowing all the details to a better state than my bungling left it.

Does she still read from my book of poems? I do, from the secondhand copy I searched bookshops for, a would-be knight faithful to his errant lady. The Esenin verses are an almond paste of sweetness and provocation, like her first smile in the bus. My favorite explains why I lathered under her impetuousness from the first moment.

You remember,
Remember every moment, of course:
How I waited, back to the wall;
And you paced the room in agitation,
Flinging stings into my face.

You said
The time had come for us to part;
That you were sick of my foolheaded ways
And had to return to real things,
While I pushed on—downward, toward my lot.

My darling!
You did not love me.
Didn't understand that amidst the city throngs,
I was like a horse foaming with exhaustion;

And goaded by a daring rider's spurs.
You did not know that the dense smoke of my disassembled
    existence
Is what caused my anguish: preventing me from seeing
Where fate's strange tricks were leading us.

Do these lines move her too? The bus slithers to a halt on Lenin Prospekt. A powerful deja-vu seizes me, and I try to understand what has prompted it before slipping into my old Weltschmerz. "What is boundless cannot be bounded"—this saying she liked comes to me, together with its image of arms trying to embrace the infinity of universal mysteries. Suddenly I recognize a signpost identifying this as *the stop*.

My thoughts stampede into planes of time and space, fate and human destiny. These mute buildings, streetlamps, stunted trees that have stayed the same while I was thrashing about in my drama harbor answers to the riddles of existence. Organic and permanent, they provide everything lacking in mortal, perishable us.

This inane grandiloquence exasperates me even as I think it; yet the sense of revelation persists, far more dizzying than mere coincidence could produce. Maybe this is the very bus. I look toward its back platform. *A girl is there*! running toward the open doors, her cheeks flushed in the frigid darkness . . .

Frost on my window blurs her badly, but I swear it is *she*. Her red scarf floated by forward notion, she is already reaching for the railing at the rear steps, which she misses only because the driver sees to it with a spiteful start. My inner ear hears "Black plague," her curse for such occasions.

My heart races the diesel's detonations. Maybe not emotion has been tilting me, but occult forces. I am aware of the bus's forward motion only when I begin cursing myself for not leaping out of the back door and seizing my miraculous second chance with her. We are at the next stop, where I searched for her that morning in the metro foyer. I fumble toward the exit, which an infuriating disorientation prevents me from reaching in time. A sharp start in a broken first gear, a missed grasp at an overhead strap and my overcoat is sopping with the floor's rusty slush.

I return to my seat and tell myself I must think. A ramshackle bus with a half-inch of window rime because of a busted heater. At the opposite end of the spectrum of the ordinary and the fantastic, the religious coincidence of her specter *there*. . . . I'll never find her if I get off now. But the driver's beer-hall bass announcing the next stop over his microphone is trying to tell me what to do: "Comrade Serigina, off at Herzen Street." That's it, *she too is going to the Conservatory*! Never mind that she's never been there on her own, and doesn't suspect that *The Rite of Spring* is the feature of tonight's program. Sheer instinct is drawing her to me; that's why she had the plastic bag in which she carries her theater shoes. Her appearance at the concert will be the proof of our inseparability.

The bus rattles across an empty October Square and down Dmitrova Street, past the French Embassy. Once she risked coming to a reception in the old mansion, during the time we couldn't keep our hands from each other. We backed into an anteroom and fondled one another, pretending to be searching the pile for our coats. Our appetites were—yes, boundless.

One chance in a million to have seen her at our stop; in a hundred million if she appears at the Conservatory. Yet I already picture her in the crowd, searching for a spare-ticket seller from the pedestal of Tchaikovsky's statue. I circle back to take her arm from behind. Her larynx laugh goes up: "Well done, clever one. I knew you'd be here."

She'll wait at my side, protecting her face with her scarf against the Bulldog Drummond fog, taking it for granted that I'll somehow get us inside. We two risking the unorthodox again, united for sensual experience. Waving my passport, I'll claim in loud American that I'm the advance man for the orchestra's New York tour.

Then our entrance into the concert hall, the eighteenth-century music room with the severe white walls and gleaming organ pipes. And the Stravinsky—even better, because its dissonances are more electrifying, than on Proposal Evening. Her face is as gold and clean as the hall. We are merged by the exquisite setting, the magnificent coincidence of our meeting, the enthralling Russian paganness of the music. The rite of *our* spring. We *will* be together. . . .

But stop. I'm tired of this tale before forcing myself to live it. At last I'm beginning to see: far from the patron of love it tries to pass for, my urge to dramatize and romanticize relationships is an unconscious wrecking device. Before we meet again, I must have an honest word with myself. Theatrical props don't work for her. She lives fairy tales too, but somehow without hamming up her own life: while I was convincing myself the episode was heaven-sent, it was enough for her to catch the Esenin book and ride on. Yes, before I see her again, I must learn to see, and see for, myself.

Besides, if I keep her as a symbol, the best of her will enrich me for years. I can spend a thousand dreamy hours pitying myself, gauging how far she departed from the Russian norm, trying to analyze how much of her glory was in my idealization. My memories are as moving as the moments themselves. I'll picture her at sleep, head thrusting out from beneath the covers and laying claim to each breath as if oxygen were one of her adored foods. Or removing her watch before sex, like an athlete before a game. Her antipathy to it in bed was so strong that if she noticed it still on, she flung it away.

I'll remember how she made herself up, examining her mirror image with a narcissism so uninhibited that it crossed the line of vanity to artlessness. Privy to the secrets of her toilet, I felt a part of her, and of the sheer physical grace I'd always wanted. What luxury to lie on the covers and do nothing but watch her minister to *our* beautiful eyes!

I'm grateful to her, even for her rejection. Even while best friends, I've always felt us competing in a strange rivalry, which there's still a chance I'll eventually win by converting this experience into some kind of elevating growth. "Man is born to live, not prepare for life," said Zhivago. She does the one and I the other—but who'll be happy in the end?

Someday I'll separate who she is from what I want of her. Meanwhile, the bus is pulling me away from her like a Greyhound on a turnpike.

VI The President's Day

The day of Nixon's arrival in Moscow dawns in fat pastel clouds. Air as fragrant as a cow's breath licks my skin through the wide-open dormitory window. What world capital can compare to the rambling village called Moscow when the spring sun shines and the smell of earth makes you free as Huck Finn? The dust won't rise for hours. The Kremlin is Disneyland on a lavender horizon. Nothing yet moves in the dormitory except Viktor's lips for his rhythmic snore and Kemal's slippers pacing the communal kitchen. I hurry past to avoid turning down his glass of tea, which comes with entreaties for advice now that M.I.T. and a university in Illinois have rejected him.

My unprecedentedly early start is to catch Zhenya on this final opportunity, and perhaps come by one of his "underground" drawings. But "underground art" can summon up more than one misleading image in this city. Some Westerners assume it is necessarily creative and good—a corollary of their supposition that persecution renders political dissenters honest and saintly as well as brave. Unsentimental critics, by contrast, have seen so much sterility, pomposity and vacuous self-advertisement—feeble plagiarism of Chagall, shallow experimentation in Op Art—that they've come to expect only exhibitionistic imitation of Western vogues in rebels' flyblown studios. And to assert that nothing more can be expected of an artistic community cut off from its roots for forty years, force-fed with Social Realist philistinism, and now painting exclusively for Western patrons of dissident art, many of whom can't tell the top of a canvas from its bottom. When they open up to foreigners, many Moscow intellectuals and artists burn with conviction that theirs are important talents, unrecognized only because of political repression. The tedious truth behind this heartwarming illusion is that some deserve as much sympathy for this conception of their meager gifts as for their relegation to the outhouses of the cultural establishment.

To all this, Zhenya the Giant is a happy exception. *His* basement studio is as foul as any, dungeon of leavings and smells. But his talent attracts even certain Ministry of Culture officials, who drop by—secretly, of course—to see his newest work: pencil drawings and canvases as divorced from Social Realism as Pasternak's poems from *Pravda* editorials. The best are oils of thrones in the cosmos and costumed girls on moonlike beaches— always with strongly understated color, hints of erotic surrealism and unsettling omissions that force the viewer to complete the work. Nostalgic, ominous, tantalizing with inexpressible perceptions and truths . . . the mood rarely fails because Zhenya, for all his dirtiness, avarice and indifference to Art—he couldn't care less about the Hermitage, let alone the Louvre—has a rare gift.

He will be leaving this afternoon for Israel via the train for Vienna: one of the year's charmed thirty thousand. When I arrived, hopes for such an exodus were dismissed as unreal, but Zhenya obtained his papers with a tenth of the trouble he'd expected. The hardship cases featured in the Western press still languished in their terrible limbo, refused both permission to leave and to support themselves; condemned by pure vindictiveness to begging and despair. ("We don't want you here; we deprive you of your jobs and pensions. But neither shall you go, traitorous Jewish scum.") But Zhenya's relatively easy success with the visa reinforced his assumption that progress toward his prosperity is the natural course of events.

Zionism still roiled him. He was rude to let-our-people-go activists who appeared with congratulations and suggestions as soon as word traveled of his application. (Without their activism, of course, it would never have occurred to him that he might go abroad, let alone emigrate.) He stormed against American Zionist committees who took it upon themselves to speak for his three million oppressed brothers, arguing that three quarters of them did *not* want to leave, and that this included the "Commie fucks": Jews in the Party and government whom Israel or any Western country would be crazy to accept. And the thought of settling in Israel appalled him. He simply knew Russia was past hope and that he'd had enough of it. The only escape was to Israel, where he intended to stay very briefly before moving on to the States. The next step was to allow his sister, a gym teacher, to pump him with sufficient courage to apply for the visa. It was taken for granted that she would go with him, to make his suppers and occasionally sweep out his room. He did not bother until later to tell his mother.

One day, I accompanied him to have a look at the application office, a division of the Ministry of the Interior run by the KGB. In the outer office, the archetypal setting for refugees at the mercy of unreachable bureaucrats, the line to see the officers in their cubicles was one hundred and forty-eight people long at 8:40 in the morning. A mean sergeant behind the reception desk was lashing out at everyone, but preferably at women over sixty. One—who was trying to visit a nephew in Belgium, her only living relative—was eighty-five, and her hands so failed her that she asked Zhenya's help in filling out the application form. "I've done it five times in five years," she apologized. "I can't remember everywhere I lived before 1905, so I keep putting down something different. Will that finish me?" There were collective farmers in cotton quilt jackets, painted tarts in foreign suede boots—they were applying to leave with their new husbands, Arab students—and elderly men wearing Brigade of

Communist Labour medals to help their chances. And it *was* democratic: emerging from their interviews, young and old both wept. . . .

Zhenya's studio in an apartment building off Dobrininskaya Square is dominated by a statue of Lenin that could serve as a parody of its genre. Evenings the courtyard is dark to save electricity, but a bulb atop Vladimir Ilich illuminates his bald dome for passersby. As a daily reminder of what to rebel against, it has contributed much to Zhenya's search for new forms, and he often touches The Leader's shoe when coming home, in thanks for the "dialectical stimulation" toward genuine art. I pass the pedestal now, hurry down Zhenya's broken steps and pound on the door. He'll be glad to see me on D-Day, especially because I have some New York addresses he's requested.

Ten full minutes later, it comes to me that my knocking might attract unwanted attention. There has been no sound from behind his door.

To kill time, I wander toward the basement of an adjoining entrance on the courtyard. It is the building's "management office," a combination of repair center, ideological checkpoint and conduit for informing about suspicious goings-on. Of course I'm accustomed to mysteries and slipups in Moscow, to little working as it's supposed to. Zhenya himself has broken more appointments than he's kept. But at this moment, he's supposed to be up to his eyes in packing for his, mildly speaking, important trip. What's gone wrong? Over my shoulder, I scan the cars parked outside: last-minute arrest of parting Jews is a KGB hallmark. None look suspicious, but an army supplies depot guarded by armed sentries across the street moves me on.

The damp management office is festooned with the usual Lenin posters, interspersed with slogans exhorting more and better work. From behind the desk, a middle-aged woman with the hat of a volunteer social worker is beseeching a workman in grimy overalls to attend to a toilet with a history, and to pull himself together and face the day. His eyes are bleary and cheeks slack: vodka-drunk at eight o'clock. And he is not about to take orders from Frilly Hat. Who says the proletariat has no real power in this country? The embarrassed lady is happy to be interrupted by a telephone call.

"Hello, Mamachka, yes, it's early but I'm fine. . . . 'The early bird catches the worm,' as they say." She is so full of bright sayings and good intentions that it seems impossible the KGB has arrested Zhenya, ten yards away.

I push off in the direction of Dobrininskaya peasant market. This section of the city, mostly untouched by rebuilding, has a small-town flavor. In a decrepit "snack room" I breakfast on kasha and gritty coffee. After eying me, the ragged man sharing my stand-up table volunteers that he spent the decade 1944–54 in concentration camps, mostly in the notorious Vorkuta complex. Fingers are missing on both hands—Vorkuta was above the Arctic Circle, he reminds me—and he has difficulty swallowing a bun; might I spare a few kopeks? His crime was to be taken prisoner by the Germans in 1942, when his unit disintegrated near Rostov. Worked and starved to a living skeleton, he escaped, made his way to his own lines, and was immediately sentenced because former P.O.W.s were regarded as probable traitors. He is the first I've actually met of the hundreds of thousands so treated, and I had no idea how badly off some still are.

"Keep well, brother," he says, and although he's a habitual beggar, this does not ring as pat thanks for my coins.

I find a working telephone booth to call Alyosha. One of the two girls using it while I wait—squeezed together, clutching briefcases, giggling—once visited him in the Juridical Consultation Office, but she doesn't recognize me. When I get through, Alyosha allows he's dejected because an actress met last evening spurned his "fraternal salaam," leaving him all alone. As if for spite, he must murder some of today's sunshine because a judge won't postpone a case he's trying. His final indignity is having to report to the hospital this morning.

"The hospital?" I respond, waiting for his punch line.

"Don't worry, I'm good at induction physicals. Cairo will hold out sans me. . . . I'll be home by lunchtime; what do you fancy?"

It is almost nine-thirty. Hurrying back to Zhenya's for another try, I bump shoulders with Lev Davidovich, the lawyer who drops by to discuss personal problems with Alyosha. He says he's now handling a deeply disturbing case, which he'd better keep confidential. I find myself walking him to his metro station while, his qualms notwithstanding, he spills the beans. He's been assigned by a court to defend a schoolboy charged with murdering his parents. Both victims were well-liked lawyers; respect for their memory makes him unhappy about appearing for the defense.

The accused is a typically pampered progeny of the professional class. The trouble began with his parents refusing permission, required for offspring under eighteen, to marry his paramour, an older shopgirl. Citing lack of common interests, the middle-aged lawyers also argued that the girl gave him her body, but not her love. Enraged by the latter imputation, the boy resolved a weekend-long wrangle by chopping mama and papa to death in their suburban dacha.

But Moscow's lawyers were even more distressed by the recruitment of sixteen-year-old Oleg as an accomplice. The aggrieved son first tried conscripting his younger schoolmate by simple bullying. "Don't be a stupider fool than you are," he blustered. "Alone, I can't be sure of finishing them both. And it's too risky if I miss one. Are you or aren't you my buddy?"

Although he did not blink at his friend's plan, Oleg was less malleable than his promise. "What's in it for me?" he asked with teen-age shrewdness.

"I'm reasonable. Name your price."

Oleg gave another moment to thought. "Don't try bargaining, I won't do it for less. Will you take the English exam in my place?"

"The written one? Yeah, I can swing that."

"It's a deal. But no welshing."

A second ax was obtained for Oleg and he joined his friend hacking off limbs of the parents he'd never seen before. Exceptional brutality put the crime in a category about which the press is silent, and for which the KGB is brought in. From the unforced entrance into the dacha, the detectives deduced that the family knew the killers and they followed the son. He brought a bloody flannel shirt for washing to his ex-girl friend; for unrelated reasons, she no longer cared to see him—and, accompanied by friends consoling him for his terrible loss, searched department stores for an identical garment. The blatancy of the evidence suggested that the boy was trying to give himself away, but when Lev Davidovich raised this during a prison interview to prepare the defense, his questions about motive elicited only shrugs.

"You don't have much chance," said Lev Davidovich in the jail's special cubicle. "Do you know what will happen to you now?"

"They'll shoot me. Got a cigarette?"

Oleg, who also faced certain execution, cried.

When Lev Davidovich has disappeared into his metro station, I spy a telephone booth. No answer at Zhenya's studio, but since once is never enough on Moscow's telephone system, I dial twice again. The final time, the receiver is lifted on the tenth ring, but my greeting goes unanswered. "Zhenya?" I ask the ominous blankness. I'm tense again: who's on the other end? Possibly a KGB captain supervising a raid. I wonder whether to call Leonid, the clique's Jewish sidekick, who introduced me to Zhenya months ago.

"Yeah, yeah, yeah," says a gravelly voice. "C'mon over. Still a few things to pack."

I underestimated the filth. Without the sketches and paintings that formerly covered its walls, the studio seems *solely* grime. Mice droppings and jars of putrid pickle brine are exposed in corners once stacked with canvases. Two hangings remain, one a drawing of the world floating in a lake that Anastasia bought, paid for with her own money, and never collected. (Nor did Zhenya remind her.) The other, centered on the most prominent wall, is a quotation lettered on rice paper—to help, Zhenya claimed, see the surrealism in daily life.

THE CLEAVAGE BETWEEN PROGRESSIVE AND REACTIONARY TENDENCIES IN LANDSCAPE PAINTING NOW BECAME PAR- TICULARLY SHARP. REACTIONARY CRITICS OF THE *1890s* TRIED TO PRETEND THAT THE LANDSCAPE WAS AN ART FORM FREE FROM THE IDEOLOGICAL STRUGGLE.

—*Russian Art from Ancient to Present Times*
Moscow, "Art" Publishing House, 1972

Zhenya too, and his rank beard, seem larger than ever against the bareness. Or maybe it's because he is full of himself. Tackling last-minute tasks with a hammer and chisel, he recounts his triumphs in the concluding stages of his emigration battle. Never mind that early this very morning, his courage had so failed him that he took refuge in a friend's flat, which explained the studio's desertion when I arrived and his later telephone precautions. Now his own dauntlessness inspires him.

In defiance of logic—they are trying to leave the country, not enter—prospective emigrants must produce letters of recommendation from the Party committees and state agencies that have supervised their lives. The clinic to which Zhenya applied for his tuberculosis certificate declared itself out of film; just as predictably, his cash bribe quickly produced the desired X-ray. But if such successes were commonplace, others demonstrated his keen mercantile imagination. Although his studio was merely on loan from the Union of Artists, he managed to sell an unsuspecting Russian artist nonexistent rights to it, using the profits to meet the blood-money charges for his exit visa and the necessary renunciation of his citizenship. Matching the government's thousand-ruble extortion with his own fraud of the same proportions heathily reinforced his self-esteem.

"I never mind their chiseling. As long as Russians stay so easy to swindle back."

The telephone rings. As with my first calls, Zhenya doesn't answer—but perhaps now out of unwillingness to be distracted rather than fear of KGB subterfuge. For he is recounting his proudest coup: "How He Evaded The People's Theft of his Paintings." It is a typical beat-the-bureaucracy tale by an opponent not branded "enemy" because in grasping for his selfish interests—behavior the authorities understand—he made no noises about struggling for freedom. Zhenya's game has always been to break the rules, not fight them.

The instrument of expropriation was the prohibition against anyone, even the creator himself, exporting an original work of art without ministerial permission. If this seemed mad with respect to Zhenya's nonconformism—what rational government simultaneously prevents the exhibition of "decadent" art *and* its departure abroad as a "national treasure"—it was only an extension of the policy under which masterpieces by Kandinsky, Chagall, Lissitzky and others are carefully preserved in storerooms closed to the public. Zhenya knew both the hopelessness of protesting on principle and the foolishness of submitting without deviousness of his own.

To the Tretyakov Gallery, seat of the commission for initial review of export requests, he sent his dutiful sister bearing fifty of his best compositions. "It's just my scribbling and scrawling," she mumbled as coached. "Souvenirs of physical therapy sessions; as you see, the stuff lacks artistic value."

The secretary suggested she go home and fetch Zhenya. Had she not personally known his work—several of his drawings were in the closed graphics repository of the Tretyakov Gallery itself—the ruse might conceivably have worked at this stage. But even the typist recognized Zhenya's use of perspective.

Arriving at the Tretyakov—with an additional hundred canvases, completing the oeuvre he wanted to take—he was greeted by the same secretary and a member of the commission, who also prized his work. Zhenya took the offensive.

"Listen, friends. If I want, I can get all my things out without you." (Part bluff and part bargaining point, this was a hint about Western customers with access to diplomatic pouches.) "I only came here to do things legally, which could save us all some bother if you're square with me."

"Listen, Zhenya," the young official answered. "If it were up to us, we could set a duty of one ruble apiece and write passes for the whole hundred-and-fifty. But you know the Ministry reviews everything. Let's be sensible and avoid attracting their suspicions, which'd be bad news for all of us."

Opening positions thus established, the two sides settled down to bargain about the collected compositions. Word spread of this last chance to see Zhenya's work, drawing members of the Tretyakov staff into the room like an auction audience. Controlling his vanity, Zhenya haggled. Setting aside only a few works as unsuitable for export, the commission fixed duty of from five to fifteen rubles on the others, and everyone present offered Zhenya handshakes and good luck.

When he arrived for his appointment at the Ministry of Culture, the list had been reviewed and prices raised by twenty per cent, in keeping with the general policy of squeezing harder. A staff expert had attended to this; the Deputy Minister himself, a veteran Party official, knew as much about contemporary art as about Harlem jargon. But it was he Zhenya demanded to see upon learning that another forty paintings had been judged too abstract to leave the country at any price.

"For God's sake, I want to *export* them, not bring them in. If they're dangerous, you should be happy to unload them."

The bureaucrat lit a cigarette and searched in a drawer. When it came, his response was in the voice of a gatekeeper whose authority to check cars had been challenged.

"What you think is irrelevant; you're not running this country. The Soviet people have a nose for your kind of depravity. And . . . you're not as smart as you think."

He called Zhenya back for his afterthought. "It's not as easy to fool me as you 'artists' think. You want to get your junk out and sell it to some 'exhibition' to discredit the Motherland. Not while *I'm* in charge of vigilance. Now *out* before I change my mind about the rest."

The following evening, Zhenya actually treated his friends to a bottle of wine. Not only had he got permission to take out more works at a lower cost than anyone had expected, but he sneaked out most of the embargoed ones too. Calculating that customs officials would be unable to distinguish one painting from another—yet unwilling to admit this—Zhenya simply crated the prohibited compositions together with the authorized ones. Sure enough, while the belongings of cowed emigrants before and after him in the freight depot were ransacked for diamonds and manuscripts, no one checked his canvases against the long, vague inventory. Nor was his exchange with the Deputy Ministry in vain: recounted in the West, it would enhance the value of his works. The whole scene in the Ministry was a smokescreen to mask his crating scheme, and the provincial thickwit suspected nothing.

"That's what I dig in good old Russia's ruling caste. Light-years behind."

Zhenya completes this parable about himself in a beard-parting, self-esteeming grin. Not mentioning his sister's version of the story—which had him messing his underpants and sleeping in railroad stations for fear of returning home—I pass him my New York addresses, together with a guidebook procured by Joe Sourian. Jamming my offerings into his briefcase, he returns to his hammer. In the months of our acquaintance, I've given him shirts and Skira art books—which he sold at top ruble to bookshops—and paid his surprisingly stiff prices for three drawings. He never offered me so much as a cup of coffee, even when making one for himself, and now he's annoyed that I haven't brought the dollars he wanted. But he's been unfailingly entertaining, and I'm grateful for his talent. I think he's one of the few self-styled geniuses who'll achieve more in the West than a week's publicity as "dissident" victim.

In quick succession, two salvos of knocks shake the basement door. Enter a translator and an editor of a medical journal: fortyish, leather-jacketed members of the joy-through-black-humor community of Moscow bohemians, as they solemnly call themselves. As if Zhenya's packing were for a weekend trip rather than the once-and-forever exodus, the three plunge into their daily *conversazione* about soccer scores, mutual acquaintances' follies and official stupidity. A program about quarterly production achievements in the Yakutsk Autonomous Republic coming from a kitchen radio augments the atmosphere's commonplace element. Learning my nationality—and, from Zhenya, that I'm okay to hear strong talk—the medical editor recounts an adventure that recently befell his best friend.

The friend is a poet whose samizdat verses about occupied Czechoslovakia put an end to his publication. Six weeks ago, he was invited to the Academy of Sciences, a bewildering honor occasioned by his consuming interest in extrasensory perception. Driven by forbidden-fruit curiosity and unrestricted by ideological prohibitions, many Russian hobbyists know more than professionals of such esoteric matters—especially, as in this case, where the subject is alien to Marxist-Leninist materialism and much Western research is written up by men, such as Koestler, who are anathema for coincidental reasons. But in this case, the poet's knowledge was not sought of and for itself. The Academy had been asked for an audience by a celebrated Californian parapsychologist visiting Moscow, and wanted to take this opportunity to interview an expert firsthand, without revealing its own weakness in the field.

Given money for new shoes, the poet was vaguely promised good things in return for playing professor for a day. His respectable English, in which he'd read most Western literature in the field, was a positive advantage. More so was his youth, which would help impress the visitor with the onrush of Soviet studies.

"How many people have you working in the field, Professor?" asked the Californian. The ingenuous man was on his first visit to Russia; but even such Americans are not *always* fooled, and a mistake would dash the poet's chances of coming out of this with something for himself. Seeking guidance, he glanced at the Academy officials flanking him. But he was on his own; all the Secretaries and watchdogs together knew less than he.

"Actually, eight scientists at the moment." He added "full-time" in a feigned afterthought.

The intention of this outrageous exaggeration was to make the old Motherland look good. But the guest perceived it on the Californian scale: eight scientists meant eight lack-for-nothing laboratories—and if he knew anything about Russians, this was a cagey understatement. Weeks after his return home and an agitated report to Washington, the Nixon administration allocated twenty million dollars of unspent Health and Education funds to emergency parapsychological research, citing the Soviet threat in this potentially sinister field. Its own emergency over, the Academy dropped its recruit "like a Bible down a Kremlin john."

A month later, a cable arrived at his apartment inviting him to lecture at the California Institute of Technology and mentioning a round-trip ticket waiting at Moscow's Pan American office. After his expulsion from the Writers' Union, he worked in a warehouse and lacked six rubles to telegram his refusal. In any case, he knew the genuine professor would not believe a word of the truth by now, regarding it only as a crude attempt to sabotage Washington's reply to the Soviet E.S.P. challenge. So much for mutual understanding. Nor does the editor now expect that I'll believe the story—although, as Zhenya can confirm, it is gospel.

By the sheerest chance, I happen to know that Soviet scientists have been experimenting with E.S.P. since at least the 1960s. But the translator obviously believed every word, and Zhenya shook his head "Yes" throughout, like a hippie listening to an exposé of middle-class pretenses.

More knocks sound at the door, announcing the arrival of several beat-looking friends who exist on cigarettes and cynicism. Soon a small party is in progress, young men and women coming and going with an air of importance prompted by the occasion, and with a sense of the tragic, for the departure of so many Jews attenuates even further Moscow's already thin cosmopolitan atmosphere.

Pouring himself a large drink from a bottle brought by a provident acquaintance, Zhenya plays host with the residue. Preschool children play with mudpies in the courtyard while their grannies try to peer through the dirt obscuring the studio windows: our gathering is producing what they hear as fascinating noise.

The men at the center of the room's knots are mainstays of Moscow's "leftwing" intelligentsia. One critic is pronouncing Nabokovian scorn for stupes who fail to recognize Vladimir Vladimirovich as the greatest living Russian writer. (Much of the fortune he gives for Nabokov's black market books comes from his own snide articles about him for a literary newspaper.) Another principal is defending Solzhenitsyn against trendy belittling of his martyr complex. When all's said and done, the intense man argues, what counts is Alexander Isaiyevich's genius.

"Yeah, genius. For religious quacks and Western boobs who convince themselves of Russia's 'grandeur.' Why can't he see real people? Why the fuck doesn't he write about *us?*"

"Of all the stupid . . . Whom do *you* represent? What the hell are *we* in this place but extraneous waste?"

"We're talking about Solzhenitsyn."

"About Jesus-pure Christ, who can't write without posing as Russia's new Savior. And who's got the answers for all mankind's salvation too, just for good measure."

"Are we talking literature or idiocy? Name one great Russian writer without a cargo of crazy ideas. You've read Tolstoy's 'philosophical' articles?"

"The vegetarian who pretends not to notice the meat in his soup. And our new Saint Alexander plays *his* poverty bit. Praises black bread, damns Western materialism—on his way to a hard-currency shop."

"Old man, you've proved my point."

Elsewhere, the exchanges heat up in proportion to ignorance of the subject being discussed: the efficacy of Scandinavian medical care, Salvador Dali's artistic integrity. In defense of "fundamental principles" against the offense of seemingly innocent remarks, several interlocutors nearly come to blows. But the main debate lingers on Solzhenitsyn, especially his lament that the Revolution's most awful destruction was of the Russian people's friendliness. Every traveler since the sixteenth century, someone claims, spoke of the Russian peasant as essentially happy and hospitable; but that was when mere hundreds of thousands, rather than tens of millions, were exterminated by the country's tragedies. Now every day is a potential danger, and the people's traditional good nature is replaced by Soviet vigilance—

"Of course *you've* always had this unquenchable love for the people," someone cuts in. "All your earlier stuff about them being 'dumb animals' was clever acting. A great passion—and how about a little idealizing of golden tsarist times to deepen the hurt?"

A decorative girl on the periphery raises the old Khrushchev conundrum: how much might have been put straight if he and his 1960s thaw had continued. An artist sporting hundred-ruble Levis ordinarily would have disdained such triteness but has taken a visible fancy to her tits and rewards her offering by arguing that it's not a valid question. Nikita's very downfall proved the impossibilities: the Party establishment is far too strong, even if the masses really cared about who paints and writes what. "Nobody but us misfits really wants freedom—and we wouldn't know what to do with it. Besides, Khrush himself was no angel: as Ukrainian Party boss, he presided over three million killings."

"One million," says the petulant girl, proving her point about the former chief's goodness.

That nothing said changes the opinion of anyone in the room, let alone in the government, helps loosen the conversational flow. The dialogues relate to the country's social life as Monopoly to Wall Street. The proof of this is the zestful iconoclasm, even though everyone knows some of the guests inform for the KGB: harmless little reports that earn equivalent little privileges. And although who actually does the dirty deed is a matter of some speculation, each party whispering about the other, almost all agree that one man—a writer now propounding Bulgakov to surrounding smaller fry—not only reports but also invents. Known as a freedom-fighter in the West and a fink here, he is simply treated with slight extra caution, rather than avoided.

"Hey Zhenya, going to get clipped in Tel-Aviv?"

Having exchanged socialist morality for superstitious Jewish ritual, Zhenya's zealously Communist father decided his son mustn't be circumcised. He, the father, now detests the Party, but can't resign unless willing to suffer revenge for a despicable insult to Soviet rule. *And* Soviet hospitals won't truck with foreskins.

"Hey Zhenya, going to treat the great Western public to lectures on the Dobrininskaya bohemia?"

The party is in full swing. An historian who writes about the unspeakable evils of the 1918 Allied intervention is drinking hard and owning up to me. "Fourteen fucking anti-Soviet armies were on Russian soil. Why oh why couldn't you crush Soviet rule before it really got started?" Next to me, two profiles lit by the dirty window do not hear each other at all, but this does not interfere with the smooth mesh of their arguments. After all they've been rehearsing for years—and one is now married to the other's former wife.

*Kandidat
of Philological Science*   *Book Illustrator*

. . . gap of political
backwardness widening as
Russia's rottenness grows . . .

. . . fleeing to the West, which *no*

longer even seeks a Lost Paradise, is suicide for an artist . . .

. . . obscurantism, misery, brutality; and the main thing—the choice of *either* tyranny or anarchic bloodshed—will take another century to change . . .

. . . rationalist-legalistic-materi- alist West: *West*inghouse refrigerators bulging with produce, and you pretend *that* feeds the soul? . . .

. . . sick to death of the romanticism that goes prospecting for nobility in Old Russian pigshit . . . the same self-deception that ruined us . . .

. . . a cynical dictatorship, yes—but *I'd* never go where the inner ethic is also corrupted . . .

The Kandidat's much advertised hangover allows his stronger adversary to carry the day. "Yes, we're ruled by bullies with their whips and Marxist-Leninist bullshit. But I say we're freer, and happier, than where everybody *volunteers* to work for General Motors. . . . Pasternak said it all in that New Year's message of his. Socialism's only our attempt to put into practice the Christianity *they* preached for centuries. We took the sermons seriously because we're backward and naïve—and of course bungled everything for the same reasons. Suffered horribly for our mistakes. But why do they hate us for this?"

I push across to the other side of the room. Not long ago, I couldn't get enough of socialism talk, but the monotony becomes as bad as the phoniness—which would be obvious enough after a few months, even if you didn't know that the book illustrator fond of proclaiming his detestation of Western corruption lives handsomely on propaganda drawings for reactionary publishing houses. He's not above some really vicious things—East German

peasants tall and happy; West Germans bent and frightened—
for children's books.

His protests that a Russian belongs to Russian culture are all
the louder because of the unspoken comparison of his talent and
future to Zhenya's. And because bright lights in all the arts—the
genuinely creative handful who have stayed uncorrupted—are
evacuating in the Jewish emigration. They leave behind the rest
of the artistic elite, much of which is slimy with dishonesty. The
dachas and club privileges for which they sell their hack stuff
seem more pitiful as better people turn their backs on them.

By contrast, Zhenya's close friends, who are bunched near the
kitchen, are reliving their trips to the provinces where, on
commission to paint murals, they fucked everyone from daughters of collective farm chairmen to convict women in lumber
camps. I used to like this talk even more. It was the real thing:
free-and-easy bohemian life, the participants dropping everything for a month of hand-to-mouth adventures because they
care about nothing except good vibes. But the truth is that they
all suck someone as a source of income, like West Coast hippies
with monthly parental checks—only the Russians live on much
less. And although the discussion of who had whom last night
and which vodka makes cunt taste sweetest can be amusing, they
worry more than many Muscovites about sex. An ex-girl of
Zhenya's once told me that if a new lady isn't impressed with
him at the first glance, he can barely talk to her. He's so unsure
of himself, she said, that he needs a fix of immediate approval,
and only after this can he be his super-casual self. In any case, I
suspect that a few of Zhenya's friends are carefully taking notes
for samizdat reportage about Moscow life, in which they
themselves will appear as the antihero heroes.

Elbowing me aside on his way to the spotlight, a movie
director bumps me into the oldest person in the room, an elfish
fat man. When I pick up the thread of his monologue, he is
reminiscing about his youth. Born in Poland, he grew up an
anomaly: a Jewish soccer-player. He wasn't "a blimp like this,
but beautiful slim as a pencil, oh boy, oh boy." Then the Nazis
invaded; he ran east to where the Red Army was carving out its
half, and was soon in NKVD hands. His prison train to Siberia
was unfit for pigs, and he existed like a caveman in the

unbelievably primitive settlement, gathering berries and sharpening stone to chop his wood. But if many died during the first winter, it was better than being gassed, like most of his family. He never lost his affection for every new day, nor his gratitude to the Russians, who didn't kill him.

While still in Siberia, he took his first flutters on the black market, to which most immigrants—Russians too—directed most of their working thoughts. Whole trainloads were sold and resold by steel-nerved operators, he says; in some lines, seventy per cent of the production went astray. Investigators arrived from Omsk or Moscow, confiscated the loot, and unloaded it at top price—to the apprehended swindler if his bid was highest. His Krakow ghetto had hardly been a cultural center, but Russia's jungle laws took his breath away.

"I learned the lessons, and quick. You have a mouth, *eat*. A prick, *fuck*. A brain, *wangle money*. Never waste a minute thinking politics. And *socialism?* What are those two"—he points to the book illustrator and the Kandidat—"talking about? Oi, don't make me laugh."

The strange thing is, he continues, that the skinny postwar years could be a laugh if you had some wits and liked physical enjoyment. These rewards no longer tempt him, but it's too late to leave, even though he has a cousin in Massachusetts or could arrange an invitation from Israel. But Zhenya's right to go. Russia's satisfactions wear thin as a man wears out. . . .

The same Zhenya is thriftily stuffing the last of his dirty socks into a suitcase. Someone wonders aloud whether he'll succumb to copying groovy styles in the West, forfeiting his own artistic vision. If he becomes the darling of salons and foundations, another voice adds, his creative future is gloomy. Next, the concerned—and envious—gathering considers his chances of sustaining his helpless artist role to persuade people to pay his way. Even in Moscow, the bearded rebel made use of the Artists' Union's "creative retreats," always leaving early and scorning the "corrupting privileges," lest someone get the wrong idea. The young scrounger will become an old one, says someone out of Zhenya's earshot; but he'll strike rich veins along the way.

The party flags. Leaving for work, some of Zhenya's friends kiss him on the mouth; others walk away with an overcasual "so long," affecting that they'll meet tomorrow. When his sister arrives, I say I must be off. Simultaneously exulting in and whining about his future, Zhenya walks me up into the courtyard, a rare gesture of hospitality.

"See you in New York, old man. You can take me to a good dinner." His handshake crunches my bones. I don't mention the little pencil drawing he's often promised in return for small favors, or the superb one of the world floating in a lake that Anastasia forgot to take—and that I want even more.

"Yeah, good old New York." Although the thought of myself there, let alone Zhenya, sounds like more of his bull, I wish him good luck.

"And stop worrying. Smart operators—and with talent too— can't lose in the Big Tent."

Alyosha has asked me to lunch. To enjoy the scent of spring leaves instead of diesel fumes, I return by a back route to the peasant market, where I want to buy a contribution. After the strutting at Zhenya's, the market's ragtag population is a relief. From a Mercedes parked outside, three spiffy African journalists make a grand appearance to select fresh vegetables for their dinner. A provincial lady remarks to her companion that a good Russian winter ought to whiten their cruddy skins.

Scrutinizing my obviously imported shoes, a wiry Georgian vendor sidles up to me in half-steps as if to offer feelthy pictures.

"Pssst," he buzzes, "wanna buy some . . . tomatoes? What's the look? I'm serious."

Several red spheres—yes, real tomatoes!—plop into his hand from their place of safekeeping in his smock sleeve. When I indicate interest in *all five,* a miniature scale appears from somewhere else, and I'm warned that the damage is five rubles, a skilled worker's daily wage. Encouraged by the transaction, the Georgian offers to show me a genuine cucumber.

No taxis are in sight outside the market, so I hail passing cars with the sign that I'll pay the standard ruble for delivery in central Moscow. The driver who stops is at the wheel of a new Volga belonging to one of the ubiquitous organizations known by a post-office box number because it is too secret even to be named. He comments on the sun and his fishing, then describes last weekend's visit to his grandmother on a collective farm in the north, where, attempting a joke, he mentioned her starchy size and suggested she eat fewer potatoes.

"That's not funny. We haven't seen a potato in months."

The eighty-year-old lady's pension was too small even for bread. Only contributions from relatives and part-time work as a farm laborer enabled her to survive. . . . The driver was skeptical of his grandmother's peasant craftiness until he saw a young lad watching him eat his picnic pork. He'll return to the farm next weekend with sacks of potatoes bought in Moscow.

"Like taking a samovar to Tula, I guess." He smiles wryly and soon is enumerating his new car's defects in comparison to the Volvo he once drove for an embassy. Naturally, neither his grandmother's plight nor the Volga's flaws dent his cheerful conviction of Soviet superiority.

Alyosha is not home. He has recently erected a tin garage in the no-man's-land behind his courtyard for when the BMW of his fantasies replaces the Volga. On a crate inside is seated a hag who used to limp the street like a stray until Alyosha gave her use of the garage to warm her feet. Her muttering that Alyosha has been taken to the hospital sounds like her usual ranting.

Two new girls in summer dresses stroll across the courtyard, mount the stairs and ring Alyosha's bell. I can't persuade them to stay but they promise to telephone later. Walking around front again, I watch the thin traffic avoiding a cavity that has sundered the roadway since the first November freeze and thaw. Soon I'm waving to the Volga's pommeled nose as it appears in its standard place from behind the bend.

I notice a slight wanness to Alyosha's complexion, probably because he has to work this afternoon or had a boisterous night, but there is nothing exceptional in his hearty arm around my waist. After a sparser meal than usual, he remains in the bathroom for an unbantering twenty minutes, but this fits the pattern of his slight indisposition and meager appetite since March. As usual, we have shady business to transact. Although the two Jimi Hendrix records I've brought—they'll be well sold to a collector by the weekend—are not expressly illegal, we effect the exchange with the gestures, unfinished whispers and micro-phone-evading step onto the staircase that lend a sense of style to our every meeting. Today's only missing element is the quip that would have set us laughing at the system and ourselves.

We are still on the stairs when up strides No-nickname Ira, whom I never see without thinking of her story. Her mother, a Jewess with a hysterical manner, was head of the French division of the Writers' Union's Foreign Department in the 1960s and also a KGB Colonel whose work included supervising the watch on French-speaking Africans visiting the country. In that capacity, she saw to it that the susceptibles met coached girls, and sometimes told her daughter about the excellent photographs she arranged of the ensuing action.

But Ira had no thought of this when, at fourteen, a young man stopped her on her way home from school, said she was extremely photogenic, and invited her to his studio to pose. Ira feared to tell her mother about the rape but a girl friend informed for her. The enraged Colonel saw to it that the rapist was sentenced not to the maximum seven years but, under the section of the law dealing with "extremely grave consequences," to death. Ira's discovery of this years later caused the final break with her mother, whom she never saw again. She lived her own life as a translator and wife to several successful husbands.

She has come now to find out whether a friend of Alyosha's who is going abroad will be free to buy some books for her in Paris. (Actually, I am that friend, but Alyosha thought it prudent not to mention this when he promised her.) Her smart spring suit prompts the thought that I've never seen her fully clothed before. But although willing to perform for us now, Alyosha alleges we must be off immediately to our afternoon appointments, and she retires in some puzzlement over not being invited in even for a glass of wine.

On time for once, we drive leisurely to the People's Court where Alyosha most often works. A former merchant's house, revolutionary headquarters, clinic and medical archive, the building has been repainted recently, but the smells of its hundred years linger in the corridors. The warm weather has lured pensioners outside to park benches, leaving only a handful to while away their day watching the spicier cases. Alyosha's is in a former maid's room rigged with three benches for spectators. His client is suing to have the room that she and her recently divorced husband continue to occupy officially divided, giving her individual rights to seven square meters.

The hearing is so routine that I look for something better in the corridor. Divorces, petty theft and the usual collection of hooliganism cases—ragged young men awaiting severe sentences for carousing with vodka and knives—predominate. One dock is occupied by a handsome, silver-haired athletics coach, the very image of his profession. While supervisor of recreation of "Post Office Box 1844," obviously a large enterprise, he allegedly swindled three weeks' salary from some forty workers on the fraudulent promise of supplying them with sweatsuits through his sporting connections. Throughout the workers' dooming testimony, he holds himself erect, a good sport in defeat.

Finding me among the spectators, Alyosha affects surprise that I should be watching such slobber. "If people learned to control their greed for sweatsuits, they'd be *sans souci*," he whispers. "And the social order would stay sound as a roach, as we say."

His own hearing ended, he takes a few minutes to consult with an elderly colleague. Then we drive off on an errand of mercy for a neat woman named Galya, who in looks and bearing is the exception to the rule of "investigators," the rigid, much disliked detectives-*cum*-examiners who assemble the prosecution case. At the moment, Galya is also so nervous that she fails to notice the back seat is still unrepaired, and she's sitting on bare springs. Two days ago, she interrogated a suspected thief in Butirsky Prison, taking along the man's pleading wife out of compassion. Because she, the appointed investigator in the case, was conducting the interview, the warders relaxed their surveillance and the wife exploited this to slip her husband some sausage. Discovered during the search before he was returned to his cell, the grave violation of the rule about transferring things to prisoners threatened at least Galya's career.

I wait in the car a block from the prison while she and Alyosha go through their paces in the office. Their main objective is to dissuade the Chief Warden from informing the district procurator, Galya's boss. Imploring, beseeching, pleading that the poor woman was tricked, that it will never happen again, that public disgrace would destroy her young family, they prevail in the end. Even in jail, even after a genuine violation of security regulations, the time-tested tactics of humble contrition—Galya's ashen face supporting Alyosha's adjuring—achieve the usual cover-up.

In the car again, the rescued damsel badgers Alyosha and me to come home to a celebratory supper. "I'll nag you worse than the warden; I'll see your clients all get fifteen years . . ." When we agree to fix a later date, Galya, still trembling, kisses us and alights at a metro station. To my surprise, I hear that Alyosha has known her only professionally and volunteered his help solely because of her unusual fairness to his clients. But he won't accept her invitation because his reputation might embarrass her with her husband.

Alyosha is oddly moody today. He chides me for lack of charity in a remark about the courthouse, then throws an arm around my neck while steering with his left hand. "You won't get a nightingale's song from a donkey," he says. "At my age, spring fever can mean 'headache.' "

Unstockinged legs lure powerfully in the warmth, but we drive past many pairs without stopping. The hard-to-get play of Alyosha's new actress would probably end on this second day, but he doesn't call, mumbling instead about the need for a good walk and suggesting we go to Golovinskoye Cemetery, in case I've never seen it.

Of course I have, when he himself drove out to show me my first Russian funeral, one of the more memorable of our early outings. A February day of a new Ice Age; Alyosha and I trying to make each other wear my hat, like two friends jousting for a restaurant check; following a brass band's dirges as it tramped over the snow to a far corner of the cemetery. The echoes led us to the burial of a factory director. The eulogy was straight out of our oldest joke: "Rest in Peace, Comrade. The plan will be fulfilled."

The hushed whiteness of that morning has yielded, wondrously, to variegated greens; but how unlike Alyosha, who can remember the course of inconsequential conversations that took place months ago, to forget! Deep inside the cemetery, we turn to a section on the right. Although the mood is less phantom-like than in winter, spiked iron fences surrounding most graves and tinctured portraits of the deceased sustain the eerie effect. Tinny crucifixes on the headstones, peacefully unkempt plots . . .

Negotiating a maze of dirt pathways, I realize Alyosha is searching for something. It is his mother's grave.

"But I thought your mother died in Central Asia." He's told me little more about her than her death from typhoid fever, and I sense he himself knows less than he'd like.

"She caught it there but came back to Moscow. Nice little train ride."

The failure of his sense of direction is as odd as his lapse of memory; stranger still is the sudden call itself to visit his mother's remains instead of catching the last hours of sun in the countryside. In the end, we don't find the grave because it is no longer there. We learn this by consulting lists in the cemetery office, then hearing a caretaker's explanation—at which Alyosha's eyes flinch perceptibly—that plots unattended for two years may be cleared for a new burial.

"It doesn't matter," Alyosha says in a voice openly betraying how much it does. Returning to the car, he tells me, as if apologizing, that he stopped taking care of the plot because of the war.

Driving back to the apartment, we pass a cinema to which Anastasia and I once journeyed to see a revival of *Lieutenant Kije*, the 1930s film with the Prokofiev music. How we liked each other that night! Even more for seeking out the old classic in the improbable theater attached to workers' housing. The sight of it by daylight reminds me of everything. It is mine, tender and private.

"Has she called?" The ritual is for Alyosha to ask, "Has who called?"

"I think you two should tie the knot and end the agony. Or, ah, vice-versa."

"Has she called?"

"She's lost my number."

I don't tell him what I'm thinking because he's still convinced I'm playing a melodramatic act. Besides, he keeps insisting that I can easily win her back—although he won't be entirely happy with this—if that's what I really want.

We turn a corner to one of the Cartier-Bresson-like scenes that seem to manifest Moscow's spirit. On a fence concealing a construction project, remnants of a "WE WILL COMPLETE THE

YEARLY PLAN AHEAD OF SCHEDULE!" banner flutter in the spring breeze. Against the warping boards, a line of dusty workers zigzags from a stall offering draft beer, for which the men cheerfully endure a twenty-minute wait and the inevitable cheating of the stout vendor blatantly whipping up the foam. But the customers are delighted with their find. Tossing the skin of their salted fish on the ground, squinting in the sun and swapping stories, they swallow their proletarian rewards with so much gusto that we leave the car to join them.

"If there's beer, just great; if not, we'll wait," quotes Alyosha as we inch forward. The old peasant saying tells everything about Russian patience and gratefulness for small treats. Pity that the brew itself is watery.

Back in the car, Alyosha reminisces about a local Fagin who bought him his first beer in 1935. We cruise slowly, dreamy with the motion, until a Moskvich dappled with repaintings stalls abruptly at the mouth of Krasnopresnenskaya Square and Alyosha must brake hard to avoid a collision. The driver doesn't even see us until we lean out of our windows to glower. Of all people, he turns out to be Ilya, one of Alyosha's old friends.

Protagonist of many yarns about motoring into potholes, the plump former dandy is the manager of a well-known dramatic theater, tickets for which he skillfully barters for everything from restaurant reservations to his frequently needed body work in the city's every official and illicit garage. Hurrying to the trotting races to crown a four-hour workday, he persuades us to join him. Alyosha and I hesitate briefly to ride in his accident-prone Moskvich, but it is microphone-free, promising easier talk than in the Volga.

Driving to the Hippodrome, Alyosha gazes passively through the window—as I often do—while the ebullient Ilya tells the morning's latest joke, a variation on the new vogue of turning everything into its opposite to spoof the Hegelian principle adopted by Marx. The scene is Brezhnev's private Kremlin den, to which, late this very evening of May 22, he will proudly lead Nixon after their sumptuous feast. Heavy eating and drinking have intensified their shared predilection to see themselves as knights of their silent majorities and noble friends, misunderstood by their own intellectuals.

"Tell me, Lenny," says the President. "How's it really going over here? The rabble, I mean."

"Honest, Dick, Russians are fabulous. We arrest the lousy dissenters—and not a word. Raise the price of bread; still nothing. Wipe out inflationary savings by voiding our compulsory bonds—still they applaud the Party. You can't beat the Russian people."

"Jesus," moans the envious Nixon. "How can I inspire some *genuine* patriotism?"

Brezhnev rests his hand on Nixon's knee. "Sorry, Dick: I've promised Kissinger not to export revolution. . . . But maybe we should bump off the meddling Jew?"

The joke pleases Ilya with its penetration into the topsy-turvy cynicism—every last principle abandoned on both sides—that cements the new Soviet–American detente. Encouraged by my chuckle, he offers a quick résumé of other new stories and schemes to beat the system. His commercial curiosity has been aroused by the enterprise of a fellow theatrical official who worked his way into a group visiting Japan. The thousand rubles for the package tour—nearly the average Russian worker's annual wage—was hell to raise, but the traveler bought two large mohair blankets in Tokyo. Cutting them into forty strips on his return, he sold them as shawls for twenty-five rubles each. This covered the trip; the felt pencils and other trinkets represented pure profit.

Whistling at the feat—or the rumor, which serves the purpose—Ilya proceeds to his own latest exploit, devised to overcome the spare parts famine. Repair of a privately owned Volga can usually be bought or bribed at a government garage, since most official agencies use this car; but mending a Moskvich can stymie even procurers of his standing. Nevertheless, his own car has just been completely overhauled. It was only necessary to extend the factory guarantee by a trifling eight months, a minor forgery performed by a steady-handed dentist for less than the price of a gold inlay. "It's morally satisfying to fool the plant that produced your lemon."

He works his way out of his usual quota of wrong turns and onto Leningradsky Prospekt. A million policemen are assembling here: this is on Nixon's route from the airport. In the wide road's comparative safety, Ilya drifts into a monologue about his family obsession, many times stronger than autos and racehorses.

Ilya's people were Jews from Odessa, Russia's prerevolutionary Marseilles of waterfront hurly-burly, racial mixtures and criminal craft. His grandfather, a society tailor who journeyed to Paris annually for designs and for the pleasure of speaking French, was a superfluous organism in the new union of workers and peasants. And indeed: a month after the establishment of Soviet rule in the city, recruits of the Cheka, forerunner of the NKVD and KGB, visited to have a look at him and to expropriate possessions that caught their eyes. When the toughs had slammed the door, grandfather set to work hiding the rest of his gold and valuables in scattered caches in the walls. Then the city soviet requisitioned six of the apartment's eight rooms, settling them with toilet-clogging members of the lumpen proletariat. Three quarters of the fortune was thus immediately lost. To try to sneak in and recover it, even to propose a deal to the new neighbors —who were whipped up with the class hatred of victorious underdogs—was unthinkable. One accusing word to the authorities might easily have the former exploiter shot.

Without even the pleasure of stealing an occasional gaze at his riches, the former baron of southern Russia's clothiers quickly aged. Besides, he now took home just enough food to feed his children: less than enough for himself. Even when provisions were available, the threat of denunciation prevented him from buying more, and he died in 1921, so near to and far from his treasure. Returning from the cemetery, the family found the seventh room occupied by new neighbors, and their remaining furniture plundered. Now led by Ilya's father, a comic writer of magazine feuilletons, the five members squeezed into the remaining room: three generations within fifteen square meters. The valuables in those four walls tided them over several unthinkable crises during the ensuing famines and purges. They triumphed—that is to say, survived.

But when Ilya's father returned from his World War Two service, it was not to that room—nor to Odessa altogether, whose large body of Jewish writers were just then being liquidated in the fearsome postwar campaign against "cosmopolitans." Provincial Kaluga, where he settled his family, was far safer from denunciation and execution. Again they survived intact until Stalin's death liberated them from terror—but the buried treasure was farther than ever from their grasp. This roiled them—especially Ilya, who himself was now grown and living handsomely in Moscow. He had started on his high life of imported clothes, expensive restaurants and glamorous women, for which jewels and gold were badly needed. Not that he hated Soviet rule—not, anyway, for the sole reason of family grievance. But politics aside, the utter waste of the money made him ill.

He made several visits to the house near Odessa's celebrated Deribasovskaya Street. His palms sweated as he gazed at it. He could *feel* the treasure inside—but could devise no way to attain it. In each instance, he paced a week and went home. Three years ago, when he learned the old homestead was scheduled for rebuilding as a historical museum annex, his agony shot up and consultations with Alyosha assumed new urgency. As today, he never misses a meeting to kick around, as he says wistfully, his collection of futile plans.

Approaching the Hippodrome, he breaks off to concentrate on driving and parking. This operation completed, we hurry on foot to join the fine-weather crowd for the final races.

Like an amusement park, the Hippodrome is fun to visit every once in a long while. The notion of gambling in the Soviet Union is a laugh, but the racetrack itself is as dreary as a jazz combo from Volgograd. Faces in the crowd are the best entertainment: shabby pensioners who spend every possible hour and their last kopeks at the track; would-be racketeers with pencil moustaches. Periodic newspaper campaigns demand that the course be closed, citing fixed races, compulsive gamblers embezzling state funds, and the "dregs of society" who swarm to this intolerable eyesore in the nation's capital. But everyone here is nose-close to his form sheet as if the indignant articles concerned some development on the African continent.

Physically too, the creaking wooden stands smack of Coney Island. Pushing past toughs and teen-agers, who run small-time operators' errands as Alyosha once did, we find a place among the enthusiasts at the rail. The afternoon is at last taking shape. I have no real wish to be here but can think of no place I'd prefer for this moment, and sense that a bit of action will clear the ambiguities.

Our first race, the ninth and penultimate on the program, is off at 3:40—and then 3:45 because the starting car stalls and the rigs must be lined up again. "Who do you like?" challenges an urgent last-minute voice above the babble, and as the seven trotters prance past, a chorus of "C'mon, *c'mon*" goes up, in a universal intonation. But when the winner is announced— Burma, driven by a muscled woman—the curses of disappointed bettors are distinctly stronger than at Yonkers.

"Shit."

"The whore."

"A cunt of a nag, she took a dive."

When Alyosha and Ilya go off to place their bets for the final race, I contemplate the woman on my right, a crone in boots and a winter overcoat. Gradually, I become aware of a man in a windbreaker nudging me on the other side. I begin the small talk. He yacks in a country dialect about luck, life and the hardships of Siberia, which he has "er, visited once," but for some reason balks hard when I ask where he hails from. At last he mutters "Odessa," but when I ask about his occupation there, thinking of Ilya's house, he becomes pugnacious. I turn away from the odd stranger, but he fingers the cloth of my pants and asks where *I* hail from, the busybody. . . .

"You're *American*. But *no*. Really-really? Let's drink to that. I want to share a bottle with you—*I insist*."

I manage to demur by citing my companions, and soon we're smiling the idiot smile of nothing further to say. But minutes later, his lips are in my ear again.

"Over there in your America—have you got crime?"

I affirm the sad truth.

"That's what our newspapers always say, but . . . well, you know. Good to hear it from a straight-shooter. Tell me, how much goes on?"

"Too much."

"Wait now, don't mix me up. For example, have you got any *karmanchiki?*"

My memory supplies the translation, but my imagination isn't working. Visibly pleased by my reply—of course we have pickpockets—the thin man turns thoughtful, only to wheel around again a minute later.

"Send them our respects. To American pickpockets from their Russian colleagues: we embrace them, in *true* peace and friendship."

When I decipher the clues—what had so interested him in my clothes, why he'd stood so close, what he was doing in Siberia—I pull an instinctive step away. The nifty professional reads my eyes. "Don't worry, for God's sake, I'm not going to do *you*. Stick up Uncle Sam? I'm no double-crosser."

It's my day for being reacted to as an American. Hearing the news, the taxi driver on the way to the University lectures me about my President, who has already arrived at Sheremetyevo Airport. Gor'blimey cap down to his eyes, the driver is lamenting the ninety minutes lost because much of the city center is closed for the cavalcade. A squad of policemen ordered all drivers on his street to the curb, ignoring pleas to move on by an alternative route until their orders changed. But despite his temper, he's surprised I'm not cheering Richard Milhous among the sidewalk crowd.

"Your own President, aren't you proud? People should stand up for their country or it'll grow weak. Take us for example. Even your American bosses come here to learn. To bargain for agreements—because we're strong."

I left Alyosha and Ilya after the last race to attend to some things in my room. Ilya had acknowledged our four-ruble winnings with a playful "Our Luck Lies in Our Own Hands," a slogan for prodding productivity—to which Alyosha retorted with an old Russian saying: "There's no such thing as luck—and don't bother waiting for happiness either." In keeping with this out-of-character pessimism, and with his odd behavior all day, he asked Ilya to pinch-hit at a five o'clock appointment with a lovely. He was going home and asked me to come as soon as I could.

The dormitory is almost gay in the spring afternoon. Before starting my nuisance errands, I respond to a note from Masha asking me to come by immediately. Gesturing to the ceiling—a bit of silliness: surely *her* room's not bugged—she steps into the corridor to tell me that Chingiz has been arrested.

She's almost certain. He was led away last night. To prevent Jewish activists from causing embarrassment, the causes célèbres were rounded up for the duration of Nixon's visit, and rumors are flying through the dormitory and the Philological Faculty that Chingiz had volunteered some services for them or was otherwise involved in the dissident movement.

We find privacy in the stairway. Masha blurts out a story that punishes me for my part in Chingiz's trouble. A month ago, he was summoned to an office in the main building and handed a manuscript. It was a draft of a newspaper article cataloguing my sins, from "debauchery" to "disrespect for elected Soviet representatives," and had been prepared, he gathered, for instant publication in case I was expelled for running with disreputable elements. Among the testimony exposing me as an instigator of anti-Soviet conversations was a quote from Chingiz. The author, a middle-aged journalist specializing in the Western colony's sins, asked him to sign.

Chingiz said he had neither heard such remarks from me nor observed me as described. Storming that this was not the behavior of a Soviet citizen, the journalist threatened him with expulsion. The rector's relative liberalism and reporter's extremely weak case convinced Chingiz that this was a bad bluff, but Masha feels the episode is connected with his arrest. Perhaps the correspondent had worked through the pro-rector, known for his Stalinist inclinations. Chingiz's selection to be one of the students "quoted" by whoever ordered the article is also ominous.

The news is like a many-pronged attack. Since Masha is not in the fraternity of temperamental opposition, I'm uneasy talking politics with her. Weeks ago, out of the blue, she accused me of considering Palestinians subhuman, "like all Americans do." Our relationship is grounded on avoiding everything separating East and West, and only such an emergency could have prompted her to open up to me about the pressure on Chingiz and the journalist's tricks. But of course the brunt of the blow is on him. All I can do for him now is do nothing; until where and why he was taken is known, bringing the story to a Western correspondent might worsen his position. Recognition of our helplessness gives Masha and me a moment of camaraderie before she returns to her resentment, silently blaming me for involving Chingiz with my foolish liberalism.

The truth is that he dismissed my political notions. Unlike other dissenters, if that's what he really is, he still regarded Marxist socialism as the ultimate hope for progress. Although more aware than most that Soviet society was less democratic in many ways than the worst tsarist reigns, he insisted that this could change if the dictatorship were displaced; whereas the outward manifestations of choice in the West—one vote for a banker, one for an unemployed black—only pointed up the impossibilities. A substructure of contradictions, hypocrisy and greed, capitalism could never support anything shining.

At our last meeting, we discussed Orwell's *Homage to Catalonia*, which he'd laboriously studied with his rudimentary English. What impressed him was not the murderous Soviet drive for control of Republican forces in the Spanish Civil War; he'd fully expected that ruthlessness. But Orwell's enduring faith in democratic socialism strengthened his own. He read me a passage he'd painstakingly copied: "In every country in the world, a huge tribe of party hacks and sleek little professors are busy 'proving' that socialism means no more than planned state capitalism with the grab motive left intact. But fortunately there exists a vision of socialism quite different from this."

Thus Chingiz nourished his idealism with Orwell as he had with Mayakovsky—despite both men's severe reservations and disillusionments. He too needed commitment to something noble. The final irony is that *Homage*, which I'd obtained for him, was a banned book. But I can't raise any of this with Masha. For all the wrong reasons, I'll be losing part of her friendship together with Chingiz, if he's truly gone.

Awaking on my trusty cot, I feel better. Maybe it wasn't the Chingiz news that made me so tired, but being up since six o'clock. The light has dropped to twilight intensity, giving the translucence of spring evening in the north. I lie still, simultaneously feeling the great freedom of an entire city at my disposal with no obligation to anyone and a larger limitation on all and any freedoms. Chingiz's trouble already seems fated.

Seeing I'm awake, Viktor turns up the radio: ". . . Brigade of Communist Labor . . . voluntary pledge . . . annual plan for linoleum production . . ." A rousing chorus of "Russia, Motherland Mine" contributes to my sense of being caught. And what of Viktor, who no doubt contributed to the journalist's quotes, yet stayed soundless in respect for my nap?

I can't bother with my chores. I feel like doing only one certain thing just now, and the knowledge that I'll succumb fills me with a mulled pleasure of self-indulgence spiced by guilt. Yes, I'll go have a look at Anastasia.

To calm a dissenting voice, I have a good gulp at a bottle I keep in my trunk, then walk to the metro, after-shower smooth. The semitrance I fall into when obeying the call to Anastasia blurs my gleaming train when it arrives: filters all sights in my line of vision from fully registering. I can only breathe in the fragrance of the swollen river as we cross the bridge. The whole earth is active, like a stimulated gland. How much closer these sensations could draw us than trysts in damp stairwells! Sweet spring, when nature calls all pairs together; when my own nature is so much happier and we could enjoy so much more together than in pinched winter.

But the train goes underground on the other bank. The ride between stations is eternal; I fight down a claustrophobic premonition that I'll never get off. The respectable citizens opposite me look as prim as a row of burghers, and I wonder whether they saw me take a nip from my pocket-size bottle. Like the old Times Square Camels ad, "Reserved for Children and Invalids" and "Do Not Lean Here!" imprint their stencils on a plate of my memory. . . . At last we're in a handsome new station and a party of tourists is appropriately agog—but what are they doing in this offbeat part of town? And why am I riding up this interminable escalator when I know the moment of self-indulgence I've come for will only drag me down?

The professor lives on First Troitsky Lane, a humpbacked side street near Alyosha's old office. My first time, I had the usual trouble finding it. Of course a Second and a Third Troitsky

Lanes wound around the First, as well as an intersecting Troitsky Street. But no one had heard of Troitsky in any form, and the man who finally did gave the familiar vague wave and laconic "over there," as if too much order must be avoided even in this. But this very uncertainty strengthens my sense of being home now that I know my way through the maze.

Bit players run through their parts against the backdrop of the mild evening. Local teen-agers are loitering, smoking, cat-calling to girls in a small playing field I pass, and in a grocery on Petty-bourgeois Second Street, customers crowd the liquor department for their joy. I join their tribute to vodka's power with a new nip at my own bottle, then take a shortcut across a lot, where a heavy woman rises from a bench to ask me to thread a needle in the fading light. Oh the artlessness of the Russian people in their large, sometimes happy family! She knows I'm high from the way I keep missing, and calls me "my son."

At the booth I use for this, I telephone the professor: no use waiting to catch them coming home if they're already there. A girl says "Hello," and before I realize it's a wrong number, I take her for Anastasia and hang up *fast*. Then I chuckle, thinking of how Alyosha would have pursued the anonymous teen-aged contralto. A gulp of white magic to steady my hand, two no-answers to establish that the prey is actually out. I take up the watch quickly before they return.

My position is inside the entrance to his courtyard. They must pass here because the front door is permanently locked, but won't see me behind the gate they themselves will open. Squatting on a layer of last fall's leaves, I check the scene across the street from under the rusty bottom frame. Nothing suspicious, no one checking *me*. The neighborhood is a mixture of new prefabricated housing and sagging log houses converted into communal apartments. The professor's prerevolutionary apartment house is the solidest building in sight except for the spire of the Soviet Army Club, which I squint to see in the distance.

There's something reassuring as well as demeaning—a link to my inner self, evidence that I'm the same person—in my still going on with these childish pranks. The eighth grade again, spying on the girl I "liked." . . . I wonder what I'm going to be when I grow up. . . . I wonder how much time has passed and why I can't stand to wear a watch. More swigs relieve the stiffness in my knees, but where the hell is Anastasia? I want to see her while my high is in balance. It's like old times: she keeping me waiting.

The Tijuana Brass blares through an open window, drowning out a Mozart piano sonata being practiced several floors beneath. In the darkest corner of the courtyard, a teen-age couple are registering the progress of his hand in her blouse. Huffing about public behavior, a burly man in a sateen undershirt appears from the back stairway to chase them off. The girl cringes, her swain retreats, muttering, "Kiss my ass." A younger boy dashes by in pursuit of a stray cat.

The burly man returns to his room to watch television on a set with a smudgy magnifying glass. I know this because I knocked on his door when first searching for the professor's apartment. The protector of socialist morals was picking his teeth with a pen knife. Eyes on a soccer game, he conversed about my accent, which I had said was Czech to allay suspicion. He informed me that Russian is the world's best language, spoken by the most developed people. "You're an example; you see the need to learn Russian. Nobody's anybody without it now. Science and culture —everything important's in the Mother tongue." I asked what other languages he knew, and was backing toward the stairway when the flush hit his face.

When he has well and truly disappeared, Irina Sergeevna clumps into the courtyard on disintegrating slippers. Ironically, I first heard of her from him, her ghastly neighbor in their communal apartment. Passing her door, he snorted gratuitously, "She's out—at the *theater*." "Theater" was obviously a dirty, class-enemy word. Actually, she was seeing *The Cherry Orchard*, her thirtieth time in forty years.

I know I'll sober up by thinking about Irina Sergeevna's life, but maybe that's better. I visualize the fading snapshots she's shown me: a lithe woman holding her husband's hand. She's wearing a flapper hat in one; in another, a lacy veil. I never used to think people cared about such things during the first Five-Year Plan.

Eight years earlier, she was a scholarship orphan in the best Kazan gymnasium. Fresh from the Civil War triumph, two

Communists—the first she'd ever seen—burst into her French class to instruct the teacher about his new, socialist curriculum. Apart from the epithet "bourgeois," neither spoke a word of French. But more than this, it was the new local lords' Russian, a riffraff patois blending thugs' jargon and malevolence toward their betters, that gave the timid schoolgirl the lesson of her life.

Until then, the school's anti-Bolshevik tattle had caused her secretly to admire the mysterious Lenin. But whatever he was trying in Moscow, one look at the types in control at the grass roots was enough to gauge the direction the country was likely to take. Irina Sergeevna knew the danger of antagonizing beer hall habitués, but neither inherent meekness nor conscious self-effacement, practiced from that revealing moment in class, saved her from the fate of millions less careful—which is why her companions are plays and books.

In 1934, she moved to Moscow with her husband, a talented engineer, and their infant daughter, the joy of their lives whom the neighbors called "Angel." Now a doctor, Mama worked double shifts in a tuberculosis hospital. Two years later, the child died of meningitis, unknowingly passed by Irina Sergeevna from a patient in her ward. Only her husband's night vigils kept her from going mad.

Her nightmares stopped on the blessed day she realized that she was pregnant again. Maybe it was wrong to bring another child into their world of terror of purges, but at a time when even faithful friends feared to exchange an honest word, the solitary couple needed a baby on which to lavish their normal instincts. Their one hope for hope itself was this replacement for buried Angel. They touched the swelling stomach, worked harder than ever, counted the weeks.

With fifteen to go, the engineer was arrested. Answering a call from Peter the Great, an ancestor had immigrated to Kazan from Württemburg in the early eighteenth century. He still bore his family's German surname: proof he was a Gestapo agent.

Irina Sergeevna joined the horde of mute and hysterical wives, mothers, daughters who swarmed around offices in hopes of hearing whether their husbands, sons and fathers were alive. Trekking from prison to prison, enduring day-long lines in winter's cold, she miscarried, losing the purpose of her life and her ability to produce another. Upon discharge from the hospital, she learned her husband had been shot. During the next few years she lived like a zombie. The war began. A niece off to the front as a nurse revived her by putting her daugher in her care, but someone—probably Burly Boy, the neighbor—denounced her as the wife of an enemy of the people, unfit to raise a Soviet child. The baby was removed to a home.

Irina Sergeevna tended war-wounded. On V-E Day, a surgeon proposed marriage, but a Party official in the hospital warned against an alliance of a tainted woman and a "cosmopolitan." The suspect Jew was sent elsewhere; Irina Sergeevna returned to tuberculosis and her eccentric lover of the theater, becoming a middle-aged pensioner before she knew it.

Remembering her tale, I yearn to do something elevating for her—and for myself. It's sacrilegious to compare the tragedies, but my loss of Anastasia has helped me understand Irina Sergeevna's deprivations. In one tiny way, I even envy her: her loneliness was caused by others' cruelty; mine by my pathetic illusions. My compulsion to make a mess of my affairs, then to pity myself—ye gods, am I a drip!

Drip, it hits me smack in the forehead—the first drop of a sneaky summer shower, blown hard by an ambushing wind. I rely on my bottle again to inure me to the soaking. My lousy luck. Or maybe some kind of rain god telling me to shut my trap; I talk too much.

The café to which I dash after a quick search for nearby shelter is a squat new one at the focus of the local shops. For no apparent reason, half the tables sport "No Service Here" cards, and the waitresses defend their empty sections by shooing me away. But it's hailing now too, and after being pelted a bit in the line, I push back inside and claim one of the free seats.

Damn clever of me, since the floor show's better than most. In full view of the drenched line-standers, a clutch of waitresses is enjoying a smoke in the kitchen passageway. The maître d'hôtel, a frowzy woman with a Lenin pin, is swallowing meat patties at the corner table. Finally a customer abandons hope for his own supper and scolds her for the scandalous mess, from driving citizens into the wet to her own "gobbling" while others wait.

"Eat?" The reply is an outraged shriek. "And why shouldn't I

eat? I've been here since six this morning. You're the only one with the right to nourishment? I should slave until I drop?"

After the usual bickering, a neat man at my table manages to order a meal, then steadily ups the volume of his fork-taps on the oilcloth to demonstrate his impatience at the dragging wait. Finally our waitress slaps down his three courses simultaneously, pleased that his soup will be cold and fish sauce congealed before he finishes his eggplant salad. Next, she takes on the woman on my other side, who has asked for a pepper shaker with pepper.

"I've got to walk my son both ways to school every day, so don't you try to needle me," the waitress hisses. "I've got a husband who drinks but never helps." The woman mumbles an apology and forgoes the pepper. By this time, the man on my right has been turned analytical by the appearance of food in his stomach. "A few drunks an evening does it," he reflects. "They make enough cheating them blind to send the rest of the customers to the mother of hell."

What they don't suspect is how much I'm enjoying this. The whole evening's been too goddam solemn. For some obscure reason—or perhaps because Nixon's name stands out on the front page of the *Pravda* that the man's making into a rain hat—the scene reminds me of the nearness of my President. A mile or so south in the Kremlin, he'll be having his State dinner just about now: caviar, sturgeon in champagne, filet of beef and smoked venison with fruit—the works. And rendering his and Pat's sincere thanks for the hospitality. I imagine his style: "The United States and Soviet Union are both great powers . . . ours are both great peoples. . . . We meet to begin a new age in the relationships between our two great and powerful nations. . . . Never have two peoples had a greater challenge or a greater goal. . . ."

Picturing the toasts in the Kremlin Banquet Hall makes me happier than ever in this dive, and I raise my chipped glass with a smirk. To sustain my cheer, I'm quaffing Crimean vino, the only alcohol not crossed off the menu at this hour. I've also ordered some hash that the woman urges me to finish because I'm "thin." . . . Suddenly, I've had too much of one or the other and must leave for air.

Outside again, I remember my uncollected change and resent

the bitch of a waitress for cheating me out of three rubles. But what the hell, I admire her too—and my table companion for his tactful warning of how it was going to happen to me. The rain lies in large puddles on the sidewalks, but other parts of the wavy asphalt are already drying. To help with my swaying, I play a game of avoiding the water, but trip into the gutter, coating my suede sleeve with a layer of muck. Hearing "He's lapped his fill," from a passing couple, I rise with dignity.

Time to call it an evening? Telephoning the professor again, I'm half sorry he's not home so I could cancel the final act. Drink claustrophobia prevents me from holing up in my hiding place, but the courtyard is soundless now and I'll hear them approach in time to slip behind the gate. I make it fine when a car turns the corner—a false alarm. I wonder if time can really move backwards, as they claim in the new physics. A bulletin board at the professor's entryway announces a free course of lectures on "New Forms of the World Class Struggle." The note underneath offers an ironing board for sale, used but cheap.

I drift into nostalgia so wistful that the score for it, Strauss's *Till Eulenspiegel*, plays in my ears. I am thinking of my first Saturday job as a paint store stockboy when the boss said that I was obviously trying but he had to let me go because business was bad. Putting aside my gratitude for the gift of memory, I'm trying to seize the key to my life offered by this forgotten incident when a taxi pulls up. I know it's theirs because I've lived this moment before.

Not fear but incomprehension paralyzes me: I can't sort out the competing impulses to my limbs. May's moon is freeing itself from the last of the rainclouds. Anastasia materializes at the gate, followed by the professor, who bumps a long leg on the frame. She's wearing the Bolshoi dress and clasping a handbag; I know they've been to a good theater. And that although loyalty and intellectual appreciation still bind her, she can't breach his aloofness; they're already unhappy together.

So my rival is also weak! I'd like to greet him before hiding but my feet are still stuck in the rain-made mud. Anastasia's every movement is profoundly familiar, like the Dvořák *Slavonic Dance* my cerebral orchestra is now playing. I want to formulate something about her looks, but can only think to say that living with a man has burnished her splendor. She's an untouched-up Catherine Deneuve.

But I've been idealizing her too long, deleting her sensuousness. The slight Asian protuberance of her mouth reminds me of her frankness in lovemaking: the unlipsticked lust. Blood is pumping away from my sodden stomach—faster now, for her reaction to seeing me is flattered delight. But wouldn't you know, she converts it immediately to what-a-foolish-youth disapproval, expressed by pursing lips.

What a mistake to be half-hidden by a tree instead of in the open! She'll think I've been trying to peep through her windows—which I did once, climbing the old poplar as I'd seen children do afternoons; but not tonight. She approaches me as if I'm the courtyard naughty boy. I yearn to be imposing yet humble, to show my new worth and to press her hand to my forehead—a hundred things at the same time. The much-tortured alleycat scurries between us and toward the gate, distracting her from the declaration she's preparing for me. I long to hear my fate from the highborn princess, now advancing to strains of *Scheherazade*. The professor catches up with her, his expression revaling he knows who I am and is flustered. The poor fellow is quite willing for me to take his difficult ward for the night, but I have no such pretensions. Dearest Nastenka, I only came to drink in your beauty.

"Dearest Nastya, I didn't mean to drink. I only came . . . to wish you well."

"For goodness sake, you don't even like it. You can't blame your tricks on alcohol."

What tricks? Does she know I still sometimes follow her in the metro?

The professor hesitates because he wants to invite me in, but Anastasia strides past and he mounts the stairs in her train. Her scent follows: a fairy's fragrance visiting the courtyard's earthy odors. And moonlit flaxen hair on black jersey, lingering on my optic nerves like a television dot when the set is switched off.

Sonorous quiet again. The moment was far too quick. I lie down on the bench favored by babysitting grandmothers. Wisps of cloud are still up there. The certainty of her rebuff cleansed my confusion; the only hurt now is that she's better than ever, more meant for me.

But it's time to move on. Roll off and take the first step. Leaves in the breeze above remind me of Moscow's huge advantages for living over New York. Green to see, air to breathe, no doormen to avoid.

I find another bench on the walk to Alyosha's. It's good to be on my way at last, but there's no need to rush. We'll have a midnight snack and listen to the Ray Charles. I forgot to tell him my news about my application for a Black Sea trip so we can spend some of the summer together on a beach before I leave forever. And I must remember to mention Chingiz, in case he can help.

He doesn't answer the bell. Strange—the car's in the courtyard and his lights are on. I play the new la-de-da, then the special, special ring only I know. A teen-age factory lass lives on the opposite side of the landing, together with her parents, grandparents, uncles and aunts. She used to sneak across to the apartment for clothes-on copulation until her older brother came searching for her one day with murderous intent. Alyosha parried so well that the brother ended by inviting us to join a team stealing tar paper from his construction brigade.

But something's ominous about his not answering. *Wait now:* something's been off all day. Pounding's out because of the neighbors. I sit down on the stairs, deciphering the random pattern of the concrete.

And I go queasy when I hear steps jerking their way to the door. Alyosha plastered? That's impossible no matter what he guzzles—and wrong, because the appeal of his dissipation is his always being in control of it, like mental breakdown depicted in art. I can be morbid sometimes, even in May.

He fumbles with the catch. I step back in horror. He's not only slobbering drunk but deranged, like a man with a family wiped out by fire. I'm not even certain he recognizes me—or cares.

Suddenly I remember the hospital this morning. The howling clues that have escaped me all day. He is SICK.

"I know it's that. For God's sake *tell* me, Alyoshinka. We'll face it together."

I am cold sober again, tasting vomit in my gullet. Something loathsome has attacked my friend. A deathly film blears the eyes of the symbol of life. He was waiting for me all these hours, drinking alone in his room.

I help him lie down, but he gets up again to look out of the window.

"Alyosha, buddy, speak to me. Modern medicine works."

He will not talk. But when he does, it is worse than I've imagined. He has intestinal cancer.

It has spread from his rectum to his duodenal tract. A young internist he knows socially and trusts more than the clinic doctors has told him, under pressure, that the malignancy looks fierce.

He opens another bottle. And I join him because he wants me to. I wish to God we could be closer now than ever, united in adversity, but we are too hopelessly drunk to be truly aware of each other. Like shapeless heaps, we grunt and bark.

We grope for each other and try to dance. I remember an odious joke the day after President Kennedy died. I was working nights as a copy boy in a radio station, and a slick news announcer appeared for his morning stint, this time to narrate a memorial documentary. He was the kind who never let you pass without a gag. "What will John-John get for Christmas this year?" he drawled. I waited; he timed the punchline. "A jack-in-the-box." *And I laughed.*

We want to walk. I think we try to go out doors. Alyosha suspects he left some rum in the car. Later we ransack the drawer with his old photographs. There are a few of him in Sukhumi during the war, posing on the beach in a white-belted bathing suit. He whimpers again.

Toward dawn, I doze off in the armchair. A movieola of vignettes mellows my sleep, and I'm troubled only by a peripheral awareness that I must wake up soon. I imagine that Alyosha will trick the hospital as he did his draft board; that he's the subject of a malicious police campaign; that these dreams are reality and the cancer is the dream.

The radio has been left on. In the far, far reaches, I hear the news. And I am no longer dreaming, but putting everything together. The answer is a Nixon plot. Why did that creep have to come here? Break into my life with his Big Government and Big Business? Do this to Alyosha?

VII Interlude

Walking the friendly half-slums of Battersea, I remembered roommate Viktor. He was all excited when I first told him I might spend the summer in London: the spy novel he was reading had a KGB captain musing that "the only people who can even try to outwit us are the Order of Jesuits and the English Intelligence Service."

I also caught glimpses of the crank I'd become. I conversed with half a dozen people during the seven weeks, each time mentioning Russia within minutes. Although my quick notification of my connection with the exotic land was intended to cast myself in a dashing light, a larger truth was that I felt incompetent to discuss anything else, even with myself. The greengrocers were full of fat avocados. I couldn't say, "Look at those nice avocados," but "In Moscow, we don't have avocados. We don't have string beans or even leeks." I remembered a man I knew in New York who'd written eleven books about other subjects, yet whose frame of reference for everything was still the Soviet Union he visited in 1935. "In Russia it's worse. In Russia they do it differently. . . ."

To my surprise, London's streets had girls who were prettier—as well, of course, as more chic—than Moscow's, and because of Moscow, I moved to pick them up. But I backed down at the last minute. "Pardon me, miss, may I stop you a moment?" would have been a washout on Bond Street. So many elemental things seemed easier in the land of hardship.

And more important. Everyone's fascination for the dominion of enigmas and mystery strengthened my impression that other countries and subjects were irrelevant to life's inner truths. Even Vietnam talk seemed abstract compared to the pull of sadness and escape in Moscow's streets and flats. The heightening of feeling, the jumble of emotion. I kept trying to place the quote—Pushkin? Gogol?—that chugged in my ear: "Oh Russia, how miserable you are, how full of senseless pain and struggle. And how I love you!"

I also felt that Russia owed me something. This sensation never left me, but since I couldn't identify precisely what was due me, I began to calculate that the debt had better be paid in cash. For weeks, I toyed with what had been called, in derision of the fallen Nikita, "hair-brained" schemes for producing some. Write an exposé of the joys of Russian girls? Tell Fleet Street what I'd heard about Raya Brezhneva, the boss's "piquant" daughter? One way or another, I had to turn a penny with my inside knowledge.

After three days in a Marble Arch hotel, I moved to a bed-and-breakfast place off the bad end of Westbourne Grove. Beyond cardboard walls, my neighbors were clusters of Greeks, Indians and Pakistanis harder up than I was and desperate for work permits because of wailing babies. A sign over the peeling portico declared the former Regency town house to be a hotel. The corridor smelled of down-and-out damp, curry cooked on hotplates and a rug tramped by bare feet making for the toilet. Even on sunny days my sheets stayed clammy. Transient London. The landlady claimed it was the rainiest summer since the war.

I might have moved to a better place if it weren't for my

misadventure. As it was, I was so broke that supper was two
portions of beans on toast in a transport café ("kaf") behind
Paddington Station. A slight story attached to the disappearance
of my money. Having left Moscow with literally the clothes on
my back—all shirts, ties, sweaters and T-shirts, everything but
my old overcoat, had been distributed to friends—I made for
Oxford Street to stock up on sweaters. My jacket rested on the
counter seven seconds while I tried on a turtleneck. The store
detective, a lady out of an Alec Guinness movie, said the July
sales were Mecca for pickpockets, but that my passport was little
use and might be returned. The wallet had contained my
summer nestegg; from then on, I had to squeeze by on the bills in
my trouser pocket.

In a way, being robbed was liberating. It released me from the
urgent missions whispered by every second Russian who'd heard
I was going abroad.

"You'll be in London?"

"That's right."

"Please help me, please. We need medicine."

"What medicine? Where's it manufactured?"

"I don't know exactly. Japan, France—somewhere in the
West."

"What's it for, then? The name of the disease."

"I'm not certain. But you must find it. If you don't bring some
back, my sister will die."

Being broke also tendered inherent rewards. From Hampstead
to the East End docks, I walked London's streets, discharging my
nervousness into the padding of perpetual motion. Sausages in
pubs cost almost as little as tomatoes in street markets. I got
tired; I could sleep. But the most satisfactory part was the
matching of my financial circumstances to my position in life.
Orwell had the answer to salon Communists telling workers that
half a loaf is as good as none at all: that type knew zilch about
the working class. On the other hand, as Orwell also knew, there
were moments of joy in feeling you had nothing to lose. I tasted a
tramp's freedom. I spent a pound in Petticoat Lane on an
umbrella for the drizzle. It was my walking stick and
friend.

Something would turn up; it had to. And did: Joe Sourian's

Betty Vogl. Earlier in the summer, she had visited Joe in Cincinnati, calling him from her hotel room and asking if he had seen The Graduate. Then she was off to London on a two-week BOAC tour. Joe wrote me of this—on Cincinnati University stationery, for he was already an assistant professor there—in case I wanted the pleasure of her company. In the event (as I was learning to say), I had a bath in her room and a supper in her hotel coffee shop. But compared to Joe, she found me thin and listless—the latter, of course, a reflection of what I saw in her. I preferred tramping.

Something else would turn up; my fate was now blessedly out of my hands. What release in semivagabonding, what aspirin for ego-tension! Besides—never mind the contradiction—I had a terrific plan. I always knew Russia would make me rich.

My miracle-product was Sunday, an unknown Tolstoy novel I'd unearthed in Moscow, which an Erstwhile recommended and I read in a spree when Alyosha was away on a case. Although not quite Anna Karenina or War and Peace, it was certainly profound stuff (and made me rather proud of having coped without a pony).

But what did my opinion matter about a new blockbuster by Lev Nikolaevich Tolstoy?! Because I wasn't in London a week before discovering it had never been translated. A Tolstoy masterpiece, and nobody even knew about it! It clinched my point about Western ignorance of Russia; but even I never dreamed the terra incognita atmosphere extended to classical literature. It took spunky me, living like a native, to dig out a cultural treasure as important as the Tutankhamen relics causing bedlam at the British Museum—and probably more valuable in hard currency. The copyright had surely expired. I'd do a quick translation to establish my rights, then a polished job—and make a crazy fortune.

You never know about life. I first realized what I had twenty-one hours after my wallet had been lifted. One accident squashes you; the next one is deliverance. A man in a Russell Square pub who, to my temporary embarrassment, knew much more than I about Russian literature, had never heard of Sunday—so much for his supercilious expertise. I checked Foyles and the Slavonic School. All the other classics were there, from

Childhood *to* The Kreutzer Sonata; *but mine might never have existed.*

The secret sounded in me like Solzhenitsyn's invocation of the four Beethoven chords. Fabulously rich and famous overnight! Specialists to restore Alyosha; recuperation in stately Riga. Through everything ran my sage insight that this was not blind luck striking, but natural law providing fair compensation. Had I plugged on with work and career in Moscow instead of squandering the year, I'd have missed this supreme opportunity. . . .

To fix the taste of poverty in my memory, I waited another day before calling a publisher. I had to map tactics too: offer world rights in one lump or sell separately in every country? A fund for any living Tolstoys would probably best express my quiet generosity. Then it was time to move. The greatest publishing coup since the Depression was up for grabs.

Which is exactly how I put it to the junior editor whose Bloomsbury basement audience I finally obtained. I reckoned a strong approach would trim wasted time before he brought me upstairs to his chief. His Etonian fingers reaching from a pin-striped sleeve to a Russian dictionary behind him was the dart to my bubble. I'd had the title absolutely right. But as his forefinger reproved, "voskrensenye" translates not only as "Sunday" but also as "resurrection." While he went out for sherry glasses, I slinked up the stairs.

To the drizzly streets again, and no sneak return for my forgotten umbrella. But the dismal episode also made clearer than ever my need to go the other way, away from riches and back to Russia. I needed Moscow's adventures and sense of struggle to bring me back to life. I'd return and recapture Anastasia whom, in London's polite foreignness, I more and more treasured as my future wife. And I had a mission. Alyosha's young internist friend had given me a list of medicines, including an experimental Swiss one, that might save his life.

Another omen was the scholarship committee's quick consent to sponsor me for a third semester. My virtual disappearance during the first two should have got me disowned, but a ten-page letter claiming I'd wangled access to city Soviet archives just before leaving in July and extolling their handling of the exchange program—in paragraphs they could quote for further funding from Ford—did the trick. The chairman published a paean to samizdat literature every three months in The New York Times Magazine, and I casually mentioned how well his (useless) sociopolitical insight had guided me. With only a few nervous reminders to me of my previous academic achievement, the committee declared faith in my judgment if I felt it important to return.

The Soviet side was less obliging. Unlike the students preparing to leave from America, for whom the committee coordinated and channeled the paperwork, I had to arrange my own visa. The mess ripened under the gaze of the Soviet Consulate's guilt-framed Lenin. Counselors Kuznetsov, Kutuzov and Rasskazov, the three musketeers of the propaganda-stacked waiting room for tourist visas, couldn't understand the immensity—or cheek?—of my request. Oh no—they were not so easily fooled. If I wanted what I pretended, how could I explain the presence of a student of the American exchange program in London? . . . They should cable to their Washington embassy to check my story? Ho ho, and would I next suggest they fly me to the moon?

No, Meester, their cables went to Moscow, thank you; they knew their own jobs. A so-called "American student" couldn't be abroad without his government's knowledge and consent; why, therefore, wasn't the proper Washington agency sorting out my problems? And if I wanted someone to check an American so-called Scholarship Committee's correspondence about me with the Soviet State Commission on Special Higher Education, why did I come to them with my dubious request? Did I know what building I was in? And that it closed at one o'clock; all, er, guests must be out."

The workings of the Soviet consulate brought everything back. Better than Moscow offices because it had a veneer for foreigners, but with the same antagonism to petitioners; the same resentment, suspicion and surliness to the public it supposedly served. To what category—rat? snooper? spy?—does this disturbing foreigner belong? Will we have to spend money on him? (Xerox copies are devilishly expensive in Moscow: a vice-minister of trade was recently rebuked for running through an unnecessary sheet to show off a new machine, thereby wasting nine-tenths of a cent of hard currency.) The switchboard operator—in central London!—answered with an angry "da" (guess where he was trained) and knew almost no English. In any case, Kuznetsov was not at his desk, Kutuzov was away and he'd never heard of Rasskazov. Better to call again in the afternoon (when the Consulate was closed).

The next day, Kuznetsov was away, Rasskazov not at his desk and nobody could imagine where Kutuzov was. I took a bus to Hackney for a new place to walk.

In mid-August, the sun shone most mornings and a committee check for expenses upgraded my suppers to take-out curry from a Queensway shop. A Soho chemist, the seventeenth I begged, sold me a dozen tubes of an ointment called "5 Flurouracil" without a prescription. They were to ease the X-ray burns on Alyosha's buttocks. But he couldn't get the Swiss medicine, and a Fulham Cancer Clinic consultant, having listened to my translation of Alyosha's diagnosis, said he could not prescribe treatment for someone not his patient. Besides, the potion itself could be lethal. I could do nothing more humanitarian now, he concluded, than to help my Russian friend prepare for his death. He was an upper-class English turd who informed me that Nixon should have leveled Haiphong.

The next day, I invaded the Embassy as well as the Consulate. (Telephoning was becoming harder. When switchboard operators heard the bleeps indicating an incoming call from a public booth, they hung up before I could push my two-pence in.) Kuznetsov and Kutuzov were on vacation in Moscow—which was no longer even faintly comic. A voice raised as high as mine said there was no word about my case and nothing to do but wait. It "seemed unlikely," however, that a consulate assigned to conduct Soviet business in the United Kingdom would be empowered to issue a student visa to an American. Why didn't I fly to my homeland? Accustomed to "logical" problem-solving, Moscow would approve this "more straightforward" approach.

I sat among Hyde Park's nannies, alternately storming and trembling. Bureaucratic stupidity—I couldn't allow myself to think it was more—was a personal insult: Russia defaulting on its debt to me. One more week and I'd have to borrow money and actually fly to Washington. Alyosha needed the medicines; I needed to be with him. We had worked on a scheme to meet in Bucharest if I couldn't return: pleading the gravity of his disease, he'd get doctors to support a petition for special dispensation to travel abroad. But his oldest medical friends, who'd signed a thousand absent-from-work chits for his girls, shrugged unhappily. They could get Alyosha a visa as easily as Pravda thunder could free the Scottsboro boys. He would go nowhere. It symbolized our relationship's unnatural change of balance that everything now depended on me. I had to find the strength to make up for the decline of his.

At the lowest point, I recognized his handwriting on an envelope from the top of my hotel stairs. "News from a foreign country came/As if my treasure and wealth lay there." Dreading the worst and hoping for the miracle, I trembled as I coped with the glue.

"Hello there, muchacho! Summer skies are blue and the radish crop gluts our markets. Accept our congratulations on the advent of Machine-Tool Workers' Day. I know I can count on you to continue saluting our patriotic holidays. For our part, we're planning a fitting fete . . ."

Corny as it was, a censor might take this at face value, predisposing him to pass the rest. But my tears were forming because these first words I'd received from him since I left showed that at least part of him was undamaged.

Machine-Tool Workers' Day was on September 29 this year, he continued. His advance warning was because all my mail to him, sent throughout July and August, arrived in one delivery the previous week. "No doubt the English mates are on strike again. It's not for me to interfere, but can you really expect an efficient postal service on exploited labor?"

He objected to two of my postcards—of Queen Elizabeth in regalia and a Modigliani nude—that had obviously pleased him, comparing them unfavorably to his enclosed one of the famous Worker and Peasant statue, which, under the guise of admiration for its sickle-waving Amazon, slipped in the sweater size of a new clothes-conscious lovely. A hilarious sketch of a visit to the Exhibition of Economic Achievement followed, the real message

of which was an account of his icon hunt in the Zagorsk
Monastery, where a sanctimonious priest talked prices between
the lines, much as he was doing now. Like a plumber discoursing
with a naturalist, they couldn't be certain they understood each
other, and the priest balked before selling.

"Oh yes, vandals swiped the Volga's remaining strip of
headlight chrome from the monastery parking place for Western
tourists. But this is not the tragedy some would make of it,
inasmuch as no purloining of ornamentation can affect the
saloon's riding qualities."

The car was enjoying a few days' rest just now, while he spent
them in a clinic—an excellent one, run by the Central Institute
for Advanced Medical Training—for an evaluation of the first
series of X-ray treatments. (First series? I shuddered when I
understood the implication of this.) The various analyses were
almost completed, and justified every hope for more decades of
honest toil. "After all, my pension is ages away." If he asked
again for the "5 Flurouracil" it was largely because his doctors
were eager to try it. He was writing this from his clinic cot, where
a dozen samaritans—including Anastasia—had visited him. The
food was fine; it was only the regularity of three daily squares,
served by well-meaning others, that indisposed an amateur cook.
Speaking of that, what was poor I eating now that the Soviet
government had bought a billion bushels of grain to save
Western farmers from bankruptcy?

Only one section revealed the deep pessimism still in him. "I
can't forgive myself for that outburst," he wrote. "Those first days
I felt I had to share my despair and therefore sloshed you with
gloom. It looms sillier than ever now that I'm in constant high
spirits (as opposed to strong spirits, which—an odd streak of
obscurantism in our otherwise progressive clinics—the chief
nurse unaccountably considers detrimental to recuperation). I'm
confident of a future of lithoid (horny) health, and since I can't
reach your shoulder without a chair in any case, promise not to
slobber again on your chest. Despondency is an enemy of the
people."

The self-reproach was superflous. We had woken at noon after
the drunken night when the disease was confirmed. That day
and the next, he occasionally cried, insisting that his strain of

cancer was unresponsive to medicine and any treatment would
be self-deceptive. His mental process of preparing for burial, he
said, had already begun. What changes happen in life! How he
loved his empty existence! But these few days were the full extent
of his "unpardonable burden" on me, for which he had already
apologized effusively before I left. After that, he took himself in
hand, declaring his optimism "incorruptible"—and this new
reference to the first blow was a bad sign.

The letter ended with a toast for my "luck, love, happiness,
richness, health; choose your own arrangement, add what I
forgot" and was signed, "Your old friend, your trustworthy
colleague." But "trustworthy" could also mean "reliable" as we
always applied it to the faithful Volga: a promise that despite
minor breakdowns, he would roll on indefinitely. And by
satirizing the Sovietese use of "colleague" with its phony
representation of a virtuous official toiling for The People, he
conjured up a dozen images of our bootleg activities together. It
was a satiric disquisition for an audience of one. And although it
contained no direct mention of my return—before I left, Alyosha
kept insisting I must get on in life, and shouldn't press my luck
by coming back—each of the four packed pages was like an
appeal floated in a bottle.

The P.S. was written with a different pen. "Big hugs and kisses
from me. (My malady is not contagious.) It's grand to have time
for reading again; any suggestions for enlightening books?
Incidentally, it's becoming chic here to pass evenings, in reading
or other useful activity, by candlelight rather than under vulgar
bulbs. So if your power shortages occasionally leave you without
electricity, you can turn to more fashionable sources of light.
Whenever you say the word, I can mail you some candles. And
resign yourself to long boring letters. With clinical greetings,
Alexei."

The term for exchange students was to begin on September
8—Tankists' Day on the "Leninist Calendar" displayed in the
Soviet Embassy. I went to the consulate immediately, knowing
that failure today, September 6, would make me miss the start: a
clear sign they had no intention of letting me back. A man who
was probably the Musketeers' M. de Tréville glanced at my file,

cupped his hand over a question on an internal telephone and slipped a visa into the pages of my passport, all within two minutes. It was somehow obvious that my permission had been in his desk for weeks, awaiting his last-minute stroke, the implication of which escaped me.

"You are going to our capital to study?" It wasn't clear whether the idea itself or my pretension to it was preposterous. "You will inform the State Committee the exact moment of your arrival. Good luck."

Mother Russia's gravity pulled me to Heathrow hours early, also dulling my senses with apprehension and relief. A clutch of Russian tourists—shoes as blunt as faces, suits screaming "Soviet" though bought specifically for Western Trip—huddled around their leader in the lobby. Years ago, I used to approach such groups to try out my Russian, but their pathetic recoiling taught me to desist. Fear of being compromised, of informers' reports, of the outside world itself . . . What drew me to the land that produced this?

(In the Embassy one morning, I had caught sight of bantam Alek, Anastasia's chum, in a delegation of medical students. When he turned and saw me, he so sustained the blank in his eyes that for a moment I wondered whether I'd made a mistake. Catching on, I pretended not to notice him, but wildly searched the others with my eyes in case Anastasia had come too. Then I remembered that her association with me was enough to keep her from ever getting out with an official group.)

"Air India, Flight 506, via Moscow to Delhi. "Are you a vegetarian, sir?" . . . "Drinks will be served, do you tolerate spirits?" . . . Never mind; the pilot was surely British-trained, and he took off on the dot. The Indian rajahs flew first-class while Soviet officials and Western tourists crowded together in economy, mutually humble victims of this third-world hoax.

The Boeing's altitude was breathtaking. The afternoon sun waned somewhere in northern Europe as we sped east, away from the giver of warmth and light. As if the plane knew its direction—at this exalted height, toward the Arctic's Holy Spirit—the cabin grew cool. Stewardesses in saris served mango juice, but the sensation of terrestrial bleakness grew with the

murkiness of new time zones. Dipping back below the clouds on
the Moscow descent, we passed mile after mile of Russia's
swamps and uninhabited forests. I wanted to reach out and
stroke the continent of enduring sadness.

We touched down at Sheremetyevo International, taxied,
stopped near the terminal—and were ignored. Four hours before,
Heathrow had been a Woolworth's-cum-World's Fair, bustling,
throbbing, hawking shiny wares and briskly shuttling passengers
to a Hit Parade of flights. Here we were the only plane in the
disembarking area, and the air quivered with abandonment, not
urgency. A skinny neon MOSCOW tried to stay alive. The crew
operating the passenger ramp bided its time: three clump-
booted workmen placidly rummaging for matches. I read their
lips.

"Nu, Fedya, let's go."

"Easy friend, I'll finish my smoke."

"I heard a big shot's on this one."

"He'll hold his water; do him good."

A huge raven perched on a radar tower. Mud, fir needles
dripping autumn rain and tommy guns greeted arrivals. And
workmen cooing over the miracle of a dispatcher's swaddled
baby. Through the airtight fittings and into the cabin seeped
Russia's smell, an oily, dusty blend of diesel exhaust, dill, tar,
sweat-soaked wool, birch sap, latrine disinfectant and Balkan
tobacco. . . . A tarted-up Intourist guide was roasting the driver
of our bus. Nothing had changed. I bathed in the fever of being
lost in desolation, yet awake to spirits that roam the land mass
like prairie wind, sighing about the futility and importance of
existence.

Finally, the hatch opened to a blast of bracing air and an
armed Army officer in the ankle-length overcoat of the full
winter uniform. Striding into the cabin, he completed an
eye-rolling scrutiny with an order for "pass-ports!", its sharpness
startling the passengers whose first word this was from a Russian
on home soil. While soldiers took up stations between the ramp
and bus, a diminutive gentleman in transit to Delhi tried to
make contact.

"It seems you have winter here already. Quite extraordinary."

His face free of a spark of acknowledgment, the officer

accepted the Indian's passport as if it were a glass of soda from a dispensing machine.

"Win-ter? So soon? But you cope, you are a hardy people."

The robot's eyeballs clicked down, locked onto the Indian and surveyed him without reply. (Where is Kemal? I wondered. Finished at the University, rejected at American campuses; I'll never see him again.) Retreating, the gentleman gasped to his wife, "Such a welcome to this land!" But from a minibus near the plane, a group of Aeroflot stewardesses spilled out to link arms, squeeze waists and kiss cheeks. "Do svidaniya, *pet, send me a postcard." "Don't forget the sweater, Sveta." "Galka, call Kolya for me, I forgot to say good-bye." Clinging to each other before separation, the girls unselfconsciously showed the other side of the coin of the country's personal relationships.*

I hadn't been mistaken: it was the home of quintessential types. The rustic soldier at the passport desk who read everyone's visa from top to bottom four plodding times. And after our misrouted baggage had finally arrived, the barmaid of a customs officer who scrutinized every scrap of printed material, confiscating my Time because of a photo of some starlet in a new headgear style called "Romanov," but winking at my two dozen pairs of tights for gifts.

"I'll take your word that the clothing contraband doesn't hide an atomic bomb," she quipped, resetting her stern countenance to daunt the next suspect.

The taxi driver grumbled about his local beer hall closing to build a theater. I cleaned my window and stared at the streets.

The Delhi businessman notwithstanding, winter was a good month off; but while Hyde Park was still emerald, fall here had bled the leaves. I'd forgotten how dim the streetlights were, and the early dusk's Halloween-like palpitations. How did it stay so poor, this Moscow without a single store to equal an Aldwych market stall? But it was precisely this lackluster I loved—for quenching any demands that I myself be a bright light. Frazzled like a genuine home, the Russian scene depressed other Westerners; but I was grateful for feeling accepted into the humbleness. Even the million slogans I liked to mock—now dunning for a fitting work contribution to honor the forthcoming

Twenty-fourth Congress of Our Revered Communist Party—welcomed me back.

The driver waited at the University gate while I dumped my things. I bulled my way through without initiating the process of acquiring documents or meeting my new roommate. Alyosha—who didn't know I had my visa, let alone that I'd arrived—was the reason for this journey. The buildings flanking the route to his place were totally alien and utterly familiar, as if families were preparing tea for me behind their granite-like façades. Alyosha's was under repair again; I climbed over scaffolding boards strewn across the shortcut to the dear, chummy courtyard. Upstairs, his door was ajar. The omen unnerved me. How far had he gone, he with the girls and the deals, to forget to lock it? Afraid to ring, I tiptoed in.

In the living room, an elderly woman was gazing upward, forcing her eyes toward heaven against the weight of disapproval and pity. Before I could follow them, I was visited by the dread—to the tenth power—of mounting the stage to read my poems to an auditorium of parents. The woman was surely the aunt who had helped raise Alyosha. I did not want to know why she was here, what had happened to him.

But the fear was unfounded. He was alive and whole! Pounds thinner in the face, but as lithe as when we had crossed a flooded stream last April, teetering on wet rocks. Now it was his dictionaries that were wobbling as they lay in a stack on the kitchen chair. His toes on the top one, he was rummaging through the old clothes heap atop his wardrobe closet. As quickly as I'd recognized his aunt, I sensed that this was connected with hospital preparations. I moved up behind him.

"What's your price for the skivvies, partner?"

This came out too softly, but for a moment I wondered whether he might not want to hear me and my banter.

"It's me, Alyosh. They gave me a visa."

He pivoted on the balls of his feet, a spaghetti of 1950s ties oozing through his fingers. Something went momentarily out of balance, almost tipping the chair. The old woman gave out a panicked bleat.

"My friend," he said, using the strong word droog, as in his letter. "Buddy-boy, I told you not to come."

I caught him under the arms, like my favorite uncle with me when I used to climb upon his fence and not be able to get down. (My favorite uncle drowned.) Alyosha's body too was much thinner, but I knew he lost weight every summer.

"Give the old man a hug," he directed with a trace of command, as if unaware that for long moments I'd been doing precisely this. He was wearing a Lacoste turtleneck, and I thought of everything it meant to be gripping one of my own shirts; of how much had changed, how little I'd suspected, when I bought it in Bloomingdale's. He kissed me on the jawbone. His smell contained a new component: cancer, I thought, recoiling slightly—but perhaps it was only medicine.

Finally, he held me at arm's length. "You've lost five kilos, you waif. When was your last hot meal?" He fiddled in the kitchen and I displayed his presents, as if we were trying to demonstrate that pan-fried beef for me and a pair of Levis for him had the same significance as ever. Like a woman who has attended too many family funerals, his aunt said only that she had to return to her invalid half-sister in Rostov next week.

I was narrating the "Sunday" episode in order to lead up to the real questions about his condition when a big white poodle bounded through the open door, almost knocking him down. By way of introduction, he plunged into a discourse on an old Russian saying about a dog's tail remaining in the same place no matter how you spin the body. It was the usual stuff, and it overcame what it had to to keep me laughing. If I didn't know, I'd have fallen for the act. There was just a whit too much interest in canine affairs—and of relief when I suggested we visit "King-size" Alla II some other day.

VIII Gold Medal

As Alyosha lost weight, the poodle gained. Like Russians interrupting the grinding year with periodic flings, she alternated between hours of slumber and minutes of dish-breaking cavorting. Outdoors, she trod between us: a third Musketeer. Although quickly accepting me as a lone companion for toilet strolls, she sulked unless Alyosha himself set out her food.

He had bought her from a private breeder in July, rechristening her from "Mini" to "Maxi" in August. But it would have been glib to call this a need for companionship in my absence last summer. The general context was a booming vogue for dogs—conspicuous evidence of prosperity after the petless war years and desperate overcrowding—among the fashionable intelligentsia in their new co-op apartments. Western leashes and collars, with stratospheric black market prices, were the ultimate swank. Alyosha had acquired a French set in matching burgundy, underlining the element of throwback to his dandy days in his whole undertaking of keeping a pet. But the handsome accessories lay unused under the laundry pile, and shaggy Maxi herself of the stamped pedigree papers went unclipped, proclaiming her owner's independence of fashion. Both approaches seemed designed to bolster his "life as usual" determination.

She cooperated perceptively. At "Maxi, for a walk," she charged the door like a battering ram, or shook her head "no," waiting for our laugh. When he was in pain, she lay motionless at his feet. And used the toilet rather than ask to go out; even lowered both halves of the broken seat with her nose, feeling safer on wood than on ceramic.

The sharpest pain was from skin burned by the current—second—series of cobalt-ray treatment, dispensed thrice weekly in a clinic opposite the Hippodrome. My London salve—the only medicine I was able to obtain, and the least important since it was irrelevant to the disease itself—helped, but the sting on his buttocks made driving arduous. He cut the spine of the driver's seat and blocked it back like a naval ship's captain's chair so he could pilot the Volga, with as much caution as he used to show daredevil, in a half-reclining position, propped up by a collection of pillows. The former combination of Hell's Angel bike and My Friend Flicka became a pathetic rather than a mischievous wreck.

Second to sex, his infirmity showed most here. My grandfather, a refugee of a Polish ghetto, used to stretch his neck manfully to peer through the bottom inches of his Nash's windshield, holding himself on guard against the outside world that was permanently preparing a missile for him. It was spooky to see the same muscle movements in Alyosha's straining for vantage above the Volga's dashboard. Playing on the slang for "outperform," which is literally "outspit," he challenged Ilya to a contest of whether they could avoid each other on a narrow street.

Maxi increased Alyosha's handicap by licking his face, easily reachable in his lowered position. And we were vulnerable to bad-tempered traffic cops as well as faster cars. The knowledge that if stopped in his condition, his license would be revoked on the spot until he passed a stiff new physical bolted him upright at the sight of a gray uniform, he commenting on his own lunge in the voice of a fervent sports announcer. If this was too late and the law insisted on a closer look, he played the radiantly healthy yet properly humble citizen, who had been creeping at twenty kilometers out of respect for Alexandra Kollontai, whose date of decease Comrade Constable surely remembered. These diverting little skits of eagle eyes and obstinate will cheered us on our way to some minor errand.

When they became more forced, I took the wheel. Eager to help, or uneasy about my inexperience, Maxi volunteered to move her bulk to the back seat, regarding us with dubious eyes from there. Fall drizzle and mud camouflaged her whiteness.

Despite the sharp risk of my driving without a license, we prepared no excuse. Somehow we assumed that the emergencies, unspokenly defined as the times when Alyosha wasn't well enough to drive, made everything possible for us, as if we were on our way to report to the War Cabinet during this time of national crisis. I thought about our escapades on last winter's ice, which took more skill than I could have imagined before handling the tank myself. Under five miles an hour, the wheel required a wrestler's strength; over five, I practically had to stand on the brake to achieve a gradual stop. And the clutch rasped for its master's touch.

What saved me was the "wingman's" directions. Alyosha allowed me to concentrate on mechanical operations by calling out obligatory right turns, unlit road signs and police traps forty yards in advance. His keen coaching on the welter of singular traffic patterns was the introduction to a campaign to impart general knowledge of the city, for he had reversed his earlier objection to my returning and now suggested I settle in Moscow, preferably as a correspondent.

"Luxury on minimum work. Five or six annual R & R's in Helsinki or the fleshpot of your choice. Of course I can't say how far you'd go in the States, but a local sinecure might be appealing. Think it over, *muchacho*."

Then we went to a dramatization of *Ballad of a Sad Café* at a theater he used to scorn for its highbrow repertoire, including a carefully pessimistic selection of Western plays. An interest in serious literature had replaced his urge for frivolous entertainment. In this, and especially in his eagerness for me to have the life of free time and easy money he used to, he was a dying man, concerned about fruitful expenditure of his remaining days and about his heir. It was a fitting twist that I was the one to get the tickets. How childish I'd been, resenting Anastasia for not praising my skill at it last year. What a big deal I made of myself; how much happier we could have been with her appetite for cultural enrichment, which was almost opposite to Alyosha's last-opportunity one. I waved my passport in the same box-office lines, but it was the November of life. And the ticket sellers were growing tired of me.

Yet in our way, Alyosha and I were happy too. We accepted the worst only at the deepest level. Some days were normal enough to fool girls who dropped by, not having heard. We shrugged off "corporal tenderness" with them: even without the general malaise of X-ray bombardment, Alyosha would not show his burns, which disfigured his lower stomach too. Instead, we joined matronly types taking constitutionals on a tree-lined boulevard near his house. And hunted for gas fittings and clean plywood: Alyosha was redoing his kitchen in contemporary studio style with a fitted unit combining refrigerator and cabinets. His plan was a *Paris-Match* advertisement that brought out his hammer and saw and brought down the wall between the kitchen and the main room the very day he saw it in August. He was sick of the pigpen style, he kept insisting. No more zinc sink, no blackened stove, no stretching across one to reach the other. A Yugoslav exhaust fan for "modern disposition" of cooking smells. "Who says technology's not for the people?"

He played his enthusiasm straight and I honestly couldn't tell—or, of course, ask—whether the project expressed faith in a better future or the desperation of doom. For we still didn't know his prognosis. If there was self-deception in this, it was partly genuine too: the specialists' unwillingness to promise anything made more credible their assurances that recovery was possible. It depended on where the cancer had spread and how it was responding to treatment—which could still only be guessed at. The doctor in direct charge of his case said it was not permitted to discuss a patient's progress except with immediate relatives; and even with them, they were usually less frank. She was bending the regulations for me in recognition of my loyalty in coming all the way from abroad to be with Alyosha, who had talked of me all summer. Besides, I'd donated three extra tubes of the salve to her department.

She was a thirtyish blonde whom Alyosha nicknamed "Luxuriant" in honor of her cherubic bottom. "You've opened the final horizon for me, Doctor. I thought I knew about positions to assume for cultivated women. And thanks to your, er, skill, I don't feel a bit embarrassed."

She blushed delicately, and accepted his box of bonbons. Like a widowed landlady titillated by a notorious lodger's charms, she took pleasure in his mellow palaver. Even she called him "Alyosha" instead of Patient so-and-so, exempting her favorite from clinical bossiness.

This helped gild the pill of the medical hours. And the cost of the treatment itself was surely a good omen. Together with the use of the capital-intensive X-ray equipment, he was being injected with a new American solution for better tissue response. From what we knew about the Soviet approach, neither would have been so liberally given if it were felt he'd never rejoin the nation's work force. And his clinic, the Central Institute for Advanced Specialist Training, was one of the country's best.

What puzzled us was why they weren't keeping him permanently there, as with most patients of his type, and as they had during his own first X-ray series in August. Now he slept at the institute only twice a week; on the other days, they merely told him to stay in bed four hours daily. Alyosha was so happy to be home that he often did rest for two or three hours, and never raised the question, in case the arrangement was a mistake.

But the real mistake was his failure to have sought help long ago. He had had a year for this. His general health and attitude conspired to preclude it.

The first sign had been a watery spot on his underpants noticed during his Black Sea vacation the previous summer and attributed to a scratch on an underwater rock. The little lesion didn't heal and some days its stain was not quite so tiny; but Alyosha ignored it—and, except for a passing wisecrack, the slight diminishment of his energy—until a month before Nixon's arrival last spring, when he saw blood on his sheets. The wound seemed to be growing deeper and there was a lump in his groin.

This combination was finally enough to overcome his distaste for medical assistance.

Diagnosing piles, his local clinic's duty doctor arranged an operation in a municipal hospital, whose chief surgical consultant confirmed the diagnosis and signed the final papers when Alyosha's turn before him came several weeks later. By then, the other groin also had a sore nodule, and he could feel the first growing from morning to evening. He consulted a medical encyclopedia, then called a brilliant young internist whose father he'd once helped on a case.

He lowered his trousers and lay on the daybed. After a minute's examination, his friend went white and looked up at his face. He called contacts to arrange Alyosha's immediate acceptance by the Advanced Training Institute, and treatment began as soon as the biopsy had verified malignancy. . . . This story, the details of which I heard only now, laid me low for weeks. *Alyosha had cancer ever since I knew him*—during the entire time I was glorying in his energy and health! *And he could have recovered easily if we hadn't been so blind.* The doctors all agreed that it began with a relatively mild skin disturbance, with over a ninety per cent chance of complete cure.

The diagnosis was *cancer spinocellulare.* Sorting out his bureau drawers months later, I saw it written as such on a postcard he'd never sent me, probably because its tone was downcast and chief message a request for more medicines. The main tumor encircled the anus, with one hundred per cent metastases to the lymph nodes of both groins. Major surgery was planned for next month; meanwhile, the X-ray assault continued as before, and on the lower intestine too for prophylactic purposes, even though it was uncertain the malignancy had reached there.

On the days I hadn't slept over, I arrived at the apartment for breakfast. At eleven o'clock, we drove toward the Hippodrome along a route I already knew without instructions. His clinic was in a cluster of medical institutes something like the grander one on Manhattan's East River. We were admitted with almost no formality and made our own way to the radiology department. It was excellently equipped, but the building itself had the curious Russian plainness of research laboratories and technical institutes, which can give the mistaken impression that the scientific apparatus is also obsolete. I felt I was back in my old high school.

Despite our purpose there, its genial efficiency had a calming effect. Only the chief administrator compressed his lips as if cancer sufferers were an inconsiderate burden, and pursed them when I identified myself. Otherwise, the novelty of professional courtesy instead of the elbows and *nyet*s of most public institutions lifted our spirits, at least until Alyosha's turn under the machine. When he was summoned inside for this, I continued waiting in the anteroom alongside patients with appointments after his. A man with the hands of a half-century of manual labor was often there, confused by the elaborate attention awarded him at this late hour of his life, craving a cigarette despite his deathly wheeze. And a nine-year-old girl whose mother couldn't decide whether to spoil her appetite for lunch by letting her open Alyosha's chocolates or to spoil her in the other sense because the doctors couldn't guarantee she'd live to be ten. To young and old, the staff was unpatronizingly gentle. Even teenage nurses whose contemporaries were already snarling from behind store counters spoke in the tones that allow the hospital sick to feel slightly less useless.

One morning, I was alone in the anteroom. Through the wall, I heard the hum of the rays penetrating Alyosha's intestines— "trembling vectors of electric and magnetic fields, unimaginable to the human mind." I was trying to think of a drive he'd enjoy in the afternoon when the door opened and I felt my face being studied. Then the disapproving chief administrator entered, choosing the inches next to me on the bench to seat himself in the otherwise empty room. I stiffened. Things had too long been too friendly here; this was my time for being thrown out.

Quite the contrary, he had taken this moment to express concern for my friend. Life's tragedies united people in a larger loyalty, he said. People of every kind. He leaned closer. Americans once helped him greatly; one day he'd explain—but Alyosha was the priority now. Soviet medicine's utter humaneness was a matter of record, but some remedies inevitably outperformed others. Especially with carcinoma, the newest ones couldn't be widely prescribed until they'd been exhaustively tested and, frankly, because of their expense. However, in certain clinics, patients died only if nothing on earth could prevent it.

He admired Americans. He knew a certain professor who had saved . . . well, some extremely important people. He couldn't promise anything, but was I willing to give Comrade Aksyonov this chance?

He took my telephone number at the dormitory and volunteered to approach the specialist. Meanwhile, it might be kinder not to arouse my friend by talking of mere possibilities. Good-bye, but hopefully not farewell.

Alone again, I thought of how little I had learned in life. To have judged the chief administrator, the one man who both grasped the scale of the tragedy and was in a position to help, by his homeliness—as if I hadn't had enough examples of saintly souls in scrawny physiques. His only increased my new tenderness toward him.

Alyosha emerged from his session, teasing a nurse about her surer skill in dropping than raising underpants. I drove to lunch at the Hotel Moscow's fifteenth-floor café where we'd had our vernal equinox meal. Looking down at the scurrying, scarf-wrapped pedestrians, I felt even higher and happier. All afternoon, I saw him as a patient who had passed his crisis. If I could be the middleman who procured the expertise for his cure, I'd never again feel cheated by Providence. This one break would be enough to explain why I was in Moscow; to justify my existence.

Like commandos cautious not to jinx a raid, we hardly mentioned the operation. The doctors had made clear that this would be the do-or-die assault, for which X-rays were mere preliminary bombardment. Wholly calm on the surface, Alyosha revealed through stress lines across his temples how much he wanted to survive his battle.

For a week, I had my own strain of waiting for the chief administrator's call without telling Alyosha, and of trying to find out why he had disappeared from the clinic after our conversation. Then a two-day hailstorm descended, which seemed to bury forever the queer waiting-room encounter with him. The raising of my hope was no more cruel than the news itself of the cancer in May; the promise of a magic cure no odder than the warnings, entreaties and riddles whispered to me last year by an assortment of strangers. All helped stipple the Russian scene with that occasional weirdness I would never be able to fathom. Alyosha and I lived out our strangely peaceful days, with some unhurried work on the kitchen and a meal in an out-of-the-way restaurant to avoid the fuss of being seen at the better places. Evenings, we were at home in candlelight, and some visitors were convinced enough that nothing serious was amiss to complain of the slack entertainment.

At this level, the entire experience of sickness and treatment was an elaborate charade we had undertaken to act out for inexplicable reasons. Or, when confronted by the smell of his charred skin, it was someone's tedious practical joke. How to make real to yourself that your best friend may be mortally ill?

Our reality was based on the opposite premise—and with some cause. The salve worked well on the burns. Much more significant, the "nasties" themselves, as Alyosha called them, had begun responding to the X-rays: the groin lumps and little ulcers that had appeared on his stomach were growing smaller and less painful. He "felt himself up" and chuckled.

"Listen, buddy, you're still a neophyte in thrills. The little buggers have had enough—behold *this.*"

I did look, encouraging myself to smile at the uncooperatively indistinct improvement. The London doctor's extreme pessimism, I told myself, had not accounted for Alyosha's strength. Besides, what did I know? I much preferred following *his* party line, which was stouter than ever. He was going to recover. His life would still be very full. He'd cut back a bit on activity and eliminate the summer trips to soak up his beloved southern sun: his own research had told him that strong ultraviolet rays were a permanent threat. But this was a blessing in disguise. He was sick of the Black Sea anyway; we'd go to the cooler Baltic coast, with its European touches. And take our best friends. "Everybody paired off according to age: Lady Anastasia with 'little dog' Maxi; you and old me."

Such talk usurped any serious discussion of his infirmity. Even if the damn nuisance did exist, which we sometimes actually doubted, the treatment would tame it for unreserved riddance by the operation—the success of which depended largely on his own positive attitude. Nothing so insignificant as "crabs" could get the better of him. Some days I even detected gratitude for a salutary change of perspective.

"Kismet's taken pity and done for me what I couldn't myself. That jostling in the market every day, the skirt-chasing—never a minute to *think*. What can be better than sitting in your own place with a mute doorbell? When this is over . . ." He never completed the thought, but it was understood the old life was finished.

Meanwhile, his deterioration proceeded in stages. In late September, we had a fragrant spell of "old woman's summer." He'd been scheduled for preoperation rest in the clinic that week, but was so buoyed by the Vermont-like days that "Luxuriant" gave him the time off, except for the treatments. Still unable to think of him as an ordinary patient, she let us drive her home for the sake of his chitchat.

Then we went to a river beach where he used to spend at least a few hours of most summer days before going south. Hundreds of bathing-suited girls were recruited here, but it was even better just to lie on the sand, cherishing the fall sun that built up under our sweaters. Just the two of us—he still looking much younger than his fifty years—shooting the breeze about his Army and my Navy days, next year's hikes together in the Carpathians. The next day we drove to Arkhangelskoye, the former Golitsin manor on the banks of the same Moscow River twenty-five kilometers from the center—far more beautiful, because simpler and more lyrical than any country estate I'd seen in Europe. The new restaurant for foreign tourists there was uncrowded because of the season, and I got Alyosha to eat a full bowl of borscht.

But he slumped when the weather turned. October arrived wet and raw; his protests were mild when he was told it was time for his complete clinic rest. After a week, he was permitted out for a few hours daily. He said he wanted to drive, but soon asked me to take over, joking about himself in terms of the fairy princess who feels the pea through twenty mattresses and twenty featherbeds. His body had begun to hurt "in general."

We took to making our outing in late afternoon; rush-hour traffic lifted his spirits. In mid-October, we came upon the tanks rehearsing for the Revolution Day parade—the spectacle Anastasia and I had blocked out with our kiss. On the way back, I had to stop the car for him to be sick.

When the call came, I had to think for a moment. Before my memory clicked, the chief administrator was apologizing for being away, soothing me like a family friend in a confidential matter. And I felt a current passing between the poles of confidence that this man would fix everything and conviction of his phoniness.

Was I listening? Although things were still in flux, they'd advanced enough to justify a meeting. This was no time to make merry, but "the tongue feeds the head": it was an old Russian custom to eat while talking. And important people had indeed agreed to talk to me. He named a time and place.

The evening was stranger than the sum of its parts: a propitious atmosphere, my optimistic side reckoned, in light of the unorthodoxy of the undertaking itself. Something was wrong somewhere—as it *had* to be in order for Alyosha to be accorded treatment reserved for the headmen. Someone was lying, as people *must* to get spare parts through back doors. The very air of dissimulation heightened my anticipation—and queasiness. It was too late when I guessed which feeling was right.

The caviar was in little iced pots at each setting. Seven double portions but six diners: early in the meal, the chief administrator returned from a telephone call to announce that the specialist had been detained. We began without him, attacking a spread of hors d'oeuvres stipulated at receptions for official guests of upper-middle importance. The numbers surprised me more than the luxury: the chief administrator had said nothing about bringing so many staff. The dinner was crowned by Georgian specialties, for we were in a private room of the esteemed Aragvi restaurant, observing the Soviet custom of approaching important business through a banquet.

One of the doctors questioned me about Alyosha's medical history; another took notes. They were far from my kind of Russians, but my kind didn't reach high places. Perhaps they weren't doctors in fact, but some sort of medical administrators, conceivably even attached to the mysterious clinic; but as in so many Soviet situations, it seemed wrong to ask. A new West

German preparation called "DMSO" was mentioned. I had tried so hard to get it in London that *dvukhmetilovaya-okissera,* the Russian translation, remained in my mind. If this was one of the prizes, it was worth any unease in this inlaid atmosphere.

"Another drop of the white stuff, young man? Come on, you need to relax." I lifted my glass—kept filled by a team of waiters from a bountiful collection of bottles—to join in their toasts to good-fellowship; and even told a few self-conscious stories myself.

No action was taken. It was agreed that Alyosha should be given an exhaustive examination, starting from the very beginning. And that we all must meet again soon—no doubt for further screening of me: the five pairs of eyes were recording my moves like television cameras as we honored the Georgian custom for downing the final glass. Maybe it was the old awe of Americans, even at this level. They were all childishly curious about my life in New York.

Outside, they were exaggeratedly solicitous about how I would make my way back to my dormitory. I said I'd take the metro and they climbed into their cars, obviously amused. At the notion of an American on foot while they were chauffeur-driven? I couldn't decide whether they cared about Alyosha or, at bottom, whether they had been shy or supercilious with me.

"He started by selling flour for something called 'French buns,' later rechristened 'Soviet buns' of course. *His* father was a serf. He made his pile by driving himself more than your ordinary muzhik, not necessarily being smarter. Everybody called him 'granny,' the employees too. It confused me for years; I thought that was his name. . . ."

We were parked alongside Young Communist Ponds, a leafy residential corner, while Alyosha was reminiscing. He mentioned his family more often now, although seemingly stopping short of the stories he wanted to tell. Feeling this would come, I withheld my questions.

Again that afternoon, his grandfather intrigued him most: a peasant-turned-landlord who had much in common with the type described by Gorky. A shrewd, sometimes imperious man, extremely indulgent to his sole grandchild and principal heir. Alyosha was raised under his roof and domination.

His bashful mother had been sent to good schools until she met his future father in an art class. When she disclosed her pregnancy to Grandfather, he thundered that the painter could barely support himself, let alone a wife and child. He gave the young artist a purseful of rubles and a train ticket to Tashkent.

When Alyosha was a year old, his mother heeded the call of letters delivered by a loyal art student as intermediary, and followed her beloved to wild Central Asia. The baby stayed home while she supposedly took the waters, planning to win Grandfather over by returning home married: loving mother and father of the child Granny himself adored. She caught typhoid fever in Tashkent and returned in six months instead of two weeks—to die. Alyosha's Rostov aunt was summoned to help raise him, but he was unmanageable by the age of twelve and grew up largely on Moscow's rowdy streets.

The only person who might have controlled him had also died prematurely. Tough old Granny's ruin was accomplished in stages, starting with the confiscation of most of his property soon after the Revolution, only to have some returned during Lenin's later policy of encouraging small-business private enterprise to revive the country's gasping economy. But Stalin shifted the line again, more violently than ever; those who had been urged to cultivate their own gardens were first to be harvested in Bolshevik baskets. Grandfather paid the punishing taxes, and new collectors knocked. He sold everything, but the assessments only rose and he was dragged to jail for nonpayment. The circumstances of his death were never established. Rumors reached Alyosha that someone had denounced him for hoarding gold and that he was starved in an attempt to make him reveal his nonexistent treasure chest; but the young boy had no way of checking. By the time he became skilled in researching such matters after the war, the records, if they had ever existed, were lost.

"And your grandmother?"

"Took off with my aunt for her old village where there was more chance to save us. They tried like hell to keep me there and raise me, but of course I ran away."

We were about to drive off to an early movie when he asked

me to circle around the back of an apartment building facing the attractive little park where the Volga had been parked.

"Know what Young Communist Ponds was *before?*" he queried.

"Something better." I remembered that he sometimes went out of his way to pass this spot—for the sake, I thought, of its touch of the Russian outdoors.

"It was Patriarchal Ponds. They changed it."

But this was more than the lead to one of his discourses on the renaming of everything evocative in the country. The building we now went out to look at had been the site of one of his grandfather's two hotels. This one, moreover, housed one of the city's best and most rollicking restaurants, an emporium of gypsy girls, lavish-spending merchants and eccentric characters, of suckling pigs and a hundred delectable, now forgotten, native dishes. A veritable microcosm of Old Moscow with private rooms for whoopee and thirty varieties of vodka—and, in fact, it had been featured in an obscure book called *Moscow and Muscovites* that celebrated the most colorful prerevolutionary haunts.

"They demolished it in 1933. Cost too much to run without Granny; and anyway, it didn't fit in with the new Soviet capital. Had the wrong associations; they stuffed it with dynamite."

Suddenly I realized many things. Alyosha would have been heir to a minor fortune if not for the Revolution: might have been precisely the kind of playboy I used to picture him in California. But until now, he'd never so much as hinted that personal loss played any part in his lampooning of Soviet rule. His complaints of the lackluster and "anti-pleasure principle" of Moscow life never mentioned his grandfather's unwilling contribution to the general sacrifice of merriment and color. Perhaps something in the story shamed him; perhaps only thoughts about life and death—the operation was coming next week—regenerated these memories. In any case, I couldn't ask: telling the story of Grandfather had tired him; he wanted to say no more for the moment.

But I had only begun to think. I felt I was approaching an understanding of how his intelligence and wisdom were related to the simple-minded wenching that first attracted me to him. Might his fondness for feeding Moscow's girls be an unconscious

link to the self-made innkeeper who provided the only model of
sturdiness in his fluid childhood? Was that the source, in any
case, of his extraordinary energy, rationalism and quickness with
figures?

But Granny's persecution reminded me of something I sensed
would be even more important when I could place it. It came
during the movie: Alyosha was closer to Till Eulenspiegel than
the Peck's Bad Boy I used to see in him. Like the German lad's,
his wandering adventures had been set going by an inexplicable
witch hunt of an innocent Grandfather. Properly interpreted, he
and *his* practical jokes had the makings of a twentieth-century
legend. And the fetes, I realized abruptly, were not foolish, but as
symbolic of Russia's condition as Pushkin's *Feast During the Plague*.
Alyosha was the sustainer of this tradition.

We drove to the Juridical Consultation Office. Having transferred his best cases, he was waiting for an under-the-table cut
from the defense of a former vice-minister's son. Party instructions to the prosecutor made it a fascinating case, but I could
only think of the epic of Alyosha and his grandfather. There was
much more here than a century of sad, wild and triumphant
episodes; even more than one peasant family's turbulent chronicle. It was a potential allegory of national life, since Granny was
the ceaselessly enterprising and ambitious kind who would have
taken over the country if the Bolshevik cadres hadn't, and under
other circumstances, Alyosha too might have been the opposite of
a pleasure-seeker.

The rest of the day, I had to keep myself from blurting out that
he *must* write his life story. At last I'd recognized its full
importance. It would be a spellbinding saga; just the sketches of
his clients alone, the long list of rogues and misfortunates,
promised a hundred amazing yarns. Mixed with a record of his
own peregrinations, it would tell more about Russia—and
whatever The Russian Idea stood for in life, politics and
literature—than anything I could think of. And he was the man
to write it. The structural elegance of his legal briefs, comic
fluency of his letters and vividness of his conversation guaranteed
a narrative masterpiece with just a bit of effort. All this must not
be allowed to die—which was precisely the reason why I couldn't
think of a tactful way to put this to him.

We picked at a snack, lit the candles and settled into chairs. As if he'd been reading my mind, he again began to talk about his grandfather's skills. The old man could predict which peasant produced the best wheat for which millers and bakers; and although hardly aware of it as a child, this expertise, all but forgotten in the country, was now acquiring a strange importance for him. He even had a notion to write about it, and put down a few things about his own life at the same time.

I jumped up to applaud. I'd smuggle out the manuscript, I pressed—and if he could prove his father was Jewish in order to emigrate, the royalties would give him life security abroad. Again and again, I urged him to begin; what I did not say was that if the operation went badly, *at least there would be a record* of the extraordinary phenomenon he was. But he sensed this too.

"You've got a deal. I've got a baby to give birth to. 'My Issue,' edited and translated by *muchacho*."

The next day passed without the promised start. And the following morning we had to be at the clinic early for an examination by the senior consultant. Trying not to nag, I mentioned the *Confessions*, as we'd already titled them, as often as I could, suggesting that he begin with the tape recorder. I had the sinking feeling that this would join the hundred projects forgotten in the chase of one more girl, the throwing together of yet another last-minute supper. But this time the failure was more understandable and less admissible. It was too late. Alyosha could continue coasting, but he was too tired for anything of such grand design.

"Yes, I must," he kept saying. "I want to." The next day he talked about pitching in after the operation, when his mind would be freer and he'd need something constructive to fill the boring recovery weeks. I soon dropped the subject until a better time. Reminders only depressed him.

I reread his summer letters to see if they might fit some literary form, but none went beyond banter to reveal the thoughts that now concerned him.

Greetings, Redcoat!
    Everyone who gets wind of your rash intention to visit an old buddy here is much taken by the implied loyalty. 'Now

there's a *true* friend'—to which I reply that no less of this virtue resides in me, inasmuch as if anything should happen to you, God forbid, I'd want to set out in your direction instantly. Furthermore, I'd even visit you over there without a convincing excuse, no indisposition necessary. . . . True, I won't be able to embark during the coming few days. I'm going for a high on something called cobalt. . . .

On he went to describe the sunglasses needed to consummate our fancy-wrought Hungarian holiday. It seemed to me that everything would be saved if only he could complete his book. But if so, he'd have no need to write it.

The final cobalt treatment was the day after tomorrow.

When our "presurgery soiree" was well started and Alyosha was drinking as he hadn't since May, he began calling his 1950s friends. They arrived within the hour in their new Soviet Fiats: movie producers, theater managers, songwriters waving bottles as they mounted the stairs, like studio stand-ins invited by a Hollywood magnate. Their mistresses swelled the ranks of Erstwhiles, and the intellectual and philosophical thrusts with which they tried to impress the scores of lovelies and themselves brought a touch of a free-wheeling seminar on the state of the arts and the soul to the otherwise sprawling blast. It was so loud that I couldn't make out even our Ray Charles theme song. When the floor space was exhausted, people stood on the stacks of kitchen cabinet plywood. It was one of those parties whose very diversity generates a unified life of its own.

Gradually the presence of two plainclothesmen became felt. They had appeared ostensibly because of the noise, perhaps to investigate why a dozen cars were parked in the courtyard and street.

"What's the excessive revelry, Citizens?"

Suddenly everyone remembered why in fact he was here, and stopped in midmotion. The silence was strained enough to convince the detective that he *had* uncovered something suspicious. Finally Alyosha himself broke the tension, in his driest deadpan.

"It's a little early this year, Marshal. We're seeing in the Jewish New Year."

A sense of relief—this was the vintage Alyosha who'd never change—spiked the roar. But having laughed, only a handful of determined merrymakers could forget where Alyosha would be tomorrow. The party slid downhill; within an hour, everybody had self-consciously wished Alyosha *merde* and left. He roamed the empty room, guzzling last drops from bottles and declaring he didn't give a damn what some fool surgeons found inside him.

The following morning, we drove to the Order of Lenin Infirmary named after S. P. Botkin, a highly reputed clinical hospital in the same cluster of medical institutes. The operation was scheduled for five days from then, after tests, rest and making ready. He was worried where I'd spend the time, and for a moment, talked of calling everything off. If he was going to die—which he didn't believe for a moment—let him, without the damned nuisance of being cut open and laid up. Then he took himself in hand again, reasserting the order-of-the-day optimism.

"Kovo ebat budyem," he said as the hospital appeared, but it came out feebly and he wished he hadn't tried.

The flower vendors outside the new building nettled me with their callousness. Some people will trade on anything. The staff was more understanding, but politely refused to let me into his ward. We parted quickly and he walked down the corridor swinging my BOAC bag, which contained his overnight things. Proud of it, he was asking a nurse for a hospital gown "of equivalent élan." Anyone who didn't know would have taken him for a peppy man in his prime.

A second Moscow fall is far gloomier than the first. With the novelty exchanged for knowledge of what awaits you, the descent to winter is like the early months of military service. As if for spite, the compensations of snow and frosty air were delayed this year; instead there was rain, rawness and the remorseless trap of grim climatic forces. Environment Determines Consciousness.

The afternoon murkiness was worst. I felt I was being sucked into whatever it was that had retarded certain parts of Europe— Slovakia, Albania, Transylvania—for centuries. My new room looked out on a small railroad depot, full of messy piles of ties and greetings to the Twenty-fourth Party Congress. How could I have thought them quaint on the day I arrived? The same slogans leered like cretins from every public room. One more poster, the very next radio program, would snap my nerves.

My new roommate was cut from the cloth of the Party banners: a fine figure of a careerist Young Communist who talked in newspaper language. We had nothing to say to one another. Joe Sourian was gone, together with his magazine- and fun-packed room, which had been like a base canteen for whenever you didn't know what to do with yourself in the dormitory. As if to underline the loss, the Edward who begged Westerners for pity because he informed on them now lived in Joe's old room. I knew none of the new crop of exchange students, nor did I want to in their initial period of mothering by the Embassy.

Forty-eight hours before the operation, when Alyosha was in an isolation ward with radioactive needles doing the final preparation on his ulcers, the suspense and loneliness in my dormitory room crossed some line of tolerance. I called the chief administrator at the institute. Whatever I already suspected about him, there was a *possibility* he might obtain what he had offered, and I damned the scruples that had made me wait this long.

He tried to make his surprise at hearing from me emerge as delight, then excused himself and promised to call the following morning—which he did. That evening, I went to the second meeting.

It was in a smaller room with fewer hosts and a correspondingly less luxurious table. The atmosphere was even odder. There were occasional mentions of mutual help, but nothing more than hints about any for Alyosha. *My* health was inquired about, as if I were the purpose of "our consultations." Many of the comments were made with the slightly overquick anticipation of an amateur group performing a whodunit play, and long silences between the lines suggested that my fellow diners were doubling as the murdered corpses. We poured our own vodka. I drank, and felt nothing.

The specialist, they said, was on an extended trip abroad. But cooperation between peoples of good will never depended on a single patient's progress. We could only wait.

The rotting bait of Alyosha's cure killed my appetite. It was easy enough to sense I was in something unclean; but not how to pull away. Someone volunteered that Alyosha's *present* treatment was devilishly expensive, but "of course" The People's State never considered such things. The threat was both preposterous and real: whoever these men were, they surely had some connection with Alyosha's care.

One murmured that everything possible was being done. He may have been a genuine doctor, and ashamed. I was given to understand I should not ask about the chief administrator, who was neither present nor mentioned. The dour man at my left took a persistent interest in where I'd tried to "acquire" the Western medicines Alyosha had asked for. I couldn't specify what trouble this might get us in, but his tone suggested he knew they came from a CIA fund, and I was already developing the facility of weighing my words from every possible angle yet giving the appearance of a simpleton abroad. Instinct told me to talk effusively—and emptily. My long, earnest description of the London clinic's coolness to foreigners was intended to convey a burning desire to damn capitalism's well-known flaws in all my American naiveté, while giving me the needed seconds to think what might be dangerous for Alyosha or me. I think my act fooled them but it also dragged me further in. The friendlier I made myself appear in order to ward off some ominous threat, the more I was their pet.

I kept thinking of the fool I'd been to rekindle their interest by volunteering to meet them again. And I slowly became aware of the man—Bastard—who was going to be my persecutor when this party was over and I'd be alone with him at a series of suppers grim as Goya on war. He said nothing, but his eyes stuck to my skin like leeches, making their blackness felt even when my back was turned. The wart on his cheek was something from an evil dream.

I thrust ahead with long, steady strides, yet made no progress toward his ward, as if I were walking against the current of an airport pedestrian conveyor. The five days of tests and rest, the operation, then four days when I couldn't see him and was told only that he was "as expected." Four days when I actually began writing a scholarly article because nothing else would kill the time. And no trick in the book of special pleas made any impression on the hospital staff.

But their permission this morning was a good sign. Postsurgical patients could ordinarily be seen only by their immediate family; this exception for me wouldn't have come if things had gone poorly for him. He was just at the end of this shiny corridor, if I could ever reach it. The thousand things I had to tell him all came down to two or three. The operation *had* to work; all alternatives were unthinkable.

I reached the ward. It was clean, uncrowded, reassuringly antiseptic-smelling. But the forms languishing on its beds broke my hope like kindling. I knew I was crossing the Styx.

Most patients retained too little strength to scream and could only join a chorus of moans, one relieving the other to keep the sound constant while the first gasped for breath. Was *Alyosha* somewhere among these tortured mutilations? He'd strolled down the corridor just over a week ago, waving. Whatever was festering inside him, and aside from the X-ray burns and occasional nausea, he had nothing in common with *them*.

Something kept me going. It was my first look at a cancer surgery ward, in Russia or anywhere else. I remembered Tolstoy's sketches of the Crimean War wounded. Part of me wanted to swap bodies with him, another part to accept that all was finished and to run. Then I saw it. Gazing toward the ceiling, the yellow copy of his face with a blankness in place of his spark. All the theory, plans and logic on which we'd lived since my return burned in one searing instant, like a strip of magnesium.

I took a breath and said his name. During the long minute between his accomplishing a turn of his head when he heard me and forcing something through his teeth, I welled up with guilt for having disturbed him. He had to repeat himself because I couldn't decipher his mumble.

"Hello *muchacho* . . . place to sit down."

The nurse had said that since the anesthetic had worn off his pain was "fairly bad." I was afraid of being sick.

His eyes tried to smile. They were the same, but looked very different, like the headlights of a wreck, still on after a hideous highway accident—because everything else had degenerated. He was encased in bandages from ankles to waist and had to lie in a persecuting scrunch designed for recovery from his operation. But it was his moisture of weakness when I bent down to kiss him that told me he would never again be the Alyosha all Moscow knew, even for the time it took to deliver a single punch line.

His face had shrunk and his mouth had begun to sink, giving him an eerie resemblance to his faintly Neanderthal Rostov aunt. The overnight aging of some men who long looked much younger than their years was only part of his transformation. He had become decrepit.

I remembered the young internist who had originally rushed him to the Advanced Training Institute. Leaving the apartment after a visit in September, he broke down under my wheedling and divulged his personal prognosis: that the cancer was furiously malignant and had already spread to some internal organs; only Alyosha's constitution was keeping him on his feet. *And the operation?* I pressed. In one chance in a million, it would help. Otherwise, it would weaken him—and spread the metastases even faster through his system. Then he, the brainy little Jewish boy who loved Alyosha, repeated almost word for word the advice of the upper-class London consultant who had urged me to "help the patient prepare for death" instead of writing the prescriptions Alyosha needed. The Englishman had straightened his Bond Street cuff, whereas Alyosha's friend broke down with me. "I'm only a doctor," he said, his face turning to baby's blubber. But both specialists feared the operation would only shorten his life. And they were right.

All this I knew before Alyosha and I exchanged a sentence. And he knew I knew. But he was also deeply grateful to see me—all the more because he hadn't suspected I could talk my way into his ward. As if it represented some important sacrifice, he asked if I could stay until the nurse told me otherwise. But well before this, he went silent: he was too weak to talk.

The staff allowed me in every day. They were the only Russians I'd ever met who were embarrassed by little gifts—not to be confused with bribes, because they *wanted* to help. And the flower vendors I'd earlier condemned seemed to be performing a noble service; all the more because I stopped bringing delicacies, which, lying uneaten on his little table, turned to the wrong kind of symbols. Besides, he was surprisingly fond of "posies," as if in compensation for his loss of appetite. Like a child waiting for a present from parents returning home, he looked toward my hands as I entered.

Bastard was a caricature of his service. All the general talk and specific stories I'd heard suggested that many KGB officers were above average in looks, intelligence and education. Masha's lover in Perm, a feckless Yalta agent who became Alyosha's friend after being tossed out for drinking—a fair share of essentially decent blokes filled the modern ranks. Chingiz once mentioned that the KGB boss of a Volga town where he worked was the most enlightened man for miles. Nothing more significant than bad luck stuck me with my repulsive hack. I kept hoping for a substitute.

The first impression he conveyed when on his own was of malevolence trying to pass for self-importance. He was permanently angry—at his own physique, if nothing better was handy; at nature's mistake in assigning a janitor's countenance to a Big Man.

Next I noticed his leer, which exposed his jaundiced resentment of me under attempted congeniality. Envy of my height, my shirt, my freedom—everything. His bile was so sour and his cover pose so weak that whatever they were supposed to be saying, his every word and gesture in fact proclaimed his relish for exercising power over me. Once he came right out and said it, pointing up to a radiator grill above our table.

"Supposing our conversations here *are* being recorded, what of it? We've got nothing to be ashamed of. This is a cozy supper with honest heart-to-heart talk among friends. Now let's drink to your health and happiness, which is all that really counts."

To his bosses monitoring the tapes, the greasy sham of revealing "confidences" would broadcast as a standard feint to put a prey at ease. But Bastard's larger purpose was to gloat that he not only had me imprisoned but could toy with me like a laboratory animal. And I had to pretend I understood nothing, for that was the role I'd got myself into—and feared to change, lest he explode and get at Alyosha by expelling me. All pretense about helping Alyosha had been abandoned, but my personal keeper clearly had the power at least to recommend expulsion to those who decreed it. Besides, playing simpleminded seemed the best way of saying too little for use if they doctored the tapes. So I sat there, faking gullibility and controlling my revulsion at his skull, which gleamed below the chandelier like Repin's painting of semi-Mongolian tribesmen petitioning the Turkish sultan.

"You're no child any more. What's this drifting around, the trying to 'find yourself' flimflam? Your parents know better. A hippie is a weakling." . . .

"I'll tell you frankly, not everyone trusts you. An American with wide circles of rootless "friends"—the facts indicate cultivation of useful *contacts*. There was that incident with a nitwit called . . . Chingiz—firing his follies, preaching antisocialism. Some dire mistakes have to be made up for." . . .

"You're not eating. Taste these mushrooms; *go on*, try them. And learn to relax. Forget my official position; I'm here as your *friend*. I left my work at the office just so we could enjoy ourselves." . . .

"The escapades with that 'medical student.' Tailing her around, convincing my colleagues of your intelligence background. And your orgies! University officials wanted to expel you; *they* argued you were no student at all. Only came here to besmirch socialist morality, violate Soviet rules. People wanted to make an example of you with a newspaper exposé. But I laid myself on the line to postpone it, because *I* think there's good in you somewhere . . ."

His lips were oily with the pleasure of both the expense-account caviar and of kicking the boot of his lies in my face. The waiter knocked and cleared the table to Bastard's self-satisfied command, glancing in curiosity at the guest in this special room, and at Bastard to demonstrate deference. This was my introduction to the intimate delights of restaurant rooms for two about which I'd often read—while Alyosha languished alone.

"I enjoy life now. I suppose you think it's not worth much to live in this condition. I can only say it doesn't work that way."

Alyosha's goal was "two or three more years of this," and he was now urging me outright to stay for this period. He had recovered his senses and was trying to accommodate them to the new circumstances.

"It's the first time I understand the main things: how good it is to live in general, as opposed to living 'well.' To breathe, see the patterns in the ceiling—you fill up with happiness. I'm glad if I'm down for a thousand days or so just looking around."

I made up my mind. I'd stay with him, whatever I'd have to take from Bastard. The doctors now looked away when I asked, but it was clear enough that two or three years was the outside guess.

"You haven't mentioned our get-togethers to Alyosha?"
"Why should I?"
"That's good. Why worry him? Very good. He has his own problems."

Bastard's use of the diminutive "Alyosha" was more repulsive even than his calling me *"tu."* But I *hadn't* mentioned him to anyone else; for once I could tell him the unequivocal truth. Meanwhile, the softening-up continued in all its rawness.

"I'll tell you straight, your chatter about 'not getting involved with politics' isn't worthy of you. Everything is political; you're not a baby or coward to pretend you can stand aside from mankind's struggle. Evasion puts you in the ranks of reaction. . . . You claim you're for peace, not any one ideology. But you have to fight for peace. It's time to prove your manhood. Show us where you stand by *doing* something for peace." . . .

"You can't live on a student stipend all your life. A man's nothing without money in his pocket. I tell my friends you're growing up and starting to think about your dignity and your wallet." . . .

"Law number one is that all states serve class interests only. The difference is we're a Peoples' State, while certain others are armed agencies of monopoly capital. No American worker ever got a fair trial. Thousands of innocent students rot in jail for refusing to join Saigon's exploitative massacre. That kind of trampling on justice, the terrible curbs on free expression, can't exist in the genuine democracy of a People's State. Your own passport is not valid for travel to China or Albania—that's what you call freedom? The FBI has powers over every American that our Constitution and citizens wouldn't stand for. Besides, we're an agency of peace, working for everyone's freedom." . . .

"This girl stuff of yours—*I* don't mind, but it behooves you to behave decorously. The Soviet people feel strongly about cleansing their society of perversions. And why advertise your weaknesses? I want to protect you against anyone who might try to exploit them."

"Be more discreet, let people know you're a serious person. With your own FBI and CIA too—don't give them a lever on you through childish excesses. What good is signing useless protests against the Vietnamese war—which only get you on a list, spoiling your chance for *real* peace work. Criticizing your own government, even to Russian students, is ill-advised for you. You don't want your officials to suspect you're not a loyal American."

He assured me that American agents in London had instructed me to return for the additional semester here, holding myself "in readiness." And explained the "real" workings of American society for me from the vantage point of his Lubyanka office. But it was his personal advice that made me feel contaminated, as if a weevil grub had crawled inside me to tell me what to do in life.

The excruciating pains lasted two weeks. Parts of his rectum had been removed, adding the humiliation of tube defecation to the pure physical anguish. Sedation provided the only intervals of relief from the burning, stinging and stabbing of his "giblets," as he tried to joke. His old blondie doctor, who was no longer looking after his case, told me that the location of the trouble put him near the top of the patients' agony list.

Some days it was easier to bear than I had feared. After all, this was the very worst that could happen and the world hadn't collapsed; we were somehow living through it. Other days, it was only part of the nightmare to call his suffering "life." I swigged at a bottle before visiting him.

Apart from twitching and writhing, he hadn't moved from the tormenting recovery position. Then the bandages were removed, providing release and the first psychological lift, which the convalescent timetable—he was scheduled to get to his feet in one more week—marginally reinforced. A tinge of color worked its way into his cheeks as he jested again, feebly.

"The entire Soviet people is toiling day and night to give labor presents to Our Party's historic Twenty-fourth Congress. This ill-timed indisposition prevents me from raising my personal production targets, but that's a mere glancing blow to my morale."

He'd asked that the crutches be brought early and liked to grip the handles, urging me, meanwhile, to procure some Rolling Stones records so we could flog them and live "a little wide" after the hospital. "You know my weakness for fine music," he said to disguise our trading intentions from an imaginary microphone under the bed—and also to convince us that he *was* going to have at least a period of non-invalid living.

"Toddle-dee day" was seventy-two hours away. All our outlook had adjusted to the "two or three more years." Then I entered the ward on a sunny morning and the terror on his face struck me even harder than his ghastliness after the operation.

"Look at this," he said like a pupil in a reading class. "See what is happening to me."

He opened his gown. His chill fingers guided mine. A new net of knots had appeared in his right armpit, and the lump on his neck was prominent enough to make out without touching.

I saw tears in his eyes: despair prying loose his party line as a killer wrenches his victim's hands from a window ledge. *Nothing* was going according to plan; the notion of even temporary recovery was a sham. He was back to May, when he first confirmed the doom of "cancer"—and again his courage briefly lapsed. He broke down and sobbed, grasping my hand, then pushing it away and turning over so that only our old mascot nose, which was becoming grotesque in comparison with the puckered rest of him, was visible. When he rolled back to see where I was, I read the terrible thoughts, the most dreadful prospect, in his eyes. There was nothing to do but to hold him, repeating my palliative phrases.

He recovered from this the same afternoon but remained dazed. He was in a bad dream, he said. He couldn't believe it could drag on *so long* without a cure. The law of probabilities said a lick of good luck *had* to slip into this year's run of punk.

The next day he settled into something between extreme pessimism and his fancy that the encumbrance would somehow disappear. "Recovery is like a horizon that recedes as I approach it," he said. "You've traveled more than I have so *you* dope it out: should I make haste or loiter?"

I knew that not answering Bastard's calls would only provoke him and that he would keep pestering me until I did. Even if his men weren't following me that day, there was nowhere I could say I'd been to explain an absence of more than several. hours. No hiding place from his advances, I thought to myself as I trudged toward one of the dormitory booths.

I picked up the telephone, picturing his smirk at the other end. He expressed his satisfaction in trapping me for another evening by breathing into the receiver before speaking.

"How's every little thing with my favorite student?"

The very unctuousness of the greeting was calculated to taunt me through demonstration of his control of my time. Sometimes he would ask where I'd been the previous evening, and if I said "a movie" he'd name the one, "casually" recommending I see it one day. Or feign surprise in a way that made it plain he had known all along and was establishing for the *n*th time that he had ways of checking my every movement. Nevertheless, the sting of his own repugnance spoiled his triumphant moment of delivering the invitational command. Despite everything, he was afraid he might be slighted, that I might refuse him. He was caught in the perversion of performing the very actions that made him most hateful.

"You've been losing weight," he drawled into the receiver held tight to his mouth. "Nothing *you* can do just sitting at the bedside: I'll take you someplace for a bit of a nibble."

The same canting generosity; the clumsy fraudulence of concern for my health, while the picture of his crapulous feeding on KGB funds during Alyosha's crisis brought bile to my throat. For the first time, I made a serious effort not to go. I wasn't feeling very well, I said, with the conviction of the truth.

His tone was transformed. Whenever he suspected I underestimated his power over me, he switched instantly from the fatherly policeman to the mean one, eager to punch.

"Don't play the prima donna with me. It's now five-thirty. Be there at seven o'clock."

The "somewhere" we went for "a bit of a nibble"—he invariably used the same laboredly coy phrases—was the Aragvi. There was still a slim chance for reprieve. Twice previously, he had called back at the last moment to cancel, emphasizing his importance as an agent summoned to something more urgent, and underlining his mysteriousness. He thought it enhanced his prominence to tell me nothing whatever about himself and would smile his pretension to a significant smile when, for distraction, I asked whether he'd ever visited Leningrad. Or would turn the question around, urging me to tell him what *I* ought to about my travels. My every personal question—his taste in Black Sea resorts, which newspaper he preferred—was an insidious attempt to crack his identity, and while it sometimes seemed prudent to ply him with precisely these queries to kill time and flatter his self-importance, there was the opposite danger he would take them seriously as evidence that I was coached by the CIA.

But I did know he worked in Lubyanka, not only through his hints—this fact made him seem important and threatening enough to be exempted from his strict secretiveness—but by seeing his black car there one afternoon with the license I remembered. I also knew that his name was not the Evgeny Ivanovich Rastuzov he supplied. Hoping to cancel once, I called the emergency number he had given me for office hours. The three-minute failure at the other end to recognize his pseudonym and amateurish whispering with a hand over the receiver were enough to convince an adolescent television detective of its phoniness.

I also assumed he worked where he logically should have, in Lubyanka's department for resident Americans. Occasionally he disclosed knowledge of a genuine fact about America—a state capital, the senatorial term of election—that had probably been imparted in a background course for junior agents. He was proud enough of this too to breach his own silence with it; even to utter such phrases as "crime rate" and "drop out" in English. But resentment of my more fluent Russian curbed his desire to display his feeble linguistic skill.

I waited for the reprieve until the last possible minute, then hurried uphill from the metro station, pushing through Gorky Street's evening crowd: he was always worse when I arrived late. Mingling in the line outside the entrance, I enjoyed my last free frosty seconds until he saw me through the glass of the door, grinning a snake's welcome as he motioned to the doorman to admit me.

His greeting chimed with delighted surprise, as if the recent telephone summons had never been. Lifting his stubby arms to help me with my coat, he moved as he thought a kingpin should—and smugly, because this fake gesture at playing gracious host was his notion of irony to remind me of who in fact was master. In the rush I had forgotten to remove my brass-buckled belt, at which he scowled. Before I learned to dress down, he resented my pastels more than anything. His bully's flush bloomed at the provocation of my pink shirt, which humiliated him while defiling Moscow. A thousand old fogies in Viennese cafés couldn't have hated a thousand hippies more.

He was in his evening suit, darker than his office one but of the same boxy cut. However, the tie blocked tight into the white nylon collar most clearly identified him and what he represented. He stuck to the skinny black band out of fear to be seen by *his* masters in a colorful Western one. It was his badge of loyalty to Marxism-Leninism and to the Soviet system that galled him: the tyranny that made him what he was also kept him from being the smart detective he longed to be. The GUM garment symbolized the petty gangsters who do the dictatorship's menial work yet can't get the pickings—the Broadway cravats—they crave.

"Shall we partake of some refreshment?"

And his cheek wart! The bartender's mien that kept him even from fantasizing about himself as he wanted! He strode down the corridor toward our room, his aversion for his physical self and itch to lash out at others tensing his fists. He disliked walking in front of me for the vantage point it gave me to look down on his bald spot, but couldn't let me go first because *he* always had to lead the way. I pictured myself sneaking off but hiding close enough to enjoy his expression when he wheeled around to no one following.

Paneled in walnut, the room was just big enough for two or three diners. Bastard felt better when the door was closed and he could assume his role without the interference of outsiders who elbowed him aside until shown the card in his wallet. He pointed to my customary chair. The table had been laid out in advance with the usual bottles and hors d'oeuvres, but the main course wasn't yet chosen because it was part of his pleasure to order for me.

"You look in the mood for something adventurous. Shashlik Caucasus-style?" (He almost always selected shashlik.) "Tell you what—make it two. It's not every day we can do the town together."

The waiter glanced at me to wonder whether I'd caught on or was still the dupe being led to slaughter. As always, Bastard chose the best Georgian red. He was much more a vodka than a wine man, but his greatest satisfaction seemed to come from the thought of the rich free feed than from the actual food or drink. Whatever else it was too, an Aragvi supper was the peak of Moscow's good life, and he reveled in it, fork spearing red cabbage, fingers splotched with the cold chicken's cream sauce. He had ordered enough for three—with the usual two half-liters of "vodka-kins"—but methodically cleaned the plates. A third of his bottle disappeared in ten minutes, and his face was florid with the gratification of a feast on a cold night.

"What's this disrespect for the savories? The salami's particularly recommended; give me your plate."

I said I was off my form, trying to repeat the words I'd used on the telephone. Excuses sometimes annoyed him, but he let this one pass, merely repeating his supposed peasant saying about the medicinal powers of "the little darling white liquid."

The trick was to take token sips of the vodka, spilling an equal amount into my napkin: he had a weak sense of smell. He probably wasn't trying to get me drunk—it would have been easy enough to slip something into my glass, after all—but simply make me join his overindulgence as part of my fealty. At some level, he knew that the sight of him masticating made me queasy, even when I fought for my honor and my stomach by trying not to eat. . . . My other dodge was to talk enthusiastically about something that might delay his importuning. The weather—but not the Russian winter, for that would give him a lead for his sermon about my affection for, and duties to, the Russian people. What I'd been doing since our last meeting—but nothing about the hospital to avoid his hypocritical questions about Alyosha. Something neutral in the news.

He finished the last of the hors d'oeuvres and tossed back more vodka. Two more hours—he liked to leave at ten o'clock—and nothing nasty so far: my luck was holding. He permitted the waiter to serve the shashlik and pronounced himself satisfied with its preparation.

Then I made my first mistake. Bastard's "g's" for "kh's" and backwoods "o's" were unmistakable signs of a cracker upbringing: something else to be ashamed of. This is what I failed to register when, to keep fending him off, I asked what part of the country he hailed from. He glowered at me for my impudence, his guard up like the dukes of a beery brawler.

"And what makes you think I wasn't brought up in Moscow?"

I was making no such assumption at all, I said; it had been a figure of speech. Still smoldering at the implied slur to his social standing, he remembered why we were here and bore down on me about my debt to the Soviet people—through him—for indulgences to Alyosha and me.

To feed his ego, I feigned disappointment not to have learned the origins of this masterful incognito operative; to make him feel smarter, I pretended be be in awe of his keen mind and Kremlin connections. Consumed by curiosity about all he couldn't reveal, I could not quite grasp his hints about the responsibility of a "true friend" to Russia. . . . Falling back on these standard defenses, I heard an echo of Alyosha's quip about sharpening the brains of the nation by "playing dumber than our sleuths."

The sleepiness of food and drink dissolved his veneer of artfully guiding the conversation. Patience gone, he snarled at the waiter and leaned his face across the table, inches from mine. Now each minute dragged like a speech to the Presidium. I had to convince him he was making progress with me, which would eventually penetrate my obtuseness and lead to what he wanted. The only way to do it, keeping clear of politics, was to talk about myself, emphasizing my self-doubts to show him how naively honest I was, how much I trusted him. Rikki-tikki-tavi came to mind and

I tried to remember whether it was the mongoose or cobra who owned Bastard's hypnotizing eyes.

The sounds of boisterous good times in the main hall faintly penetrated the door. Russians celebrating with the usual abandon, Georgians singing their clannish songs, Western tourists enamored of their artlessness, as I once was. I sweated and stole a glance at his watch. I even profaned my feelings for Alyosha by talking about them to consume another quarter hour. The tactics worked in the sense that he was satisfied with the evening's reapings but only through the humiliation of opening more of myself to him, and supplying more to be used against me next time. Parry, cover up, pretend to forget . . .

He ordered his favorite pastry. The worst was over: he always ended on a lighthearted note, with which the next invitation was supposed to harmonize. My response to his attempted joke about a haircut for me pleased him. What prompted my chuckle was in fact a memory of calling him "Doctor" during our first meetings.

Walking down the corridor, we passed the closed doors of six or seven small private rooms like ours. Bastard sighed. In a mellow mood now, he helped me with my coat and tipped the old cloakroom attendant handsomely for his bow. Outside the driver, who'd been waiting the three hours, scrambled to open both doors for us, but Bastard never pressed his offer to drive me home. I was grateful for the small mercy.

He removed a glove and squeezed my hand with a show of intimacy.

"What are your plans for tomorrow? Oh yes? Have fun, we've opened this country to you to show our trust. But remember your goal is establishing yourself."

I walked the whole way to the apartment. Spooky in the yellow of the swaying streetlamps, nighttime Moscow was both cruel and comforting for its assurance that "nothing can be done about it." I thought of Alyosha *and* Bastard urging me to stay; of Alyosha, even now, enjoying my hair after a shampoo and Bastard hating me for it. Maxi watched while I sandpapered the kitchen cabinets.

More surgery was immediately scheduled, to be followed by a third series of cobalt treatments. Alyosha submitted without interest. The declaration "To prevent further metastases" turned his head awry, as if it wanted to escape from his body.

The day before the second operation, he asked me to help him with his bath. I arrived early and wheeled him to the bathroom. When he undressed, I had my first acquaintance with the horror accompanying the tragedy. The incisions of the first operation were still unhealed. They had had to be reopened when the stitches were removed to drain lymphatic liquids gathering there. The effect of the radiation on the surrounding tissue prevented the clefts from knitting.

I had feared this moment since I first saw him mummy-like in the bandages. And the wounds were indeed fearful, but only momentarily, until my eyes did what was necessary to move to the greater awfulness of his groin. Three-inch cavities stared at me from both sides, like a revolting joke about the green eye of gangrene. The bottom of the hollows was raw meat, covered by blotches of puss.

I straightened up. A smell that I could hardly believe came from a living body was eating into my nostrils. "Sorry, old man," he apologized. "It's really rotten."

But the worst was what he as a whole had become. A desiccated, tormented body, hunched under the weight of his head. My sadness came in the Russian word *gorye*, with its connotations of human frailty and limitless hurt.

I washed what I could of him and shared his noontime soup. We talked about the time he had produced two pairs of roller skates and we whizzed down the whole of Gorky Street, dodging pedestrians and incredulous traffic cops. "I didn't want to grow up," he said. "Into what? 'Je ne regrette rien'—but you can do better."

"So while we're the vanguard of the proletariat, we simultaneously defend the interests of civilization as a whole. We represent the toiling masses *and* mankind's future; that's what real men want to serve."

He had started the dunning earlier this evening. Perhaps his bosses had told him to speed things up. I wished I could remember their faces at the group dinners: Bastard surely planned nothing on his own. But that was a diversion. There were a hundred and forty minutes to go, and I had to think of something embarrassing but unexploitable to confess, without making any slips that might contradict my half-truths of last time.

The second operation caused less relative damage because Alyosha was too feeble for drastic decline. It only made a very sick man sicker, which was less shocking and more exhausting.

The hope was correspondingly shorter, for his thighs had new lesions within two weeks. The doctors theorized that the startlingly rapid spreading might somehow be driven by the same remarkable vigor that was keeping the patient alive. Alyosha's cancer was in the image of himself. This probably meant little in terms of life expectancy, since the two forces would tend to cancel each other out, but it made the battle and pain exceptional. Yet the nurses still heard no more than an occasional gasp from him.

Not fortitude for its own sake moved him, but a desire to salvage something worthwhile of his remaining time. He stopped talking about the two or three years, transferring all his expectations to a final spring we'd enjoy together. Meanwhile, he wanted to read—*Cancer Ward* first. I brought him a copy of a pocket edition, convenient for sneaking past customs guards. Early the next morning, he was three-quarters through the long text; I realized he must have read most of the night. He was holding up the outlawed novel to the light, a photograph of triumphant factory smokestacks on the newspaper bookcover he'd made to avert questions. Two thin arms propping up the five-ounce volume as if it were a dictionary: this was Alyosha in his own cancer ward, devouring the account of patients in the other one facing their approaching deaths. I waited in the doorway, grateful that his concentration was undisturbed by the tiny print and the pain.

The brainstorm struck as he was greedily spooning the last of the caviar-chik, but I held back to polish the details. First let him know how impressed I was by his last lecture about the inevitable triumph of the world working class. Then keep a straight face when I came out with it, in my searching-for-the-truth-under-his-guidance voice.

"Evgeny Ivanovich, I'm all confused. History says the Revolution will win in the end, but is this the right moment for a new popular front in France?"

And finally knit my brows in earnest interest as he dragged himself from his morsels, wiped his fingers into a napkin and undertook to reply.

He couldn't refuse. The same microphone that plagued me was keeping a check on him, and failure to answer well in terms of the current line might alert his bosses to *his* political unpreparedness. Nor could he vent his anger on me: the question, after all, seemed prompted by the success of his own indoctrination of me. Here was I, expressing an interest in the advance of the Communist movement, revealing a secret desire to be on the winning side!

But he, of course, didn't give a damn about France as a whole, let alone its stupid working class. He stared in frustration and disgust at this American punk with his idiotic curiosity. Hating the goddam Frogs, sweating over his ignorance of European politics, angrily suspicious, despite everything, that I had trapped him, he offered a rambling, incoherent "analysis" of French Communist intentions. In the end, he was so tangled in his doubletalk that he could only mumble, then half-shout, that our job was to leave the ideological challenges to the Party experts.

"Don't you worry, we've got lots of them—the best. They don't make mistakes."

I watched him squirm, surprised I could enjoy my little triumph. Its best part was the twenty minutes I'd managed to kill. Next time, I'd ask him about socialism in China and hear him gnash his teeth. Pavlov confirmed!

When it reached the lungs, neither X-rays nor surgery could be used. The last resort was chemotherapy. Somewhere I heard that it worked in sixteen per cent of such cases.

Rumors weaved their way through his ward: a miraculous new Swiss substance, West German ampules, an experimental Japanese pill. . . . Cursing myself for not having tried harder in London, I put a call through to the Royal Institute consultant I'd seen. He was abroad, and the man who took the call understood neither who I was nor what I wanted from Moscow. The American Embassy doctor, a bland last-straw, knew less about intestinal cancer than I did at this point. Abruptly, I remembered how Bastard entered my life. Perhaps there *was* a VIP clinic somewhere in the country—in which case it was only a tremolo to our curse.

The old Alyosha would have flirted and probed his way to the source of the rumors in a morning. His shadow waved a hand to indicate I shouldn't bother. He no longer believed in cure. The X-rays, operations, false leads had been a grand illusion to mask the theft of his numbered months. Although he had come to terms even with this, further effort would be "a profanation." He wanted only to keep free of escapism and to live until New Year's Eve, his champion holiday. To see the new year in together would be a fine finish and a portent of good luck. We'd celebrate in fitting style, at the Sovietskaya, where he first invited me to join his party for the actress and models. I placed a deposit on a table.

And passed on his attitude to the doctors in case he was unable to make himself clear. They agreed that the operations might better have never been performed; but medicine could not work in hindsight, only on judgment of what seemed best at the time. Now as then, their obligation was to continue pursuing every available means.

They were going to try an extremely powerful drug, used when other treatments fail. Perhaps because of my intercession, I was told he could not have visitors during the first two days. This was going to be so hard for him that I said nothing about it. On the third morning, I was ushered directly into an atmosphere tenser than ever before. He had been so weak, I was told, that he collapsed after the second injection and was heart massaged back from clinical death.

He himself knew nothing of this until later, but thought he'd been under sedation. His dreams were so compelling, he said, that he resented waking up. The cough that had been bothering him for weeks was now a steady series of salvos convulsing his body and threatening to burst his lungs. I tried reading to him, but my mistakes in Russian seemed to worsen the hacking and I let him doze.

When Bastard got to the message for which he'd been preparing me—for which his entire operation had been mounted—I almost enjoyed another forbidden laugh. I knew perfectly well, he enlightened me, that I had invested too much in learning Russia's language and ways to waste by shifting to something else. Yes, and loved it too much; my heart would always be here. But neither sacrifice was necessary: I could settle in Moscow with my friends and my interests *and* earn the livelihood that would make me a real man. Never mind that my research had flagged; I wasn't cut out for scholarship anyway. My real interest was life itself, not egghead books. And he had convinced his colleagues to make everything possible by not opposing my presence in the capital.

"You'll always be welcome. Doors shut tight to other foreigners will open to you. Because we've come to like you. . . ."

What I must do, he confided, is return home after the semester and get a job that would quickly send me back. Become a Moscow correspondent or join the diplomatic service; I was free to choose the best path for myself, and once here they would provide me with information to advance me further. And as a full-fledged member of. Moscow's American community, I'd be party to Embassy talk—precisely the "real life" he'd just mentioned. It went without saying that I would want to tell him about plans to wound or slander the Russia I loved.

"It's what you've always wanted as a person searching for himself through truth. Don't think I'd dream of asking you to perform espionage. We stand on the principle that you must do nothing against your own conscience—yes, and it's exactly the scheming that *violates* your conscience you'll want to discuss with people you trust. You can help us be sure of who is our friend and who isn't. Because a huge spy network is plotting against us here. . . ."

To the extent that the crudeness exceeded my expectation, I was relieved. The trick now was to avoid undertaking the smallest errand for him, which would lead to instant blackmail, yet not to prompt their revenge by refusing: more than ever, my job was to stay with Alyosha. Thank God, I'd begin with a week or more of clear sailing. I'd tell him I needed at least that much time to think, and ask for a copy of the Twenty-fourth Congress's declarations on how the Party is pursuing its goal of world peace.

Word had gone around. Well-wishers came regularly, the new ones with the apprehensiveness of first visits to a cancer clinic. They sat briefly at his bedside, trying to cheer him up with snippets of news, or, if he was dozing, peeked from the corridor and talked to me about the incredibility of what was happening, with reminiscences about escapades with him to prove this point.

Most were happy to leave quickly, either not to tire him or to escape his coughing. Some said silly, self-serving things, such as reminding him of some favor they had performed in the business of acquiring him cloth for a suit or a reservation in a hotel room. Many fought not to disturb him by crying.

The mainstays were from the eclectric collection—the Ilyas, Ediks, Lev Davidovichs—he'd seen most often during the past four or five years. But some of the cultural achievers present at the preoperation soirée also came, as well as former clients he'd assumed, as he sometimes quipped on their way out, were still in the clink. And a smattering of Erstwhiles bearing touching, useless gifts.

And his former wife, who came twice a week since I first brought her at his request, and was less pleasant than I'd imagined from our brief meetings last winter. I wondered why he had taken such pains to continue seeing her all these years. Keeping her new husband away, she spoke of herself as Alyosha's closest living relative, a weakly disguised hint about inheritance, accompanied by eyes on the Volga.

Anastasia had been coming when I wasn't there. Ever since my plane touched down in September, the knowledge that I was near her again—that she was still here, in this closed world and within my reach—was my comfort as I tried to comfort Alyosha. Alek came by to apologize for his London behavior and to tell me of Anastasia's parting from the professor. I sensed we would start almost anew when we met again, for something had happened to make me want to know her, and not my dreams about us.

But we could not talk about our future during his ordeal; and to avert my old tendency to play a noble role, I did not want her to see me at his side. We cooperated by avoiding each other, until I caught sight of her leaving the building one evening, her head hung, her hat askew. I remembered the hiding behind tree trunks to spy on her, and she looked up just then as if she'd known I was there. We smiled, perceived the importance of our forthcoming meeting, nodded. Everything took a long time, as though we were moving through water, whose current bore her off to a street on my right.

Still feeling obliged to try, the doctors asked the chief chemotherapist of the prestigious Blokhin Institute to examine Alyosha personally. The day before his appointment, I entered the ward to see him sitting up in bed.

"Give me your hand." The absence of greeting revealed how impatiently he had been waiting for me.

His ribs were like the struts of a Japanese lantern. On the damp skin stretched across the middle ones, I felt a lump the size of a meat ball. I wasn't startled, because I had noticed it two days before when shifting him to a more comfortable position.

"It's all over," he said, settling back into the pillow. "Nature taking its course." In the next minute I felt him making his peace not with his fate as before, but with death itself. He was utterly calm.

"It might not be so bad," I ventured weakly.

"Oh, *muchacho*, I don't need *that*."

Silently, he showed me more lumps on his back and stomach, then broke into a grin like the limey POWs photographed when first catching sight of liberating British troops.

"What are we waiting for? Time to vacate the premises."

He knew that some terminal patients were allowed out and resented losing a single extra hour to bureaucratic delay. *Home* beckoned so powerfully that strength returned for plying me to get him discharged. But I hesitated about leaving medicine's keeping.

"It's going to be harder if I have to be cute with you too," he said impatiently. "I understand you think it strange, but I know everything and am prepared for everything. Let me go out with a memory of real life, as opposed to this hospital imitation."

Feeling I had no further duty to encourage him with

treatment, I argued his case to the doctors, who met informally the same afternoon and concurred that keeping him against his wishes served no purpose. The last X-rays had shown large voids in his lungs, and the disease was still spreading "as if it had something against him." The tricky question was who was going to look after him, but despite the extreme irregularity, I convinced them to accept me. I fetched his ex-wife, who still bore the name Aksyonova, despite her remarriage. It was agreed he be signed out to her official care, while the nursing procedures were explained to me.

I hurriedly packed his things. The doctors said that curative measures could be resumed at home in two weeks, but Alyosha did not need this pretense either. He thanked them warmly, each with a personal mention of what they did best. They slumped, as if not thoroughly used to this. The final examination and writing of the discharge would take place in the morning.

Bastard was drinking more than usual, probably because it was too early to expect my final decision, and this meal was merely to keep his presence felt. More for the microphone than for me, he was mouthing his old monologue about giving me the chance to atone for my mistakes. Some of his colleagues were still demanding retribution for my joining Joe Sourian as a CIA scout, inciting Chingiz to defect, using Alyosha's illness as a front for—

"For God's sake, stop," I said. "Why do you need the lies, what good do they do?"

I wondered why I'd snapped. He'd long been stuffing me with worse junk and graver implications. But there was no time to puzzle over this. In a flash, he was cold sober and ready for action, as if he'd never touched a drop.

"Watch your tongue and don't ever try to call me a liar. You're on the territory of the Soviet Union, not your Harvard playground. And I'm sick of your stalling, make up your mind."

For the first time, I thought I must forget the complications and go to the Embassy. But the cultural attaché's lie when I had told him about Anastasia meant they trusted me as little as I them. They'd only suspect me of cooperating with Bastard—and in any case, KGB microphones in the Embassy building would probably give me away. . . . No, drawing them in would only worsen everything. *They'd* see to it that I, tainted, was expelled.

The fear of Bastard's threat the night before extended to every little thing. I was afraid of Maxi's attitude toward Alyosha, not having seen him since before the first operation. But the minute I wheeled him through the doors, she sent a howl of anxious greeting from inside the car. An assistant and I negotiated the chair down the ramp and settled the patient under his blankets.

He reached across to run a circle over the steering wheel. Passenger cars were beginning to crowd some streets, but when he had wangled the Volga thirteen years ago, he was the one Russian in a million with private wheels and his kind of grin in the driver's seat. In a cap I'd bought for the occasion, he now looked like John D. Rockefeller in his last, wizened years.

I had wanted to take a taxi because of a snowstorm and the doctors had ordered an ambulance, but Alyosha pleaded to go in the car that had taken him to the Black, Baltic, Azov and Caspian Seas in the days when that alone was enough to provide an illusion of freedom and indulgence. Now we intended to defy doctors' orders and drive out to the river beach where he used to swim every summer before his annual trip to the subtropical south. It was to be just a look, but he was deprived even of this because the motor stalled and neither of us could restart it. Alyosha was scrunching into the ball in which he had lain after the first operation and turning greener with each round of coughing. Appalled at my foolishness in helping with the discharge, I ran down the street, waving wildly for a push from passing cars.

At last the nightmare was over; we turned into his street. Neighbors in the courtyard whispered the feared word "cancer." Very slowly, I helped him up the stairs, Maxi following a step behind like a trained pointer, although Alyosha's new scent had made her nervous during the drive.

I plopped him into the daybed, which I'd moved beneath the window for his reading. But after a rest, he asked to "tour" the apartment. His weight on my arms, he shuffled down the corridor, in and out of the bathroom and across the living room to the kitchen. I'd completed the remodeling a few days before, painting the cabinets with a good semigloss I'd managed to obtain. I had sometimes worked late into the night: the term project to end term projects. Alyosha's smile was reward enough.

"A new kitchen is a fresh . . . Let's think of a nifty proverb, *muchacho*."

He was bathed in sweat, like a white trader with tropical fever. Shifting his grip to hug me in thanks, he suddenly began trembling. "Can't walk any more," he said abjectly. Slipping away from me, he leaned against the wall to rest, only to jerk straight up because of his sweat splotches on the new wallpaper.

"*Oi*, I've queered your beautiful job."

I helped him negotiate his last steps back to the bed.

He offered me a smoke—partly as a stand-in for this evening's carrot, for he had dropped the stick. But it was also to show off his access to the American cigarettes sold at the special stores for his Service. His attempt to do it casually—to convince me he saw nothing extraordinary in a pack of Marlboros—only accentuated his fawning regard for the red-and-white box.

"What's this hesitation? Why don't you trust us? Don't think we'd ever blackmail you, that's the last thing that would occur to us."

The homecoming was a shot in the arm. I caught myself hoping again. Alyosha himself spoke of his condition as "stabilized," and reckoned the chemotherapy had done some good after all. Again, he seemed to read my thoughts.

"All right, I do believe in miracles. I'll go on believing until the last day. But that's wildly futuristic, so will you please hatch a smaller commercial wonderwork to sanctify the redecorated kitchen with meat and potatoes?"

Ignoring my admonitions, he applied himself to an approximation of his old activity. I had to move back the bed in reach of the telephone, which he used constantly, calling business contacts to raise money, giving legal and personal advice to old friends together with medical reports about himself. These highly exaggerated his improvement: he was sensible enough not to encourage an exhausting stream of well-wishers.

Besides, he was planning to see everyone on New Year's Eve. Changing his mind again about the party—it was now to be a "recluse's extravaganza" at home—he sent me out for the LP's to finance it. Bastard's knowledge that I had no license provided another little lever for blackmail, but also an odd measure of protection against ordinary traffic cops.

One day, I returned to find a girl washing up in the kitchen, a homemade beret pulled over her ears despite the indoor warmth I maintained with extra heaters. Like a maid of many years, she moved on to the bathroom, stopping only for a comment about a scratch in the new sink. This was my introduction to Nina, an old Erstwhile. Tall and once probably attractive, she was already growing peasant-thick at twenty-three. But her very unobtrusiveness gave her dignity. And her wide-lipped smile, which appeared at unpredictable moments, was the outward indication of an original sense of humor.

From then on, she was with us every day, taking over most of the domestic work, knitting in a corner when nothing was needed. She came at dawn, directly from the telephone exchange where she worked, and left in time for her night shift. At first she said nothing about her attachment to Alyosha; I thought she was simply a kind girl who, in the best Russian tradition, offered her large red hands for sweeping and scrubbing in a tragedy.

Bastard resumed his coaching after a short pause for effect. Back in America, he explained, I would overhear anti-Soviet plots. Contemptible articles being planned, "nefarious" agents preparing to pose as diplomats or tourists. But first I had to place myself in earshot.

"Travel around some: you're an active person, you don't like sitting in one place. To Washington, for example. You should know your own capital anyway, and also the State Department experts; you're curious about what makes people tick.

"And when you get wind of some filth, you take the next plane here. Forget the expense, the Soviet people aren't stingy defending peace—or rewarding peace fighters."

My head ached with envy of Moscow Americans who avoided this pimping by living "clean." And I had to clear it for something freshly timewasting.

"All right, Evgeny Ivanovich, I'm in Washington. And I hear something urgent but don't have enough money on me for a ticket; I can only contact you. Should I use the telephone number I have?"

His smile sagged into a grimace. Propelled by his shout, flakes of horseradish were splattering my jacket.

"No. I forbid it. Not from abroad."

His black eyes blazed in revenge for this attempt to take the initiative with *him*, the counterintelligence expert. But he wouldn't be tricked; *he* knew no one would ask for such information without CIA coaching. Yet this quick counterstroke did not abate his inner fury: not he but his superiors would have to take any decision about contact from the States—and he hated me for revealing his lowly status.

The question grew sorer with his puzzling delay dealing with it. Surely the KGB had dozens of suitable fronts? But during our next meetings, his admonitions that he would instruct me about contact procedure at the proper time only made it more obvious that he hadn't received his own instructions.

Finally, he produced the address and telephone number of an apartment and ordered me, as if he'd thought of the idea, to call or cable there if I had to make an emergency contact. Passing a telephone booth the same night, I wondered whether he'd named his own place. The test was so simple: I'd hang up when someone answered. No one did. There was no such number, and, as a quick taxi ride proved, no building at the given address.

Prone Alyosha was cocking a snoot at doomsday: propped high on pillows, declaring he thought he'd licked the pain, taking pleasure in the telephone's constant chiming. The talk was about tickets for Duke Ellington's forthcoming visit and about the weekend dog show, for which members of Moscow "society" were already grooming their entries. Suddenly he cupped his hand over the receiver and announced that Maxi was going to cop first prize.

A rush of pity and dismay washed over me. This was the sign I had been fearing: his unnatural cheeriness was working into mania, from which the inevitable plunge would leave him in unreachable depression. The Maxi fantasy was an unmistakable symptom: however impeccable her breeding, it was unbalanced to expect even a mention for the never-groomed whelp in a first show. But Alyosha prattled on about painting one wall white for better display of the gold medal, almost snarling when I tried to talk sense to him.

Depressed myself with the futility of it and all it represented, I spent the rest of the day crisscrossing the city for a new head to fit a prewar German clipper he'd bought together with Maxi herself, but never used. It was one chance in ten thousand that his contacts could supply this recherché item, and I tried to think of a substitute distraction of some worth while going through the motions of searching. His new urge to spruce up his life-style, as in last week's insistence that I buy him "California-thick" bath towels to replace his stringy ones, had bogged him down in pathetic trivia, wholly detached from his future.

But I actually found a suitable shaving head. Gripping it in my fingers, I momentarily felt the queasy exhilaration of a powerful coincidence, as if fate were guiding me and anything were possible.

When I returned, Alyosha reached out as if I were handing him nothing more unusual than a glass of mineral water. I was immediately redispatched for every library and Central Canine Breeders' Association booklet on the care and training of poodles. The same evening, I was holding that bathed and carefully dried Maxi on the bed while Master and Nina bobbed her on the pattern of the books' photographs.

There was a trace of the old, Yankee-ingenuity Alyosha in his tackling this new, improbable project—but a reservoir of hysteria underneath. Last year, he'd have come no closer to a dog show than a choice bon mot. Now he was freakishly tense about the clipping, and although faint with exhaustion, snapped an-noyance when I tried to make him rest. At the last minute he heard of someone with a new "championship" shaving head, and threatened to "write off" our friendship unless I promised to launch a new search in the morning.

With some new source of strength, he began training her, his voice and my body doing the work. For four days the room was a kennel. He had memorized the booklets and taken notes on a searching interview with the breeder while I held the telephone to his ear. Mastering commands and movements, Maxi's intelli-gence amazed us; I could have sworn that she understood what was at stake and wanted to give him a big gift. Like her master, she worked her heart out.

But it was Maxi's love of life, revived by this new interest in her, that delighted us most. And her charm—which Alyosha nourished— "You're a splendid lady," he kept croaking to her, "the purest representative of your sex and breed—remember that, my darling."

As he weakened, his line of encouragement became more defiant. "You're not going to take it on the nose just because I am," he said. "You're brimming with beauty and health, you're meant to *win*."

On the Sunday of the show, his pain was back full force. I knew I shouldn't leave him; with an eerie combination of mock gruffness and feeble defiance, he insisted I go.

"And don't bother coming back without the gold medal. You *or* Maxi: handsome is as handsome is judged."

The Moscow Exhibition of Auxiliary Service Dogs was held, with all the confusion of a nonmilitary Soviet event, in an outlying field house. With Maxi's "passport," Alyosha's notarized authorization deputizing me to serve as her handler in the competition convinced the head-scratching officials I had the right to enter her. Maxi's medical certificates were also accepted, although at that moment she herself looked as unhealthy as I had ever seen her. The first sight of the thousands of competitors and spectators—bored time-passers and fanatic enthusiasts, the usual Russian ragtag of total amateurism and the most pedantic expertise—badly startled her. The first hour of barking, snarling and shouting then reduced her to cringing.

I wanted to go home even more than she did but dreaded the empty-handed return. Alyosha's kidding about the prize had been much too serious. Deepening as the moment of truth approached, my despondency about how to cope with his fantasy led to daydreams about bartering my sheepskin coat for someone's first prize. It was the kind of enterprise—like how to handle Bastard—that cried out for the finesse of Alyosha himself.

German shepherds, Great Danes, Spaniels; morning dragged into afternoon while patriotic speeches substituted for postponed decisions. The field house was a mass of whining puppies and children, nagged by exhaustion and thirst. At last it was the turn of the poodles and a hundred of them, chiefly brown and black, were going through their paces, all more neatly than the uncomprehending, irritable Maxi of the conspicuous new whiteness.

Then she came alive. With a cock of her head, she seemed to realize that the hours of waiting had been nonsense; this was the Big Show. Her flair grew every time she jumped one of the necessary barriers, climbed a ladder as we had coached her, gave her paw and—now like a circus performer—barked at my request. Her college try was suddenly so moving that a section of nearby fans began cheering for her. I loved her as never before for this: I could tell Alyosha honestly that she hadn't disgraced herself.

I had heard that the judges were amenable to bribes, but when we began our parade around them—seven or eight relatively clean-suited men in the center of a dirt expanse—they seemed to belie this, for they kept advancing us, as if to toy with my hope against hope, from near the rear of the four-abreast column where we'd started toward the front, where the winners would be. Maxi held her neck as never before; she was brighter than the country snow outdoors. "You're a splendid lady," I kept saying in Alyosha's rasp, and she agreed with her shining eyes. We were moved up from nineteenth place to eighth to fifth to third. That was more than I dared think of out loud, but only the gold medal would do for Maxi, who began prancing, even smiling at the judges. They submitted to this winsomeness; she was *the winner!*

In glee, we dashed to the table, ignored our instructions to stay for the walk-past of best-of-breeds and ran for the exit. Driving back to the apartment, I pushed the Volga almost as hard as Alyosha used to. My key had hardly touched the lock when he cried out from bed.

"Where's that medal, lad? Hurry, I *told* you I want to see it."

Maxi bounded in to lick his face furiously. To spice his reward with a second's tease, I said the judges had been blind.

"*Muchacho,* how *could* you?" he howled, pushing Maxi away. "Not even the silver? What for, why have you dishonored us so terribly?"

Lifting Maxi back up to him, I apologized for the bad joke and produced the gold medal. He was as triumphant as if vindicated of a Dreyfus-like wrong.

"Aha, what did I *tell* you?"

He took a sip of brandy with us to celebrate. The day had been like a "happy" episode in a very sad film I'd already seen. If only his uncanny guess about the prize were a symbol of something.

"I'm not asking you to steal your Embassy's codes. Join the CIA and hand me a list of its spies. I'm giving you a chance to prove your own principles and construct a real life for yourself."

The slump that ended his upswing seemed largely psychological. His mood changed again: he was detaching himself from all reality apart from his immediate surroundings and his reveries, which he kept to himself. I wondered whether the growth had reached his brain.

In the middle ground of the outside world, his intelligence shrunk. Too short of concentration for books, he took to newspapers, itself a dismaying regression, scouring them for human interest items which he reported to us like a cleaning woman telling movie plots. An Irtutsk man who had been sentenced again and again for drunkenness until it was discovered that a malfunctioning pancreas was secreting alcohol into his bloodstream. A counter woman in a Moscow department store who had won a public commendation for actually being polite. A group of factories in Rostov that received fifteen thousand railroad cars of gravel annually from Stavropol, two hundred miles away—while neighboring quarries in Rostov shipped an equal amount of the same material to Stavropol plants. . . . We tried to know whether to restrain or feed this giggly appetite for such babble.

His temperature fell and the tormenting cough virtually ceased, but was replaced by fits of agonizing shortwindedness, during which his eyes threatened to pop out in the effort to draw a breath. If he had to suffocate, I said to myself, let it come quickly to end his gruesome gasping. The spectacle of the shriveled thing writhing in pain was sometimes too horrible to watch.

Occasionally he reached for Nina's or my hand; other times he begged us to go away, and for me to return to America. Why did we subject ourselves to his "performances"? But he clamped together his yellow teeth and still did not cry.

Nights were sometimes better, although Nina was away and Alyosha had no more than three hours' peace at a stretch despite the hospital's pills. I slept on the divan, moved near the bed. Before dawn one morning, a foreboding woke me. The lamp was on, as always. Alyosha of the starving Biafran's shoulders was sitting up in bed, pajama top removed and pressed up against his stomach.

Before my eyes focused, I was struck by the reek—the same as in the hospital bathroom weeks before, but concentrated to a new degree of putrid awfulness. I was about to go to him when I saw. Discharge from an open fission below his rib cage was soaking the pajama. Attending to himself silently, he looked for something dry, which is when he caught my eye and turned away. Stifling the urge to retch, I cleaned him with a fresh towel and held his face in my hands to drain away his horror of himself. Then I switched off the lamp to erase the ghostly light and shadows.

Soon we were used to this. The broken fistulas served as channels for blood, puss, endocrine fluids and unidentifiable liquids. New reddish-blue tumors were growing on the soil of the old, then opening up to spread the poison. He was rotting alive.

He named a prominent Yale professor of international relations who had arrived in Moscow two weeks ago for research. Before congressional committees and in popular periodicals, the professor had been urging caution on détente because, he warned, long-term Soviet intentions remained unchanged. And two years ago he had tried to do the right things for a Soviet exchange student who defected in New Haven, later announcing that Soviet diplomats threatened his family with reprisals. Bastard suspected that the professor had "played a dark role" in that "trumped-up" affair. "And in general, he's a corrupt man, paid to blacken socialism and poison Soviet-American relations." But he wasn't "absolutely certain," and wanted my help "exposing the truth."

"For your own sake, I urge you to see him. Take a couple of your girls to his room; why shouldn't two countrymen have some fun together?"

But the wile of photographing sex on a hotel bed was too obvious even for him. He lowered his sights.

"Just go meet him, find out how he sees things in today's changing world. A serious conversation will be rewarding for you. Believe me, there's nothing more noble than removing suspicion from an innocent man."

Whose suspicion, you aberration? But this was no time for tripping him up in his double-talk; Bastard's very lack of threats that evening told me his bosses had decided to test me. I had reached the end of the stalling line.

As it happened, I had met the prim professor at a seminar. But even at Yale, he would hardly have understood my need for a social call, let alone questioning him about détente. Yet I couldn't fake a claim to have met him; surely Bastard was having us both followed.

He was staying in the new Rossiya Hotel. On my way, I stopped in the Lenin Library, displayed my passport and obtained back copies of the *Congressional Record* from a closed archive. An hour of shaky searching produced one of his articles, on which I made notes. Then I went to his room, from which I had to extract him to prevent our talk being recorded. The bait—an invitation to sample "real" Soviet life through a foreign-policy harangue at the University—was genteelly swallowed and we were together two hours, hopefully seen but not overheard.

When I presented my summary of the professor's article as notes on our "free-ranging, off-the-record" conversation, Bastard's eyes bulged with excitement over his success, tinged with angry suspicion because he understood almost nothing of my handwriting in English. Shuffling the pages, he grumbled that I had not "developed sufficient detail." But the fake won me my breather: I heard no more about my "report" nor the professor himself.

Alyosha stopped mentioning New Year's Eve, both the party and the date. "Let's talk about more important matters." But even more than contact through words and thoughts, I sensed he wanted the solace of touch: reassurance that his unstanchable discharges had not made him disgusting. I got into bed and lay with his bones as something inside them tried to assert a claim to life by recalling images from one life story.

He rambled, repeated, forgot; he recounted the visit of a string quartet to baffled tank crews resting from battle only to fume because he couldn't remember where the incongruous concert had taken place. Many recollections seemed too much for his narrative power; while he gripped my hand in silence, I felt him reliving literally stirring episodes. He kept saying he wanted to make something clear about the days of "riding errands" with Granny in his wagon, but digressed into less significant vignettes. He explained he had left Moscow "society" ten years ago because it was a depressing collection of little people trying to be big through dachas, entrée to the Cinema Club and the regime's pathetic privileges, but I sensed he was omitting the truly important memories for sheer lack of strength, and was unhappy with himself for waiting too long to try to put his life into some kind of perspective.

Occasionally a brilliant cameo emerged of a recollected person or place. A streetcorner in wartime Sukhumi where, among Parker pens and Remington shavers, you could buy battlefront decorations, impeccable draft exemptions and diplomas from any university in the land. A high-school dropout he once defended who had passed himself off as a chess master, ace fighter pilot, champion parachutist and high-school inspector, presenting medals in stadiums, collecting pensions as a Hero of Socialist Labor and touring the country in style as a hotel director, Aeroflot manager and financial inspector. Replacing a friend's head on his torso after a tank battle; collecting parcels for a violinist too terrified to go to the post office because they came from a sister in Paris.

Although trying to convey something with this jumble, he only commented "That's the way it was in those days, the screwy way it was." I had moved his bed back to the window. He looked up at it from upside down, his spiked nose like a bustard's beak. Despite the snow, a few leaves had freakishly stuck to the courtyard tree.

"And that's what is left. I keep hoping they'll continue to cling. What nonsense!" And to Nina: "You must find your man, Ninochka. I get such pleasure from your health."

I studied his glinting skull through half-closed eyes, trying to decide whether I hated it enough to kill him if he pushed me. The paradox was that he was actually helping me "grow up," as he never stopped urging. I felt myself emerging from a prolonged childhood of witless optimism, grasping for the first time that at least half the world was hardship and evil—and that *this* is what made me feel, from the first weeks last year, that I had come home to Russia. I was learning to accept pain as the country did, to put my own defects in perspective, to recognize my American compulsion to be—to pretend to be—the strong, smiling success type for what it was. As centuries of senseless tragedy had taught Russians, even the most terrible failures need not outrage or shame you. This was not a meager lesson for an exchange student.

On the courtyard bench sat two women of the same certain age. The talkative one's Bronxlike voice was working up the scale of indignation.

"So I said to him, *what* presents did you ever give me? A skinny box of chocolates once; a pair of stockings? Some snapdragons—until it came out that you got them from your own students on graduation day. Let me assure you, I said, you should be ashamed to mention such 'gifts.' . . . And between you and me, darling, what it *cost* me, *oi*, to wring even them from him."

I looked to see if she was serious. Most certainly. Life was going on—and, I supposed, in Washington, where Nixon was enjoying his re-election; in Paris, scene of Kissinger's preparations to end the Vietnamese war; in Moscow itself, where Jews were still mourning the deaths of the Israeli Olympic athletes. But I couldn't think beyond this courtyard. From one window giving onto it, a thin man who looked like a former bookkeeper gazed down with a pensioner's blankness. He twiddled his thumbs—first this way for hours, then the other way. This helped him pass the winter; and it helped me, in my breaks for air, to pass mine by looking up at him.

I had gone down while Nina was dealing with the putrescent sheets. Only she could have coped with Alyosha's wastes day after day without the slightest thought of sacrifice nor any need, as I had, for periodic escape. Her deep Orthodox faith inured her to just such earthly awfulness. A peasant child, she had been raised by an illiterate mother on a dishwasher's wages in a room of candles burning in front of the icons and adoration of Stalin. Alyosha stopped her five years ago as she was leaving a church. Her religious faith had kept her pure to share her life with one single man. When her few days with him were over, she was tortured by guilt as well as by desperate longing, and tried to throw herself under a car. Alyosha took her in for another fortnight, patiently coaching her to accept the facts of his life. At last she did, but prayed for him constantly from then on, never even imagining that she might ever love anyone else.

He motioned me back into bed with him. His voice was so weak that I had to hold my ear near his mouth. Something in his thorax reverberated at each word, like beads in a Raggedy Andy.

"Sometimes I don't have the slightest regret. This insipid, dingy, dreary life—who cares about pulling out of it? We have no art, no literature, nothing true. Only propaganda to keep us morons. . . . And my work was a travesty. I defended murderers, robbers, doorway rapists every day. Instead of redeeming that scum through enlightenment, we knout them; they end as animals. I had no profession, lived a useless life . . ."

The shaking of his inner beads ended in a fit of convulsive coughing. Finally he resumed in a softer tone, with long breaks between sentences.

"I wanted to talk about this to my friends. Why we live so purposelessly. They looked at me with bewilderment—with suspicion, mistrust. As if they didn't understand. Then it came to me: almost no one did. So *I* learned—to shut my trap.

"And to shag skirts. You're so much like me in some ways; yet it's been only a diversion for you, not a life. See a girl. Take her home, watch her undress. Cuddle her—but it's a pose; she doesn't really interest you. Next day she looks at you, puzzled: 'Is that all?' Yes, that's all. And it's when you wish you'd been born a century earlier, before the desecration called Soviet rule. Or a hundred years from now, when the specter of some civilization may again haunt our land. I popped up in the middle."

That night: "Good God, I'm saddling you with all my anger. Making it even tougher for you, which is crazy; you've no reason to be bitter. But you'd have found out for yourself. If you stayed here, the bastards would eventually have dragged you under. Made you pimp for them; they kept on trying with me . . ."

When did they try? Again I couldn't ask.

The last-chance visitors included Erstwhiles too shy to come to the hospital and former clients with caps in their hands, like peasants at Tolstoy's funeral. When Alyosha recognized them, he was happy to pronounce their names.

At the beginning, I cherished a hope that Anastasia would come one day, like Nina, to help me nurse him. But when her blanched face appeared, I was very tired. The last time she was in this room, she stroked my hands while I sniveled about my heart. I thought more about her first time, when she succumbed to her inventive suitor, now the sack on the bed. All the genuine pain endured since then made even my conviction about our future irrelevant.

She sat down beside him, without tears or poses. I went out to leave them alone. She emerged later with the expression of what she had learned showing on her face and joined me on the courtyard bench. We watched the afternoon turn dark and talked.

"He's totally dependent on you. You're his son, and his parents—that must be some comfort to you in this madness."

"Six months, can it be true? If he lives to New Year's Eve, it will be seven. And he knew he was finished from the first."

"You've changed. He needs *you* when it's roughest. You're different, do you know?"

I remembered how I had longed for these words from her. Then recognized life's trick: the very change, if that was what to call it, had diluted their importance.

She said the winter was empty of everything. She had less interest than ever in medicine and a feeling that nothing was going to work out for her. She was talking of switching to an institute of literature when I realized what I owed her.

"If you ever want to leave hére, I'll do it for you," I interrupted. "You know what I mean."

"And I can count on you now?" But she pronounced this more as a declaration than a question, while her eyes thanked me for my offer.

"What a pity," she said matter-of-factly, "if you marry someone else." She squeezed my hand and left.

"Please, Alyoshinka, what harm can it do? Try a little corner."

Nina was pressing him, as she had been for days, to partake of a specially consecrated monastery hardtack reputedly able to absolve a dying person of unconfessed sins. Although this worked only on the eve of Easter, she had convinced a sympathetic priest to make an exception for a good man who might not last.

"You'll feel much better; a weight will be lifted."

Shivering in pain, he dropped his exception to the "black magic" and took a bite.

"Well?" she asked tremblingly.

"It's true. I feel better already."

His whisper was too feeble to tell whether it indeed had some psychological effect, or whether he was trying to comfort her.

"Hard to make sense of nature. Bestows perception upon *Homo sapiens* and forces him to contemplate his nonexistence the whole of his life. One way or another, we all wait for the appointed hour, knowing we're doomed." . . .

"Maybe that's the source of the excess anger in human nature. Evolution should have stopped a level or two earlier."

Later: "We'd enjoy life far more that way, because we wouldn't know the implications of time. I've been working it out: you're a wildcat; Nina's a llama. A platypus for me—they choose the right climate. And Anastasia's also from the lynx family, so your brood won't sprout tails where they should have ears."

That evening: "My biggest mistake: not to have children. I miss my girl and boy. . . . Remember my mother looking down at me the night before she left. Very tender, incredibly beautiful; she thought I was asleep. The forbidden sweet of my life. Don't even know whether I remember or dreamed that scene. . . ."

His heart beat furiously with the effort.

Bastard's exhalation into the receiver on the afternoon I dashed to the dormitory to change clothes disabused me of my notion that he had stopped calling out of consideration.

"And I've got something else imperative for a week or so. Some of your countrymen keep me busy, heh. But we'll catch up on everything when I return."

Somehow, his threats were less real and he himself seemed less disgusting. But it was Providence that drew him away just now. Distracted by this thought, I heard myself wishing him a good trip.

"What?"

He demanded an explanation of my levity.

When the resident who visited him every other day on her ambulance rounds saw the agony was intolerable, she prescribed morphine, instructing me how to inject and leaving supplies enough to last until her next visit. Bastard was still working his blackmail and elsewhere the bureaucracy remained as stupidly rigid as ever; but as a member of the little medical family caring for Alyosha, I was trusted with narcotic drugs.

He had been looking forward to this stage as a man with a broken leg awaits removal of his cast. Happy to be spending his last days "in modern comfort," he perked up enough to hatch final schemes. To pay part of his debt to Nina, he wanted her to inherit residence rights to the apartment—which could happen only if she married him.

"Use your stubborn brain, Ninochka. What's good for you *is* the only way I can do something good for me, can't you see?"

But she believed that since the healthy him hadn't needed her, marriage now would be collusion in his death. She beseeched him to retract his wish.

He turned to me. "Thank God you don't need a boost," he said, oblivious of our old icon talk. I'd make my own way, he assured me—to the top. But Maxi should ride with me. On American hamburger, she'd live a good twenty years, a living symbol of our friendship.

Notarizing his bequest wasn't enough; he wanted to see with his own eyes a document certifying that she could leave the country with me. In his dozing hours, I coaxed the Volga—dying too without his repairs—to half a dozen offices that, each according to the previous ones, were empowered to sanction the emigration of a Soviet pet. I hurriedly filled out forms, composed affidavits, told the story at the Central Canine Breeders' Association, Central Customs Bureau, Ministry of Sport. Alyosha awoke and pointed to the gold medal as proof I'd eventually succeed.

There was no regulation against Maxi leaving; it was simply impossible to obtain permission. Never having heard of such a case, everyone spontaneously said no. One minion observed that Maxi was a medalist of an official body that was simultaneously a sporting association and a volunteer auxiliary corps. In other words, she might be needed in a state emergency, and in this sense was the People's property. Finally, a senior customs officer demanded a three hundred per cent duty on her estimated value: naked extortion of five hundred rubles for the Soviet treasury. Before I could deliver it, a Ministry of Foreign Trade official vetoed the deal.

Such benighted patriotic obstinacy brought back all Alyosha's old talk about a "normal" country. I cursed Russia for denying a dying man his last wish of willing his dog. Its fulfillment soon seemed as important as his recovery had once been. The more time I wasted away from him, the more compelled I felt to succeed. I rushed from one hulking building to another, pushing past the supplicating public, shouting at torpid faces behind petitioning windows. I *had* to snatch this final victory—and reassure Alyosha that I had the stuff to carry on alone.

I touched his eggshell of a forehead, assuring him we'd win. But his interest expired as my determination grew. Maxi was beginning to annoy him. Tail wagging and talk about walking her was too much for his system; he asked me to find her another home. I darkened the room with blankets to ease the stress on his eyes. Anastasia came again, but he did not acknowledge her.

He now cared only about his morphine, which I was injecting every three hours—into his arms, despite all the previous punctures, because of the open stew of flesh elsewhere on his body. The doctor supplied two supplementary pain killers; I used all three together, steadily increasing the dose to his more and more hopeless imploring. Laced with drugs, mouth open like a geriatrics patient, he descended into oblivion.

We stared at the bump under the quilt. It had stirred.
"Not gone, still thinking."
An hour later, another move.
"Had so few friends . . . we met so late."
The next day, he tried to pull himself back.
"Always feel good when thinking of you. Inasmuch as this is often, I'm usually happy. . . ."

Nina stayed home from work and stretched out on the divan. I used the Black Sea mattress. He barely looked at us with his drugged eyes, sometimes as if we were strangers.

He took a spoonful of egg one day, a glass of tea the next. A few sips of tea the day after that, then he couldn't swallow. Thirty-six hours passed with four words from him: "bitter" and "crazy, still here." Each breath was drawn with a noise like a death rattle past parched lips and a desiccated throat. Unable to stand this sound any longer, Nina put a teaspoon of water into his mouth. It remained there, swishing back and forth until it dribbled away.

The doctor said nothing could be done. Alyosha fell into what passed for sleep and I convinced Nina, who had been eating hardly more than he, to go out for bread. The dark wobbliness of the room was like a submarine stranded without power. When he awoke, I saw he had suffered a further drop, even from his previous level. The least possible quotient of life still flickered in him. I took his hand and words rushed past my lips.

I said that whatever happened to me, wherever I would be, I'd never have a friend like him, with whom I was so deeply happy just to be with. Just to sit and talk—or not to talk, like now.

My grief gushed out as if it stood for all the feelings I too often suppressed. "Dearest Alyosha, why are there so few good people? So little genuine friendship? I'll think of you always. Of the man who changed so much for me. . . . Alyoshinka mine, you're the rare presence that makes other things glad to live. The gift you have, the gift you give."

He summoned all his strength to look at me. I think he understood.

Immediately, I felt guilty about tiring him, and urged him to relax. But my words began haunting me even before the sentence ended. To my horror, my injunction to sleep tranquilly came out as the punch line of our old joke about the factory director's funeral.

"Dearest friend, rest in peace."

The faintest wince crossed his face. It might have expressed either hurt for my indiscretion or appreciation of the black irony. I longed to explain that it had been unintentional and return to the spirit of my eulogy, but it would have been asking too much of him to listen to more from me. Clearing myself was not the most important consideration now, nor even what he thought of me. I had to live with the inexplicable burden that my last words to him—the last he would understand from anyone—had been a slip of the tongue. The gap between us was unbridgeable. The world was as meaningless as the floorboards. I knelt on them because this night I couldn't stand the use of a chair. . . .

After midnight his breathing became a ghastly convulsive rasp. I called the ambulance service again. A young doctor gave him a mercifully quick examination and an injection. I looked hard at him, trying to establish contact. Surely he knew these were the last minutes. But there was nothing but blankness and decay. An hour later, he drew a breath that gashed my ears. Then the room was silent. Perhaps the unimaginable would not come if I did not move. Alyosha was no more; Alyosha would never be.

The lifelessness of the aged rag doll on the bed added fear to paralyzing sorrow. Nina spoke to it as to a younger Alyosha. She told it about her fresh bread and rearranged the blankets. Suddenly she threw herself to the floor and banged her forehead against a leg of the bed.

Choking over her words, clinging to the body, she asked why he was depriving his friends of his goodness, abandoning us to darkness. She wailed in anguish—and I prayed she had enough strength to keep it up, because I had too little to cope with the numbness that would follow.

When it was light, we washed the body, slowly, to protract our contact with him. Nina was already growing distant from me. The great emptiness had begun.

IX Come Again?

I switch off the light and draw the half-curtain in case I'm being watched from a dormitory window overlooking mine. If the KGB acts, I think with surprising calm, it must be in the next few hours. December's predawn darkness affords a margin of safety, and anyway it's got to be now rather than never; left behind, the icon would be a trail of evidence.

In the glint of streetlamps on snow, I remove the square foot of crumbly gesso and wood from its hiding place and stash it between some legal journals and balalaika records near the bottom of my trunk. Although everything is still proceeding according to plan—New Roommate will be another ten minutes frying his breakfast in the communal kitchen—the suspense of what probably awaits The Madonna and me spikes my blood with adrenalin.

So I'm leaving Moscow as I arrived: edgy because of the country's harsh rules and my impulse to flout them. To cheat by sneaking out contraband. One day—if I slip through at the airport— I'll no doubt attribute these palpitations to totalitarianism. I picture myself lecturing to college audiences about the Soviet citizen's subliminal dread. I alone will know that shouting at Kremlin evil helps drown internal whispers of my corruption; that there is a selfish temptation to diligently expose—and make capital of—the system's crimes.

The icon will rouse the customs crew to search for more. The real trouble will come from an envelope of Alyosha's notes about himself that I found in his wardrobe, including papers about cases he had tried. Classified as theft of state documents, they could teach me all about labor camp starvation for five years. And keep me from visiting Russia ever again: a severe sentence too, even though the thought of leaving—yes, for corny freedom! —has made me like a puppy whimpering for a walk throughout this last week.

I haven't time for that mood now. For the dream of getting out, breaking loose, *escaping.* Of freeing myself from the debasing fear that a capricious "they" will sooner or later get me—for doubting Communism, liking women, *being me.* After the funeral, I sometimes had to hold myself back from charging down the corridor, shouting my pride in being a lick-spitting dog of imperialist capitalism.

To assuage the longing for reprieve, I spent days in the offices of KLM and Air France studying timetables, rechanging routes —all to assure myself I could leave when my time was up. Just being in the office of a Western company bolstered my spirits. As with everything else, it took four times longer than in a normal country to fix a ticket; but while railing at the red tape and security mania, I was secretly pleased. For I could waste more time in an activity that passed for important and demanded no thought.

Yet the icon is a bleeper signal alerting officials to unmask me and keep me here, stamping their boots on my yearning to leave. A Virgin and Child with a tarnished brass cover and smells of unwashed generations in a peasant cabin, it would fetch no more than two hundred dollars if I ever thought of selling. Yet I must court this risk for it. All Russia's riches—never mind that they're riches of poverty—and I'm departing empty-handed after these feverish sixteen months. A smuggled icon: token compensation. Besides, it's the last survivor of the lot Alyosha was collecting for our get-rich scheme. We peddled most of the others for living expenses during the fall, and someone—probably a friend come to cheer him in his pain—made off with a few when I was out on an errand. Only this greenish one, with its touch of a souvenir-shop Christ, came down to me. And the flannel shirt for its wrapping, which Alyosha used to wear while greasing the Volga.

Locking the trunk, I look for things left behind. Thank God I got rid of the last of my dangerous books, the Khrushchev memoirs and emigré editions of samizdat. After the funeral, a stranger in a bus line whispered imploringly that my room had been searched in preparation for a trap. Although his scare might have been on instructions, I took no chances, quickly distributing a few copies to trustworthy people and mailing the rest to a professor who used to harangue Joe Sourian and me about Truman's wickedness.

The picture of the power-hungry academic frenziedly concealing the parcel of prohibited books from faculty colleagues awards me with a grin and I think of Heathrow, where my flight arrives in exactly twelve hours. Maybe I'll transfer straight to New York; might as well spend New Year's Eve in a plane, pretending Alyosha's with me for his last party. Or I'll stay a few days and walk the London streets I did when he was alive.

But now to finish packing before New Roommate reappears. How tiny this room is when you look at it; how barren compared to last year's. A final cigarette, then out to tackle my check-out documents. Since I first started planning this day, the main priority has been an early start for a long last walk around town.

I reopen the curtains. Sweatsuited enthusiasts are jogging into the winter dawn. Soon the nine o'clock news will be on, with announcers I know better than Walter Cronkite. The current broadcast is entitled "On the Soviet People's Vigilance Against Imperialism's Subversive Activities." The West is one large school for spies, the commentator is explaining. Détente is being used to train thousands of visitors to Lenin's homeland in espionage and psychological techniques to lower *your* ideological guard. . . . The communal kitchen is a babble of pans and sleep-grumpy voices. Someone is cursing the buffet woman for not having opened last evening, leaving him breadless. How familiar everything seems; how much hollower than it used to. My old "cosmic" ache fills only part of me.

The morning snow is heavy and wet. A woman with a walking stick asks directions to the "petitioning office" of the Supreme Soviet, then laments her husband's arrest as if I'm from her village. I point her toward her destination and unbutton my coat, despite the wet. Working people grumble that it started ten years ago, this ruining of Russian winters. "Sly Khrushchev was up to no good."

At the back of Soviet Square, I take a downhill street. Who lives in this building? Oh yes, "Uncle Grisha," the old cobbler who spends his fat profits entertaining pretty girls in restaurants. Who took me here? Yes, last semester's dusky Masha. She's in a different dormitory wing this year and I've hardly seen her, except when she's dropped by for Tampax. Once we slept together as a lark and my awkwardness was gone, so maybe I've gained something. Forfeited something too: she seemed less wholesome, and her stories of Perm life were turning stale.

Masha told me that Chingiz wrote from his Siberian exile, sending his regards to her "neighbor," a code word for me. He's coping, but I'll never see him again. Or the voracious book-borrower Semyon, who avoids me. Or Alyosha's Ilya, who's on a "working vacation" in Odessa, making a last try for the family gold. Half my friends have disappeared. When I bumped into the nicest of last year's clique, he said he'd like to talk now that he's learned a few things in the provincial radio station where he's working, but he'd better not. And Lev Davidovich of Alyosha's old Consultation Office begged me not to come again when I dropped in on him. We slunk away from each other like guilty ghosts.

Why are some people still happy to see me while others have been explicitly warned to stop? Leonid was told he'd never get the newspaper job he sought if we continued to meet. This was the straw that prompted his emigration application, despite his vows that *he'd* never trade Russia for Israel. His larger motivation was the general political situation, which he considers more hopeless than ever. Convinced that trade with America is only a new means for preserving the old dictatorial power, he sank into morbid pessimism.

After his application, he was summoned to the office of the editor he'd been seeing—who, as he knew, was also a KGB captain. The older man, a family friend, made a reference to "you Yids." The Leonid who had endured years of the clique's insults spit in his face.

Putting away his handkerchief, the editor quickly summoned the police while the documentary evidence of "Disrespect for an Official Person" was still on his cheek. The police's first order to Leonid was to expectorate on a paper for chemical analysis of his saliva. During his two weeks of jail for hooliganism—a reduced sentence because the editor-vigilante pitied his parents—his head was shaved and his resolve reinforced.

Shortly after this, he got a letter from Zhenya, whose sister is helping him sell canvases hand over fist to American tourists in Tel-Aviv. The Bearded Giant dislikes Israel less, but far more volubly, than he ever did Russia, abandoning all his Moscow caution about criticizing in public and spending much of his time lobbying to emigrate to New York. He blesses "Soviet humanism" for sharpening his wits in the matter of wringing an exit visa from a "miserable bureaucracy"—and this newfound flipness in safe surroundings angers Leonid, the new Zionist.

Thus do attitudes change—in keeping with the country's persistent search for nonexistent solutions. But, as always, its personal lessons are far more important than the social and political hash of new dreams from old it tries to offer up. Not only Alyosha is gone forever, but a close handful of others. The wisdom of the country where people disappear overnight is not merely that life goes on because it must. I sense I have been loaned a few friends to love—who have been taken away again so I will know how to behave with others in the future.

On old Stoleshnikov Lane, a man in an ankle-length overcoat pulls me toward a telephone booth. It's very important, he can no longer see well, I must help him dial. I get the same wrong number on three attempts and he clumps away without a word.

Stoleshnikov Lane is more crowded than ever today. Like sperm wriggling in the street, a hundred thousand shoppers are hunting New Year's Eve treats. Incredible even by Moscow standards, the jewelry and liquor departments are thronged with gaping, glowering customers, faces set as if they do not recognize each other as being of the same species. Thirty rubles for a lacquered Lenin in his bank clerk's suit, forty for a crude clay plate: where do these working people get the wads for their splurges?

The humbler street stalls have temporarily lost their attraction; fat women peddling political pamphlets have time to gossip with fat women peddling stamps. A line stretches around the block to Petrovka Street from a clothing store with a supply of fedoras. A mother near its end is peeling an orange for her son with all the emotion generated by a land where each globe of fruit, each touch of mama's hand, is a tangible link to human existence.

I'm falling into a familiar mood again. The orange reminds me of the obsession of Chekhov's Trigorin. "Night and day, I'm a slave to a single inescapable thought," he complained. "I must write. *I must write.*"

I see that cloud over there, shaped like a piano. And I think: in a story somewhere I've got to say that a cloud floated by, shaped like a piano. . . . Worst of all is that I'm in some kind of stupor, and often don't understand what it is I'm writing. . . . I feel I must write about everything.

I wonder why I too feel compelled to see and memorize every detail. The brownish shawl on the woman slogging on in front of me—one of ten million exactly like it, in which every working-class woman over fifty is wrapped from October to May. I know it stands for *something* and must fix it in my memory. Somewhere I must record how snow lands on the nubby, soiled wool. How she walks, this block of a woman, clutching her canvas bag and wedging the phalanx of blocks ahead of her.

And that drainpipe—a tube of dented tin from which ice water dribbles to the wavy asphalt sidewalk. I'm constrained to study it too lest it disappear from my consciousness—which I equate with being dead.

The drainpipe belongs to a jumble of yellowish buildings whose submissive acceptance of fate provokes pity and love for them, myself, the human race. Here they stoop, asking only to share the same air; and the huge mural of the handsome Soviet Woman harvesting wheat and the confident Cosmonaut Conquering the Future leaves their essential humbleness unchanged. The cafeteria in the adjoining basement has good chicken soup: this is my last day, *I must remember.* Must remember the stories too that otherwise will be attic letters fed to an incinerator. Such as Alyosha's note from a fifteen-year-old Erstwhile made pregnant by a classmate. "Dear Alyoshik," she wrote from the maternity ward. "I wish little Natastinka were yours. People still make me feel ashamed. Please come see us if you're not busy."

Perhaps this episode must survive because of the dresses he bought mother and daughter. Yet deeper reasons lie in the Russia I'm leaving. Walking these self-effacing streets, I have been nourished by communication with the fire, water, air and earth that constitute the universe. These organic materials; this homemade planet. The atoms of that weatherworn fenceboard over there are related to mine. I have come to understand that I belong to the weary, all-forgiving whole known as Mother Earth.

I chide my feet for having taken me here; Red Square is for tourists. The Historical Museum, a fairy-tale witch's castle, which rumor says will soon be razed in Moscow's massive rebuilding into a "Communist" city of steel and glass. A busload of smart French tourists being guided toward the mausoleum. And the Central Lenin Museum—where, before meeting Alyosha, I used to take my first pickups to escape from the cold, and to feel them up furtively in the shelter of bunched listeners to eulogies to The Leader.

The square's expanse is fuller than I've ever seen it except during State parades. Holding their children close, provincial tourists gawk at the landmarks or enjoy a break from the madness of GUM. Just before two o'clock, thousands bunch to see the changing of the mausoleum guard, the hourly celebration of the country's existence that blends the police state's religious idolatry with its veneration for arms. The clock produces its famous chime; the soldiers goose-step to their places, bayonets fixed, fanatic devoutness imposed on village faces. The crowd watches in boredom or awe, but not, apparently, with my queasiness. I wonder what they really think of their iconic mummy on the slab inside.

"Won't their feet freeze?" a young girl asks her mother about the soldiers, now statue-like at the crypt's entrance.

"It's not cold today."

"What about other days?"

"Yes, it's hard for those boys to stand there without moving."

Behind them, one provincial man is enlightening another: "Stalin used to be there too. Now it's Lenin alone; things change."

An older mother is comforting her braided daughter: "Are you hungry, Tanyechka? We'll go home and fix you some nice soupchik."

So here too, at Leninism's sanctum sanctorum, the human element intervenes. It is this childlike innocence I'll sorely miss: the long-exploited, everlastingly misled Russian people falling for vast religious and political con games, yet retaining the purity and artlessness that can make you feel clean. It's still not too late: maybe I should stay here as a translator, subservient forever, but in contact with this gift.

Sounds of a disturbance interrupt this familiar musing. I push through to see a scarlet-faced major flaying a young dark-suit-and-white-dress couple celebrating their wedding with the traditional Red Square visit. The officer commands the hidden vantage point from which the holy place is kept under constant surveillance.

"So you like jokes?" he bellows. "This one won't go unrewarded. "Let's see your papers."

The mortified pair beg forgiveness. Their transgression was photographing each other with a bathroom cabinet, a wedding present just picked up in GUM, with the teacher's mausoleum *"right there,"* in the background. Softened by a new fall of sodden snow, the major's threats of punishment for the sacrilege ring in my ears as I leave the Square my last time. Lenin is indeed "more alive than the living."

Winter's daylight ebbs; my time expires. The banality of the symbolism does not embarrass me: in a thousand ways, unspoiled

Russia's movements are still determined by the angle of the sun. But my compulsion to exaggerate has had its own day. I walk up Kalinin Prospekt past the Lenin Library, remembering Ilya Alexandrovich, the aged prince. One look at the British Museum's listings on Admiral Kolchak was enough to recognize that Ilya will never produce more than an outline of White Russian records preserved abroad. The brave man's risky, crusading research has all been written up long ago, and better. Only in this closed world did his secret labors seem original and important—and I was quite willing to be taken in.

Have I blown up Alyosha too in this conspiracy to boost myself? But the truth is that Moscow withered after his death. The spark was gone; the common touch. Even people who hadn't known him well felt adrift. And phrases about him that propaganda overuse would otherwise have made extinct kept circling through the intelligentsia. Alyosha was "life-loving," "bubbling with life," "irreplaceable."

The morning I left for London the previous July was like a Three Stooges film. Although late as always, Alyosha and I had to conclude a last-minute deal involving a tie-clasp. Then stop for a pretty girl. Then race to the Tretyakov Gallery and talk our way in with a nutty pitch: we'd left our long-planned icon inspection for the last minute and it turned out to be the museum's monthly "sanitary day." Then to Gorky Street for the makings of blini, my last-lunch wish; but empty counters meant that the smoked salmon had to be bribed from the manager of the nearest restaurant.

Hurrying home, we drove right off again to a local foodshop for additional supplies: two girls waiting in the courtyard had to be co-opted to the party. The toasts split our sides. The blini were downed still sizzling from the pans. Leave the country without a proper celebration? Hell no! better to gorge, guzzle and joke against the clock.

Suddenly it occurred to us that empty valises—I'd sold or given away everything except the suit on my back—would alert customs as surely as if they'd been bulging with icons. Climbing on chairs, ripping at ancient cartons, Alyosha ransacked the room to supply me with "London outfits"—anything too old or ripped even for the secondhand stores—and taking the occasion to proclaim to the microphone that the Soviet people spared the naked Western proletariat nothing. He crammed my bags with rags, grandly topping the pile with a sweater I myself had given him, now full of holes. Wide ties of the 1940s still bearing Western labels were best: how could a customs officer prove *this* stuff wasn't mine? "Pacesetting bon ton, sir; imitators years behind." Alyosha's double-talk sales spiel mocked everything we were and were trying to be, turning the incongruity of the clothes into a riotous, yet tragic, representation of our fated topsy-turviness. We doubled up.

This was only six months ago, when the cancer was already marching toward his lungs.

We downed the last blinis in the car. A tire gave out in sight of the airport and he tried to fight off my help because I was going "there" and my hands should stay clean. Racing my things to the counter, he whispered facetious instructions for London life in my ear. Only his eyes betrayed a hope that something would cancel the flight.

Winter's daylight ebbs. Last laughs echo off the overcast.

She is just inside the little post office off October Square, the spitting image of a Siberian girl who urged me, an aeon ago, to hop on a train and play house with her in Irkutsk. She has the telltale look of having nowhere to sleep, no money to spend, nothing to do until something comes along to snap her boredom. I visualize her nipples as she dutifully exposes them; I remember my exultation of our parade. All the giving girls marching into the category of the people I'll never see again . . .

Inside, I think of filling my hollowness by handing her the rubles I no longer need. I go to the telegram counter and send them to Nina, trying to decide whether signing my name will slow her healing.

I couldn't get him into the cemetery where his mother had been buried, so the funeral was held here, in this new one. A rambling tract beyond a housing development's skeleton, but he'd have liked the name—Vostyakovskoye—for its old Slavic ring. Might have been touched, too, by the crowds: the caretakers said it was one of the largest private burials they could remember. He was a whitish death mask in his rough coffin, attended by colleagues, criminals, Erstwhiles, troupes of friends from various classes. The line for the ritual kiss of the cold forehead stretched into the muddy slush.

Then the eulogies: tender, funny, intensely personal yet universal. Subtle and honestly sentimental in the Russian oral tradition; worthy of him. The Chairman of his Juridical Consultation Office lauding his legal mind, a movie director reminiscing about the 1950s cafés, when the entertainment was either Alyosha himself or talk of his talent. . . . The wind blowing snow into eyes helped me drift into my private memories. I saw him bent under the lamplight, sewing his underpants as he sometimes did after returning from a gala evening, touched by the sad-humanity pantomime that makes a great clown. I remembered him backing out of the apartment one night when a girl wanted to be alone with me. I thought he had gone for a drive, but when I went to the bathroom afterwards, found him asleep in the tub, weary after a long day's running around. He looked at me fondly over the water and raised his fingers to his lips, "Shh . . . ," clowning that I needed reminding not to frighten the girl.

"The final moments slip by, one by one, irretrievable." Suddenly I was aware that his first wife was up on the little mound, denigrating his "juvenile behavior." Explaining that *she* had grown up but—this was his trouble—he never did. Everyone gasped but no one answered. I tried to make a speech, but my Russian went blurry just when it had to be most precise. Of the hundred pairs of eyes looking up at me, I recognized Anastasia's, thanking me because *she* understood.

His wife's attack was garnished by a moment of horse-trading by one cluster of mourners for the pitiful pickings of his possessions. Then two separate friends from his dandy days whispered that he had been reporting on me to the KGB all along. Their fables and faked concern bore all the marks of Bastard's touch. A country where people have to do that, even to the dead. And they didn't even *have* to: they had sold out for some little privilege.

The next day, Nina and I were alone at the grave. Our wreaths had been stolen. It was the work of teen-agers who sell them to mourners arriving an hour later at the cemetery, making more this way than they could in a factory. This in the country that has "eliminated the objective causes of crime" and sentences people for questioning the dictum. Alyosha so liked flowers in the hospital. We had built little tents of fir branches to protect these from the frost.

The grave must wait a year for a headstone. I stand by its side until it gives me the power to go. No place on earth is so peaceful.

The icon is now in two trunks: mine and the car's. The bulbous Chaika cradles me as if I were one of the potentates for whom it was designed. We circle the Hotel Moscow, its heavy suspension cushioning the lean. We accelerate after a red light on Prospekt Marx, the front end dipping down before we surge ahead of lesser machines. Ours is from Intourist: I was instructed to go to the airport in their car rather than make my own way—and to be ready three hours before flight time.

These arrangements are a dead giveaway. Why the pointed gesture of sending a car for me? A Chaika limousine, the Central Committee's handmade chariot, for which policemen clear the way through ordinary traffic like Cossacks whipping their way through the rabble? Alyosha once showed me a leaflet distributed to Moscow drivers.

COMRADES! From Time to Time, You Will See "Chaika" Automobiles on the Streets of our CAPITAL. They Are In Use for Elected Officials of our PARTY and Government, and the Soviet Union's Foreign Guests. Whenever You See a "Chaika," Pull to the Curb Immediately, Waiting Until It Has Completely Passed.

The driver's explanation—that the party of tourists scheduled to go with me canceled at the last minute—was clearly rehearsed. Loading my things, he scrutinized my face with an agent's curiosity about his quarry that dissolved the last uncertainty about what's waiting at the airport. Yet the trip out has already become one whose end can't be imagined, so perhaps won't come. I settle back to enjoy it. The seat nap smells like my father's new Buick when he first drove it home in 1950. I've had a fine snack of mushroom soup, *pirozhki,* and vodka in a restaurant called The Central. What's so serious about a four-hour flight?

The ironies alone are worth the ride. The intrepid explorer of backstreet Moscow leaving in a Chaika limousine. And accompanied not by the Russian friends in whom he's invested his emotion but by an American bachelor returning from his Christmas vacation to a London bank, who tries to strike up a conversation about the best hard-currency bargains.

The strange thing is that I don't resent this buttondown stranger as I would have a year ago. Unassumingly, he forces me to think about what I ought to. In the real world where I'll be tonight, who cares that in the Central Post Office we're now passing on the left, a dead man called Alyosha and I composed comic telegrams to each other while waiting for likely girls to waft into sight. My fellow passenger has *usable* know-how—in contrast to my inside knowledge of Moscow, which is worth far less than I pretend. I'm tired of being a bigger deal here than on the outside, just because I don't belong.

Besides, it's his chance to discover Russia. He's the type of American who's moving in and taking over. Moscow offices—of the First National City Bank, Rockefeller's Chase Manhattan, Univac and the rest—are opening everywhere, their expense-account staffs reserving the best restaurant tables. Beneath Lenin's portrait, the Minister of Foreign Trade contracts with Pepsi-Cola to produce millions of bottles annually, Comrade Brezhnev boasting he'll drink the first one. The Russian people will stand on line all day, and with Pepsi and chewing gum—yesterday's arch symbols of American vulgarity and imperialism—finally in their grasp the new revolution will be postponed another fifty years. They'll have made it; Orwell was right.

The penetration of the organization men started that day last May with the visit of Richard Nixon, former counsel to Pepsico International. Very soon "my" Moscow won't be the same.

The pleasant young banker moves closer to his window as I to mine. The street lights are on: evening at four o'clock. The Chaika's plush ride conspires to isolate me from the passing blur of shops and shoppers, but I concentrate on this last chance for refreshing my memories. The joyful moment when Anastasia and

I pressed against each other in that doorway over there, the labyrinthine entrance to the Bookshop Number One. "Let's get a taxi to Sokolniki Park," she said, instantly aroused. "I know a place for standing up."

Up the hill of Gorky Street, a favorite site for strolls. Past Mayakovsky Square and the Hotel Peking, where my bottle of scotch last winter for Ivan Petrovich, the restaurant manager, will always get me the table I no longer need. The driver's in a hurry to take me to his leader. Past the fortress doors of a store called "Armenia," where a hundred yards of well-dressed customers wait in thick sidewalk slush for baklavah to adorn their New Year's tables.

The line curls past massive façades and pathetic shop windows, gloomier than ever in the afternoon dark. The sodden snow soaks shoulders as it lands. Suddenly the key to this scene comes to me in a monologue of Prince Myshkin, Dostoyevsky's "Idiot," who explains that Russians subject themselves to extremes because they are driven

> by fever, by burning thirst. . . . As soon as we Russians reach a shore, as soon as we're certain it is a shore, we're so happy that we lose all sense of proportion. . . . It's not only we who are surprised by our passionate intensity in such cases, but all Europe. If a Russian converts to Catholicism, he's sure to become a Jesuit, and a rabid one at that. If he becomes an atheist, he'll surely demand that belief in God be eradicated by force. . . . Why such sudden fury? Because he has found his motherland at last, the motherland he has never had here; and he is happy. He's found the shore, the land; and rushes to kiss it. . . . Socialism too is the child of Catholicism. . . . Like its brother atheism, it too was begotten of despair . . . In order to replace religion's lost moral power, to quench parched humanity's spiritual thirst and save it not by Christ, but by violence . . . "Don't dare believe in God! Don't dare own property! Don't dare have a personality of your own. *Fraternité ou la mort!*"

This is the explanation for the willingness to wait two hours for the Armenia's sweets. No matter how small-minded some of their outward goals, no mere material comfort has ever driven Russians. Ten times more intense than the American dream, the

Russian one is laced with religious notions of suffering for spiritual salvation. This world's meanness prompts fantasies of a braver one, for which they allow mad tyrants to starve and shoot them in their striving to attain it. I know because I feel this fever in me.

But as we stop for a light, the vulgar exaggeration in this turns me off. For every Dostoyevsky analyzing the anguished Russian soul and Solzhenitsyn demanding repentance, ten million Pavel Ivanovichs are troubled only by what movie to see on Saturday. Just off this very Gorky Street, I know an engineer more typical of the new urban masses than anything—by Russia-lovers or Soviet-haters—I've read. He cares about his children and his car, not guilt for the purges.

"All the brain-fucking, what's it for?" he once challenged me. "It's a myth that we go around agonizing. Talk of old troubles may precipitate new."

His truth cut me short. Only people who are themselves disturbed work at probing this country's hackneyed riddles and enigmas. Muscovites pick their noses, haggle over prices, steal everything not nailed down. At evening parties, so-called intellectuals take personal affront over matters of "principle"— Gorky's real nature; Dali's motives—about which they know next to nothing. They argue sullenly or lunge with ignorant blows.

I had enough of this, and of the "soul-searching." The Russian people themselves don't really care; the endless contemplating of Great Questions—Who am I? What is Society? Whither Russia, and therefore the world?—is camouflage for their indolence. For their inability to cope with the simple things—unpolluted bathrooms, zippers on trouser flies—that the normal majority wants. The truth is that only against the poverty of my own emotions, as against that of daily Russian life, did the spiritual rummaging appear exhilarating. And this final hot-air discharge has me robbed of my last look at the Hippodrome and Alyosha's cluster of hospitals.

We've left Gorky Street and with a Chaika's immunity to police whistles are building speed on the Leningradsky Motorway. Past the boat station on the reservoir, where you can board a river cruiser for a day of the Russian countryside's magic. Past the Ring Freeway, on which the old Volga could circumnavigate the city in an hour on a clear spring night. The city limits. The airport highway, an asphalt strip bearing the usual military-looking trucks, and the only memory of which I have is of a winter night when a young party I met celebrating a birthday in a restaurant took me out here, to a drunken orgy in a ramshackle cottage near the road. Discovering the following noon that literally our last kopeks had gone for the taxi out, we ransacked the room for something to peddle to a neighbor for bus fares back. Then the girls peered through the ratty curtain and went out to scout before I stepped outside, even though all such precautions were a farce if the police or KGB had followed us from the restaurant. Those days of simple-minded pleasures!

The driver's eyes on me in the rear-view mirror snap the memory. He handles himself as skillfully as the car, for although we both know his work, he is self-confident enough not to need small talk. Alyosha's notes about himself are mostly brief descriptions of time and place, but the legal materials are genuinely incriminating. His most recent murder file documents a case of startlingly sloppy work by an investigator, prosecutor and judge, which an appeals court confirmed out of aversion to "indulging" a man already sentenced. Alyosha's innocent defendant got ten years, having been told by one official to "stop whining—you won't be shot."

Zoom! we overtake a black government Volga, its chauffeured functionary parting his curtains for a look at us as my fellow-passenger and I exchange weak smiles. Next we swish past a tanker truck serving as a snow plow, its kerchiefed woman driver straight out of a World War Two film. That's fine, but as the caught hostage being driven to the hoods, I'm an equally clichéd movie character.

I'd rather think about summer, when everything changes. When sun bakes sultriness even into these fields, and the best Moscow evenings are all balmy air and strolling in summer dresses. Baseball gloves—worn by jabbering Cuban students— appear on the University's soccer grounds, Yanqui imperialists having cleverly forced the game on exploited Cuba decades ago so that Cubans would infect the Soviet homeland with it. The sound of ball and bat, of insects and nightingales; the profusion of Russia's wild flowers and heady smells . . .

The turnoff to the access road. Another two minutes cutting across a Vermont postcard of unbroken snow and statuesque firs, each branch gloriously coated. Past the old airport and to Sheremetyevo International—right up to the front door, for this is not your honking Kennedy. The new terminal is full of the usual warps, fissures and cracks. They build things so badly here, brag so loudly about the results—and thank God: this same puffing weakness of theirs may make it easier for me inside.

Besides, it's New Year's Eve: maybe the customs staff will be too busy covering for each other's backdoor bottle-nipping to organize serious searches. Good old Russian bungling may save me, and the lifeless terminal entrance looks like confirmation that nothing sinister is planned. I control my thumping impulse to hurry inside and dump the icon in a toilet.

The quiet American retrieves his streamlined suitcase and disappears with visible relief. The driver methodically helps me with my heavier things, but won't even take a ballpoint for a tip—which removes all doubt that he's no ordinary driver.

He watches in disbelief, almost stops me because I'm not making my way inside as I should but to a telephone booth at the corner of the building. I know he's convinced I'm about to pass the word on him to the American Embassy or someplace. But the hell with him, I've heard the signal I've been waiting for. I'm going to say good-bye to Anastasia again.

Not good-bye, really, but a genuine hello. Someday, somehow, I'll come back for her. I can't yet visualize how, but I know she will be my link with this land—because she represents its beauty and truth.

There's a danger of my old self-delusion here, but I'm fortified by a truth I suddenly realize about every great Russian writer. The government of the period may be cruel, the muzhiks drunk, the gentry or intelligentsia sniveling; but the *women* are noble. They rule the Russian novel because their inborn commitment to honesty lifts them above the daily muck. My own thoughts about Anastasia have been fumbling toward this psychological insight of Russian literature; I've *felt* this for months.

I won't burden her with this but will just remind her of our talk after the funeral, which she'll know excludes false promises. She needs just a bit more reassurance, and I can give it now. I'll say that one reason I want to go home is to see where we might fit in—into a semblance of the "real things" of our Esenin poem, not just summer idyls in Norway. That if I don't write through the mails, she must never doubt this. When the time comes, I'll find a way to get word to her.

And I want to know where she'll be so I can raise my glass at midnight. Luckily, I still have a supply of two-kopek coins for the phone, the last fruit of Alyosha's lessons. My fingers dial her number without having to think. Between the dark and the daylight: she'll be home at this hour. Damn, her dorm always takes a year to answer. At last someone does—wrong number.

I dial again. The same woman answers, this time cursing me before flinging down the receiver. What's this, of all madness? I know her number in my deepest sleep. Russia's million daily mechanical breakdowns checkmate you even when you know how to be a man. I've got to make the call of my life and of course it doesn't get through—because there's a *system* of right- and dignity-robbing obstacles that reduces you to insignificance in ways you hadn't even imagined.

But before my outrage boils over, a wiser voice tells me that railing at the telephone's flaws is an old device to shunt anger from my own. Setting down my stuff, I fish out my address book on the off chance I've transposed figures in her number. Glancing frequently inside the terminal for instructions, my driver is making himself as obvious as police plants in the hard-currency stores. Last night, in preparation for disaster, I ripped out pages from my little black book identifying people the KGB might not be certain I knew. But the old listing under Jonquil is there, and my memory hasn't bungled her number.

Fluorescent lighting casts a ghastly glow from the terminal windows to the crusting snow and the silence is extraordinary, considering the place. It's amazing how a new challenge appearing just before a long dreaded one can disarm the second by changing your perspective. When I was twelve, I couldn't sleep for weeks because a store owner who caught me shoplifting threatened to come to our house. All that fear for nothing: when he did appear, my parents had just announced their separation and no one bothered with him. Now the trouble waiting at customs, even any punishment afterwards, is receding in the same pattern. The maximum sentence they'd dare is a couple of years, whereas putting things clearly to Anastasia and myself might affect our entire future.

My only fear is that something—a KGB device to foil communication from the airport?—has jinxed this telephone. I dial a third time: the number's busy. Then one try after the other, without interruption. The roar of a taxiing plane comes just at the wrong moment, when it will drown us out if our connection is bad. Still in the doorway, the driver actually nods his head in my direction. But I stick to my guns—and win!: the number rings. I somehow sense Anastasia herself will answer.

My God, *it's the angry bitch again!*

"Wait, please don't hang up!" I blurt this out before she can slam down, instinctively resorting to the most effective bid for attention from operators, gatekeepers and other strangers. "Don't cut me off again, *please*. I'm a foreigner and I can't understand why your number keeps—"

"A *foreigner!*" The woman's panicky shriek tells me she is an officer worker in her sixties widowed by the purges and pinched by decades of grind; still living by the Stalin era's laws—according to which a foreigner's call is a Mafia kiss. She hurls down the loathsome instrument in her hand, saving even her gasp until the danger is past.

So I'm beaten? Without knowing why? I wait for the solace of the new scheme that switches on automatically when my preceding one breaks down, but fail to discover anything sensible, let alone positive, in whatever it is that has thwarted this last word with Anastasia. If I really wanted to reassure her, the inspiration should have come in time for more than a stagy call from the airport. I will have to reach her another way, without the instant reward of her voice and new friendship. Anyway, for once I'd rather do something for her than promise it.

Life goes on. My hat goes on. I remember Alyosha's joke when he sewed its crown an inch smaller because I'd bought it too big. From the depths of his memory, he dragged up the phrase "swelled head" in English, adopting it to the reversed circumstances and simultaneously satirizing Malenkov. But the trick is to shunt some of this nostalgia-generating energy into the physical variety, since dreams won't get my trunk to the check-in counter.

It strikes me as odd that I haven't seen this final scene before. Free of déjà vu, I lug the trunk toward the entrance, also coping with all my other gear in a clumsy gavotte of strained arms and stretched fingers. Although it has turned colder, my underwear is sweaty. No, I won't return to the telephone booth for my sheepskin gloves.

I reach the entrance, conscious of the eyes following my progress. The driver is talking to a younger man posing as a fellow chauffeur, but neither makes a move to help me with the double portals. Heavy doors again: I *must* write that essay. Although I should be supremely indifferent to the opinion of these two musclemen, something tells me to display fortitude by tackling the doors and struggling without resting. More than any possible arrest inside, I fear the humiliation of dropping my bags.

The numbness that relieves my arms also pleasantly unfocuses my vision. It's the well-known phenomenon of split-consciousness sundering my conscious and acting selves. The first thing I notice inside is that this is no international departure building, but a Mosfilm set for an espionage potboiler supposedly set in the West—the kind old roommate Viktor liked so much. Good old Viktor, whom I appreciated only after he was replaced by tougher types, just as Moscow intellectuals grew fond of Khrushchev during Brezhnev's reign.

A detachment of soldiers is crossing a large area of new flooring, its warps rippling in the fluorescent glare. A tourist couple searches nervously for the document listing their ruble purchases, which must be surrendered before they can leave the country. My fellow passenger in the Chaika is staring at me as if I'd risen from a bloody accident. What's on my face, I wonder, to cause his startled concern? How I admire him, that straightforward American with nothing to smuggle and no Russian illusions to defend or shatter.

Cleaning women, pudgy counter women, a few porters sustaining the motions of work. A microphone voice squawking about botched transportation for incoming passengers. But like a wildebeest's eyes fastening on a waiting lioness, my vision is drawn to an immobile object in this kaleidoscope of everyday disarray. Bastard is standing like a bludgeon under the messy sign announcing "Flight BE411, Moscow-London," gloves folded in a stubby hand like a collaborator imitating his Gestapo boss.

Bastard at the airport? Of course, as you knew he'd be. Since we both knew the Intourist girls had instructions to tell him before writing my ticket, his arduously blasé questions about when I "might leave" was his usual phony dissembling to demean me. I'm just as sure now that New Roommate informed long ago about the icon—proof of Alyosha's judgment in urging me never to take one to my room.

I remember thinking that Bastard's itch to punish identified him as the type who supervised the mechanics of the purges. He wanted revenge in general; and in my case in particular, I always knew I'd have to pay for "spurning" him. I wonder whether he knows I'm Jewish; whether he swallows the newspaper stuff about the "Zionist conspiracy" to subjugate a hundred million Arabs *and*, by "impugning President Nixon's integrity," to sabotage the Soviet–American détente. He's the type to believe he's on the trail of an agent of Tel-Aviv and of the Pentagon simultaneously.

Even from here, I can make out the facial moles: plugs for spraying the vinegar of his countenance. He's checking his watch now, and the silliest of words—*escape!*—whispers itself to me. But where could I flee to or hide in? Assuming I somehow sneaked out of the building, should I try for the Turkish border? The notion makes me smile—a mistake because Bastard catches sight of me at this instant, and Bastard wants humble recognition of his mastery on my face. While he inspects me, the smile, to my dismay, becomes one of bumping into a shit in the subway and faking pleasure to conceal embarrassment. The triteness of this role I'm about to play with him makes me sheepish.

He grimaces and nods to his henchmen, seven or eight dicks in the uniform of customs officers or equally distinguishable KGB mufti. An announcement of a flight arrival in delightful Mata Hari English breaks my concentration. A woman waddles out from her currency-exchange booth to whisper to a passing stewardess, oblivious to everyone's opinion of her dignity. That's what I love in these people. Russians squabble in a packed bus if they want to, slurp their soup in a crowded restaurant—because they're simply not selfconscious . . .

And I'm contemplating the Russian character even now, making me realize that this has encroached on everything I've done here, preventing me from thinking straight about Anastasia not as a type but *as a person*—and about myself. For some reason, I sought in this country's ambiance the missing keys to what I wanted to be and wasn't.

The joke is that one of the needs it promised to satisfy was my old one for punishment. It's not simply, as I used to reflect at my window, that Russia relieves neuroses by providing external adversity; even that it reminds you daily of the tragic essence of existence. Its subtler gift is a sense of retribution to fill out the primordial human knapsack of guilt. And if the underlying melancholy I welcomed is utterly contradictory to the happy Russian childhood I also sought—just like extolling Russians *being themselves* with Bastard striking his ludicrous pose twenty yards away—I can only venture that contradiction is the stuff of human nature. That by laying bare some of my own, Russia has brought me alive. I feel closer to my own paradoxes, wiser because what I don't understand about myself has come nearer to the surface; some day I may grapple with it. The last irony is that I'll probably have my first taste of real persecution now, when I have less need for it because I want to go home, plant my feet on the ground, stop falling for illusions.

As I drag the trunk toward the counter, Bastard deploys one of his plainclothesmen. To reconnoiter? The deputy circles toward my blind quarter, eyes wide as if waiting for me to pull a gat, and at the same time trying to look inconspicuous, no doubt in accordance with his training. The guy's actually on his tippie-toes, and when I stare directly at him, continues snaking through the nonexistent grass, pretending he's still undetected. Meanwhile, the customs men clear a space to do a job on my luggage.

Outside this burlesque, life plods on. A middle-aged tourist is gushing awe of the Soviet people because a luggage-conveyor mechanic has handed her a glove she dropped. At a counter next to mine, a would-be Russian passenger, unmistakably a techni-cian going abroad, is ordered sotto voce to stand the hell aside *quick* and let the foreigners check in first. An Aeroflot pilot appears, uniform crumpled and picking his teeth: surely the spitting image of the one in command at the time of Joe Sourian's crash.

Another deputy sallies forth. Certainly the airport personnel know what they're up to with me; it's old hat to them. But I'm amazed that none of the foreigners have an inkling. So this is how the 1930s roundups worked: no opposition because each marked man was totally alone. Cut off from all help—even here, at ye international airport. I'd shout, but what's the point of frightening innocent tourists? As it is, even the pilgrimage-to-socialism ones are nervous about getting out of the country. Besides, I'm guilty. Attracting their attention to the icon's exposure would propagandize them exactly the wrong way.

Better to go it alone. This isn't the challenge I'd choose if I had a new chance, but it's mine. Bastard picks up a telephone, announcing something as if this were his moment in Marxist-Leninist history. I don't want to hear the drawl he himself despises. Or look at his eyes.

He sneezes and turns angrier. *That* look I remember when he kept repeating something I couldn't understand one evening while I sustained my diffident "Pardon me." His thin amour propre corroded, he pressed on grimly with the word. Suddenly I deciphered "the leadership of Spiro Agnew" through his Laugh-In accent and laughed so hard that I spattered him with wine. Georgian red on Russian purple: gorgeous!

Now his plainclothesmen are badly blanched. Crazy man, what can they fear from the prey? But I can't miss it, even in my own nervousness. Maybe they're afraid they'll botch everything, like Bastard with his phony cable address.

The funny thing is that I'm in this having had almost no contact with the dissidents so important to most other Americans here. Sometimes I felt the names in the Western headlines were the least representative Russians, but the reason I didn't get involved was simply that I didn't happen to meet them. The one celebrated "opposition" writer I did run into once later defected during a trip to London, earning himself pages of hailing publicity—and doing me dirty in a way I then couldn't believe. To demonstrate his loyalty and avoid a last-minute cancellation of his visa, he concocted information about an American who'd supposedly tried to sell him dollars, choosing a real name—mine —for maximum verisimilitude. While the world press was extolling his gallant honesty, two men were slyly grilling me in the University—which is one reason Bastard wanted to meet me even before Alyosha got sick. But try to explain *this* mix-up, where I shared Bastard's opinion—but for very different reasons —of the I-chose-freedom hero to Bastard's one-track, enemies-of-the-Motherland mind. Try to explain it, for that matter, to Western worshipers of any Russian who hates Soviet rule, seeing him as a gloriously noble Dissenter in every instance.

No, I must steer clear of all such complications, and everything else too true to be invented. My job is to cook up a bluff for Bastard about the legal materials. I've done it before with him; can do it again in the clinch. I'll say I need a few real cases for worming my way in with Washington's Soviet experts, the better to ferret out information for him. "Evgeny Ivanovich, you yourself taught me how terrible our censorship is. We can never read about your legal system. All America will go wild over these priceless examples of true justice in action. . . ."

But you know something, I'm tired of mouthing stories. I don't even want to shout; don't even hate him any longer. In an odd way he's been preparing me to face my real conflict once I'm past his tackle and home, trying to find something more "me" to commit myself to than professorial briefcases and mortgages. The Russia he represents has helped me see the other one—of simplicity, instinct, fantasy—more clearly, and to accept that it's not all one nation; everyone must pick and choose. Partly through him, the limits of my feeling have been extended and I've learned the Russian lesson that it's all right to be yourself. Bastard, the emancipator from emotional inhibition!

What I resent is that he'll be pawing the papers that are the private, intimate property of Alyosha and me. And that I'm wasting final thoughts on him. All the people I've known, the episodes I want to contemplate—and he's the last Russian I'll talk to. I feel enormously beholden to the country, but the joke is that only the KGB is left to receive my thanks.

The counter has been cleared for me. I sense that I've straightened up and that this confuses Bastard, who likes his charges to lay their heads on the block. He's under my nose now, with all his symbolic power somehow gone.

"Let's not go through the song and dance, Evgeny Ivanovich." My voice surprises me with its mellow confidence. "You'd really rather sing and dance at some party tonight, wouldn't you? Somewhere, old chap, you're nice enough to dislike your work."

His reaction is amazing—yet commonplace. His eyes blaze but his feet pedal backwards, like those of any challenged bully. In this second, I see that I'm going to make it past him; that he'll only go through the motions of a search because he knows that if it comes to a trial, I'll disclose everything I know about him instead of playing along to reduce my sentence.

"I want to board as soon as I can. Please have someone help with my things."

Yes I'm nervous, but if necessary, I'll start telling what I know about him right here—and in loud, clear English too, for the benefit of the passengers. He knows this; he sees in my posture that I'm stronger than he. My only restraint will be for Anastasia's sake: a big fuss now would keep us apart for too many years.

Too many years. I think my need to postpone the real things has expired. I'm not afraid to give, to see, to feel, to *be*. To cherish her even though she is both purer than I and less perfect than my ideal. To love as I loved Alyosha, accepting that part of all such happiness must die. To know—and not shrink at the triteness of it—that whatever I eventually do in life is less important than what I am. I remember Maya at the counter of the Lenin Library. *It doesn't matter now, I have my baby.* I'm full of joyful gratitude for the power, at last, to understand her with more than my mind.

Still grimacing, Bastard is trying to think of a scare tactic to deprive me of this. But he doesn't want a confrontation with me, especially in front of witnesses. If he does find the contraband, he'll confiscate it quietly. And in the long run, this doesn't matter. I'll take the real things with me.